To Pops
One day my name will be on the front – not just the credits. But see! It was a real book! Merry Christmas!
♡ Big One

WE FACE THE FUTURE UNAFRAID

School of our fathers, known of old,

Our Alma Mater we revere.

We give thee loyalty untold;

We love thee more and more each year.

And when sweet memories of thee return,

of lessons learned, of friendships made;

Thy spirit in our hearts doth burn,

We face the future unafraid.

Hymn to Evansville

WE FACE THE FUTURE UNAFRAID

A Narrative History of the University of Evansville

George Klinger

UNIVERSITY OF EVANSVILLE PRESS
Evansville, Indiana

Published by the University of Evansville Press
1800 Lincoln Avenue
Evansville, Indiana 47722

Printed in the United States of America on acid-free
paper by Cardinal Printing, New Albany, Indiana.

Library of Congress Cataloging-in-Publication Data

Klinger, George, 1928 -
    We face the future unafraid : a narrative history of
    the University of Evansville / George Klinger.

        p. cm.
    Includes index.
    ISBN: 0-930982-56-8
    1. University of Evansville – History. I. Title.

LD1761.E62K55 2003
378.772'33–dc22

                                                    2003061334

Parts of chapters 1, 2, 3, and 4 of the present work
appeared in different version in *From Institute to
University,* Olmsted. © 1973 University of
Evansville Press.

Table of Contents

Preface

When Wallace B. Graves became the University of Evansville's first president, he observed that the institution, already well over 100 years old, "lacked a written history which would convey to all its constituents the school's long and honored tradition," noting that such a history would enrich both present and future generations. Accordingly, he commissioned retiring business manager Ralph Olmsted, a member of the first Evansville College graduating class, to compose such a chronicle, which was subsequently published under the title *From Institute to University.*

The earlier chapters of the present volume are largely drawn from Ralph Olmsted's book and I am greatly indebted to his work in organizing and classifying the institution's historical records. Because his book has long been out of print, I have incorporated material from it to the extent that space allows. In this way, I hope to make his legacy available to twenty-first century readers.

Although, in its time, Olmsted's history served its purpose well, the sesquicentennial anniversary of our school's founding seemed an appropriate occasion to attempt the task anew, as well as to provide a chronicle of all that has happened in the intervening years.

The resultant volume has been a collaborative effort in every sense, made possible because many people generously contributed information, effort, and energy to bring the project to a successful conclusion.

Past Presidents Wallace Graves and James Vinson, Executive Vice President John Byrd, and President Stephen Jennings have given their enthusiastic support. Rebecca Dillbeck and Patricia Lippert in the president's office have gone far beyond the call of duty to be of help.

In addition, recent and current members of the faculty, staff, and administration were extremely cooperative and gracious in providing information pertaining to their discipline or area of responsibility. My sincere thanks for their contributions.

Academic Affairs
Linda Bathon, Jennifer Graban,
Vicky Potts

Alumni Relations
Sylvia DeVault

Archaeology and Art History
Patrick Thomas

Art
William Brown, Les Miley

Athletics
Robert Boxell, Jim Byers,
Lois Patton

Biology
Michael Cullen

Business Administration
Ray Arensman, Ronald Faust

Chemistry
William Morrison

Communication
Dean Thomlison

Computer Services
Manfred Schauss

Continuing Education
Bonnie Daly, Barbara Graves,
Lynn Penland, Eulalie Wilson

Education
Rex Brown, Ralph Templeton

Engineering
Philip Gerhart, William Hartsaw,
Mark Randall, Mark Valenzuela

English
Margaret McMullan

Financial Aid
JoAnn Laugel

Foreign Languages
James Talbert

Geography
Jerry Kendall

Harlaxton College/Study Abroad
Suzy Lantz

History
Philip Ensley, Thomas Fiddick

Human Resources
Gregory Bordfeld, Rhonda Holder

Institutional Advancement
Jack Barner, Jamie Elkins,
Thornton Patberg

Law, Politics, and Society/
Women's Studies
James Berry, Deborah Howard

Library
Kathryn Bartelt, Marvin Guilfoyle,
William Louden

Mathematics
Gene Bennett, Clarence Buesking,
Clark Kimberling

Music
Jeannie DePriest, Edwin Lacy,
Douglas Reed, Roberta Veazey

Nursing and Health Sciences
Rita Behnke, Thelma Brittingham,
Paul Jensen, Helen Smith

Philosophy and Religion/Religious Life
Anthony Beavers, John Brittain,
Richard Connolly

Physics
Benny Riley

Psychology
William Weiss

Student Life
Dana Clayton, Robert Pool,
Howard Rosenblatt

Theatre
Sharla Cowden, John David Lutz

University Relations
Marcia Dowell, Marsha Jackson,
Cynthia Simmons

Further assistance was kindly provided by

Sue Baldwin, Andrea Brown, Rand Burnette, Robert Byler, Etta Clark, Donald Colton, Leland Dierks, Isabella Fine, Jo Frohbieter-Mueller, Orville Jaebker, Dee Kalena, Earl Kirk, James MacLeod, Cheryl Michie, Melba Patberg, Mary Pritchard, Gary Rigley, Judy Steenberg, Susan Watson, Sylvia Weinzapfel and Robert Wilson. Adrienne Harr successfully completed the formidable task of preparing the index.

Finally, I am greatly indebted to Galen Clough for invaluable stylistic suggestions, to William Louden for tirelessly looking after the many details involved in producing a publication of this scope, and to my wife, Fran, for contributions far too numerous to mention.

Even with this impressive list of participants, the author bears final responsibility for the finished product and for any errors or omissions it may contain. Readers are encouraged to contact the Office of University Relations regarding suggestions or corrections for future editions of this book or future histories of the institution.

Special thanks are due to

Joyce Clough *Editorial Assistant*
Susan Heathcott *Designer*
Cynthia Knudson *Editor*
Suzy Lantz *Photographic Editor*

George Klinger
September 2003

Space limitations prohibit listing all the faculty, staff, and administration associated with the institution over its 150 years. The general criterion for inclusion has been service of five years or more or sufficient time to have had a lasting impact on the institution.

A limited number of persons have been chosen for fuller, more in-depth discussion. They provide a cross section of the background, experience, and talent so many individuals have brought to the school.

———

Thousands of people have contributed to the University's success, and the University is grateful to all for their part in furthering its mission.

———

In editorial matters, University of Evansville publications follow the guidelines found in the Chicago Manual of Style (14th edition).

For the reader's convenience, bold face type is used to indicate the first time a faculty member is mentioned in the text.

Moore's Hill Male and Female College,

LOCATED AT MOORE'S HILL, DEARBORN CO., IND.,
On the Ohio & Mississippi R. R.
40 MILES SOUTH-WEST FROM CINCINNATI.

This Location is free from the vices and evil associations incident to larger places.—Students have no inducements to spend money unnecessarily.—A more healthy location is not be found in the State.—Students can obtain rooms, where they can board themselves at a small expense.

ANNUAL CHARGES FOR TUITION.

Scientific Collegiate, $24.00   Preparatory Department, $18.00   Classical Collegiate, . . $32.00
Primary, ... 12.00   Classical P ratory, . 26.00   Instrumental Music, ℬ term, $10.00
Use of Piano extra charge, per term, $2.00   Janitor's fee 50 cts. per term.
French, German, Drawing, and Painting, extra charge.

BOARD OF INSTRUCTION.

Rev. S. R. ADAMS, A. M., Pres't.   Rev. S. J. KAHLER, A. B., Prof. Math.   Mr. B. P. CHENOWORTH, Prin. Prepar'y.
Mrs. H. P. ADAMS, Mod. Lang.   Miss V. HOLBROOK, Ins. Music.   Miss J. S. CHURCHILL, Ass't Preparatory.

Fall Term commences Monday, August 29, closes Friday, Nov. 11.—Winter Term commences Monday, Nov. 14, closes Friday, January 27.—Spring Term commences Monday, January 30, closes Friday, April 13. Summer Term commences Monday, April 16, closes Friday, June 29.

For particulars address the Secretary,

MOORE'S HILL, JUNE, 1859.

J. McCREARY.

1859 Advertisement for Moores Hill College

Noteworthy are the "sales pitch" (small print near center of the ad) and the 50¢ per term janitor's fee

CHAPTER ONE

Our Roots: Moores Hill College

Top: The Moore family home

Bottom: Millstone from Adam Moore's mill

BACKGROUND

The University of Evansville traces its roots to a picturesque pioneer town far away from its present location. Our university is the direct descendant of a small college established in 1854 in Moores Hill, Indiana, about 200 miles east of Evansville and forty miles west of Cincinnati. The town was named for its founder, Adam Moore, whose son, John Collins Moore, became the town's leading businessman and one of its wealthiest citizens.

Although the younger Moore had little formal schooling himself, he believed strongly in the value of education; his family, in fact, owned the only dictionary in town. So, in 1853, when a representative of Brookville College (some twenty-five miles from Moores Hill) called on him for a contribution, Moore began to think of the need for a school in his own community. Before the year was over, several of the town's leading citizens had met at the Methodist Church to explore the possibility of organizing a college to serve the needs of Moores Hill and its surrounding area.

An act of the Indiana legislature, passed only the year before (1852), required "the incorporation of High Schools, Academies, Colleges, Universities, Theological Institutions, and Missionary Boards" and the public sale of shares in such institutions. Accordingly, the founders of Moores Hill College decided to sell shares in the new institution for $20 each.

1

Moore immediately purchased fifty shares ($1,000) and each of the town's three lodges – Masons, Odd Fellows, and Sons of Temperance – bought twenty-five (total $1,500). An additional twenty-one shares were sold at the original meeting, and by October of 1855 a total of $3,670 had been raised. Moore then donated twelve acres of land on which to establish the college, as well as pledging to double the highest amount subscribed, a promise which the records confirm that he fulfilled.

On February 10, 1854, the school's founders filed a certificate of incorporation with the state of Indiana, establishing Moores Hill Male and Female Collegiate Institute (almost immediately known as Moores Hill College, although the name was not officially changed to that until 1887).

More than two years of preparation were required before the doors were opened for classes in 1856. It should be noted that, in addition to college courses, the school offered an elementary and high school program designed to prepare students for the college curriculum.

John Collins Moore (1854)

From its inception, Moores Hill Male and Female Collegiate Institute had close ties with the Methodist Church. It was, indeed, an institution of the church's Southeast Indiana Conference, and every president of the College was a member of the conference, as were a number of professors. Chapel attendance was compulsory for many years, revivals were held on campus three or four weeks each year, and at times as many as one-fourth of the school's male students were preparing for the ministry.

However, from the beginning, other denominations (especially Evangelical Lutherans and Presbyterians) were represented in the faculty and student body, and one of the founders of the College was the local Baptist minister. Overall, Moores Hill took great pride in being, as the catalog stated, "non-sectarian but Christian."

Moores Hill was one of over 130 colleges founded in the Midwest between 1830 and 1860. Among others were Franklin (1834), DePauw (1837), Ohio Wesleyan (1842), Baldwin-Wallace (1845), Earlham (1847), Butler (1855), Valparaiso (1859), and Kentucky Wesleyan (1860). However, of over 500 colleges founded in the Midwest at some point during the nineteenth century, just under one in five (nineteen percent) survived into the twentieth century.

As might have been expected, financial difficulty was the leading cause of this high failure rate. Moores Hill College certainly suffered its share of financial – as well as other – setbacks, but it managed nevertheless to retain its place among the survivors, operating until 1917, when it was moved to Evansville.

ACADEMICS

When Moores Hill College first established its curriculum in 1856, there were two courses of study: the classical and the scientific.

The classical stressed Greek and Latin composition and literature (Herodotus, Virgil, and Cicero), mathematics (algebra, geometry, and trigonometry), geology, natural philosophy, logic, American history, political economy, rhetoric, and modern languages (French or German). This curriculum generally required four years of study and led to the degree of Bachelor (or Mistress) of Arts.

The scientific curriculum excluded Greek and Latin but added courses in history, composition, and prosody to such standard scientific subjects as algebra, botany, and physiology. This program generally required three years of study and led to the degree of Bachelor (or Lady) of Science and English Literature.

In 1894, a third curriculum, the philosophical, was added. In 1905, this changed to a course of study emphasizing literature and the humanities, leading to a degree called a Bachelor of Letters.

In addition to its traditional liberal arts-oriented programs, Moores Hill College offered vocational training in a variety of areas. The first of these, begun in 1871, was a "normal" course for teachers. Because the institution's new president, John Martin, had been a school superintendent before coming to Moores Hill, such a program was a priority for him.

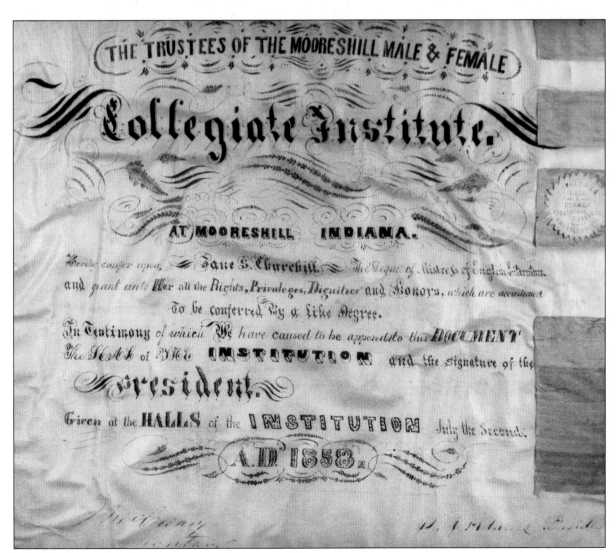

First diploma granted by Moores Hill College

3

Moores Hill College library (1890)

Graduates of the four-year normal course received the Bachelor of Scientific Didactics, renamed the Bachelor of Pedagogy in 1905. The state of Indiana, however, required only a license, not a four-year degree, for those wishing to teach in public schools. Teachers could take the licensing examination after only twelve to twenty-four weeks of instruction; needless to say, many chose this option.

Business courses entered the Moores Hill curriculum in 1882, with classes offered in book-keeping, commercial law, and penmanship. No degree in business was ever available at Moores Hill, and such courses were dropped entirely in 1911.

A year later, a department of agriculture was organized, offering courses in animal husbandry, agronomy, horticulture, forestry, and farm management. To provide students with practical experience, a fifteen acre plot was used as an experimental farm. This program continued until the College closed in 1917.

4

Moore Hall, the main college building, built 1854-1856, destroyed by fire in 1915 (not actually named Moore Hall until 1906, thirty-four years after Moore's death)

Moores Hill College Faculty 1909-1910

Other special programs included music (voice, piano, organ, violin, mandolin, and guitar) and, beginning in 1876, elocution. The stated purpose of the elocution program was to "teach naturalness, ease, distinctness, variety, and force of expression."

Finally, some graduate degrees were also offered by Moores Hill College. The Master of Arts degree is first mentioned in the college catalog in 1872, and the 1887 catalog specifies that a master's degree candidate must either pass an examination or submit a thesis of at least 3,000 words. By 1902, candidates also had to fulfill a residency requirement of one year.

In 1888, the faculty decided to offer the degree of Doctor of Philosophy, but only two persons completed the program and it was dropped in 1904. Honorary doctorates, however, were bestowed, beginning in 1873, and from then until 1916 seventy honorary doctorates and thirty-seven honorary master's degrees were given, mostly to Methodist clergymen. The majority of the doctorates were Doctor of Divinity degrees, but the Doctor of Philosophy, Doctor of Laws, Doctor of Science, and Doctor of Literature degrees were granted as well.

5

In the nearly sixty-one years of Moores Hill's existence, 487 persons earned academic degrees, of which seventy-nine went on to become ministers and 125 were teachers. At least nine Moores Hill graduates became college presidents.

STUDENT LIFE

For many Hoosiers in the mid and late nineteenth century, earning a college degree was an all-but-impossible dream. Moores Hill College offered to make this dream a reality. Many of its students were town residents while others came from nearby villages and outlying farms. Some young people walked fifteen miles to the campus, to live during the week in small rooms in the town's boarding homes.

Education at Moores Hill College was synonymous with moral instruction. For its founders, academic success must be accompanied by adherence to strict religious and ethical principles. Faculty were expected to be more than dedicated and excellent teachers; they must also serve as role models for their students. Students, in turn, submitted to a code of conduct that would be regarded as oppressive by their counterparts today. Thus, the college catalog sternly decrees:

- **All correspondence between the sexes is forbidden.**

- **Card playing, the drinking of intoxicating liquors, profanity, and all games of chance are forbidden.**

Moreover, incoming students were required to sign a pledge agreeing to be governed by all the institution's laws and policies, promising:

- **I will be present at the morning devotional exercises and be seated in my place in chapel at the ringing of the bell.**

- **I will pass quietly without communication to my room either from chapel or to or from recitation.**

- **I will not spit tobacco spittle on the floor of the halls, of the recitation rooms, or of the Chapel.**

- **I will refrain from cutting or marking desks, benches, buildings, or outbuildings with a pen, pencil, knife, or otherwise.**

- **I will carefully observe the hours that may be appointed from time to time for study.**

Women's residence hall

Moores Hill College band

- **I will refrain from visiting, from attending parties or other like public diversions except by permission of the teacher in charge.**

- **I will refrain [from] leaving town during term time without permission of one of the teachers.**

- **I will attend church Sabbath morning and the lecture Sabbath afternoon.**

- **I will avoid spending time in standing or sitting around stores, taverns, corners of the streets or other public places.**

In addition, all students were warned that "absence from recitation and church will be strictly recorded and reported to the parent at the close of each term." The College also strongly recommended that "all jewelry be left at home or otherwise laid aside lest the jewels of mind be forgotten in the adorning of the body." Regarding pocket money, the catalog informs students that they will have "very little occasion for it" and hence it would be much better "if all funds of the student were committed to the President or one of the Professors, who will in turn attend to the wants of, and settle the bills of, the student."

In conclusion, the catalog states:

The discipline of the Institution is strictly parental, and designed to lead the student, by mild, yet unbending measures, to the correction of evil and to the cultivation of all that is desirable in human character. It relies upon the moral sense of the student, his consciousness of right, and his disposition so to do.

Yet, if these fail, the means of correction are at hand. Students who persist in violation of the regulations of the Institution will not be allowed to remain in the Institution.

Moores Hill music students

College records indicate that offenses did indeed occur from time to time, but many were little more than pranks, such as concealing a hen in the president's desk drawer. It is also noteworthy that one of the students most often summoned before the faculty for misconduct, including "going skating with a group of girls at a late hour of the night," later became a prominent Methodist minister (North Indiana Conference) and served for several years on the Board of Trustees of Evansville College.

The "association of the different sexes in and about the College buildings," to use the terminology of the college rules, was a frequent cause of friction between the student body and the administration, yet the school's acceptance of women students (Moores Hill was only the fifth coeducational college in the United States) was also a source of great pride.

Its commitment to coeducation was specifically stated in its full title, Moores Hill Male and Female Collegiate Institute. In its first catalog Moores Hill states that it admits women "to an equality in privilege and an equality in honor, recognizing no distinction in mind." In contrast, both Indiana University and DePauw University did not admit women until 1867 (more than a decade after Moores Hill College opened) and then, in both cases, only after a long and bitter debate among members of the board and over the objections of many male students.

During the Civil War, being coeducational proved to be Moores Hill's salvation. Many all-male colleges lost a majority of their student body to the armed services, forcing them to close – some never to open again. But Moores Hill College, although it had only been in existence for five years when the war began, was able to enroll a sufficient number of women during the years 1861 to 1865 to survive the conflict intact.

The 1899 editorial board of Moores Hill College yearbook, the **Melange**

As might be expected, by the time Moores Hill College relocated in 1917 most of the rules and prohibitions of previous years had long since disappeared from the catalog. For example, church and chapel attendance were no longer required, and there were fewer restrictions on the association of men and women. Nevertheless, dancing, card playing, and cigarette smoking were still strictly forbidden (rules which continued to apply during the early years of the College at Evansville).

Despite the array of mandates and prohibitions Moores Hill students had to contend with, several extracurricular and recreational opportunities were available, especially in the College's later years. Picnics, parties, "term socials," contests, athletic events, and banquets were frequent. Stage plays, however, were frowned on by the faculty and administration, and there was no student newspaper until 1889.

Although the first student newspaper was edited by a faculty member, the weekly *College Life*, which began publication in 1909, was apparently edited by students, though with faculty supervision and perhaps even censorship. Each edition informed students of college activities and athletic events, and its editorials campaigned vigorously against the evils of smoking, drinking, and dancing. *College Life* continued to be published until Moores Hill College closed in 1917.

9

From time to time students were dismissed from classes for a day. Then, armed with rakes and shovels, they gave the campus a good cleaning.

A group of Sigourneans (1903-1904)

A college yearbook, the *Melange*, was published intermittently, the first annual not appearing until 1894 and the last in 1913. Many years in between, however, are unaccounted for, perhaps because the books have been lost.

The most highly organized social activities on the Moores Hill campus were the literary and debating clubs. The first of these was actually formed more than a year before classes began by a group of young men planning to attend the school. Called the Philoneikean ("love of debate") Literary Society, it sponsored numerous debates, orations,

and readings. The women of the College formed a similar society the following year, the Sigournean Society (named for the then-popular poet Lydia Huntley Sigourney). At first, it specialized in original poetry and essays, but after the turn of the century its focus changed to oratory and debate. It is notable that in contests with the men of the College, the women often carried off the first prize.

In 1869, a second association for men was established called the Photozetean ("seekers of light") Society, focusing on religious inquiry. Some men belonged to both the Philoneikean and the Pho-

Moores Hill cycle club (1899)

tozetean groups. Although other clubs started on the campus at various times, none lasted for more than a year or two until 1905, when the Castalian Literary Society (named for an ancient Greek fountain of wisdom) for women was established.

For many years, the societies owned the only library books on the Moores Hill campus. In addition to pursuing the literary activities for which they were originally formed, the four major organizations also played an active role in boosting athletic events as well as promoting May Day activities, queen contests, and campus parties.

Alumni consistently spoke of the societies as a highlight of their college experience at Moores Hill, and these organizations also provided the roots from which national fraternities and sororities on the Evansville campus later developed.

Moores Hill international student Masih Charan Singh and family (Class of 1915)

Moores Hill College football team (1898)

ATHLETICS

Athletic activity developed very slowly at Moores Hill during its early years, a situation not uncommon among similar denominational colleges in the Midwest. Most of the activity was intramural, with the first intercollegiate teams beginning their competition no earlier than 1894, forty years after the school's founding.

Only after several years of student agitation and energetic fund-raising efforts was the first gymnasium completed in 1900. Costing $1,645, it measured forty feet wide and seventy feet long, larger than Indiana

11

Moores Hill College baseball team (1902-1903)

University's first gym, which was built in 1892 and measured forty by sixty feet.

In the late nineteenth century, baseball was the most popular sport in America, and this was apparently the case at Moores Hill as well. Until 1894, instead of competing against other colleges, the baseball squad played teams from surrounding high schools or villages. After 1894, Moores Hill began to play neighboring colleges, such as St. Xavier of Cincinnati, Franklin College, Hanover College, Earlham College, Indiana State Normal at Terre Haute, Wilmington College, Rose Polytechnic Institute, and Butler University. Although the Moores Hill team never achieved any special recog-

The Moores Hill College tennis team (1894)

nition on the baseball diamond, the sport remained popular at the College for several years. (It is notable, however, that even the high moral principles of a church-related college did not prevent Moores Hill from stretching a point when it came to winning in sports. In a baseball game with the University of Louisville, the coach substituted himself for a weak hitter, made two home runs, and won the game for Moores Hill.)

A football program began sometime between 1898 and 1900 (the records are unclear) but was then discontinued until the fall of 1909. During that interlude, the College, for the first time, established eligibility rules for athletic participation, requiring that a student player must be passing in at least twelve hours of academic work. Shortly after football resumed in 1909, the College decided to employ a paid coach for the first time. E.E. Patton was hired in 1911 and served through the 1912 season, achieving a combined record of four wins, six losses and three ties. When he left in 1912, the team was coached by student team members in exchange for tuition. In 1915, the trustees, citing financial diffi-

Happy times – the women's basketball team (also known as the Moores Hill Bloomer Girls) before the 1905 faculty ban

culties, voted to eliminate football as an intercollegiate sport and suggested that more attention be given to the "finer" sports, such as tennis and track.

13

Moores Hill College basketball team (1904-05)

Basketball was also popular at Moores Hill, but again there is no precise record as to how or when it started. Between 1899 and 1905, games were played on an interclass level by both men and women. The faculty, however, was not comfortable with women playing basketball and in 1905 banned them from participating in public. Despite opposition the sport continued, but in 1913 the women's team was refused permission to compete against the University of Louisville.

Men's basketball, in contrast, was eagerly supported and a 1908 report to the Board of Trustees proudly notes that the men's basketball team that year went undefeated. By 1912, the team was holding its own against strong opposition from neighboring colleges. Thus began the tradition of successful performance on the basketball court which continued when the institution moved to Evansville and indeed extends to the present day.

FINANCES

As was usually the case with small denominational colleges, financial woes at Moores Hill occupied the major share of the administration's time and energy. As the late Ralph Olmsted, longtime business manager of Evansville College, states in his chronicle of the school's earlier years: "From the day it opened in September 1856 until its closing in June 1917, there was scarcely a day when the College was able to meet its bills promptly, pay its professors as their salaries became due, or provide for its other needs." The phrase "poor in purse, rich in spirit" perhaps best describes this hardy but often troubled institution.

For several years, it was largely thanks to the generosity of its founder, John C. Moore, that the College was able to meet its obligations at all. Moore paid salaries and bills, treating them as loans to the school from his store account. As a result, ten years

1913 Women's Basketball Team

"The expressions on these faces aren't very happy. This was the girls basketball team. Professor Zenos E. Scott was our coach and manager. Our one and only game was with Louisville. Although the score was 18-6 in favor of Louisville, we had a date for a return game. We practiced hard and long and thought we had a good chance of winning, but only a few days before we were to go there the Moores Hill faculty decided it would be very unladylike for ladies to go to another school and play before strangers. Accordingly, our game was cancelled, and that ended intercollegiate basketball for girls."

Stella Barclay (far right) provided this account (1915)

Three generations: Mary Ewan (left), Moores Hill student in 1856; Ewan's daughter, Mrs. A.J. Bigney (right), Class of 1894, Moores Hill College; Ewan's granddaughter, Mary Ellen McClure (center), Class of 1925, Evansville College

Payments to faculty – even to the president – were erratic, and faculty members were forewarned that an institutional deficit might reduce their salaries. At the end of the 1880-81 school year, for example, $316 in faculty salaries remained unpaid; the following year this amount increased to $453, and in 1902 it was $1,000. Similarly, the school owed its president $559 at the end of the 1895-96 academic year ($107 unpaid from the previous year and the remainder from the current session).

Yet, despite their meager earnings, professors and administrators often contributed labor and donated their own money for the benefit of the College. A professor and a vice president worked together to landscape the campus, transplanting more than 100 trees from the woods surrounding Moores Hill. And, in 1900, a professor reported that he had spent $60 for a furnace to heat his science laboratory.

Not all faculty were so generous, however, and many pressed their claims for back wages. In that event, the administration sometimes took out a loan to obtain the necessary funds. Even more common was the practice of passing a collection plate at the commencement ceremony for the benefit of the College. On these occasions, the long-suffering faculty was also expected to man the refreshment stands!

At one time, the Southeast Indiana Conference of the Methodist Church offered to assist the College in establishing an endowment fund of $20,000, whose income could then be used to cover future deficits. This plan failed, however, when the school had to draw upon the principal in order to cover its current operating expenses. By 1916, the College owed $21,200 to its endowment fund, $14,500 to the bank, $2,900 to its faculty, and another $220 in miscellaneous unpaid bills; yet at this time the College had a grand total of only $343 in the bank to meet all these obligations.

after opening its doors, the Institute owed Moore nearly $12,000. It is estimated that during his lifetime Moore's contributions amounted to about $30,000. Borrowing from his business continued even after his death in 1871, so that by 1874 the College owed the family an additional $8,955.

The major continuing cost in the operation of the College was staff salaries although, even making allowances for living costs then as compared to the present day, faculty salaries at Moores Hill College were scandalously low. The president himself earned only $1,200 per year and the standard professor's salary during most of the nineteenth century was about $700. By comparison, at DePauw (then Asbury) University, professors earned $1,700 annually by 1873; yet at Moores Hill, it was not until after 1900 (with one exception) that a faculty member earned as much as $1,000.

Six options (short of closing the school forever) were available for dealing with the institution's heavy financial burden:

■ **Pass on the cost to the "consumer" by raising tuition.** Interestingly, this solution never received serious consideration. For a period of fifty-four years, tuition remained unchanged; indeed, one major program (the classical course) cost less in 1910 than in 1856. Average tuition during this period was $30 per year, which finally rose in 1911 to $42 and, in the last year of the College (1917), climbed to $45 for two semesters. The apparent rationale for holding the cost of instruction constant was fear that an increase would lead to a drop in enrollment, which the struggling institution could ill afford.

■ **Canvass the Board of Trustees for contributions.** This method was attempted but failed. The board consisted mainly of Moores Hill residents and Methodist ministers, not people of means. Even as late as 1916, when the board was asked to assume $1,000 of that year's $5,000 deficit, only $800 was pledged, and some of that was never collected.

■ **Request additional funds from the Southeast Indiana Conference of the Methodist Church,** especially since Moores Hill was the only college located in its district. This method also proved unsuccessful, particularly after 1894 when the Southeast Indiana Conference merged with the Indiana Conference. Even before that date, however, Methodist leaders preferred to support DePauw University. As the older, larger, and academically stronger school, DePauw was the conference favorite, and it seemed to make better sense to church leaders to channel available resources for the benefit of that institution, even if it meant reducing Moores Hill to little more than a feeder school. As a result, church backing for Moores Hill ranged from a low of $17.25 in 1887 to a maximum of $1,225 in 1912. (Expenses for the latter year were $12,000.)

■ **Merge Moores Hill College with DePauw University.** This idea is first recorded in the College minutes for 1879, but was not pursued. It reappears, however, some twenty-five years later (1904), when the board appointed a committee to "look after the matter of the affiliation

Moores Hill College: Class of 1912

of DePauw University and Moores Hill College." Again, no action followed, but the possibility was raised once more eleven years later (1915) when a specific and detailed proposal for merger was brought to the Moores Hill Board of Trustees and adopted. By February of 1916, however, the board report describes the entire subject as a "closed incident." (There is no recorded evidence that DePauw University ever wished for or looked favorably upon the proposed alliance with Moores Hill.)

- **Eliminate all third and fourth year programs,** which traditionally had much smaller enrollments than freshman and sophomore classes and were thus less cost-efficient to operate. The change to a junior college actually went into effect in the fall of 1916, but the anticipated substantial savings failed to materialize; in fact, by June 1917, the indebtedness of the College rose to an all-time high of $39,796.

- **Relocate the institution.** By 1917, it had become apparent that this was the only possible salvation for Moores Hill. The decision to relocate was hastened by a disastrous fire on November 4, 1915, which destroyed Moore Hall, the original College building erected in 1856. It was unrealistic to believe that funds could be raised to repair the damage, and the financial problem was compounded by a decision at the national level by the University Senate of the Methodist Church. By church decree, all four-year Methodist colleges were required to have an endowment fund of $200,000 by January 1, 1916. At the time of the great fire the stated endowment of Moores Hill College was

Historic marker at the site of original Moores Hill College building

between $67,000 and $75,000, but much of this was in unpaid pledges, so the actual amount was quite a bit less. Although a major financial campaign was attempted, it failed to reach the goal. In brief, both physically and financially, Moores Hill College was in shambles. Thus the stage was set for a fresh start at a new site.

ADMINISTRATION

Setting administrative and financial policies for Moores Hill College was the province of the Board of Trustees. When classes began in 1856, it had eight members, all of whom lived in the town. The number increased gradually so that by 1896 there were twenty-seven trustees, only a small minority residing in Moores Hill.

From 1856 until the college closed, 127 men served on the board, of whom fifty-six were ministers. The record for years of service on the board was set by George W. Wood (son of a charter trustee), who served for fifty-two years. Hanson D. Moore, son of founder John C. Moore, served for forty-eight years, and two other persons served forty years or more.

At times the board was blamed for the failure of the College to survive at Moores Hill. When it closed in 1917, board president E.C. Hawkins wrote in a letter to the school's president, Alfred Hughes: "The deplorable financial condition of Moores Hill College is a plain indication of either lack of capacity or outright neglect on the part of the trustees." In his reply, Hughes agreed, asserting, "Your statement is the exact truth and sentiment that has been clear as daylight to me for months."

In defense of the trustees, however, it should be remembered that their task was formidable and their resources – both of money and of time – extremely limited. Their achievement is put in perspective when we realize that in 1873 twelve colleges in Indiana operated under the auspices of the Methodist Church, but of these twelve, only two remain today: DePauw University and the University of Evansville.

The major responsibility for the day-to-day operation of the College lay with the president. There was a constant need to recruit new faculty, since Moores Hill's shaky financial situation forced most faculty members to leave quickly in search of more secure positions. (The average faculty stay was three years.) This problem, added to frustration with the school's other financial difficulties, helps to explain the very high level of turnover at the presidential level.

Here are sketches of the many individuals who dealt valiantly with Moores Hill's many problems and somehow succeeded in keeping the institution afloat some sixty years.

1856-1862

First President
SAMUEL R. ADAMS

Samuel R. Adams came to Indiana from New England to teach at Wilmington Seminary, only a few miles from Moores Hill. After three years at Wilmington, he was appointed president of the new Moores Hill Collegiate Institute at the age of only thirty-one.

Five years later, in 1861, when many of the male students were enlisting for service in the Union Army, Adams declared: "If my boys are going, I'm going, too." A year and a half later he died of exposure and disease in an army hospital.

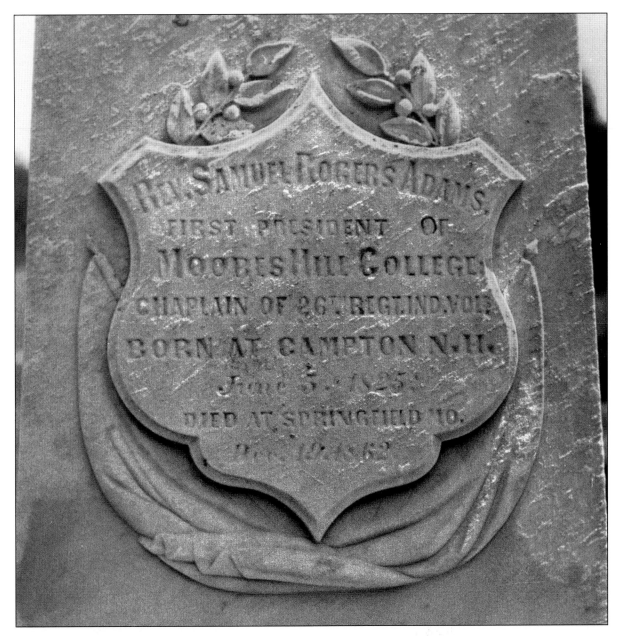

Tombstone of Samuel R. Adams

1862

Second President
ROBERT F. BREWINGTON

Robert F. Brewington, in addition to serving as its president, is notable as the College's first male graduate (1859). In September 1862, he resigned to enter the Union ranks.

1863-1864

Third President
WILLIAM O. PIERCE

William O. Pierce also left Moores Hill for military service (at which time Hannah Adams, the late president's widow, took charge of the college). Pierce was wounded in an early military action but recovered to return to Moores Hill for the 1863-64 year. During his tenure, he was able to double enrollment, but he resigned his position to enter the ministry of the Southeast Indiana Conference.

1864-1870

Fourth President
THOMAS HARRISON

Thomas Harrison was a native of England who came to the United States in 1835. After working as an editor and educator in Ohio, he served as minister of various Methodist churches in southern Indiana and was regarded as an outstanding preacher.

Harrison was chosen as president of Moores Hill College in 1864, just before the end of the Civil War and, like his predecessor, was successful in raising enrollment at the College to new heights. It is thought that the eloquence of his sermons was instrumental in stimulating interest in Moores Hill among young people and their parents.

Harrison resigned in 1870 to return to the ministry and in his later years also served as president of Brookville College.

20

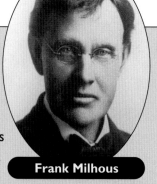

Frank Milhous

During the 1867-68 school year, during Harrison's term as president, Frank Milhous was an honor student at Moores Hill College. A century later, his grandson, Richard Milhous Nixon, was elected president of the United States.

1870-1872, 1890-1897, 1903-1904

Fifth President
JOHN H. MARTIN

John H. Martin holds the distinction of being Moores Hill's president during three separate periods: 1870-72, 1890-97, and 1903-04. Before his first term and in the eighteen years between his first and second terms, he was superintendent of schools in Franklin, Edinburg, and Madison, Indiana.

Martin was one of Moores Hill's most popular and personable administrators. A favorite anecdote relates to a Halloween prank involving several boys who planned to pull the president's carriage to the depot and then abandon it. Somehow Martin learned of the plot and concealed himself in the carriage. When the boys reached the depot after an easy downhill pull, the president surprised them, saying: "Thank you, boys; I enjoyed the ride. Now you may take me home." The pranksters labored up the steep hill to the president's home but, characteristically, that was the end of the episode. No apologies were required, no penalties were threatened, and no punishment meted out. (It must be said, however, that like many another good yarn, this story has come down with several variations, including attributing the incident to Martin's predecessor, Thomas Harrison, rather than to Martin himself.)

As president of Moores Hill, Martin was especially concerned with the College's teacher training curriculum and with the institution's physical plant. He solicited funds from Moores Hill residents to pay for campus repairs and improvements, and he also gave generously from his own pocket to benefit the College. When he retired from his second term as president, the Board of Trustees commended him for "his personal sacrifice in carrying the current expenses of the institution." Even after his final retirement, he continued to raise money for repairs and other College projects.

mons, but meanwhile enrollment at the College declined each of Hester's four years to its lowest point since the Civil War. Decreased enrollment led to even more severe financial difficulties than usual and after Hester began to experience serious health problems, he thought it best to resign.

1872-1876

Sixth President
FRANCIS ASBURY HESTER

Francis Asbury Hester filled the office of president from 1872 to 1876, but his first love was preaching, and administrative work was not really to his liking. Some Sundays he delivered three ser-

1876-1882

Seventh President
JOHN P.D. JOHN

John P.D. John was the most accomplished and most widely recognized of all Moores Hill's presidents. A native Hoosier, he was a college graduate at the age of sixteen and was appointed professor of mathematics at Brookville College at the

Moores Hill College Alumnae Reunion (1977)

21

age of twenty. By the age of twenty-three, he was its president.

Before he was thirty, he became vice president and professor of mathematics at Moores Hill and at thirty-three (1876) he was appointed president.

A new feature of John's years was that the College began to do some advertising. Each year he was authorized to have 1,000 postcards printed extolling the advantage of Moores Hill College and in 1877, he was allocated $75 for publicity.

Despite his efforts, his tenure was marked mainly by financial crises and low enrollments, leading to his resignation in 1882.

After leaving Moores Hill, however, John enjoyed many notable successes. After serving as a professor of mathematics at DePauw University for several years, he became that institution's president in 1889 and held the position until 1895. Widely known as lecturer, preacher, and writer, John crossed and re-crossed the United States several times giving lectures, in addition to writing five books.

1879-1880

Eighth President
JOHN H. DODDRIDGE

John H. Doddridge served as president of Moores Hill College for only one year (1879-80), replacing President John while the latter traveled and studied in Europe. Doddridge came to the College from the Methodist ministry and returned to the ministry as pastor of several major churches in southern Indiana until his retirement in 1924.

1882-1887

Ninth President
LOUIS G. ADKINSON

Louis G. Adkinson was a trustee of Moores Hill College before becoming its president in 1882.

His five-year term was generally uneventful, except near the beginning when, for the only time as far as can be determined from available records, the College decided to dismiss a professor. Responding to bitter student complaints about Professor J. W. Caldwell's methods of instruction only one month after Caldwell joined the faculty, and despite a spirited defense from Caldwell himself, the trustees decided to offer him $200 in return for his resignation, and the offer was accepted. (Having taught for slightly less than one month, Caldwell thus became the highest salaried teacher in Moores Hill's history.)

Adkinson resigned in 1887 to become president of New Orleans University.

1887-1890

Tenth President
GEORGE P. JENKINS

George P. Jenkins had taught mathematics at the College (1864-66) and, like his predecessor, was a member of the Board of Trustees at the time he was appointed president (1887). At Jenkins' suggestion, the cost of the annual catalog was financed by selling advertisements in the book. Sixteen advertisers participated and by 1894 the number had risen to twenty-six. This practice continued until 1900.

In Jenkins' last year as president (1890), the treasurer reported a surplus, a rare occurrence indeed. Unfortunately, the surplus amounted to a mere seventy-four cents!

1897-1903

Eleventh President
CHARLES W. LEWIS

Charles W. Lewis was educated at DePauw University and Moores Hill College, receiving a Master of Science degree from Moores Hill in 1893. Like two of his predecessors (John and Jenkins), he was a professor of mathematics and was vice president of the College when he was selected to be president (1897).

As president, Lewis recommended an aggressive program to solicit funds and increase the school's meager endowment. In his report to the trustees, he proposed that the College apply "modern business principles to the management of the College. The day has gone when we can do business on sentiment." Moreover, he warned, "the College that seeks patronage under the guise of Christianity and then attempts to run the institution on inadequate salaries and equipment is doomed." His rhetoric fell on deaf ears, however. The board ignored his recommendations and, consequently, he resigned in 1903 to become president of the University of Wyoming.

1904-1908

Twelfth President
FRANK C. ENGLISH

Frank C. English was born and educated in Ohio, taught in its public schools, and was pastor of several churches in that state. As president of Moores Hill College (1904-08), English proved to be the most successful fund-raiser in its history. This was due, at least in part, to his mastery of emotion-laden appeals. In the College bulletin, for example, he wrote:

Readers, have you ever inquired what you may do for the College? Do you not see that the President and faculty are straining every nerve to bring Moores Hill to the high water mark? Are you content to look on and do nothing while the sinews and nerves of others are almost snapping?

English also acted on his convictions. A direct visit to Andrew Carnegie to solicit money for a new science building resulted in a pledge to match whatever the College could raise. A vigorous financial campaign, supplemented by a sizable bank loan, enabled the College to erect an imposing three-story building, housing a library and administrative offices as well as science laboratories. At its completion, Carnegie Hall was regarded as the finest building of its kind on any college campus in Indiana. (Today Carnegie Hall is on the Historic Register, its basement holds a daycare center, and the building houses the town library, a museum

23

with Moores Hill memorabilia, and a shop which sells handicrafts.)

To crown his achievements, in his last year English reduced the school's deficit to $16.50!

returned to that institution after only one year (1908-09) at Moores Hill.

1908-1909

Thirteenth President
WILLIAM S. BOVARD

William S. Bovard was a Hoosier but came to Moores Hill from the University of Chattanooga, where he was dean of the School of Theology. He

1909-1915

Fourteenth President
HARRY ANDREWS KING

Harry Andrews King came to Moores Hill College from Baker University in Kansas. During his tenure (1909-15), he made a valiant effort to raise funds for the College but met with little success. When the Methodist Church issued its edict

Carnegie Hall, completed 1908

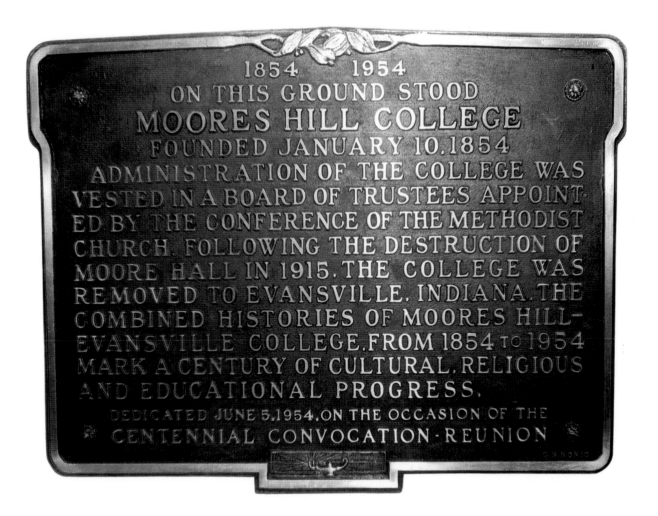

1854   1954
ON THIS GROUND STOOD
MOORES HILL COLLEGE
FOUNDED JANUARY 10, 1854
ADMINISTRATION OF THE COLLEGE WAS
VESTED IN A BOARD OF TRUSTEES APPOINT-
ED BY THE CONFERENCE OF THE METHODIST
CHURCH. FOLLOWING THE DESTRUCTION OF
MOORE HALL IN 1915. THE COLLEGE WAS
REMOVED TO EVANSVILLE, INDIANA. THE
COMBINED HISTORIES OF MOORES HILL-
EVANSVILLE COLLEGE, FROM 1854 TO 1954
MARK A CENTURY OF CULTURAL, RELIGIOUS
AND EDUCATIONAL PROGRESS.
DEDICATED JUNE 5, 1954, ON THE OCCASION OF THE
CENTENNIAL CONVOCATION · REUNION

requiring all Methodist-related colleges to have a substantial endowment fund ($100,000 by September of 1913 and $200,000 by 1916) it was apparent to all that Moores Hill could not possibly attain such a goal.

With the proposal that Moores Hill become a two-year extension of DePauw University, King believed that a solution to the College's problems had finally been achieved, and he felt free to accept the presidency of Clark University in Atlanta. However, as mentioned earlier, the affiliation with DePauw fell through and, in November 1915, the school was hit by the disastrous fire which destroyed Moore Hall. Nevertheless, the College graduated twenty students at its commencement in 1916, the last class to complete a four-year course of study. Also, the trustees decided to continue the institution at the junior college level and to seek a new president.

1916-1927

Fifteenth President
ALFRED F. HUGHES

Alfred F. Hughes was Moores Hill's last president, serving from the fall of 1916 until the College closed its doors the following June. During the school's final year Moores Hill offered mainly basic survey courses. Enrollment exceeded expectations and hope arose that a four-year standard college could be reestablished. The decision to relocate was now irrevocable, however, and most of Hughes' attentions were devoted to facilitating the institution's move to Evansville, where he would continue as president of the new Evansville College. Therefore, further discussion of Hughes will be delayed until the chapters to follow.

25

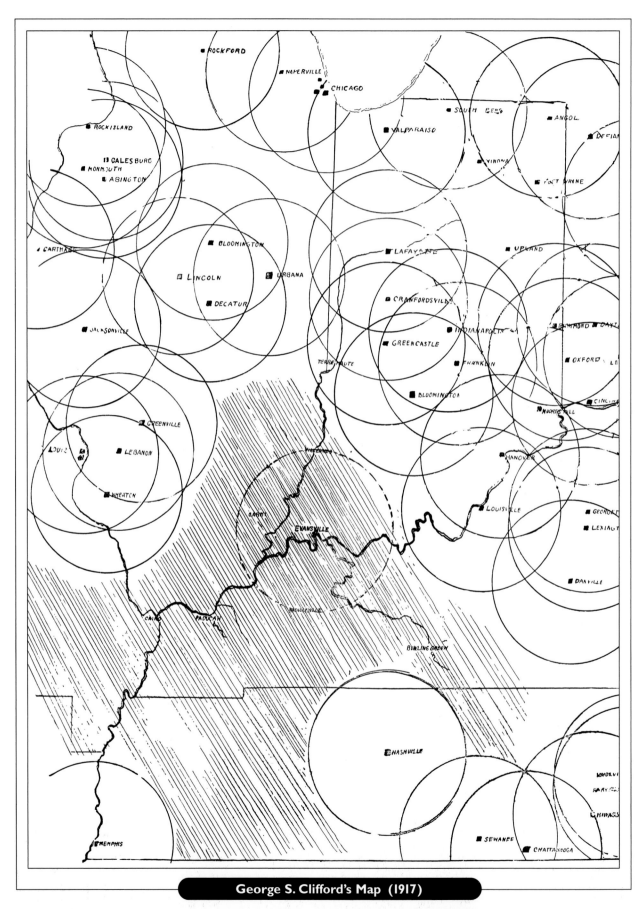

George S. Clifford's Map (1917)

Clifford's map of circles was an important sales argument for the establishment of Evansville College

CHAPTER TWO

Transition: The Move to Evansville

George S. Clifford

In view of the financial exigencies described in the preceding chapter, the need to choose a new location must have been abundantly clear to everyone connected with Moores Hill College, yet no one seemed willing to initiate the process. Whatever thoughts might have been in the minds of the Moores Hill administration, there were no public statements on the subject and nothing was ever set down on paper. Instead, the first recorded words on the subject came in the form of a letter of inquiry from Evansville industrialist George S. Clifford, a local business leader with a strong interest in education and science.

Civic leaders in Evansville had long been distressed by the lack of an institution of higher learning to serve the needs of the largest city in the state south of the capital. Clifford had read a newspaper account of the disastrous fire at Moores Hill and recognized a possible opportunity for Evansville to acquire a college of its own. With the encouragement of the Evansville Chamber of Commerce, he dispatched a letter to Moores Hill in December 1915, proposing that the College be rebuilt in Evansville.

His letter was ill-timed, however, since Moores Hill College was then in the midst of negotiations with DePauw University concerning a merger of the two institutions. Clifford soon received a brusque reply requesting that the idea be dropped immediately as it might interfere with the anticipated merger.

27

Group of Evansville citizens launch campaign

Fortunately, the letter was not destroyed and was found in the College files by Alfred Hughes when he became Moores Hill president the following year. As has been noted, the union with DePauw University failed to materialize and the idea of relocation was then, for the first time, considered in earnest. John Hancher, associate secretary of the Board of Education of the Methodist Church, suggested moving the College to Seymour, a town of 7,000 located about 45 miles west of Moores Hill, where he felt the school would enjoy excellent prospects for success.

The bishop, William F. Anderson, however, considered Evansville more suitable and proposed that President Hughes schedule an exploratory meeting with the Evansville Chamber of Commerce to determine whether Evansville was "serious or only flirting." This session, occurring in January 1917, went well; accordingly, another meeting was scheduled for the following month in Indianapolis with the Joint Educational Commis-

sion, representing the three conferences of the Indiana Methodist Church. On this occasion, delegations from both Seymour and Evansville were invited to make presentations.

George Clifford represented Evansville and impressed the commission by displaying a map of a four-state area which included Illinois, Indiana, Kentucky, and Tennessee. The map showed the location of every accredited four-year college or university, and around each he drew a circle having a radius of fifty miles. The circle drawn around Moores Hill intersected ten other circles, perhaps helping to explain why a college there had failed to compete successfully for students. But the circle with a radius of fifty miles drawn around Evansville touched no other circle in any state. Indeed, it showed that the accredited four-year colleges nearest to Evansville were well over 100 miles away, while the area around Seymour was already served by many educational institutions. Moreover, the population of the circle around Evansville was con-

28

sidered sufficient to support as many as three colleges. Clifford's reasoning carried the day and, with no dissenting votes, the commission recommended relocation to Evansville.

The following month, a group of Evansville citizens offered to launch a campaign to raise $500,000 for the new college if the Indiana Conference would pledge a matching amount. Before the conference pledge could be obtained, however, there were objections from DePauw University supporters that needed to be addressed. They argued that to speak of moving Moores Hill College to Evansville was sheer nonsense, that in fact there was no college to move since the school's liabilities greatly exceeded its assets. More important, DePauw University and the Methodist Church itself were engaged in major fund drives, both of which might be harmed at this time by a competing effort to support a college in Evansville.

George R. Gross, president of DePauw University, helped the Evansville cause by declaring that it would be neither Christian nor charitable for him to

oppose the move to Evansville. Others, however, sought to persuade the Methodist Board of Education to withhold the services of Hancher, the most expert and most successful fund-raiser in the Indiana Conference. This move led Bishop Anderson, ever an Evansville booster, to state that in such an event he would lead the campaign himself. Such was the bishop's prestige that the opposition collapsed and Hancher came to Evansville to conduct a campaign that would enhance his already outstanding reputation as a fund-raiser.

But before the campaign could get fully underway, a major international event intervened when, on April 6, 1917, the United States declared war on Germany. This action led to calls to delay any further efforts until the end of hostilities, but Mayor Benjamin Bosse was persuaded to proceed. In support of his decision the mayor explained, "I never want it said of me that I failed to do all in my power to provide for the boys and girls of Evansville the educational opportunities which I did not receive."

Although he was writing in 1970, Ralph Olmsted's words concerning the 1917 campaign remain true today: "It is doubtful that Evansville has ever experienced anything before or since to compare with the half-million dollar establishment fund campaign, which began April 15 and was concluded at midnight on May 3, 1917. In the early negotiations there were those who were quite sure that to attempt to raise $500,000 was at least folly if not insanity." (Up to this time, the largest sum ever raised in Evansville for non-commercial purposes was the $150,000 contributed five years earlier for the YMCA building.)

Come On – Bring Him Home!

Win the College and the Opening Ball Game Today

Cartoon by Karl Kae Knecht

29

Reproduction of an April 23, 1917, Evansville Journal-News advertisement

What a College Will Mean For Evansville

A QUARTER OF A MILLION DOLLARS spent here annually by faculty and every 500 students.

INCREASED POPULATION by establishing one new home on an average, for every fourteen students who come to Evansville.

AN INCREASE in the value of property.

BOOSTERS FOR EVANSVILLE in the company of young men and women who graduate each year to go out over the country.

A STANDARD COLLEGE EDUCATION for the Evansville boys and girls who could not afford to leave home to get it.

TRAINED LEADERSHIP for the industries of Evansville.

AN ELEVATION of intellectual and moral standards of our city.

AN ADDITION to the culture and efficiency of our citizenship by drawing into our city many splendid young men and women who would remain after graduation.

EVANSVILLE'S BECOMING KNOWN as a college town.

Detail from advertisement on previous page

Leading the 1917 drive for Evansville College was the city's popular and dynamic mayor, Benjamin Bosse, ably supported by J.R.A. Hobson, manager of the telephone company, and Howard C. Batton, a prominent businessman. Also lending much-needed media assistance were Howard Roosa, editor of the *Evansville Courier*, and Karl Kae Knecht, the newspaper's leading political cartoonist. These men made sure that, for eleven consecutive days, the college made the front page, both in word and in picture.

Enthusiasm rose as over 400 people joined the fund-raising effort, and before long people who had earlier been skeptical of the campaign's chances of success became eager and ardent supporters.

Contributions from the lowly and the mighty flowed in. Grade school children gave their pennies, dimes, and quarters for the college, and high school students donated nearly $1,000. Almost all Evansville school teachers gave amounts totaling several thousand dollars. At Fulton School, for example, every teacher pledged $50 and even the janitor gave $25. Industrialist G. A. Trimble contributed the $5,000 which he had saved to buy an automobile, and a railroad brakeman walked seven miles from Howell to the Courier Building to personally deliver his gift of five dollars.

As in any major fund-raising effort, it was the large donors who dramatically brought the campaign closer to achieving its ambitious goal. Bosse and his business associates at the Globe-Bosse-World Furniture Co. contributed $28,500, and $42,000 came from Haller T. Chute in memory of his father, Daniel Chute, a distinguished Evansville school teacher. Other sizable donations were made by William H. McCurdy, president of Hercules Buggy Company (later Servel), who gave $25,000 and the Samuel L. Orr family, who contributed $12,000. In addition, there were several gifts of $10,000 and $5,000 each.

31

Today Is Your Last Chance

The College Campaign Closes at Midnight

Will men point their fingers at YOU and say:

That fellow kept a standard College out of Evansville. He is so self-satisfied, so self-centered, that he refused to give, or did not give as he should.

He had money enough to help educate hundreds who lacked the necessary funds.

He makes his living out of Evansville, but would not help others make better livings.

He pushed the town back instead of pulling it forward.

He was a brake when power was wanted. He deserves nothing from US.

Will they point their fingers at you and say those things, OR

Are you doing your part — giving your share — urging others to give to bring the College to Evansville?

Today—Give Your Answer

This Advertisement was written by J. Kornblum, Adv. Mgr. Strouse & B

Reproduction of a May 3, 1917, **Evansville Journal-News** *advertisement*

To record the progress of the drive, a huge thermometer was mounted on the ten-story Citizens Bank Building at Fourth and Main Streets. Each day, campaign leaders rode a fire truck to the building, and a sign painter ascended a ladder to paint the red mercury column up to the amount that had been raised thus far.

By May 3, the last day of the campaign, the total – though impressive – was still $50,000 short of the goal. Raising this amount was absolutely critical because, under the terms of the campaign, if the full $500,000 could not be raised, all contributions would have to be returned to their donors and all the effort expended would have been in vain.

Bosse decided that the person best able to save the day was Francis Joseph Reitz, president of National City Bank, one of the city's wealthiest men and a leading Catholic layman. Bosse gathered a delegation which included Bishop Anderson, President Hughes, Pastor M. P. Giffin of Trinity Methodist Church, and Rabbi Max Merritt.

Reitz was initially skeptical of the delegation's claim that his help was desperately needed but finally agreed to give $25,000 if the group and their friends could raise a matching amount. With little time remaining, the canvassers redoubled their efforts to meet the challenge. The Trinity Methodist Church board authorized an additional contribution of $10,000, and telephone solicitations continued throughout that fateful evening of May 3, 1917.

A mass meeting held at the Soldiers and Sailors Memorial Coliseum was attended by more than 1,000 people who were gathered to hear the solicitors' reports of their progress, the results coming in by telephones which were installed especially for the occasion with the telephone number 500,000. Finally, just a few minutes before midnight, the mayor was able to announce to the jubilant crowd that the goal had not only been reached but had been exceeded with a total of $514,000!

Evansville would have its college – but only if the Indiana Conference of the Methodist Church could successfully raise its share, a matching $500,000. A closing date for this effort was set for December 20, 1917. The terms of the Evansville campaign (namely, that none of the pledges would be valid unless the full amount was raised) would also apply to the church fund drive, and it was further specified that if the conference campaign failed, the pledges given in Evansville would likewise be invalid.

The new drive soon encountered a serious obstacle when Hughes, weakened by the physical and emotional strain of the year's activities, fell ill and had to spend the better part of two months in a sanitarium.

With the arrival of winter, fund-raising efforts were hampered again, this time by unprecedented snowstorms which closed many roads for long periods. As the December 20 deadline approached it was abundantly clear that the $500,000 goal would not be attained.

Only drastic action could save the day, and the measure that was adopted was indeed bold and probably illegal, but it accomplished its purpose.

On December 19, 1917, the superintendents of the eight districts of the Indiana Conference met with Bishop Anderson in Indianapolis and, acting on behalf of the conference, signed a promissory note for $240,000, thus technically completing the campaign.

The declared intention was to pay the note in full by May of the following year, but this failed to happen. Nevertheless, in September of 1918 the full Indiana Conference officially voted its support of its bishop and the district superintendents in this matter, and the four leading Evansville banks accepted the note as collateral for loans to the College. Lawsuits were brought against the College, claiming that the conference had, in actuality, failed to raise its share of the required money, and the issue was finally appealed to the Indiana Supreme Court. The state's highest court resolved the issue by ruling in favor of the College.

It would be several years before the promissory note was finally liquidated but, meanwhile, plans for the fledgling College had to be implemented quickly so that classes could begin in the fall of 1919.

First, for the College to operate legally, it had to apply for a charter from the state of Indiana to

Governor James P. Goodrich signs the charter on February 17, 1919

33

Physical education class at the YMCA (1919-1920)

replace the one granted to Moores Hill College some 65 years earlier. The charter was duly approved by the Indiana General Assembly and was signed into law by Governor James P. Goodrich on February 17, 1919.

The charter specified that Evansville College be considered the legal continuation of Moores Hill College rather than a new institution and that alumni of Moores Hill henceforth be regarded as alumni of Evansville College. The charter also required that a major building on the new campus should bear the name of John C. Moore "in order to honor and perpetuate the memory of the founder of Moores Hill College." (This did not actually occur until 1960, when the first women's dormitory on campus was named Moore Hall.) Further, the charter stipulated that "Evansville College shall maintain perpetually a historic museum in which shall be sacredly kept all records, pictures, and other articles which are intimately associated with the history of Moores Hill College."

Finally, the charter established a Board of Trustees of twenty-one members, fourteen of whom would be elected by the Indiana Conference of the Methodist Church, and the remaining seven by the Evansville Chamber of Commerce. Although the inclusion of the chamber was unusual for a church-related institution, it was deemed appropriate recognition for the significant role played by the chamber in raising the required $500,000 two years earlier. (Representation of the chamber on the Board of Trustees continued until 1974.)

Building a college campus would, of necessity, be a time-consuming process, and Evansville was

YMCA building (1919)

34

impatient for its new institution of higher learning to open its doors, so a temporary location had to be found. The downtown area offered many possibilities, and a committee finally devised the package that seemed most feasible.

The Young Men's Hebrew Association on Vine Street between Fifth and Sixth Streets offered to rent space to the College in its three-story, thirteen-room building for $200 per month. Directly across the street was the YMCA, which could provide both a physical education program as well as housing for men. In addition, nearby Lockyear's Business College offered to rent the College a large basement room suitable for a biology laboratory and a classroom. A block away, Central High School provided space for chemistry classes for the first three years. The YMCA cafeteria was available at mealtime, and a women's residence hall, Sweetser Hall, was opened in rented quarters in the 700 block of Southeast (then Upper) First Street, about ten blocks from the classroom buildings. (It continued as a women's residence hall for two years after the move to the new campus.)

On September 16, 1919, when Evansville College opened for instruction, 104 students were enrolled. By comparison, when classes began at Moores Hill, sixty-six college students were registered; during the final year of its existence, only twenty-five were enrolled.

Tuition was set at $25 for a full quarter of study. In addition, there were laboratory fees for science and home economics courses, and $2 per quarter was charged for each hour beyond the standard sixteen which constituted a full load.

At the head of the line on enrollment day was

Norman D. Beach (standing), first student enrolled at Evansville College, with associates (1920-22)

Norman D. Beach who, two years before, had made a one dollar advance payment on tuition to ensure his claim to being the first student enrolled at Evansville College. (After his graduation from the College, he served for many years as a Latin teacher at Central High School.)

Eleven faculty members initiated the academic program at the new Evansville College. Hand-picked by Hughes himself, all were graduates of leading colleges and universities, had previous teaching experience in higher education, and were persons of "upstanding character" in accordance with Hughes' firm belief that teachers exert a profound influence on the personal lives of their students. Four members of the new faculty had earned doctoral degrees and three had previously been at Moores Hill.

Sixty-three years and seven days had elapsed from the opening of Moores Hill College to its reincarnation as Evansville College. Students, faculty, and administration were joined as one, sharing the exhilaration of establishing a new institution and forging fresh traditions. The future seemed promising indeed!

35

Administration Hall under Construction

Administration Hall Shortly after Completion

CHAPTER THREE

Evansville College: 1919 to 1940

Students pulled a plow to break ground for Administration Hall; Helen Busse, first Evansville College graduate leads

BACKGROUND

The founders of Evansville College were keenly aware that the beginning of their school coincided with an important moment in world history. The first publication of the new college, *Information for Prospective Students*, issued in May 1919, states:

This institution comes into existence at an auspicious time. The new world-to-be will call for thousands of well-equipped leaders. The educational demands of today and tomorrow are not those of yesterday. The late war has laid new emphasis upon the kind of education that equips young people for definite tasks of practical service. The war has, likewise, taught the danger of education without a soul. … Evansville College will endeavor to provide a background of rich ethical culture and spiritual values, while at the same time affording its students the training needed for specialized tasks.

37

Mayor Bosse, chairman of the building committee, at the plow breaking ground for Administration Hall; James Scarborough, contractor (bow tie), at far right

A NEW HOME

While the downtown location of the College was a reasonably adequate temporary makeshift, Evansville was eager to find a permanent home for its newest treasure. Selecting a site, however, proved to be a highly contentious issue. Several locations were proposed, but eventually the options were reduced to three: one on the west side, the second near Akin Park on the city's south side just west of Kentucky Avenue, and the third a seventy-acre tract just west of Weinbach Avenue between Lincoln Avenue and Division Street (then known as Slaughter Avenue). Evansville's mayor, Benjamin Bosse, favored the second of these but was persuaded to change his position in favor of the third, which ultimately was chosen for the new campus. Since the Akin Park area was under eight to ten feet of water during the 1937 flood, this proved to be a very fortunate decision.

In November of 1919, a building committee was appointed, both to develop a comprehensive long-range plan and to initiate construction of the first building. The mayor chaired the group, which also included Howard Roosa, George S. Clifford, Richard Rosencranz, and Alfred E. Craig. The architects' proposal was ambitious, calling for the construction of twenty-two buildings of Indiana limestone, arranged in a quadrangle and joined by covered walkways. This elaborate plan was approved by the Board of Trustees, but only one structure – the administration building – ever got beyond the drawing board.

Until its purchase for the campus at a cost of $83,000, the seventy-acre plot had been used as farmland; indeed, as Administration Hall was being constructed in 1921, the corn rows from the previous summer were clearly visible.

With enrollment under 550 at all times until 1945, this building was adequate for nearly all of the institution's needs.

It should be noted that in addition to being extremely functional, Administration Hall also made architectural history. Constructed of Indiana limestone, its stones were of variegated hues and of

38

SCHEDULE FOR CONSTRUCTION OF ADMINISTRATION HALL

MARCH 15, 1921
Contract signed

MAY 9, 1921
Official groundbreaking
President Hughes, Mayor Bosse, other officials, and several students took turns pulling the plow. This traditional ceremony was used previously in 1906 at Moores Hill College for the groundbreaking of Carnegie Hall.

JUNE 21, 1921
Laying of the cornerstone

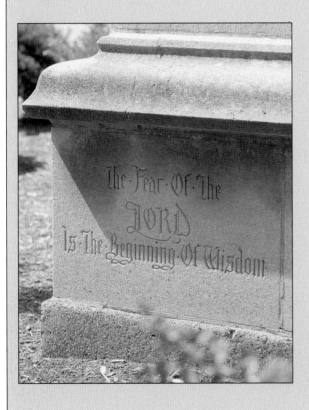

JUNE 12, 1922
First classes held in the new building

JUNE 16, 1922
Official dedication ceremony, together with commencement exercises for the Class of 1922
Speakers included Bishop Frederick D. Leete, president of the Board of Trustees; Reverend William N. Dresel, who delivered a tribute to Benjamin Bosse, recently deceased; Mayor William Elmendorf, Bosse's successor; Joseph R. Harker, representing the Board of Education of the Methodist Church; and other dignitaries. The program also included a song with words and music written by Mrs. Albion Fellows Bacon. The commencement address was delivered by William Lowe Bryan, president of Indiana University.

Construction of Administration Hall required just over one year and cost $315,000. The *College Bulletin* glowingly reported:

> **In this commodious edifice are to be found an auditorium seating 600, trustees' rooms, four administrative offices, two fireproof vaults, ten professors' offices, five laboratories, two seminar rooms, four music rooms, a library reading room seating 100, stack space for books, restrooms, three locker rooms, and seventeen classrooms.**

39

random widths. The ends were broken, not sawed, thus eliminating the straight vertical joints which were customary in such buildings of the period. It is believed that this is the first time Bedford stone was used in this fashion in the United States.

The overall design of the structure so impressed distinguished architect Ralph Adams Cram that he wrote:

> **I knew nothing of Evansville College. I did not know what to expect of its first building. I found it to be a structure of most positive beauty. Its style is Collegiate Gothic, yet it has a beautiful balance between its tower and other masses. I should describe it as modern in every sense of the word and one of the most beautiful of its kind in the country.**

House donated by Mr. and Mrs. John L. Igleheart for use by the president of Evansville College

Until 1947, the only other buildings on the seventy-acre plot originally purchased for the campus were a "temporary" frame gymnasium (which, from 1946 until 1962, also housed the music department) plus a small heating plant, both built in 1922, and a fully furnished president's house, given to the College in 1928 by Mr. and Mrs. John L. Igleheart.

Because of the tight financial situation, little was done to improve or beautify the campus in the first few years. Both the driveway and the sidewalk in front of Administration Hall were made of cinders. A cement sidewalk running halfway from the street to the building was constructed by the Class of 1926 as a graduation present to the school, but the remaining half was not completed for another three years. (Plans for a paved circular driveway extending to Lincoln Avenue did not come to fruition until 1948.) There were no electric lights on campus until the early 1930s, and campus grass was cut with a horse-drawn field mower.

Students participate in an annual attack on dandelions

40

A minor but continuing annoyance was the "sea of gold" filling the campus each spring when it became overgrown with dandelions. In 1926, at the suggestion of President Hughes, classes were dismissed for a day so that students and faculty could attack the dandelions with butcher knives and any other implements available. Prizes were given for the largest number of dandelions dug up by one person and for the largest dandelion plant.

For several years, care of the campus and maintenance of its buildings was the responsibility of College custodian Neeley Strayhorne, assisted by students (some competent but others not up to the jobs assigned to them). In 1929, a full-time professional superintendent of buildings and grounds, Clarence M. Schultz, was appointed. He served in this capacity for the next twenty-one years.

Max B. Robinson, Engineering, 1920-1928 (see page 48)

Henry J. Bassett, Latin and Greek, 1920-1929 (see page 60)

ADMINISTRATION AND ACADEMICS

The 1919 bulletin for Evansville College announced seventy-two courses to be given the first year, representing fourteen departments. The course distribution was as follows:

Education	10
Biblical Literature and Religious Education	8
English	7
History	6
Latin	6
Home Economics	6
Greek	5
Mathematics	5
French	4
German	3
Spanish	3
Biology	3
Physics	3
Chemistry	2
Economics	1
Total	72

So that the new College could offer the greatest possible diversity of courses during an academic year, President Hughes chose the quarter system rather than the semester plan. In 1928, however, the College switched to semesters and remained on this system for the next twenty years.

In addition to regular day classes, the College offered late afternoon classes intended to serve the community. English literature was the most popular of these (see page 54), with economics the second. Classes in astronomy, the Bible, French, government, home economics, psychology, and oral English (speech) also attracted interest. Total enrollment ranged from 245 to 289. After 1924, community classes were known as extension courses, and the emphasis shifted from general interest subjects to classes intended primarily to serve the needs of teachers. Most of these met at Central High School downtown.

41

On June 8, 1920, these Moores Hill College alumni, photographed on the courthouse steps, had their diplomas endorsed by Evansville College

Left to right, first row E. C. Strickler, Mrs. A. J. Bigney, Harriet Barker, Otto L. Curl, Virgil Thompson, J. C. White; *Second row* Mrs. W. T. Jones, Lillie Fosbrink, Gladys Shipman Graham, Louwillie Kessler Smith, Willard C. Patrick, Roy H. Valentine, Charles Deich, Victor B. Hargitt, W. E. Cissna; *Third row* W. T. Jones, Earl H. Mitchell, Harry R. Glick, Walter B. Grimes, W. E. Fisher, Josie Campbell, Lucetta Ferguson Burnett; *Fourth row* Curtis B. Michael, Samuel J. Copeland, Lela Mary Schooley, A. J. Bigney, Lillian Miller Nagle, Fannie Dashiell Orebaugh, Ora Belle Stevens Brown

Since the role of the College was to provide educational opportunities for the community, the school operated under an open admission policy. There were no entrance requirements and very few applicants were ever rejected.

Tuition at the new College was $75 per year, an increase of sixty-five percent over the tuition last charged at Moores Hill College. (A discount, however, was available to "children of ministers of the gospel," who were allowed a reduction of $15 per quarter when enrolled for fifteen hours of course work or more.) It is notable that, while tuition costs at Moores Hill College remained nearly unchanged for fifty-four years, fifty years after Evansville College opened, tuition costs had increased almost 1,500 percent!

During the winter and spring quarters of 1919-20, enrollment was slightly over the 104 registered in the fall, and a record 128 signed up for the sum-

mer session. After eliminating duplications, 303 different persons enrolled during the year and an additional 241 attended various late afternoon and community courses (many for teachers), making a grand total of 544 persons.

In June of 1921, as part of the ceremony laying the cornerstone of the new Administration Hall, Evansville College conferred its first degree – the only one for that year – to Helen Busse (later Mrs. Carl Wolflin), who had previously attended Indiana University for two years. In future years her daughter and granddaughter would also graduate from Evansville College.

The following year, twelve persons graduated, although all but one had begun their college education elsewhere. The exception (who was able to complete four years' work in three) was Jane Elizabeth Wright, who thus became the first person to graduate having done all her work at Evansville

College. She was also the first person to be graduated magna cum laude. Later to become Mrs. Ralph Olmsted, she went on to teach English composition at Evansville College for more than thirty years.

Of the fifty-four persons who entered as freshmen in 1919 (the other students who enrolled had taken classes elsewhere), fifteen were graduated four years later, together with ten transfer students, to make a total of twenty-five in the Class of 1923.

By this time, it must be noted, the College had seen fit to increase its tuition from $25 per quarter to $45 (with the summer session priced at $35). In defense of this not inconsiderable increase, the *College Bulletin* states:

> **Evansville College does not care to be known as a "cheap college" … It prefers to be known as a college where students are sure of receiving high grade instruction from men and women of professional reputation and recognized ability, and where the very best in the way of physical equipment is provided.**

The Evansville College Alumni Association was organized in June of 1920 but at first consisted entirely of Moores Hill College graduates. Since all Moores Hill graduates were, by state law, alumni of Evansville College, Moores Hill alumni were invited to attend the 1920 commencement exercises to receive an endorsement to their diplomas certifying them as Evansville College graduates. Forty-one persons attended, and the commencement address was delivered by Bishop Anderson.

In 1925, the Alumni Association issued a newsletter called the *Alumnus*. At first it was a four-page mimeographed bulletin, but beginning with the second issue it was printed.

Dean Torbet (left) and President Hughes at President Harper's inauguration (1928)

THE PRESIDENTS AND THEIR ASSOCIATES

The tone of an institution and the image it projects to the outside world owe much to its president. Evansville College was fortunate to begin its life with a president noted for his openness, confidence, and optimism.

1916-1927

Fifteenth President
ALFRED F. HUGHES

Alfred Hughes, a native of Ohio, was a Methodist pastor in Columbus, Ohio, when he was chosen president of Moores Hill College at the age of thirty-four. When Hughes announced that it would be necessary to relocate the institution, many Moores Hill citizens were angered. To appease them, he proposed that the campus and buildings be turned over to the town for public use, and this was done. (For many years Carnegie Hall was used as Moores Hill High School.)

Hughes was inaugurated as president of Evansville College at a ceremony held in the Memorial Coliseum in November of 1919. His associates were:

Charles E. Torbet, *Dean and Registrar*
(Came with Hughes from Moores Hill; had taught English and history there since 1901 and also served as librarian, registrar, and for a time as vice president)

43

Charles P. Beard, *Executive Secretary*
(business manager)
(An Evansville businessman who had recently completed a term as county auditor)

Lucy Jenkins Franklin, *Dean of Women*
(Also a full-time teacher)

Completing the administrative staff were two secretaries and a bookkeeper.

When Franklin resigned in 1924, she was succeeded by **Wahnita DeLong**, who remained in the position for twenty-three years. In 1925, Hughes added **Ralph Olmsted**, a recent Evansville College graduate, to the administrative staff as assistant to the president, charged mainly with public relations. Three years later, Olmsted was appointed executive secretary (business manager) of the College, a position he held for thirty-nine years. In 1926, an additional part-time position, dean of men, was created.

Hughes' personal magnetism can be credited with attracting some of the school's most distinguished students and faculty members. For example, **Guy B. Marchant**, a highly esteemed professor of engineering and mathematics for thirty-three

Dean Wahnita DeLong (left) and former Dean Lucy J. Franklin at DeLong's twenty-five year recognition dinner

years, first came to Evansville in 1924 to be interviewed for a position in electrical engineering. His initial impression of the College was so unfavorable, however, that he determined to leave without delay. College campuses he was accustomed to had fine buildings, broad walks and drives, and professional landscaping. Instead he was chagrined to see a lone building surrounded by a weedy, unkept lawn and approachable only by a cinder path. Nevertheless, Marchant felt duty-bound to honor his appointment with Hughes, and when the president conveyed his plans for the school's engineer-

President Hughes at work (note the "modern" telephone)

A VARIETY OF DUTIES

In the early years of Evansville College, when the staff was small, each administrator performed a variety of duties. For example, in addition to his work as business manager, Ralph Olmsted was superintendent of buildings and grounds, alumni secretary, admission director, and placement officer.

One of Hughes' "extracurricular" activities nearly cost him his life. While posting signs around the campus, the president fell into an old well. Fortunately, he was able to grasp the sides of the well with his hands and climb out unharmed.

ing program, he communicated his vision with such enthusiasm that Marchant accepted Hughes' job offer immediately, remaining at Evansville College until his retirement in 1957.

Hughes often repeated his credo that "a college, whatever else it does, should serve and enrich the community where it is situated." In keeping with this philosophy, he sought ways to improve Evansville's quality of life. One way to achieve this goal, in his view, was for Evansville to adopt the city manager plan of government, which was working successfully in many localities across the nation. Hughes led a vigorous civic movement, drawing up a petition and securing the signatures necessary to hold a public referendum on the issue. Both political parties opposed the plan, however, and the final blow was a ruling by the Indiana Supreme Court declaring the petition invalid because of legal technicalities. Frustrated by this defeat, Hughes resolved to leave Evansville at the first opportunity and did so when he was offered the presidency of Hamline University in St. Paul, Minnesota.

Hughes was one of the most popular presidents in the institution's history. Administration Hall, in which he took particular pride, was largely his design. In 1954, the College bestowed on him the honorary degree of Doctor of Humanities, and four years later, when the school erected its first

permanent residence hall, it was named in his honor. Hughes died in 1962 at the age of eighty.

1927-1936

Sixteenth President
EARL E. HARPER

Earl E. Harper, like Hughes, was a minister by training. When he came to Evansville College in 1927 at the age of thirty-two, he had no college administrative experience and lacked business training and experience as well. His first love was for the liberal arts, with a particularly strong interest in music and art, but he was realistic enough to

January 18, 1928

President Harper with Antarctic explorer, Commander (later rear admiral) Richard E. Byrd
_____

45

Inauguration of President Earl Harper on March 22, 1928

recognize the importance and value of vocational and professional training. His practicality served the institution well, since it fell to him to lead the College through the century's major depression.

After leaving Evansville, Harper spent three years at Simpson College (where current UE president, Stephen Jennings, was president from 1987 to 1998) in Indianola, Iowa, before moving on to become director of the School of Fine Arts and director of the union at the University of Iowa, serving that university for twenty-five years.

In 1940, he received the honorary Doctor of Humanities degree from Evansville College, and three years before his death in 1967, at the age of seventy-two, the new College dining center was named in his honor.

1936-1940

Seventeenth President
FRANCIS MARION SMITH

In 1936, when Harper resigned, a search committee of trustees was formed to find a successor. For the first time in the institution's history, a faculty committee was also chosen to "advise and consult" with the trustees in the selection process. The salary being offered was $5,100 per year, and the committee's choice fell to forty-one-year-old Francis Marion Smith. Smith was then minister of

46

Trinity Methodist Church in Springfield, Massachusetts, a large and progressive church which he had served since 1930, after receiving his Doctor of Philosophy from Columbia University.

Smith's tenure proved to be a turning point in the history of the College. Details of the major events of his administration will follow later in this chapter.

Although not involved with day-to-day operations, the work of the Board of Trustees is vital to the success of any college. Happily, Evansville College enjoyed the services of a dedicated and supportive board.

The original board had twenty-one persons, as specified in the school's charter granted by the state of Indiana, and included a newspaper editor, an attorney, a rabbi, the mayor of Evansville, several Methodist ministers (including the bishop),

Emily Orr Clifford

EMILY ORR CLIFFORD
JULY 26,1866   FEBRUARY 9,1962
AS A DEVOTED WIFE SHE INSPIRED
HIM TO REALIZE HIS DREAM AND
WITH EVER INCREASING DEVOTION
TO HIS IDEALS AND TO THIS IN-
STITUTION SHE CONTINUES TO BE
AN INSPIRATION TO ALL WHO
ENTER HERE

The first woman to serve on the board, Emily Orr Clifford, served for twenty years and was awarded an honorary Doctor of Humanities degree by Evansville College in 1940. She was elected in 1928 to replace her late husband, George S. Clifford. An active civic leader, Clifford was noted for her work with the American Red Cross and served as the first president of both the Public Health Nursing Association and the Evansville Musicians Club.

As a trustee, Clifford served on a committee that handled faculty and staff appointments. On a stifling summer day the group was to meet at the McCurdy Hotel in the Coral Room (a dining area which also served alcoholic beverages) and was at the time its only air-conditioned space.

A long-time Presbyterian (and a Sunday school teacher for many years), she sternly announced that, "at the age of 71, I have never been in a saloon in my life, and I don't intend to set foot in one now." In a display of gallantry, the group agreed to forgo air-conditioning and to meet in a (hot) hallway instead.

numerous prominent business leaders, and the president of the College, ex officio. Members of various Protestant denominations, the Roman Catholic Church, and the Jewish faith have served on the board over the years.

Despite this diversity, broader representation – both locally and statewide – was desired and, therefore, in 1921, the Indiana General Assembly was asked to authorize an increase in board membership to thirty-six (plus the president of the College, ex officio). The change was approved, and henceforth nine members were chosen by the Evansville Chamber of Commerce, eighteen by the Indiana Conference, and nine at-large members were selected by the other twenty-seven members of the board. This composition of the board remained unchanged for thirty-six years.

Members were elected for three-year terms but could serve multiple terms, as many have. For example, charter member Richard Rosencranz was elected secretary of the board in 1919 and held the office for the next forty-two years. (After 1934, Rosencranz was the only one of the original twenty-one who was still a member of the board.)

As the need arises, the Board of Trustees selects the president of the institution, but its primary responsibility is the school's financial health. Accordingly, trustees have usually led the campaigns necessary to erect new buildings, augment the endowment, and raise funds for operating expenses. During the period under discussion, major fund drives were led by the following trustees:

1917	Benjamin Bosse
1924	William H. McCurdy
1932	Walton M. Wheeler
1933	John L. Igleheart
1934	Clarence Leich
1935	W. A. Carson
1940	Richard R. McGinnis

ACADEMICS

PROFESSIONAL PROGRAMS

The curriculum initially offered by Evansville College resembled that of any liberal arts college of the time and was essentially a continuation of what had been offered only a few years before at Moores Hill. Before long, however, President Hughes came to realize that the Evansville community also had vocational needs, requiring additional programs tailored to the school's new urban clientele.

Engineering

The first effort in this direction was the cooperative engineering program (usually known as the co-op program), begun as early as 1920. Under this plan, students were grouped into two sections. While one group attended classes, the other was at work in Evansville industries; later, the two groups exchanged places. Students carried heavier than average loads, were required to attend school year round, and usually needed five years instead of four to graduate; but through the program they gained invaluable practical experience. Fourteen persons were enrolled in the program in the fall of 1920, but only five years later this number had increased to 100, almost one-fourth of the school's total enrollment.

For eight years, the program was headed by **Max Robinson.** A 1912 graduate of the University of Cincinnati, he modeled Evansville's plan on that of his alma mater. Professor Robinson was succeeded by **R. E. Robb,** who had joined the Evansville College engineering faculty in 1922, but after only a year he resigned.

His decision may have been influenced by persistent reports that the co-op program was about to be disbanded. It was known that President Harper favored such an action, despite protests from many outraged engineering students and alumni. Pending a final resolution of the issue, the College engaged **Lawrence Hoyt** to head the engineering department, but upon termination of the co-op program, Hoyt was not re-appointed. Indignant at becoming unemployed through no fault of his

First engineering laboratory (1927)

own, he threatened legal action, but after obtaining an appointment with Mead Johnson and Company, he willingly withdrew his threat.

Two considerations lay behind Harper's final decision to discontinue the co-op engineering program. First, the United States was in the midst of a depression, with many family men desperate for work. Employers, therefore, were understandably reluctant to give what few jobs there were to college students.

Second, Evansville College was eager to gain accreditation from the North Central Association of Colleges, the official accrediting agency for the Midwest area. The College had already applied in 1926 but was rejected because it lacked sufficient endowment. Crucial to its new effort was the support of Purdue University, the leading engineering institution in the state system. Because of reservations concerning the co-op program, Purdue withheld approval, causing the Evansville College administration to decide it would be wiser to drop the program and thus improve its chances of securing NCAC accreditation. Their reasoning was apparently sound, since shortly thereafter (March

1931) Evansville College was admitted to the North Central Association of Colleges.

At the same time, the College's engineering program was reduced to two years. Students who wished to earn a degree in engineering had to transfer to Purdue University for their final two years of study. During the years the degree program was offered, however, many of its graduates enjoyed highly successful careers. Charles Day, who became Evansville's city engineer, designed and built Dress Plaza at the city's riverfront. William Dress, son of an Evansville mayor, became manager of Igleheart's milling operations; D.W. Vaughn (later a member of the Evansville College Board of Trustees), after serving as manager of Whirlpool's Evansville plant, became president of SIGECO (Southern Indiana Gas and Electric Company). Perhaps it was successes such as these that led the College in time to reconsider its position and, in 1946, a four-year degree program in engineering with a co-op component was reinstated. Once reestablished, the co-op program has continued until the present day.

49

Business Administration

With the co-op program in engineering firmly established, President Hughes turned his attention to developing a strong program to meet the needs of Evansville's business community. By 1922, a business administration department had been formed, offering what the *College Bulletin* described as "not just courses in typewriting and shorthand, but a complete course in finance, banking, and the larger problems of modern business." To head the department, the College was able to attract **Waldo Mitchell**, the University of Chicago's first Doctor of Philosophy graduate in business. As the only full-time teacher in the department, Mitchell was responsible for a staggering range of subjects. Twenty-seven courses were listed in the 1922-23 catalog, with the promise that all would be offered within a four-year period. They were as follows:

Industrial Society
Business Economics
Agricultural Economics
Accounting (three courses)
Budgeting
Banking
Business Statistics
Business Cycles
Corporation Finance
Foreign Exchange
Credits and Collection
Risk and Insurance
Public Finance and Taxation
Secretaryship
Retail Administration
Purchasing
Advertising
Domestic and Foreign Trade
Rail and Ocean Transportation
Sales Administration
Personnel Administration
Business Research (three courses)
Business Law

Each business major took every one of the twenty-seven courses offered.

Mitchell served the College as the head of business administration for three years and was followed by three men, each holding a master's degree in business from the University of Chicago, but each remained only a short time. Then, in 1929, **Dean Long**, who had earned a Master of Business Administration from Harvard University and was at the time a member of the economics department of DePauw University, came to Evansville to teach in the summer session. Long never returned to DePauw, choosing instead to spend the remainder of a long and distinguished career in Evansville.

Like his predecessors, Long taught courses in accounting, economics, management, marketing, and finance, including classes for the American Institute of Banking, a non-credit program given under the auspices of Evansville College. For the first twenty years of his tenure, he served as head of the business administration department and for nearly twenty years after that he held a variety of administrative positions (discussed in further detail in Chapter 4).

Education

When Evansville College opened in 1919, the state of Indiana required all elementary school teachers to complete two years of college work in order to be licensed; high school teachers needed four years. In addition, many teachers licensed under earlier laws needed or desired further education. To accommodate these teachers, the College scheduled late afternoon, night, and Saturday education classes, as well as offering an extensive summer program.

Prior to the coming of the College, the city's Board of Education conducted its own teacher-training program but discontinued it in 1919 when its director, **Ethel Burton**, joined the College faculty. With her death the following year, after surgery, the College lost its first faculty member.

Beginning in 1922, **Alfred Cope** chaired the department for six years (but remained a faculty member of Evansville College until his retirement in 1952), followed by **Homer Humke**, who had taught education at the College since 1923; he also

The Evansville College Faculty 1926

Seated, left to right Howard F. Legg, Bible; Charles E. Torbet, Dean; A. J. Bigney, Biology; Dora States, Education; Josephine Hardy, Languages; Marjorie A. Porter, Librarian; Hilda Minder, Speech; Hazel May Snyder, Home Economics; Wahnita DeLong, Dean of Women, English; A. F. Hughes, President; A. B. Cope, Education; Henry J. Bassett, Greek, Latin; *Standing, left to right* Ralph Olmsted, Assistant to President; C. C. Regier, History; Oscar P. N. Zopf, Business Manager; John Watkins, Business Administration; Guy B. Marchant, Engineering; P. H. Nichols, English; Olaf Hovda, Physics; Alvin Strickler, Chemistry; John M. Harmon, Coach; Robert E. Robb, Engineering; and Max B. Robinson, Engineering

51

Professor Homer L. Humke (standing by wall) observes a student teacher at an Evansville elementary school

served for six years. His successor, **Charles Reeves,** who held a master's degree from the University of Chicago and a doctorate from Columbia University, remained in the position until 1940.

ARTS AND SCIENCES

With the steady growth of its professional programs, the liberal arts emphasis which had characterized Moores Hill College markedly diminished at Evansville College, but the arts and sciences were by no means neglected. Indeed, a wide diversity of liberal arts classes was offered, many of them required.

Biology

Besides Hughes and Torbet, a third member of the original Evansville College faculty came to the institution from Moores Hill. **Andrew Johnson Bigney** was, in fact, an 1888 graduate of Moores Hill and taught biology there from the time of his

Andrew Johnson Bigney

graduation until the College closed, a total of twenty-nine years. In addition, Bigney twice served as acting president and for several years was vice president and registrar. In 1917, while waiting for the new college to open, he served as a laboratory assistant at Harvard University. (His salary was $4 a week – proving that even Ivy League positions do not guarantee prosperity!)

At Evansville College, Bigney was head of the biology department for ten years until his death in 1929 at the age of sixty-six. For the first two years in Evansville, while the College searched for a suitable candidate to head the chemistry department,

52

Bigney also taught chemistry and later taught courses in astronomy and geology as well. (It might be noted that such versatility was in keeping with the Moores Hill tradition. Even its first president, Samuel R. Adams, besides his administrative duties, taught ancient languages and modern sciences.)

While the College was downtown, there was no space for a biology laboratory until a room was made available in the basement of Lockyear's Business College. It is notable that for equipment Bigney informed the administration that he could do nicely with "a few frogs and some dissecting pans, microscopes, an aquarium, and some glassware, tables and stools" – probably the most modest budget request ever submitted by a department head!

Although he studied at Johns Hopkins University, Bigney never earned a doctorate; however, an honorary Doctor of Science was bestowed on him by his alma mater in 1910. He taught three generations of students over a period of thirty-nine years and was widely regarded as an outstanding and inspiring teacher.

Dr. and Mrs. A. J. Bigney at Harvard (1917-18)

Plaque in Olmsted Administration Hall

FEBRUARY 15
1864

NOVEMBER 13
1929

IN MEMORY OF
ANDREW JOHNSON BIGNEY
STUDENT AT MOORES HILL COLLEGE 1882-1888
INSTRUCTOR IN SCIENCE, MOORES HILL AND
EVANSVILLE COLLEGE 1888 UNTIL HIS DEATH
SCHOLAR – TEACHER – FRIEND
AN EXEMPLARY CHRISTIAN CHARACTER AND
GREAT TEACHER WHO BY LOVE AND SERVICE
MADE HIMSELF IMMORTAL
IN THE LIVES OF THOSE WHO KNEW HIM
"AND YE SHALL KNOW THE TRUTH AND
THE TRUTH SHALL MAKE YOU FREE"

53

Two years after Bigney's death, **Floyd Beghtel** came to Evansville College as head of the biology department and remained for twelve years, when he resigned in protest because a history professor was released after sixteen years of service. For several years afterward, Beghtel worked in the building construction industry.

Another member of the biology department during this period, **Ima Russell**, is noteworthy as one of six people to receive a master's degree from Evansville College during the brief period (1924-29) that the College offered such a degree. Russell began teaching in the department after completing her studies in 1926 and served until 1941.

Chemistry

The two-year search for a suitable person to head the chemistry department paid off handsomely with the appointment of **Alvin Strickler**. He held the position for thirty-three years.

Strickler was well versed in his field, with a particular interest in new scientific discoveries and developments. Quartz glass, ultra-violet lamps, and chlorine therapy were but a few of his experimental interests. In addition to being an excellent science teacher, Strickler was an honorary member of the Philoneikean Literary Society and, in 1930, he founded the first police training school for the city of Evansville, writing the first police training manual before leaving the project in 1936. A civic-minded person, Strickler also served as president of the Evansville Kiwanis Club.

English

54

The English program at the new College benefited enormously from the work of **George Bruce Franklin**, newly returned in 1919 from France where he worked in support services with the American Expeditionary Force. His master's and doctoral degrees were from Harvard University, and he had taught at Georgia Institute of Technology, Simmons College (Boston), and Colby College (Maine) before entering the military.

At the new College, besides teaching various courses in composition and English and American

literature, he was the Evansville College journalism instructor and was advisor for the *Crescent* and *Linc*. In the community, he was best known for his lectures on literary subjects given in the late afternoon, an offering which often enrolled more than 200 people.

His wife, Lucy Jenkins Franklin, taught oral English (public speaking) and physical education and was, as previously noted, the first Evansville College dean of women.

The Franklins, both noted for their engaging personalities as well as strong academic competence, left Evansville in 1924 when Mrs. Franklin became the first dean of women at Boston University, where she was responsible for 11,000 young women, and her husband was appointed a professor of English.

Another early English department faculty member who made a lasting impression on the College

---

A PIONEERING IDEA

Perhaps Professor DeLong's most memorable course was her creative writing seminar, the format of which was a pioneering idea in its time. Instead of meeting during regular class hours, DeLong met individually with students throughout the day. In the evenings, she opened her home for informal group sessions. During these get-togethers, students critiqued each others' literary pieces while DeLong served dinner "to the hungry hordes."

In addition, she started a poetry workshop composed of fifteen adult members who met once a month for more than fifty years.

In 1986, DeLong received the Honorary Alumna Award, the highest award the University of Evansville Alumni Association gives to non-alumni.

When DeLong died in 1987 at age ninety-eight, her former students, wanting to give her a lasting memorial, raised money for an annual writing workshop, conducted in the DeLong manner and led by a nationally recognized writer. These seminars continue to the present day.

was Wahnita DeLong, who came in 1920 and served for nearly forty years until her retirement in 1958. She was dean of women for twenty-three years (1924-47) and again briefly during her final year. As dean, she was instrumental in establishing national sororities on campus.

DeLong was one of the school's most highly respected English professors and head of her department from 1950 to 1957. Her specialty was creative writing, and she published two books of poetry and several pieces in national literary journals. Many of her students won prizes for their poetry, essays, and short stories.

From 1925 to 1931, the English department was served by **Pierrepont Nichols**, who (like George Franklin) held both a master's and a doctorate from Harvard University. He resigned to be head of the English department at Lincoln University in Pennsylvania.

His successor, **Ernest Van Keuren**, served Evansville College for fifteen years. During his tenure, course offerings were expanded in such areas as creative writing, great books, American biography and poetry, Victorian literature, semantics, modern drama, and Oriental literature. He was long remembered as an absorbing lecturer and dedicated teacher.

Foreign Languages

In the early years of the College, a foreign language was required only for Bachelor of Arts candidates, generally about one-third of the student body. Despite the strong German heritage in the Evansville area, French was the only modern language to be taught for much of the period, a reflection of France having been our ally in the recently ended First World War. German and Spanish were offered from time to time, but then dropped from the curriculum; indeed, Spanish disappeared altogether for fully fourteen years.

History

After coming to Evansville from Moores Hill, Charles Torbet served as professor of history and acting head of the economics department. But also, as noted, he was dean of the College and registrar. After only a few years, he chose to relinquish his teaching duties in favor of his administrative responsibilities, retaining his positions until he retired in

Charles Torbet

1939. (Torbet died in 1967 at the age of ninety-seven.)

In 1922, **Charles Vannest**, a Phi Beta Kappa graduate of the University of Chicago, was appointed to teach history, followed in 1927 by **Heber Walker**, a native Hoosier and a graduate of Indiana University. During his sixteen-year tenure at Evansville College, Walker ran for state representative (1932) but was defeated.

A LINCOLN SCHOLAR

Charles Vannest, a popular professor, was greatly missed when he resigned his position after only three years. An Abraham Lincoln specialist, his book *Lincoln the Hoosier* developed the thesis that the fourteen years Lincoln spent in Indiana, from ages seven to twenty-one, formed and developed his character and philosophy of life, contributing to much of his greatness.

In an effort to retain Vannest on the faculty, President Hughes promised him an honorary Doctor of Laws degree when his book was published, but with the stipulation that he must remain at Evansville College. Although Vannest chose to leave, he requested the degree anyway; but President Harper, pointing out that the professor had failed to uphold his end of the bargain, firmly declined. (Apparently, Vannest operated on the theory that it never hurts to ask!)

Music

According to the first *College Bulletin* (1919), music instruction would be available, but there were no music classes as such. Instead, part-time instructors were hired as needed to give private lessons; in return, they received a percentage of the fees collected. (This plan was a common practice at many colleges.)

At first, the college music program was headed by **James Gillette** who, in addition, was Evansville's municipal organist. The College also owned a share in the great $30,000 organ – one of the largest in the nation – recently installed in the Vanderburgh County Soldiers and Sailors Memorial Coliseum. The school's commitment was $5,000 which, because of budgetary problems, was paid in yearly installments of $1,000. Very little use of the instrument was actually made, either for instructional or any other purpose.

From 1922 to 1927, the College music program was headed by **Herbert Heidecker**. He was assisted by his wife, the former **Lillian Ellerbush**, a native of Evansville and a voice teacher with additional experience as a concert performer. In the first year, the College's financial commitment to music education exceeded its revenues from lessons by nearly $2,400. The following year, the deficit rose to $3,289, and losses over a period of five years exceeded $11,000. Therefore, in 1924, the music department was terminated, and in its place the Evansville School of Music, "affiliated with Evansville College," was established. Financially, the sole responsibility for the Evansville School of Music lay with the Heideckers. When they left Evansville, the school was disbanded.

During his tenure, Heidecker organized a choir for the College, and, in 1927, President Harper himself assumed its direction (with various assistants who took over during the many times that College business prevented his active participation). Harper also organized a large community chorus which he directed in performances of several major oratorios. Because of his love for music and exceptional competence in the field, Harper was tempted to establish a full-fledged music department with an expanded program which the College would sponsor and support. However, he recognized that the idea was not economically feasible and therefore made no attempt to implement such a plan.

The College music program was greatly enhanced, nevertheless, with the coming of Professor **Gaylord Browne** in 1934. Browne held a master's degree from the American Conservatory of Music in Chicago, where he had been awarded a gold medal for highest honors. During his eight years at Evansville College, Browne added courses in harmony, counterpoint, conducting, music history, and music appreciation. In addition, college credit was offered for participation in the choir and orchestra. Himself a violinist, Browne successfully turned what had been mainly an amateur community assemblage into the Evansville Philharmonic Orchestra. He became the orchestra's first conductor, and many Evansville College students became part of the organization.

Philosophy and Religion

No course in philosophy was listed in the 1919 catalog, but because of the school's strong church connections twenty-one courses in biblical literature and religious education (to be offered alternate years) were included. (A census of religious affiliation taken early in the 1919-20 school year showed fifty-seven Methodists out of the total student body of 104. In the ensuing years, the percentage of Methodists declined, while that of other denominations increased.)

A course in religion was not required for graduation from Evansville College until 1927. The requirement continued until 1936, when Bible study was made optional but philosophy was required. A year later, this was changed to either religion or philosophy at the student's discretion.

Olaf Hovda (left) and the physics lab he equipped

Physics and Mathematics

Mathematics was not treated as an independent discipline during this period. There was no mathematics department, all math courses being part of the physics department. Except for mathematics classes required in the engineering curriculum, courses listed in the catalog were often cancelled because of insufficient enrollment.

When the College opened, physics and mathematics were taught by **Olaf Hovda**, a Phi Beta Kappa graduate of the University of Minnesota with a doctorate from the University of Goettingen in Germany. After arriving in Evansville, he applied his exceptional mechanical skills to enhancing the rather minimal physics equipment available to the College at the time. Hovda was also an inventor, holding two patents (one for an automatic dishwasher which was highly advanced for its day). In the early days of World War II, he developed courses in aviation and aerodynamics, employing a wind tunnel which he built himself.

Hovda was an ardent supporter of the school's athletic program and was faculty sponsor of the Photozetean Literary Society. With his death in 1942, after serving Evansville College for twenty-three years, the institution lost the last member of its original 1919 faculty.

Psychology

Like mathematics, psychology was not an independent department during the institution's early history. Rather, courses pertaining to psychology were taught under the auspices of the education department. These included educational psychology, child psychology, and the psychology of elementary school subjects. Although the department name was changed in 1930 to the Department of Education and Psychology, another sixteen years would pass before psychology would become a separate department of its own.

Sociology

Similarly, there was no sociology department as such during the early years of the College. Classes

57

in this field were offered from the very beginning, but they were not sufficient in number to constitute a major.

A course in rural sociology, however, assumed particular importance in the College curriculum. When the College began, the family of A. C. Rosencranz donated $50,000 to endow a department of rural economics. Thought was also given to having an agriculture department, but the idea of a rural emphasis was discarded in favor of a curriculum more suited to an urban economy. Nevertheless, a course in agricultural economics was offered by the economics department for three years (1923-26), and the course in rural sociology was ongoing from 1920 to 1931.

In 1931, **James Morlock**, a 1927 graduate of the College, returned to his alma mater as an instructor and built a more substantial program in sociology. Courses were added and the class in rural sociology was changed to rural-urban sociology. In 1936, Morlock was also appointed dean of men, replacing **Howard Fifield Legg**, who had served since 1929. Morlock held the position for the next thirty-six years.

Speech and Drama

Debate was an extracurricular activity of great interest among Evansville College students during the 1920s and 1930s. Two students, Herman J. Stratton (1923) and O. Glenn Stahl (1931), placed second in state contests. In 1924, the Evansville College team debated a team from Oxford University of England. The event took place in the

Memorial Coliseum and attracted a crowd of 2,500. An Oxford team returned in 1931, and Harvard University's debate team came to Evansville in 1939. Other schools Evansville College debated included Northwestern University, the University of Wyoming, Cornell University, and several Indiana colleges.

Like debate, theatre during this period was strictly extracurricular at Evansville College. Students participated in dramatic productions from the very first year. These plays were sponsored by the city of Evansville's Drama League, the College literary societies, the YWCA, the Sweetser Hall residents, and others. Then, in 1924, a dramatics club, the Thespian Dramatic Society, was formed on campus. Since its first production, *The Importance of Being Earnest*, occurred just before April Fools' Day, the *Crescent* made light of it, stating that it "played before a pitifully small audience which booed throughout the performance." No serious account of the production survives.

Various faculty members directed plays each year until 1926, when **Pearl LeCompte** came to teach speech and coach the debate team. She also assumed the role of theatre director, a position she retained for twenty-one years. LeCompte held a mas-

Pearl LeCompte

HAPPY ENDING

In 1929, the Evansville College thespians were invited to a competition at Northwestern University. On the journey home, their car – a big, seven-passenger Hudson owned by President Harper – skidded on an icy road and was demolished. There was no insurance on the car, but Harper rejoiced in the fact that no one was seriously injured.

Home economics class (late 1920s)

ter's degree from Northwestern University and had considerable college teaching experience before coming to Evansville College; in addition, she had directed the Little Theater in San Antonio.

In her first year at the College, LeCompte inaugurated the annual tradition of presenting *Eager Heart*, a play concerning the Nativity. A part of this tradition was not to announce the names of cast members in order to focus attention on the religious message of the play rather than on the actors. A freshman assigned a role in the play kept that part until he or she graduated. The Christ child was always played by a real baby, usually the child of a faculty member, and the music department provided the choir and orchestra. *Eager Heart* was performed every year at Christmastime for forty-three years.

LeCompte was long remembered for her weekly play reading sessions at which she served her students Russian tea and gingerbread. She has been described as a teacher who "inspired, prodded, awed, directed, and loved generations of students"

and, like her colleague Wahnita DeLong (see page 54), she was among the most admired and beloved of all Evansville College faculty members.

She retired in 1952. Upon her death fifteen years later, her former students, as well as many drama patrons in the community, banded together to establish the Pearl LeCompte Scholarship Fund, specifically intended to assist students aspiring to a career in theatre. The program, under the auspices of the University of Evansville Theatre Society, continues to the present day.

Other Areas

Among other areas of study, early Evansville College catalogs listed home economics, classics, and physical education.

Home economics classes included such diverse fields as food, millinery, home nursing, household accounting, sanitation, and decoration. By 1928, this list was augmented by courses in costume design, gardening, nutrition, and child welfare.

59

Classes in Latin and Greek, although always marked by low enrollment, continued to be offered, the former because it was needed by high school language teachers, the latter because it was important to the institution's pre-theology majors.

From 1920 to 1929, the teaching of classical languages, mythology, and culture was in the hands of **Henry Jewell Bassett**, whose doctorate was from the University of Michigan. Equally renowned for his huge handlebar mustache and his amazingly wide scholarship, he was a member of Phi Beta Kappa and served as secretary of the faculty during his tenure at Evansville College.

During the decade from 1932 to 1942, classics were taught by **Imri Blackburn**, whose doctorate was from Indiana University. As interest in Latin and Greek declined, Blackburn also taught classes in ancient and medieval history. His deep interest in religion led to his ordination as an Episcopal priest. He served as rector of St. Paul's Episcopal

Church in Henderson, Kentucky, and then of St. Paul's Episcopal Church in Evansville; the heavy duties associated with these positions led to his decision to resign from the faculty of Evansville College.

An organized program in physical education began in the fall of 1923 when **John Harmon** joined the faculty as instructor of physical education and also athletic coach. This enabled the College to offer classes leading to a high school teaching license in physical education. Many Evansville College graduates later became coaches in Tri-State and other high schools.

Women's physical education was taught by part-time instructors and also by senior-level students, including Mabel Dillingham Nenneker, who would later become associate registrar. (See also the Athletics section of this chapter.)

The Evansville College Faculty 1930-1931

Left to right, front row seated Walter Guy Parker, associate professor, religious education; Howard Fifield Legg, dean of men, professor of Bible and philosophy; Charles Edgar Torbet, dean and professor of history; Earl Enyeart Harper, president; Wahnita DeLong, dean of women, associate professor of English; Alfred B. Cope, professor of education

Middle row Olaf Hovda, professor of physics; Dean Long, professor of economics and business administration; Charles C. Delano, professor of Latin and Greek; Gladys Curry, instructor of home economics; Pearl LeCompte, assistant professor of oral English (drama); Irene Welke Place, instructor of modern languages; Alvin Strickler, professor of chemistry; Sarah Lee Lloyd Snepp, instructor of English; Mabel E. Inco, instructor of mathematics; Marjorie Porter, librarian; Heber P. Walker, assistant professor of history; William Labry Brown, instructor of civil engineering; Howard C. Abbott, professor of biology

Back row Herbert W. Fillmore, instructor of engineering; William V. Slyker, professor of physical education and athletics; Mabel Dillingham, assistant in physical education; Guy B. Marchant, assistant professor of electrical engineering; Paul G. Cressey, assistant professor of sociology; Lawrence B. Hoyt, professor of civil engineering; Ima S. Wyatt, assistant in biology; Lucile Jones, assistant professor of education; Isabel B. Reeves, assistant in education; Homer L. Humke, professor of education

Members of faculty not in the picture Paul Warren Ashby, assistant in music; Fred W. Davis, assistant in education; Clara Lieber Harper, instructor in voice; Ralph Olmsted, business manager and instructor of English; Herman Watson, assistant in chemistry

DEGREES

During the early years of Evansville College, the trend was toward a multiplicity of degrees, each specifying the graduate's area of study. By 1931, the College was granting the following degrees:

Bachelor of Arts

Bachelor of Science in
    Business Administration
    Education
    Civil Engineering
    Electrical Engineering
    Mechanical Engineering
Bachelor of Industrial Science
Bachelor of Religious Education

In 1932, a sweeping change consolidated all these degrees to only two, the Bachelor of Arts and the Bachelor of Science, and for two years (1941 and 1942) only the Bachelor of Arts was awarded. (Courses and curricula, however, were not affected by changes in degree titles.) By the late 1940s, most of the specialized degree titles were reinstated.

It also should be noted that in the late 1930s President Smith, with the approval of the Board of Trustees, instituted a major structural change, organizing College departments into three major divisions: humanities, social sciences and physical sciences. The four-year program was then divided into two two-year segments: the junior college and the senior college. After the first two years, the degree of Associate of Arts was conferred upon the graduates, who could then continue in the senior college to receive their baccalaureate degrees. However, these changes proved to serve no useful purpose; consequently, they were soon abandoned.

61

THE LIBRARY

In 1919, the College library totaled 3,823 volumes, mostly brought over from the College at Moores Hill. Before the year was over, however, the College library became affiliated with the Evansville public library, which numbered over 100,000 volumes, and books from the public library could be borrowed by the College for periods of up to eighteen weeks. Thus, the entire resources of Evansville's public library were at the disposal of the student body. In addition, students could borrow from Willard Library, an independent collection not part of the public library system.

During the first year, a city library employee, **Dorothy Heins**, worked half-time for the College, but later the College employed its own librarians: **Marjorie Porter** (1924-35) and **Anna Louise Thrall** (1935-46).

The budget for the College library was always comparatively meager. Although $3,500 was allocated for books in 1921, by 1924 the figure had dropped to $650, and during depression years it was usually $500.

On the other hand, the College was able to enlarge its collection with gifts from private donors. Among the many who contributed a substantial number of volumes were J. F. O'Haver, George S. Clifford, and the widow of Levi P. Gilbert. Also, in 1925, Sallie Bruce Cooke gave $10,000 specifically for the purpose of augmenting the College library.

For three years, the library was housed in a room in the College's temporary building at 517 Vine Street. When the new Administration Hall opened in 1922, the library was moved to three rooms on the second floor, gradually expanding into three additional rooms. The reading room was inadequate, however, having only 100 seats.

In the ten years from 1930 to 1940 an average of 700 books was added each year so that by 1940 the collection totaled 19,725 volumes. Clearly, a library building was desperately needed but, unfortunately, no funds were available to build one.

62

STUDENT LIFE

With an academic program firmly in place, students at the new Evansville College were soon agitating for the activities that had long been a traditional part of college life: athletics, fraternities, a newspaper, a yearbook, a school song, cheers, and a student government.

The first of these to become a reality was a student newspaper, the *Crescent*, a name suggested by faculty supervisor George B. Franklin because of Evansville's location at a crescent-shaped bend in the Ohio River. The initial issue bears the date of October 21, 1919, and the student editor-in-chief was Ralph Olmsted, later a journalism instructor as well as assistant to the president and business manager of Evansville College. Until the 1960s, the paper usually ran to four pages, but page size varied from year to year.

Within the first year of operation, a student government association was formed at Evansville College, with election of officers held in the spring of 1920. In 1932, at the suggestion of President Harper, the student government was changed to a student-faculty federation under a plan which provided for joint student-faculty committees (eight in number) with equal representation.

Moral Standards

Continuing along the path well established by Moores Hill, Evansville College was deeply concerned with the character and conduct of its students. As early as 1920, the *College Bulletin* contains this stern warning:

> **Students who seek only a good time, and who mistake the social activities of the campus for the serious business of hard study and the mental discipline acquired by the mastery of their study, are not especially urged to attend Evansville College.**

A journalism class gives careful attention to the latest issue of the **Crescent**

In a similar vein, a brochure issued by the College in 1926 states:

> **The aim of Evansville College is to build character and to train for service ... To this end it maintains a wholesome religious atmosphere. Its faculty is made up of men and women of Christian character. It was founded and is supported by godly men and women. It is a Christian college.**

Accordingly, presence at Chapel services was required of all students, and a standing faculty Committee on Chapel Absences monitored attendance. Still, the College continued to state in its bulletin (as did that issued by Moores Hill College) that the school is "in no sense sectarian. Its doors are open to persons of any faith."

Restrictive policies were in effect, however, regarding such matters as smoking and dancing. Smoking was prohibited on campus until 1940, when the Evening College started and adults wished more freedom than that granted to college-age students. But even then, students were encouraged to use the restrooms for smoking or were urged to smoke outside the buildings. (The large number of

cigarette ads which came to be a major source of revenue for the *Crescent* in later years would have been unthinkable in the 1930s.)

The prohibition against dancing at campus functions was highly controversial during the 1920s, with articles and editorials critical of the administration's position appearing frequently in the *Crescent*. By 1928, President Harper felt that the Board of Trustees needed to take a firm stand one way or the other on the issue and indicated that he was not personally opposed to dancing as a social diversion. The board's decision was to pass the matter back to the president and faculty. Finally, after many years of student agitation, the prohibition was abolished in 1931 and dancing quickly became an integral part of the College's social program.

Also discarded was an honor system adopted by the student body stipulating that, no professor being present, "every member of the student body pledge on his honor ... that he will not receive or give unauthorized aid in any written examination, test, or quiz, and is pledged upon his honor to report any violation which he sees." The honor system was dropped when it proved unworkable because of student reluctance to report violations.

63

Fraternities and Sororities

Also controversial was the issue of social fraternities and sororities; such organizations were frowned upon by the College administration for many years. An early bulletin declares:

The College, having no fraternities, is free from those divisive organizations which so often break up colleges into unfriendly groups, add greatly to expense, and often detract from scholarship.

In place of fraternities, President Hughes strongly preferred reviving the literary societies which had provided the dominant extracurricular activities at Moores Hill College, believing that these societies would serve to bind the many hundreds of Moores Hill alumni to the new institution.

For a few years, the revived literary societies carried on in Evansville much as they had at Moores Hill. Programs were held weekly, consisting of speeches, debates, readings of essays and poetry, and music. Gradually, however, the literary activities faded and the organizations became almost entirely social clubs.

Meanwhile, there was considerable student agitation in favor of local fraternities. In 1929, the administration agreed to strike the word "literary" from the names of the literary societies and to replace the current names with Greek letters. It refused, though, to allow substitution of the word "fraternity" for the word "society." Accordingly,

Philoneikan Literary Society **became** Pi Epsilon Phi,

Sigournean Literary Society **became** Gamma Epsilon Sigma, and

Photozetean Literary Society **became** Phi Zeta.

(Only the Castalian Literary Society continued under its original name.)

In the mid 1930s, a movement arose to allow the building of a "clubhouse" which would also serve as a student residence, but the plan never materialized.

The first honorary fraternity at Evansville College, Tau Kappa Alpha, a national society in debate and public speaking, was established in 1927 and continued for about ten years. In 1929, a chapter of Pi Gamma Mu, a social science honorary, was organized on the campus, followed in 1932 by Phi Beta Chi, an honorary fraternity in the natural sciences.

The Literary Society of 1923; later it was the local chapter of Phi Zeta and then the national chapter of Lambda Chi Alpha

Residence Halls

During its first decade, in lieu of dormitories, the College used converted residences to house those who could not or preferred not to commute to school. From 1919 to 1924, one of the large old homes on Southeast (then Upper) First Street was home to about thirty women. It was known as Sweetser Hall (from the name of the owner).

During the first year, many male residential students lived at the YMCA across from the College. But the men preferred a home of their own; therefore, a house was rented on Southeast (then Upper) Third Street. It was known as Excelsior Hall, and it housed a future college professor, a future dean, a future business manager of Evansville College, future high school teachers and a principal, a prominent attorney, and at least three future ministers.

HELL WEEK

Like other schools, Evansville College had its annual "Hell Week" activities to mark the time of initiation. After the "battle" between freshmen and sophomores ("the class scrap"), freshmen were required to wear green "beanies" for the whole year if they lost. Among the men's societies, hazing was normal, and punishments were enforced with paddles. One women's society imposed punishments such as washing windows, carrying a large box of matches which had to be scattered on the ground and then picked up each time the pledge met a society member, pushing a baby carriage with a doll in it, searching cemeteries at night for a certain headstone, wearing green hats, addressing society members as Miss, carrying a carefully wrapped brick and a can of worms, using only the side doors to all buildings, and picking dandelions. (Fortunately, no pledge was required to perform all these tasks.)

The women's lounge, located on the first floor of Administration Hall (1926)

PRANKS

As might be expected, college pranks soon became a part of campus life in the new institution. To cite only one example, two residents of Excelsior Hall were sentenced to moving 100 bushels of coal from the street to the cellar as punishment for painting the hands and faces of their unsuspecting comrades with indelible ink in the middle of the night while they slept.

Excelsior Hall closed after the second year, most of the students returning to the YMCA. After the new College building opened, some residences near the campus were used as dormitories (at various times, two of these were named Hughes Hall in honor of the school's president) but, by 1929, these too were closed and eventually sold.

Lectures and Broadcasts

Community outreach was already important to the College at this early period of its history. For example, in cooperation with the Evansville Federation of Teachers, several outstanding speakers were brought to the city. During the 1919-20 season alone, students and the community were able to hear former President William Howard Taft, journalist and biographer Ida M. Tarbell, novelist Sir Hugh Walpole, novelist and critic John Cowper Powys, and poets Jessie Belle Rittenhouse, Cale Young Rice, and Vachel Lindsay.

In addition, radio being a new medium at this time (Evansville's only radio station was less than two years old), the College was eager to participate in the new technology. The first Evansville College radio program, carried by WGBF on October 23, 1925, was an hour in length and was hosted by the Photozetean Literary Society (now Lambda Chi Alpha fraternity). The broadcast included selections for banjo, violin, piano, and voice, as well as spoken comments. The following year, the Thespian Dramatic Society hosted a series of monthly programs consisting of both dramatic and musical material.

In 1929 and 1930, weekly programs were presented involving President and Mrs. Harper, both skilled musicians, and Evansville College music students. Ralph Olmsted, the College business manager, was in charge.

Beginning in 1931, radio programs were broadcast from a small studio on campus and transmitted by telephone lines to the radio station downtown. Programs during this period included quiz shows as well as broadcasts prepared by area high school students.

School Seal and School Song

At one of the first faculty meetings in 1919, the subject of designing an appropriate pictorial seal for the new College was raised. The issue was considered again in 1921 and in 1923, and two years later cash prizes were offered for a suitable design, but without success. The following year a new attempt was made but still with no results. Finally, in 1928, Gordon Legg was declared the winner in

YOU CALL THAT ART?

A controversial modern art show on campus in 1934 upset many students. The questionable art contained images that looked like several different objects, depending on how the painting was viewed. One such painting looked like a cross between a diamond ring and a set of false teeth, but many students complained it resembled a rusty bear trap.

Student Gordon Legg displays his design for the Evansville College seal (1928)

a competition for the best design. It showed, within a circle which read "Evansville College, 1854," a representation of the doorway to Administration Hall. In the doorway stood a multi-branched candlestick, each with a Greek letter, the initial of a word describing such elements of a full and well-rounded life as intellect, love of beauty, health, fellowship, and spiritual aspiration. The seal of 1928 served the College for nearly forty years, being replaced in 1967 by a new seal for the University of Evansville.

The search for an appropriate school song, like that for a seal, produced no immediate results. After at least two false starts, a contest for an offi-

cial Evansville College song was held in 1926, with the winner to receive free tuition for two quarters. Ironically, the song which was awarded first place by the judges is long forgotten, while the runner-up (second place winner) has been the preferred school song ever since. The music was written by Mary Ellen McClure, a graduate in the Class of 1925 (and the niece of Professor A. J. Bigney), with words by McClure in collaboration with Evaline Tureck. Because this song, now known as the "University Hymn," has played such an important role at institutional functions for many years and is also the source of the title for this volume, its text is found on the title page.

67

ATHLETICS

During its first year in Evansville, the faculty debated the establishment of intercollegiate athletics for Evansville College but delayed a decision until later in the year. When a basketball team was organized in January 1920, the faculty allowed it to play against neighborhood teams, but not against high school or college teams. Early in the fall of 1920, the Committee on Athletics reported its plan for "competitive and universal" athletics which permitted scheduling not more than ten basketball games with colleges in Indiana, Illinois, and Kentucky.

Two years later, a temporary physical education building was erected, a frame structure 100 by 100 feet square, large enough for a regulation-size basketball floor with space remaining for bleachers, locker and shower rooms, offices for physical education instructors, and a cafeteria for students and faculty. The original campus plan called for replacing this structure (popularly known as "termite heaven") within five years but, in fact, it remained in use for forty-one years until Carson Center was completed.

With a building – albeit temporary – in place, attention could now be given to developing an all-around athletic program. To deal with the costs of developing and maintaining such a program, the trustees, in 1923, established the Evansville College Athletic Association, a separate entity composed of trustees, faculty, and students. In 1930, this association was disbanded, and the athletic program was turned over to the physical education department. Two years later, a student-faculty committee on athletics was created to promote the interests of intercollegiate athletics, and, in 1936, a Board of Control for Athletics was established, representing trustees, faculty, students, and alumni. Despite the board's best efforts, however, it was unable to generate the income needed to cover athletic costs.

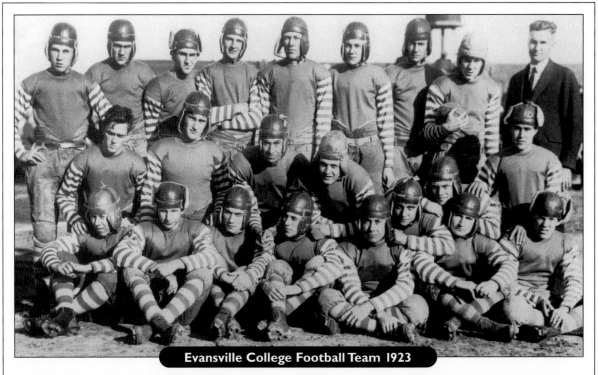

Evansville College Football Team 1923

Left to right, front row Russ Gudgeon, George P. Wright, Edgar Lee Marynell, Charles Taylor, Albert Schmitt, Arthur Coffman, LaVerne N. Gill; *Middle row* John G. Dunville, Rupert G. Roth, Edward S. Stuteville, Luther C. Small, Willis W. Reinke, Albert L. Fisher, Charles F. Tismar; *Back row* Edward J. Ruminer, Ed. J. Small, Fletcher Williams, Orville H. Fletcher, Irwin Whitmoyer, Hal E. Dudley, Willard H. Hoyt, William E. Bakewell (captain), Coach John M. Harmon

Football

Football began at Evansville College in 1923 when the Board of Trustees voted in January to begin intercollegiate football that fall. Although there were only 160 men enrolled in the College, thirty turned out for practice. The first intercollegiate game in Evansville was played at Bosse Field on October 18, 1923, against Union Christian College of Merom, Indiana, a game won by Evansville 19-0. The team, coached by **John Harmon**, set a respectable record of three wins, three losses, and one tie. In seven seasons, from 1923 to 1929, Harmon's teams recorded eighteen wins, thirty-five losses, and one tie.

Arthur Dick (Socko) (c. 1927)

Evansville College athletes were known by their nicknames, which included Cowboy, Stumpy, Tails, and Bounce

JOHN HARMON

John Harmon was a star athlete who competed in football, basketball, baseball, and track before coming to Evansville College in 1923 as director of athletics and coach of all sports. He turned out to be an excellent coach, too, leading Evansville's basketball team to a record of 59-50 from 1923 to 1930. Prior to Harmon's arrival, Evansville had won only seven games in the program's previous four years of existence.

But Harmon was much more than a "jock." He left Evansville College to earn the first doctoral degree in health and physical education ever granted by Indiana University. In 1932, he joined the staff of Boston University and eventually created a doctoral program there that supplied athletic directors to hundreds of colleges and universities.

Today, the Dr. John M. Harmon Memorial Installation Banquet is held each winter on the University of Evansville campus to induct members into the UE Athletics Hall of Fame.

"Dad loved Evansville, and I'm told that he often lugged me as a baby to football and basketball practice," says his son, Millard Harmon. "He obviously was fond of athletics, but academics and religion meant a lot to him, also. And he really cared about the boys he coached. They didn't use the term back them, but I think Dad was an excellent role model."

William Slyker, formerly at Reitz High School but coaching in Cleveland at the time, became the next coach, serving for thirteen years through the 1942 season when he resigned to enter a war industry. His record during those years was about the same as that of Coach Harmon, with thirty-four wins, sixty losses, and nine ties. The team played several new, strong opponents, such as Southeastern Missouri State College, Butler University, Valparaiso College, and Southern Illinois University. Between 1936 and 1938, the College had the dubious distinction of playing in twelve consecutive games without scoring a point!

WILLIAM SLYKER

As a student, Bill Slyker played in the 1921 Rose Bowl for Ohio State, went to law school, and became a licensed attorney. But his love for athletics guided him into coaching and eventually into the position of director of athletics for Evansville College in 1930. Even though his football teams usually finished with losing records, Slyker was responsible for bringing Aces athletics to a new level against tougher competition. Success came more quickly in basketball. Slyker's predecessor, John Harmon, began a winning tradition, and Slyker maintained that success. In thirteen years as basketball coach, his teams compiled a 123-96 record.

Slyker lived only seven more years after leaving Evansville, passing away at the age of fifty in 1949. But his name lives on. In 1954, Slyker's friends and former players established the William V. Slyker Award, presented each spring to the Aces' most outstanding male athlete.

William Slyker

Basketball and football coach, director of physical education (1930-1943)

LET THERE BE LIGHT

The year 1929 introduced a first in Evansville College athletics: night football.

The field was then situated on the present site of Hughes Hall. Field lighting was then in its infancy, but Coach Harmon was willing to experiment. During the summer, he obtained a quantity of old four-inch boiler tubes and had them welded together to form thirty-foot poles. Atop each pole was placed a reflector holding a 1500 watt light bulb. It was a rather crude system, but the twenty-eight poles gave off a surprising amount of light.

The lighting system was a success, but unfortunately the Aces lost their game 25-0. Indeed, for the entire season under the lights Evansville went down 7-1.

Baseball

Baseball, which had been the most popular sport at Moores Hill College, did not achieve that distinction in Evansville. It began in 1924 under John Harmon and continued for four years with a record of sixteen wins and twenty-eight losses. In 1928, baseball was dropped as an intercollegiate sport, primarily so that Harmon's football team would have more time for spring practice. Baseball was not played again until 1946.

Basketball

Although basketball was the sport which put Evansville College on the athletic "map," the beginning of the basketball program was not auspicious. The team had a 1-3 record against local independent teams in 1919-20. When the faculty then decided to allow intercollegiate competition, the team finished its first year (1920-21) with a 3-8 record. During its first four years under part-time coaches, the record was an unimpressive 7-28. Under its first full-time coach, John Harmon, however, the team's record in the five years from 1923 to 1928 was 54-21, thus establishing the reputation of the College as a basketball power in the state.

During the Slyker years (1930-42), the Aces compiled a winning record of 123-96. He also

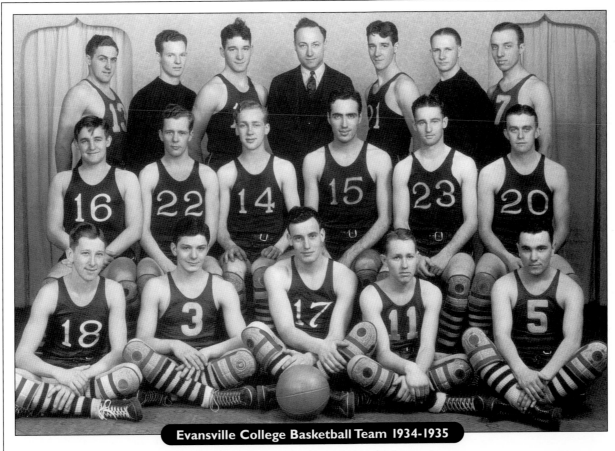

Evansville College Basketball Team 1934-1935

Left to right, front row Emerson O. Henke, Chris P. Maglaris, Joe Theby, Bruce Lomax, Robert Polk; *Middle row* Fay V. Johnson, Otto P. Thuerbach, Loren Bailey, Colby Pollard, Constant Hartke, Walter R. Riggs; *Standing* Hugh R. Thrasher, Ron Jacquess, Howard Selm, Coach William V. Slyker, Harold Selm, Melvin Seeger, Alfred Rose

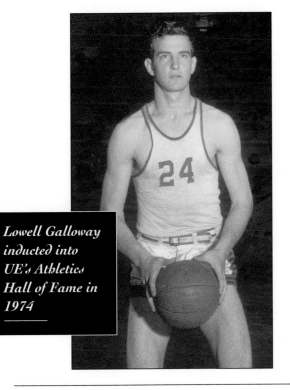

Lowell Galloway inducted into UE's Athletics Hall of Fame in 1974

raised the level of the competition, with Evansville playing Ohio State, Indiana, Western Kentucky, Ball State, Western Michigan, Kansas State, Boston, Southern Illinois, and Murray State.

Local support for the team continued to increase; however, finding an adequate facility for home games proved to be an ongoing and frustrating problem. Originally, the team played in the campus gymnasium, but in 1924 games were moved downtown to the Agoga Tabernacle. In 1935, the site changed to the Memorial Coliseum and from there to the National Guard Armory near campus. As the team's fame continued to grow, even that facility proved inadequate; as a result, fans often had to be turned away. Only with the opening of Roberts Municipal Stadium in 1957 was the problem solved.

71

ACES

The "Aces" came to be the nickname for Evansville College athletic teams in the mid-1920s, thanks in large part to Louisville's basketball coach. In the fourth game of the 1924-25 season, Evansville beat Louisville 59-39. After the game, Louisville's coach told Evansville coach John Harmon, "You didn't have four Aces up your sleeve, you had five!"

Harmon related the comment to *Evansville Courier* sports editor Dan Scism, and both Harmon and Scism agreed they liked the sound of "Aces" better than "Pioneers," the Evansville College nickname up to this time. Scism also had a personal reason for promoting the use of "Aces;" those four letters fit into his headlines more readily than the longer "Pioneers."

Since the Evansville College colors were purple and white, "Purple Aces" soon became the school's unique nickname that is now known all over the country.

Also dating from this period is the Aces' official fight/pep song, "Evansville, All Hail to Thee," with words by Emilie Thuman (Heberer) and music by Mary Louise Mueller.

Women's Basketball and Other Sports

Women's basketball also enjoyed considerable success during the early years of Evansville College. In eight seasons, from 1920-21 to 1927-28, the team had a record of 37-20-2, although only five games were played against other college teams. The sport was abolished in 1928 and replaced with a program of diversified intramural sports, including archery, hockey, hiking, interclass basketball, horseshoes, and volleyball.

Other sports received only passing attention during this period. Track was actually the first intercollegiate sport in which Evansville College participated competitively (a meet against Oakland City College in 1920), but Evansville track teams did not fare very well over the years. Tennis and golf entered the intercollegiate schedule during the late 1930s, but Evansville's athletes were hampered because the College lacked both a tennis court and a golf course.

By 1940, there could be little doubt that football and basketball were the sports that would dominate at Evansville College.

Evansville College Women's Basketball Team (1927-28)

Left to right, front row Ruth Huegel, Mary Flo Siegel (Niednagel) (captain), Naomi Huegel; *Middle row* Iris Sullivan, Ruth Smith (Warren), Hilda Dawson, Kathleen Guthrie, Melba Schlueter (Veneman), Ruth Hock; *Back row* Mary Davidson (Fierke), Mabel Dillingham (Nenneker), Verna Hasseries, Alice Lytle (Taylor) (coach), Mary Fitzsimmons (Keneipp), Harriet McCutchan, Dorothy Hunt

FINANCES

Financial difficulties plagued the new College, just as they had at Moores Hill. Construction of Administration Hall strained available resources, forcing the board to borrow $125,000. The loan was to be repaid in five years, with the campus property to serve as collateral; interest was set at $7,500 annually.

Hampering the school's efforts to achieve financial stability was its inability to actually collect the $1 million that had been pledged in the campaign of 1917. By January 1, 1924, only $787,868 had been received, and only an insignificant amount was turned in on outstanding pledges after that.

The College plant (campus and buildings) cost just under $597,000, leaving an inadequate amount for the endowment fund, operating expenses, and income to pay the annuities which the College owed a variety of creditors.

Tuition alone was far from sufficient to meet the school's operating expenses. Tuition income for the first year totaled about $12,000, yet costs were $45,000. Even with $6,000 from the Indiana Conference and $4,000 promised by the Board of Education of the Methodist Church, it was clear that about fifty percent of the operating budget still needed to be found elsewhere.

In 1923, plans were formulated for a joint fund-raising campaign involving Evansville College, DePauw University, and two Methodist hospitals, but when DePauw withdrew from the effort and the Evansville YWCA launched a major capital fund drive to erect a new building, the College decided to postpone its plans until the following year.

When the time came, however, the College lacked sufficient funds to mount a major campaign. Bank loans of $150,000 were finally secured, but only on the condition that all funds collected from the campaign would be used first to repay the loans. As collateral, the College was required to turn over $89,000 of its meager endowment securities.

The campaign goal, as in 1917, was $1 million, but only $737,500 was pledged, and of that amount less than $500,000 was ever collected. Overall, the effort must be labeled a failure, since it yielded immediately usable funds of only $13,000 over the cost of the campaign. On the other hand, pledges were obtained for considerable amounts of money which the College would receive at the death of the donor. Unfortunately, the estates of many of these benefactors were wiped out or greatly diminished in the market crash of 1929 and the Great Depression which followed. On the positive side, though, Evansville College was able to pay its final installment to the architect and the contractor in September of 1924 for the building they had completed more than two years earlier.

At the suggestion of business manager Oscar P. M. Zopf, a different approach was then utilized to resolve the institution's financial problems. His proposal to the Board of Trustees called for combining all of the school's obligations into one loan and then floating a bond issue of $175,000, the money to be paid back over a period of ten years. Again, however, the Great Depression intervened. Even though bond holders agreed to accept three percent instead of the promised six and Evansville banks reduced their interest rate from six percent to five, the College required extensions and, in the end, took twenty years (until 1945) rather than the original ten to pay back the bonds in full. And even then $80,000 had to be taken from the College endowment and $20,000 from current operating funds.

In 1929, another fund-raising campaign was attempted but it fell short of its $250,000 goal, yielding pledges of only $187,000, a little over three-fourths of the amount hoped for. As a result of the market crash, even some of these pledges could not be fulfilled.

The following year, however, with the death of Evansville industrialist and College charter trustee William H. McCurdy, the institution was left a substantial legacy, in addition to his many previous gifts, totaling $60,000. Although McCurdy's will specified that his estate could not be distributed

Originally a farmhouse, this building (the first one on campus) served as the College cafeteria and men's lounge; later, it housed the music and biology departments, and finally the School of Nursing; it was demolished in 1972

until 1945, the College received income from it amounting to $48,000 in the meantime.

As previously noted, the president's home was given to Evansville College in 1928, a gift valued at about $37,000 from Mr. and Mrs. John Igleheart. The next year, $150,000 was received from the estate of Preston Kumber, a Washington, D.C., attorney who had lived in Evansville as a young man. In 1931, $80,000 came to Evansville College from the estate of Leslie G. Igleheart to support the school's engineering program, and, in 1932, Louise Graessle of Rushville donated a grapefruit orchard at McAllen in the Rio Grande Valley of Texas, valued at $33,750. Unfortunately, the orchard proved to be a liability and eventually had to be sold for only $14,000.

Finally, in 1933, a gift of $25,000 was received from the estate of John L. Igleheart. Although there would not be another major contribution to the endowment for twenty years, the fund had now grown to $408,000, an impressive gain over the 1921 total of $109,000.

Annual solicitations continued in an effort to assist the College in meeting its operating expenses, producing the following pledges:

1932	$17,800
1933	$36,000
1934	$19,000
1935	$50,000

The 1935 campaign was especially crucial since the 1935-36 budget projected a deficit of nearly $50,000. President Harper described the situation as "a question of life or death for Evansville College" and trustee William A. Carson reinforced this by declaring flatly in a statement to the newspapers that unless $50,000 was raised, the College would close. Thanks to the efforts of many people and a generous pledge by trustee J. Giltner Igleheart, the goal was achieved.

It was a close call, though, and in 1936 Harper persuaded the board of directors of the Evansville Community Fund to accept the College as an annual fund recipient, an arrangement which lasted until 1940 and yielded Evansville College a total of $168,414. At the time, Evansville College was the only institution of higher learning in the United States to depend on annual gifts from a community chest fund, causing the College to appear as a charity, and creating what many viewed as an extremely humiliating situation.

Early in 1936, citing the "constant strain of trying to keep the College alive" and the resulting inability to focus his attention on the "educational, civic, social, and cultural services of our College," Earl Harper decided to resign as president of Evansville College.

Faculty Salaries

Faculty salaries during this period correlated closely with the institution's financial condition. In 1919, a full professor earned $2,500 for four quarters of twelve weeks each. For 1922-23, the salary was raised to $3,000 for the standard academic year of three quarters; summer work received additional compensation. Just two years later, though, in view of the school's severe monetary problems, the faculty was asked to accept a salary reduction of $200. Full salaries were restored in 1929 but, in 1932, national economic conditions led to a ten percent cut in salaries (which, incidentally, the president accepted for himself as well), with a further five percent reduction imposed the following year. Even then, the trustees refused to guarantee any specific amounts, agreeing to pay only what the College could afford after absolute necessities, such as utilities and coal, had been covered. All remaining funds were then divided among the faculty.

In 1934-35, the salary was set at seventy percent of the pre-depression level. Two years later, salary payments were again guaranteed, but only at eighty-five percent of the pre-depression level. In 1937 and for eight years thereafter, payment was at the ninety percent level, reaching the $3,000 level in 1945. Nonetheless, faculty morale remained

> ### COLLEGE EMPLOYMENT
> In January 1939, Evansville College field secretary G. R. McCoy conducted a survey concerning employment among college students. At the time, fifty percent of Evansville College students worked, and although a high salary of $30 a week was reported, the average weekly wage was only $7.37.

high throughout the Great Depression, in part because millions of people throughout the nation suffered similar reductions in salary and many others had to contend with no salary whatsoever.

The Proposed Merger with Indiana University

In 1937, President Smith proposed a two-year campaign to raise $600,000, one-half for new buildings and one-half for the endowment fund. To determine the feasibility of such a campaign, the New York firm of John Price Jones was consulted at a cost of $2,750. After a thorough survey and analysis, the consultants predicted failure under current conditions and suggested that Evansville College either be reduced to a two-year junior college or be offered to the city of Evansville, to be operated as a municipal, tax-supported institution.

The latter plan was favored by the president, the faculty, and the trustees. Indiana Conference approval was also needed, an enabling act would have to be obtained from the Indiana legislature, and a city-wide referendum would probably be necessary as well, since additional taxes would be required to support the College.

Conference approval was forthcoming without significant opposition, but at this point trustee C. B. Enlow put forth an alternative proposal, namely that the College become a state institution. His reasoning was based on the fact that Evansville taxpayers were already paying to support the state's higher education system but were receiving nothing in return.

Although Smith appeared to prefer the earlier idea of municipal ownership of the College, the

75

Indiana Conference, by a vote of 99 to 59, lent its support to the plan of making Evansville College a division (school or college) of Indiana University.

The presidents of independent and church-related colleges in Indiana, however, firmly opposed the merger, fearing that it would be only a matter of time before all private colleges would be absorbed by state universities. Moreover, many Indiana University officials and alumni also opposed the proposal, fearing that resources intended for the main campus would be siphoned off to Evansville, causing Indiana University President Herman B Wells to revise his original stand and suggest that the Evansville campus become a two-year extension center instead of a four-year college.

At this point, both Evansville College and the community began to reassess their options. The Indiana University plan would mean that only lower-level courses would be offered in Evansville, and that such programs as student government, health services, athletics, social organizations, and the alumni association would all be eliminated. Furthermore, teacher training – an important part of the Evansville College curriculum – would no longer be available, since it required four years.

Balancing all the ongoing financial problems the College continued to face were numerous positive achievements: Evansville College was a four-year, North Central accredited college with strong programs in liberal arts, education, business administration, and engineering. It had a student body of over 400, a loyal and able faculty, more than 1,200 alumni (many of whom had been accepted by leading graduate schools), an endowment fund exceeding $400,0000, and a seventy-acre physical plant valued at $1,000,000.

Following extended consultation and discussion, Smith, although he had originally supported the idea of changing Evansville College from a private to a public institution, now reversed his stand and

declared: "It is the unanimous judgment of the administration and faculty of Evansville College that the acceptance of the [Indiana University] proposal would be a backward step for Evansville College and would limit higher educational facilities for Evansville."

This position, stated publicly at an Alumni Association banquet, was carried in a report by the Associated Press, and thus reached President Wells. Assuming that the newspaper account expressed the official position of Evansville College, Wells quickly issued a statement that he understood the reasons for the action, that the decision was probably in the best interests of both Evansville College and Indiana University, and that Evansville College could count on Indiana University for its cooperation and support. The subject of a merger was then quietly dropped, never to be mentioned again.

With the possibility of tax funds from either the city or the state now eliminated, College officials feared the public perception might be that the College would be forced to close its doors. Accordingly, letters were sent over the summer of 1939 to all students, assuring them that the College would be operating as usual in the fall. Newspaper articles and brochures reiterated the point, resulting in an increase in enrollment from 429 in the fall of 1938 to 461 in the fall of 1939.

President Smith, feeling that his mission in Evansville had been fulfilled, resigned in May of 1940 to become the minister of Central Avenue Church of Indianapolis, one of the largest in the conference, and, in 1947, Smith returned to his home state of California.

When the school's alliance with the Evansville Community Fund came to an end in 1940, the College conducted its own maintenance fund drive. This time, the campaign goal was exceeded by $3,000!

76

CHAPTER FOUR

Evansville College: 1940 to 1967

May Queen and attendants (1948)

BACKGROUND

During the twenty-six-year period under discussion in this chapter, Evansville College was under the leadership of two presidents.

1940-1954

Eighteenth President
LINCOLN B. HALE

77

The first, Lincoln B. Hale, a native of Connecticut, was trained as a machinist and, after military service in World War I, spent two years as a draftsman. Before long, however, his interests shifted to education and the ministry. Even though he had never attended an undergraduate college, the Divinity School of Yale University accepted him. He received a Bachelor of Divinity, a master's, and a Doctor of Philosophy from Yale University. (That he was a Presbyterian, however, rather than a Methodist, remained a source of friction with the Methodist Conference during his years in Evansville.)

Hale worked in education in Greece, was a parish minister, worked for the YMCA in Connecticut, and in student services at Carleton College before coming to Evansville in 1939 as dean and registrar (following the retirement of Charles E. Torbet, who had held the position since the College began). When President Smith resigned the following year, Hale was appointed acting president and a year later president. He served until 1954, a tenure longer than that of any previous president of the institution, ultimately resigning in order to head a United States mission in Israel.

His fourteen years were momentous ones for the institution, embracing the Second World War, the post-war enrollment boom, the school's first major building program in nearly twenty-five years, and a greatly expanded curriculum.

As President Hale's term began, the College was at a turning point. Without any chance of merging with Indiana University, the opportunity for receiving tax dollars was permanently doomed. This setback, coupled with the expiration of a five-year affiliation with the Evansville Community Fund, meant that in the future Evansville College would have to depend on its own efforts and resources for continued survival and expansion.

The War Years

As noted earlier, the fund-raising campaign of 1940 was a great success, but within two years the community's priorities shifted as attention became focused on America's involvement in World War II. As enrollment inevitably dropped, tuition income dried up as well. Enrollment fell to 280 in 1944, the lowest since 1921 when the College was still downtown.

The war also brought many curriculum changes. New courses in mathematics and physics were added, and the physical education requirement was extended from two years to four. Special classes were offered in first aid, radio communication, and meteorology; the summer session was extended; and a trimester plan was introduced in 1943, providing for three terms of sixteen weeks each. This adjustment enabled a student to complete four years of work in three years or less.

78

Engineering Defense Management class in radio communication (1942)

In addition, Evansville College was involved in several training projects which contributed to America's war effort. Under a contract with the Civilian Aviation Authority, in place since September 1939, the school provided pilot training. Then, from 1941 to 1945, the College participated in the Engineering-Science Defense Management Program (later called the War Management Program), the purpose of which was to train and upgrade workers in Evansville plants holding government contracts. During the four-year period, 192 evening classes were offered, with a total enrollment of 3,851. Participants came mainly from Republic Aviation, Servel, Sunbeam Electric, and SIGECO (Southern Indiana Gas and Electric Company), with instructors also drawn from these industries. The College took charge of this plan for fourteen counties in southern Indiana and also, under the leadership of Dean Long, head of the business administration department, cooperated with Indiana University in a similar, although smaller, program related to business management. These courses enrolled 1,111 persons in fifty-six classes.

Another major wartime project for the College was a navy pilot-training program consisting of eight weeks of ground school and forty hours in the air in light civilian airplanes. To facilitate the program, the city of Evansville leased 140 acres of level land off Outer Division Street north of Burkhardt Road. Lieutenant Colonel Lyle V. Courtney (retired) was the military officer in charge for the College; Emerson Henke, an instructor in the business administration department, was the manager. The facility opened in April of 1943 with fifty cadets; later, enrollment went to approximately ninety per session. By January of 1944, when the navy determined that it had enough cadets for its foreseeable needs, the College had trained 335 navy cadets, for which it received an official commendation from the Department of the Navy. The total number of men trained to fly by Evansville College – combining the Civilian Aviation Authority, the army, and the navy – was 639.

It must be added that the income received from these various government contracts helped immea-

Loren Bailey, first Evansville College student to lose his life serving in World War II

surably in avoiding deficits during this period of extremely low full-time enrollment. Indeed, Evansville College successfully operated "in the black" every year after 1932-33.

Nearly 1,000 students, graduates, and College personnel were involved in wartime service. Of these, thirty-two are known to have died while on active duty, the first being Loren Bailey '37.

In 1942, Alvin Strickler, chemistry department head since 1921, volunteered for military service and was commissioned a captain in the air force. He worked in the Chemical Warfare Service and returned to Evansville at the end of the war, with the rank of lieutenant colonel. Two other department heads, William V. Slyker (physical education and head coach) and Gaylord H. Browne (music), resigned to take positions in war-related industries. (Neither returned to the College after the war.)

Six members of the Board of Trustees, including its president, Richard R. McGinnis, were also in uniform. Others were Rufus Putnam (lieutenant), Norbert G. Talbott (lieutenant), Ralph Irons (major), Samuel Orr (captain), and Ellis Carson (lieutenant).

Athletics was also affected by the war. Football completed all but the final game of the 1942 season but was then abandoned until 1946. Basketball continued throughout the war, but with a considerably abbreviated schedule.

Finally, the formal inauguration of President Hale, planned for February 21, 1942, was cancelled.

The Post-War Era

When World War II ended, veterans were granted free college tuition under the act popularly known as the GI Bill. Although college enrollment across the nation soared, Evansville College grew even more than most, undergoing the most dra-

matic transformation in its history. It was Hale's policy that every qualified veteran wishing to attend Evansville College should be admitted. During the war years, enrollment was between 280 and 400 students. Classes were taught in one building by a faculty of twenty-seven. In the fall of 1946, registration climbed to 1,505 and the next year burgeoned to 1,722.

Needless to say, a shortage of classroom and library space developed, soon growing to critical proportions. Large numbers of part-time instructors augmented the small core faculty, and classes were scheduled from 7:00 a.m. to 10:00 p.m., not only in the classrooms of Administration Hall but also at the nearby National Guard Armory, Bosse High School, the auditorium stage, and even the president's reception room. In addition, as we shall see later, a new classroom building was under construction, and one wing was sufficiently completed to accommodate classes in drafting and physics.

Happy veterans return home, eager to attend Evansville College

Finally, part of the frame gymnasium was remodeled for use by the music department.

A further problem involved finding housing for students from outside the Evansville area. Eight buildings near Mesker Park, formerly used for war industry workers, were made available to the College by the Federal Public Housing Authority which, in addition, provided buses for transportation to and from campus. Closer to the campus, thirteen two-family pre-fabricated structures on Rotherwood Avenue were also provided by the government. They continued to be used for student housing until 1961, when the College purchased four apartment buildings at Weinbach Avenue and Walnut Street.

The Hale Administration: An Overview

Hale was regarded as less personable than his predecessors and inspired less affection. In fact, an associate once described him as "always an explosive individual with a short fuse." Nevertheless, he had amazing energy and worked hard to promote the goals and ideals of the College, especially in the area of community service. He was deeply devoted to the liberal arts as well as to the school's professional programs. His fourteen-year tenure saw the creation of the Evening College, the Center for Advanced Study, the Center for Industrial Relations, the Preparatory Music School, and the School of Nursing, as well as a revival of the co-op engineering program and more extensive cooperation with the Evansville Philharmonic Orchestra. In short, he wished to put the College at the service of the community, not only to benefit the community but also to increase financial support for the College.

Two important milestones occurred during Hale's administration. In 1944, a large civic banquet was held celebrating the twenty-fifth anniversary of the College in Evansville, but wartime priorities precluded further festivities. Ten years later, however, it was time to mark the centennial of the founding of Moores Hill College. This time an extensive celebration was planned, with the trustees setting aside $10,000 to cover the costs. It

began with a centennial convocation in September and continued with an artist and lecture series, a vesper series, television and radio programs, newspaper stories, club programs, a centennial calendar, and the publication of a book by John W. Winkley '05, *Moores Hill College: An Intimate History*.

On January 11, 1954, a centennial banquet took place in Evansville with President Herman B Wells of Indiana University as the principal speaker. Among many other participants was former President Alfred Hughes, and greetings were read from President Dwight D. Eisenhower.

On April 3, an all-sports dinner was held, attended by John M. Harmon, the College's first full-time coach (1923-30). At this event, a new award honoring the memory of William V. Slyker (coach from 1930 to 1943) was announced. The first recipient was Robert Martin.

On June 5, at a convocation on the old campus in Moores Hill, honorary degrees were conferred on nine graduates of the school, and a large stone and bronze tablet was dedicated marking the site of the former College building. Mrs. Harry Andrews King, wife of the president of Moores Hill College from 1904 to 1915, unveiled the tablet, and a service was led by President Hale. Later, at the commencement ceremony in Evansville, former President Earl E. Harper delivered the main address.

The centennial year was also marked by the departure of President Hale. His resignation was accompanied by some unpleasantness, perhaps occasioned by the fact that his often abrasive personality had irritated many faculty and trustees, who questioned both the methods and the manner of his leadership. In any case, Hale's announcement of his invitation to head the United States Foreign Operations Administration mission to Israel was accompanied by a request for a year's leave of absence, with the possibility of a further one-year extension.

The Executive Committee of the Board of Trustees rejected the request, arguing that "the continued success and development of Evansville College make it necessary that the institution have an active and permanent head" and that, therefore, his term as president of Evansville College should be terminated. The full board later concurred with the committee's verdict, leaving Hale upset in part because, although an ex officio member of the board, he had not been notified of the meeting.

The program Hale was called upon to direct involved American technical assistance and economic aid to the recently formed nation of Israel. In his new job, Hale served with distinction for three years, and even after returning to the United States his strong interest in the Middle East continued. Indeed, he was addressing a meeting on the subject in New York City in 1958 when he collapsed and died. In accord with his wishes, his ashes were scattered over the Holy Land.

1955-1967

Nineteenth President
MELVIN W. HYDE

When Hale's request for a leave was denied, Dean Long (vice president since 1949) was named acting president while the College searched for a new president. Trustees, faculty, and alumni were represented on the search committee, which spent several months and considered sixty-five candidates before making its selection.

Its choice was Melvin Watson Hyde, then fifty years of age, an experienced high school and college teacher, a former dean at Dakota Wesleyan University and Mount Union College (Alliance, Ohio) and assistant president at Drake University (Des Moines, Iowa). Hyde, a native of South

Dakota, held advanced degrees from Columbia University and, although an active Methodist layman, was not educated for the ministry. He thus became the first president of Evansville College since its founding in Moores Hill who was not a minister. (Interestingly, despite being the school's first non-clerical president, church support increased significantly during Hyde's administration.)

In addition, enrollment increased dramatically during Hyde's tenure, from 1,091 full-time day students in 1954 to 2,859 in 1966 – an increase of 160 percent! This influx of students demanded an extensive building program, requiring a total commitment of Hyde's energies and abilities. (Details of his achievements in this area follow.)

Hyde was also an active and accomplished civic leader, in recognition of which the Evansville Rotary Club proclaimed him the Outstanding Citizen of the Year for 1958. The community suffered severe economic reversals during this period, highlighted by the closing of Servel, one of the city's largest employers, and the removal of the Chrysler assembly plant and the Briggs body plant from the Evansville area. To counteract these losses, the Evansville Future organization was founded, with Hyde as its first president.

Hyde resigned when he believed that the time had come, in his words, for "turning over the responsibilities of leadership to capable younger minds, hearts, and hands." In June of 1966, Hyde announced that he would retire a year hence, allowing the board more than twelve months to find a suitable successor.

Upon his retirement, Hyde was elected president emeritus. The Hydes moved to Estes Park, Colorado, but Hyde continued as a consultant to various colleges and as an examiner for the North Central Association of Colleges. He died in Colorado in 1978 at the age of seventy-four.

McCurdy Alumni Memorial Union near completion (1950)

BUILDINGS AND FINANCES

Throughout its history, the financial goals of the College had centered on the institution's survival. Therefore, it was gratifying indeed when the school reached a point where mere survival seemed assured. However, for the College to flourish academically and serve its student body effectively, it required a greatly expanded physical plant. Although a single building had proved sufficient to meet most institutional needs, it will be remembered that, from its beginning, the founders of Evansville College had envisioned a multi-structured campus. Now the time was right for a new financial plan to make the vision a reality.

As early as 1940, trustee William A. Carson had strongly urged his fellow trustees and President Hale to initiate a building program. The American City Bureau of Chicago, a professional fund-raising agency which had recently assisted the College in its campaign, also encouraged the trustees, saying that, despite the war then raging in Europe, it was a good time to raise money, thanks to the federal tax structure, which allowed companies generous deductions for donations to nonprofit organizations.

By the time active fund-raising began in 1943, America was fully involved in the worldwide conflict. Despite the shortage of building materials, which made actual construction impossible, incomes were much higher than they had been for years, tax-deductible gifts flowed in, and many friends of the College, after purchasing government bonds to support the nation's war effort, then gave them to Evansville College.

From 1943 to 1946, Evansville businesses and industries were asked for contributions, much of the solicitation being done by Hale himself. The total raised was $520,000, of which $7,500 came from ninety-eight men and women in military service, many in combat areas. At least two of these contributors did not return from the war. Meanwhile, the student body, then numbering only about 300, pledged more than $5,000, and the faculty and staff, comprising about forty-five, gave $4,250.

Hale's priorities were to construct an engineering building first and then a union building, the former to meet the technological needs of an urban society and the latter to provide a more pleasant environment in which students could live and work. Before the war, a lounge in Administration Hall had been adequate for most social needs, but a greatly increased student body required more recreational space. As a start, a former Red Cross canteen was moved to the campus in 1946, and an addition was built on to it the following year. This temporary union building (nicknamed the TUB) served its purpose while the permanent union building was under construction. Later it was taken over by the ROTC until it was razed in 1965 (to make room for Hyde Hall and Shanklin Theatre).

In 1947, a city-wide building fund campaign began, headed by Robert D. Mathias, executive vice president of Old National Bank, and assisted by Louis Ruthenburg, president of Servel, and manufacturer and banker William Carson. John R. Feigel led the effort for alumni support. Donations from alumni, students, and faculty reached $58,000, and a $50,000 gift from Servel spurred other industries to contribute generously as well. By far the largest single gift was $300,000 from the estate of William H. McCurdy. By October of 1947, a total of $1,265,000 had been secured.

The success of this campaign boded well for the institution. After so many earlier drives had failed to raise even enough to meet costs, the success of this drive, as well as the school's ability to cover yearly expenses from its annual operating budget, assured its future financial health. During this period, for the first time in its history, the institution was not confronted by a serious financial crisis.

In appreciation of the contributions to the fund drive made by alumni, students, and faculty, it was decided to dedicate the new student union building to alumni who had served in World War II and as a memorial to those who had died in the service. In recognition of Colonel McCurdy's generosity to the College, the building was officially named the McCurdy Alumni Memorial Union. It was completed in January 1951.

Besides the two permanent structures, three temporary buildings were erected with government funding, providing an additional 33,000 square feet. These facilities housed classrooms, faculty and administrative offices, a dispensary, and a library reading room seating 300. The first of these temporary structures was removed in 1955 (to make room for Clifford Memorial Library), but the others remained in service until the 1970s.

Hale's original plan called for a new gymnasium first and a library sometime later but, predictably, many faculty disagreed and in time Hale was persuaded to reverse his priorities. The College library, located on the second floor of Administration Hall, had been overcrowded almost from the very beginning and conditions continued to deteriorate with every passing year.

By the early 1940s, the fourth floor attic had to be used to store those books and magazines least often used. During the peak years of the veteran enrollment (1947-50), an extra reading room, as mentioned above, was set up in one of the temporary buildings. Although three additional rooms in Administration Hall were also given over to the library, these, too, soon became full. Finally, although a happy problem, as the budget for reading materials increased, overcrowding grew even worse.

Clearly, there was a critical need for a new library. Before Hale's tenure ended, he was able to secure a $200,000 challenge grant from the Lilly Endowment of Indianapolis, the grant being conditional upon the College raising an additional $450,000. Then, under the leadership of Leland M. Feigel '29, the first Evansville College alumnus to serve on the Board of Trustees, a successful campaign was mounted. Ninety-four pledges of $1,000 or more were secured and, of these, sixteen were for $5,000 or more. The largest donation, $20,000, was from SIGECO.

A groundbreaking ceremony was held on November 22, 1955, the same day Melvin Hyde was inaugurated as president; the cornerstone was laid the following year. For the event, the Student Association prepared a historical cache to be placed in the cornerstone. More than ten million words and thousands of pictures were recorded on microfilm to give future generations a picture of the

Clifford Memorial Library under construction (July 1956)

Clifford Memorial Library 1957

world of 1956. The box was sealed after the air had been replaced with nitrogen, a process designed to help the documents and films resist deterioration. Included in the box was a tape by Elvis Presley, despite some complaints from those maintaining that such a hip-shaking entertainer should never be part of a package purporting to represent civilization. Final judgment on whether this selection was appropriate will have to rest with posterity.

During construction of the building, an engineering error was discovered when the architect's office realized that only half the correct number of reinforcing rods was being used. To bear the immense weight of thousands of books, library floors require twice as much steel as a classroom building, a factor which had not been properly considered. Eventually, the error was corrected, though at considerable cost, and the building was completed.

A.C. Biggs

The next problem was to move 45,000 books, periodicals, and other library materials from Administration Hall to the new library. A.C. Biggs (see page 117), director of physical plant, designed an ingenious scheme to accomplish this task. He rigged a cable car connecting the old library to the new. Attaching two cars to the cable caused the loaded car to pull the empty car back for reloading. In two days, the entire library contents were removed with a minimum of effort.

Overall credit for bringing the building project to its successful fruition must be awarded to the College librarian, **Thomas Harding** (Ph.D., University of Chicago). Harding came to Evansville in 1948 and remained until 1966. His outstanding organizational skills proved invaluable, and he was as successful in guiding and expanding the library's collection as he was in planning its new facility.

The new building was named in honor of Mr. and Mrs. George S. Clifford. In addition to originating the idea of bringing Moores Hill College to

Evansville, Clifford served on the Board of Trustees from 1919 until his death in 1927 and received its first honorary degree, that of Doctor of Laws, in 1922. His widow assumed his position on the board shortly after his death, becoming the school's first woman trustee.

On March 19, 1957, Clifford Memorial Library was dedicated. The principal speaker was the Cliffords' son, James L. Clifford, professor of English literature at Columbia University. (His extensive personal library is now part of the University collection.)

Included in the new building, the first on the campus to be air-conditioned, was a small auditorium seating 100 and named in memory of longtime trustee Henry C. Kleymeyer.

The growth of the Evansville College library collection was very nearly as impressive as its new facility. One of the earliest private contributors was Sol Esarey, an Indianapolis attorney and a Moores Hill College trustee from 1903 until 1916, who had one of the finest private libraries in Indiana. His first gift to Evansville College, as early as 1921, consisted of 175 books, rising to 2,675 by 1954; and, after his death, his widow augmented this amount.

In 1959, the Lilly Endowment gave the College $20,000 to increase its book collection, and three years later an unusual and valuable gift came from Karl Kae Knecht, who for fifty-four years drew cartoons, mostly political in nature, for the *Evansville Courier*. Approximately 10,000 original cartoons were included in his donation which, in 1979, were edited by Phillip Ensley of the history department and published by the University of Evansville Press.

By the early 1960s, the College library had grown to 55,000 volumes, but in less than a decade this number doubled, filling the building to capacity. In addition to books, the number of journals and newspapers also increased, and a host of new technologies – microfilm, microfiche, computers, etc. – started to appear. With the coming of the information age, the facility proved less adequate than originally hoped and, with enrollment continuing to grow, the need for more library space (and funds) grew increasingly acute.

THE BUILDER

During Hyde's twelve years as president, seventeen buildings were added, earning him the apt title of "the builder." In order of their completion, the structures erected or acquired during Hyde's tenure were as follows:

Clifford Memorial Library 1957
(Hyde completed the campaign begun under Hale to raise the $450,000 needed to claim the Lilly Endowment challenge gift of $200,000.)

Hughes Hall (Residence Hall) 1958

McCurdy Alumni Memorial Union Addition and **Bookstore** 1959

Moore Hall (Residence Hall) 1960

Bigney, Franklin, Hovda, and **Torbet Houses** (student housing) 1961
(These buildings, already constructed at Walnut Street and Weinbach Avenue, were purchased for College use.)

Krannert Hall of Fine Arts and **Wheeler Concert Hall** 1962

Carson Center (Health and Physical Education) 1962

Moore Hall (Addition) 1963

Hughes Hall (Addition) 1964

Harper Dining Center 1964

Neu Chapel 1966

Hale Hall (Residence Hall) 1966

Brentano Hall (Residence Hall) 1966

Hyde Hall (Classroom Building) and **Shanklin Theatre** 1967

Also, additions were made to the heating plant and maintenance building in 1956, 1961, and 1966. The total cost of all of these buildings and their equipment was approximately $10 million, of which more than $7 million was debt free.

Carson Center

ACADEMIC BUILDINGS

The buildings for fine arts and physical education were financed through a citywide campaign led by Evansville businessman Kenneth C. Kent and supported by a $400,000 gift from Mr. and Mrs. Herman C. Krannert. (Mr. Krannert was the founder and president of Inland Container Company, a major Evansville industry. Walter G. Koch, vice president of Inland Container, was at this time a member of the College Board of Trustees.)

Another large gift, $275,000, was received from the Lilly Endowment of Indianapolis. A portion of this gift honored the memory of its recently deceased general counsel, Walton M. Wheeler Jr., also a member of the Evansville College Board of Trustees. It is noteworthy that Wheeler's father, Walton M. Wheeler Sr., had been a College trustee and was College attorney from 1919 to 1939. The concert hall in the new Krannert Hall of Fine Arts was subsequently named Wheeler Concert Hall.

Other large gifts to the building fund included:

87

W. A. Carson
$100,000
Mead Johnson and Company
$100,000
Old National Bank
$30,000
Whirlpool Corporation
$30,000
Vanderburgh County Savings and Loan League
$25,000
Citizens National Bank
$20,000

Wheeler Concert Hall and Krannert Hall of Fine Arts

The orchestra performs in Wheeler Concert Hall

88

So generous was the response of other large companies, alumni, students, faculty, public school teachers, and friends of the College that the campaign was over-subscribed by $210,000, the total pledged being $1,735,000.

The Krannert Hall of Fine Arts, in addition to Wheeler Concert Hall, houses the music and art departments and the Krannert Gallery. Carson Center includes three gymnasiums, an Olympic-sized swimming pool, classrooms and offices. The total cost of these two buildings, dedicated in 1962, was slightly less than $2 million.

Four years later, Neu Chapel, made possible by a major gift of $350,000 from Mr. and Mrs. Adam J. Neu, was dedicated by Richard C. Raines, bishop of the Indiana Area of the Methodist Church. Until that time, religious services were held in the Administration Hall auditorium or, after 1949, in

a renovated portion of one of the temporary buildings erected just after World War II.

Neu Chapel, constructed of Indiana limestone, has an interior marked by an arched wood ceiling. A balcony houses a fine Holtkamp organ, the chapel will seat as many as 500 persons, a ground floor meeting room seats about 200, and the exterior features a large illuminated cross. Religious services for students and the community are scheduled weekly during the school year, and special events such as concerts and lectures are presented frequently in the chapel. Neu Chapel has also proved popular for weddings, with 70 to 100 ceremonies performed most years.

With enrollment reaching new heights, there was a pressing need for additional classrooms as well as for an improved theatre facility to accommodate Evansville's expanded and nationally recognized drama program. Although the original plan for Evansville College theatre was to renovate and modernize the auditorium in Administration Hall, costs proved prohibitive. Since a new classroom building was then in the planning stage, it seemed feasible to incorporate a theatre. A further advantage was that **Sam Smiley**, theatre director, strongly favored an open or thrust stage in which the audience is seated on three sides, placing everyone closer to the action, as opposed to the conventional proscenium arch or "picture frame" stage, as in Administration Hall.

Constructing one building proved far more economical than two separate buildings, and the new structure was completed in the spring of 1967. Lighting and sound controls were made possible by a gift from the Junior League of Evansville, and nearly all of the 486 seats offer an excellent view of the stage. The theatre opened on April 14, 1967, with a performance of Shakespeare's *Hamlet*, the title role played by Evansville College graduate and drama department faculty member **John David Lutz '64**.

The theatre was named in accordance with the will of Robert F. Shanklin, which had established a trust fund to benefit Evansville College specifying that it be used for a building on campus if the College would agree to name a building in memory of the Shanklin family. Many family members had distinguished themselves in a variety of areas: James M. Shanklin, Robert Shanklin's father, had served as a colonel in the Civil War; his uncles, George W. and John G. Shanklin, owned the *Evansville Courier* during the last quarter of the nineteenth century; John G. Shanklin was prominent in state and national politics and public service; finally, another uncle, John Marshall Harlan, was appointed an associate justice of the Supreme Court of the United States in 1877. (His grandson, who bore the same name and was Robert Shanklin's cousin, also became a Supreme Court justice, serving from 1955 to 1971.)

Hyde Hall, named in recognition of Melvin Hyde's twelve years of outstanding service as president of Evansville College, became home to the business administration and education depart-

Neu Chapel

89

Moore Hall

ments as well as housing numerous classrooms, offices, and special-purpose rooms.

With the opening of Hyde Hall, Administration Hall finally became what its name implies, the offices of the president, deans, and other administrative personnel. In 1965, the auditorium was removed and subsequently, that space was used by central duplicating, the mail service, supplies, and computer services.

Residence Halls

As Evansville College continued to attract a greater number of students from outside the Tri-State area, the need for on-campus residential housing became increasingly acute. President Hale had repeatedly requested the trustees to consider a campus residence hall, but it was not until President Hyde began his campaign to launch an extensive building program that serious action was taken. In October 1957, construction contracts were signed for the school's first residence hall, and the following September – nearly forty years after the College began – the building was ready for students.

The new four-story residence hall had room for 128 students. In addition, there was a large lounge, a recreation room, a head resident's suite, a guest suite, a laundry room, and storage areas. Total cost for the facility, which faced Weinbach Avenue, was $486,000. The building was named Hughes Hall in honor of the school's first president. Hughes and his wife were present for the opening ceremony and occupied the guest suite, as they were to do again on a later visit to the campus.

During its first two years, Hughes Hall was a women's residence but, in 1960, a second residence hall, a near replica of Hughes Hall, was opened; it also provided housing for 128 students. The new structure fulfilled a long-standing promise to name a campus building for Moores Hill College founder John Collins Moore. The Indiana Conference of the Methodist Church raised $500,000, and their contribution made it possible to construct the building at no expense to the College. Moore Hall became a women's residence hall, and Hughes Hall housed male students until 1972, when it became a residence for both male and female students.

*Hughes Hall under construction
(early 1958)*

Hale Hall 1966

91

Hughes Hall 1958

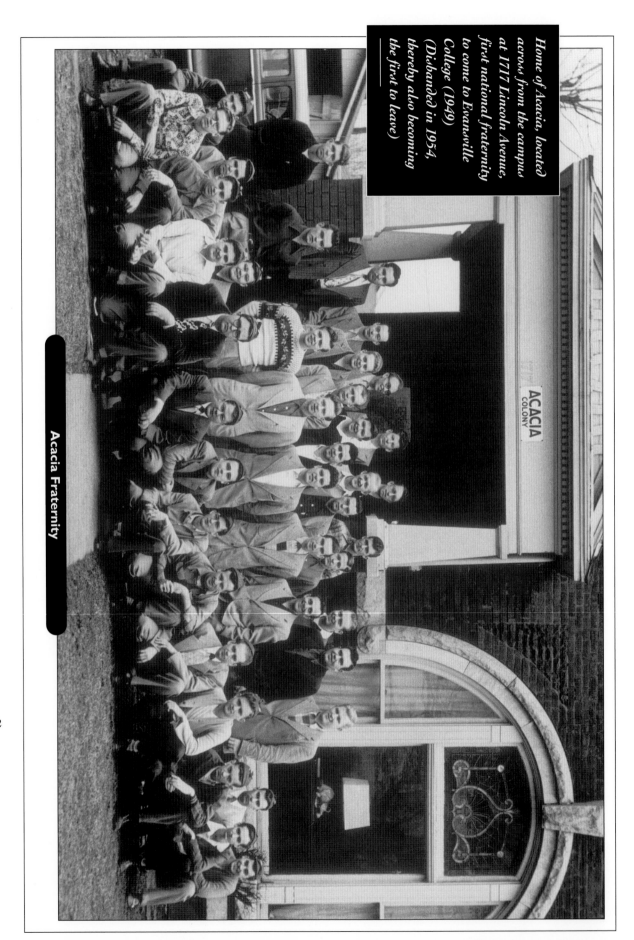

Home of Acacia, located across from the campus at 1717 Lincoln Avenue, first national fraternity to come to Evansville College (1949) (Disbanded in 1954, thereby also becoming the first to leave)

Acacia Fraternity

ACACIA COLONY

Both Moore Hall and Hughes Hall soon proved too small, and additional wings were added to each (in 1963 and 1964 respectively), thus more than doubling their capacity. The two residence halls were then able to house 584 students.

In 1961, just after the completion of Moore Hall, the College also acquired four brick apartment buildings located at Walnut Street and Weinbach Avenue for a total of $220,000. Since each apartment had a kitchen, they were easily adapted for use by married couples as well as for single students preferring not to live in residence halls. Each building was named in honor of an original Evansville College faculty member: George B. Franklin, Andrew J. Bigney, Charles E. Torbet, and Olaf Hovda. (These apartments were later razed to provide space for three fraternity houses.)

Increasing enrollment inevitably required even more residence hall space. In 1966, Hale Hall for men and Brentano Hall for women were completed, the first Evansville College residence halls to be air-conditioned. The men's hall honored former President Lincoln B. Hale, and the women's hall was named for August A. Brentano, a trustee from

1940 until his death in 1961, treasurer of the Board of Trustees from 1948 to 1961, and chairman of the Development Committee from 1955 to 1961.

Meanwhile, 1964 saw the completion of a campus dining center named in honor of another former president, Earl E. Harper, who attended the dedication ceremony with his family.

Buildings and Grounds: Other Aspects

▪ Landscaping plays an important role in making a campus attractive to visitors and prospective students. Beginning in 1937 and for some thirty years thereafter, Ben Wolfe, the owner of a nursery and an ardent supporter of the College, supervised the care of shrubbery and trees on the campus. As new buildings were erected after 1947, Wolfe designed the landscaping and furnished many plantings, often without charge.

▪ Although the new library was the first building on campus to be fully air-conditioned, air-conditioning began at Evansville College in 1951. Since funds for that purpose were not then available, the business office staff decided to sell candy bars at the cashier's window and use the

93

Harper Dining Center

profits to buy a window air conditioner. The plan succeeded, and within a few months, the business office made campus history by installing the school's first air conditioner.

■ From the time the College moved to its Lincoln Avenue location until the early 1950s, the entire campus was one tract with no street dividing it. Walnut Street stopped at Rotherwood Avenue on the west side of the campus and resumed at Weinbach Avenue on the east. Then, in 1953, Walnut Street was extended so as to bisect the campus, providing additional entrance and exit points to College buildings. Subsequently, Walnut Street became a major artery connecting the east side of Evansville with the center of town. (In 1997, however, the University of Evansville proposed returning to the original plan by closing Walnut Street from Weinbach to Rotherwood Avenues in order to unify the campus and provide greater safety for its students, but community protest was so strong that the proposal was quickly dropped.)

■ Also in 1953, the trustees were asked for the use of approximately four acres of the campus as the site for a county auditorium. Although this proposal was accepted, several downtown merchants and many west side residents objected to the east side location; accordingly, the plan was dropped and eventually the auditorium was constructed at a central location downtown.

■ With an eye toward future development needs, board member Guthrie May recommended in 1964 that the College purchase sixty-two acres at the southeast corner of Lincoln Avenue and Burkhardt Road. Three years later, forty acres on Vann Avenue between Lincoln Avenue and Division Street, part of the grounds of the Indiana State Hospital, were acquired from the state.

FUND-RAISING

In 1940, after five years with the Evansville Community Fund, the College resumed its own fund-raising efforts, the first campaign bringing in an impressive $38,000.

In the following years, many new approaches and initiatives were attempted. Until 1944, there had been only sporadic, tentative solicitations of Evansville College alumni, but in that year an alumni drive for the proposed student union building raised over $57,000, handily exceeding its goal by $7,000. In 1951, a formal annual Alumni Fund drive was begun, and only a few years later more than 1,100 alumni contributed $66,395 to build Clifford Memorial Library.

Beginning in 1962, solicitation of alumni by telephone (Telerama) was used successfully to supplement mail solicitation, with long distance telephone lines furnished by Whirlpool Corporation. In a typical year, 1966, 182 alumni made 6,200 calls and received pledges from 1,776 persons for a total of $16,500. In the twenty years from 1951 to 1971, the Alumni Fund raised more than $370,000 for the institution.

In 1950, the Lilly Endowment of Indianapolis began making annual gifts to the school, under Hale totaling $235,000 and under Hyde reaching $1,218,200. This included $445,000 for the library building, the fine arts building, and the physical education building, as well as grants for faculty development and other educational purposes.

In 1952, Evansville College became one of eleven charter members of the Associated Colleges of Indiana, organized in part through the efforts of President Hale. Henceforth, instead of each private college in Indiana clamoring for an individual gift from a business or industry, only one annual solicitation would be made and all resulting gifts would be divided according to a formula agreed upon by the members, although donors had the right to designate that their gifts go to a particular college if they so wished. Two additional schools joined later and the Lilly Endowment agreed to pay the association's office expenses so that all the money contributed by business and industry could be used for educational purposes. Between 1952 and 1971, Evansville College received more than $1,250,000 from this source.

In 1956, Evansville College received $290,500 from the Ford Foundation, which specified that the money be used to increase faculty compensation and augment the endowment fund. This emphasis on endowment was especially welcome since Evansville College, like its predecessor, Moores Hill, had traditionally lagged in this critical measure of an institution's stability. Money had always been so desperately needed for operating expenses and later for campus buildings that the endowment received only meager attention. For example, in the twenty years from 1932 to 1952, total assets in the endowment fund increased by only $36,000.

In 1961, President Hyde set $6,700,000 as his goal for a healthy endowment fund. Although he was unable to attain this figure, within a decade the fund had achieved a book value of $3,349,000 and a market value of $4,076,000, a significant amount considering the financial commitments involved in the various construction projects undertaken during his tenure.

The sound financial condition of Evansville College during this period is due in large part to its major donors. These include those already mentioned whose gifts made new buildings possible: William H. McCurdy, William A. Carson, Mr. and Mrs. Adam Neu, and Mr. and Mrs. Herman C. Krannert. A further significant gift from McCurdy's estate consisted of securities and cash valued at $210,000, plus a one-half interest in the large four-story building at Fourth and Sycamore Streets housing the Sears and Roebuck retail store. Rental income from this building proved invaluable to the College for many years.

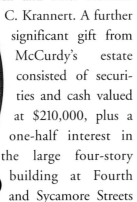

William H. McCurdy

Additional gifts were scholarship funds given in memory of trustee Samuel L. Orr and his wife, Louise Dunkerson Orr, by their children, and by trustee Henry Kleymeyer and his sons, Ralph, Clifford, and Henry.

Faculty Salaries

Faculty salaries across the nation rose sharply during the period under discussion. At Evansville College, salaries showed a steady – and at times dramatic – increase and, beginning in 1947, professors were guaranteed year-round employment with every third summer free of teaching responsibilities to be used for advanced study or recreation at full pay. In 1955, a full professor received $6,000 a year under the above plan, but by 1966 this had climbed to $13,400 for a nine-month academic year, with additional pay for summer teaching. Other faculty ranks also saw substantial salary increases.

In addition, faculty were offered a wide range of fringe benefits. For its first twenty-five years, the College offered no retirement plan, but in 1945, Evansville College joined the Teachers Insurance and Annuity Association, a national nonprofit company organized specifically for college and university staff members. Faculty contributed five percent of their annual salaries with an equal amount deposited by the College. Seven years later TIAA established a variable annuity plan, providing for investments in a common stock fund, rather than the more traditional bond-and-mortgage investments which characterized TIAA. Membership in the new organization, known as the College Retirement Equity Fund (CREF), was optional, but most faculty elected to have at least one half of their retirement premium placed in CREF. Beginning in 1966, non-academic employees were also admitted to the TIAA retirement plans. Since all College employees were already enrolled in Social Security, the combination of TIAA (and CREF) plus Social Security provided Evansville College faculty and staff with a highly satisfactory retirement income.

In 1946, a Blue Cross/Blue Shield health insurance group was formed for employees, with the College paying one-half the premium. In 1960, a major medical plan (catastrophic insurance) was added, with the College again sharing half the cost. In case of sickness or accident, a faculty member received full salary for three months. Beginning in 1966, a low-cost plan also became available to pro-

95

vide income for anyone suffering permanent disability; in this event, sixty percent of the professor's salary is paid until age sixty-five and both his and the College's share of the retirement premium is also paid. Then, at sixty-five, retirement benefits begin just as though employment had continued.

Group life insurance began in 1955 with a $3,000 policy for each faculty member, increasing to $10,000 by 1963. Policies with lower benefits were available to non-academic employees. All employees paid approximately one-third of the premium. Also beginning in 1955, faculty and staff dependents received free tuition. In addition, full-time staff members were able to register for up to five hours of class work per quarter at no cost. Finally, to encourage research, scholarship, and professional growth, the College began providing financial assistance for those attending professional meetings or working on advanced degrees.

In 1964, the College instituted a paid sabbatical leave program for faculty holding the rank of associate professor or professor. Applicants were asked to submit an acceptable plan of study, research, or educational travel, and were required to return to the College for at least one year (or repay the amount received).

Overall, the closing years of Evansville College were the best, financially speaking, in its history up to that time. During Hyde's presidential tenure, income from tuition and fees increased nearly five-fold, from $583,000 to $2,869,000, and total income also rose five-fold, from $1,064,600 to $5,306,550. Endowment income went from $30,930 to $109,110. Support provided by the Associated Colleges of Indiana rose from $31,000 in 1954-55 to $100,000 in 1966-67, while annual support from the Methodist Church rose from $8,200 to $113,450, and Lilly Endowment support from $35,000 to $100,000.

To top it all – except for bonds on two self-liquidating projects, Hughes Hall and Harper Dining Center – Evansville College was now debt free!

96

ACADEMICS AND ADMINISTRATION

PROFESSIONAL PROGRAMS

From 1931 to 1940, the Bachelor of Arts and Bachelor of Science were the only degrees granted by Evansville College and no field of study was designated. This system proved unpopular, however, and by 1950 nine specific degrees were being awarded.

Business Administration

The Bachelor of Science in Business Administration, for example, was reinstated in 1946, and majors were established in economics, accounting, finance, management, marketing, and secretarial science.

A key figure in the development of a strong business program at Evansville College was Dean Long, who headed the business department from 1929 to 1949 and again from 1951 to 1955. For thirteen years, he conducted an evening class on corporate policy and management, a seminar enrolling 369 executives and various management persons from ninety-one firms. Participants unfailingly agreed that the course was highly useful and worthwhile.

In 1953, Long was instrumental in establishing the Center for Industrial Relations, developed in cooperation with the University of Chicago. Evansville College became the first of about twenty institutions to take part in this program, which was particularly timely in view of the turmoil and conflict occurring in cities such as Evansville with substantial manufacturing operations. Strikes, lockouts, and inter-union rivalries led to several incidents of violence during this period. Evansville College hoped to resolve some of the troubling issues faced by local industry by offering services to all levels of management in dealing with supervision, communication, cost management, work performance, and human relations. A major project of the Center for Industrial Relations was the establishment of a joint Labor-Management Relations Council, which sponsored an annual two-day conference featuring prominent national labor relations officials as session leaders and keynote speakers. The conference continued for fourteen years, longer than any other such conference in the country. In addition, the center helped employers measure work effectiveness and employee job satisfaction, and it conducted extensive testing programs. For example, an important service to the city of Evansville was the annual testing of policemen who had applied for promotion.

In its first year, the Center for Industrial Relations had programs for six Evansville industries. Less than twenty years later, this number had reached ninety-five. As vice president for adult education, Long was responsible for promotion of services offered by the center. **William Affolder** (M.S., Indiana University) directed the day-to-day operations of the program from 1954 through

1965, when **Joseph Holt** (M.S., George Peabody) assumed the position of director.

For the final decade of Evansville College the head of the business administration department was **Ray Arensman**, a 1943 Evansville College graduate whose master's and doctorate were earned at Indiana University, where he was also a faculty member for six years. Arensman published extensively, was a visiting professor at various universities, and was a consultant to numerous Indiana corporations.

Nursing and Other Health Services

Evansville College made many important contributions to training students interested in the health care field.

In 1940, the school began a cooperative program with Deaconess Hospital providing classroom instruction in the arts and sciences for the hospital's nurses in training. The first graduate of this five-year

---

BUSINESS ADMINISTRATION FACULTY

Also joining the department during this period were:

Lawrence Anderson
(M.A., Northwestern University) 1945-67
Economics, Finance

James Julian '41
(I.A., Harvard University) 1947-73
Industrial Management, Business Policy,
Business Statistics

Edward Hauswald
(Ph.D., Indiana University) 1954-64
Economics

Robert Martin
(M.B.A., Indiana University) 1956-87
Office Administration, Management

Clifford Stone '39
(Ph.D., University of Iowa) 1958-86
Accounting

Frazer Rodman
(M.B.A., University of Pennsylvania) 1959-67
Management

Millard Pace '56
(M.S., University of Illinois) 1959-85
Marketing

Allen Bess
(M.A., University of Missouri) 1963-98
Accounting

Mau-Sung (Maurice) Tsai
(Ph.D., Southern Illinois University) 1964-97
Economics

Ronald Faust
(Ph.D., Indiana University) 1964-present
Management

Miles Taylor
(M.B.A., University of Chicago) 1966-71
Management
(Taylor originally joined the College in 1963 as
Colonel Taylor, commanding officer of the U.S. Air
Force Reserve Officer Training Corps [ROTC] program on campus.)

program was **Thelma Brittingham**, who was later an Evansville College faculty member. The arrangement with the hospital continued until 1982.

In 1944, Evansville College began a new four-year degree program, a Bachelor of Science in Medical Technology. After three years in the classroom, focused mainly on biology and chemistry but including general education classes as well, the student then received a full twelve months of instruction in the pathology laboratories at Deaconess or St Mary's Hospitals. A.W. Ratcliffe, an Evansville pathologist, was the College's resource person in developing this program, which successfully reduced the shortage of trained personnel in this field.

In 1953, Evansville College joined with Welborn Baptist Hospital for a program which was to grow into one of the most prestigious and successful in the institution's history, the Evansville College School of Nursing. Through a carefully constructed and demanding four-year curriculum, students were able to earn a bachelor's degree which combined a strong liberal arts component with high quality professional training. The faculty was drawn from the staff of Welborn Hospital and, although at first they were given the lowest possible academic rank, visiting assistant instructor, as the nursing program grew in importance and reputation they became bona fide, respected faculty members.

Mildred Boeke was appointed head of the nursing department (officially named the School of Nursing in 1959), a position she held until her retirement in 1968. Boeke's leadership was deeply appreciated by students and highly regarded by her professional colleagues, one of whom described her as "multi-talented, an entrepreneur, and a risk taker," adding: "Failure did not exist in her books."

Mildred Boeke

As a result of her efforts, enrollment in the program increased dramatically, rising from a freshman class of twelve in 1953 to eighty-five fifteen years later, when total enrollment in the program was 269. The curriculum was especially strong in integrating clinical experience with academic instruction and made extensive use of various health agencies and community resources.

Of particular significance was the contribution of Genevieve Bixler, who guided the School of Nursing's effort to secure accreditation by the National League for Nursing. When this was successfully achieved in 1960, Evansville College became the first four-year nursing school in Indiana to be nationally accredited.

Education

Teacher training played a major part in the Evansville College curriculum, nearly one-third of the institution's enrollment being in this area. (Between 1940 and 1966, it ranged from a low of seventeen percent in 1947 to a high of thirty-eight percent in 1963, between twenty-eight and thirty-five percent being typical.) In the late 1940s, veterans from World War II swelled the ranks of potential teachers, with an especially sharp increase in male candidates.

Embarrassed by the success of the Soviet Union in space exploration during the 1950s, the federal government began pouring money into state and local coffers to upgrade science and mathematics programs. Preparation of teachers in these two areas was later expanded to include reading, the language arts, and social studies. The Evansville College education department held many workshops and special courses to help teachers become more knowledgeable in these disciplines; Mead Johnson sponsored science workshops; and NASA supplied material for units on space.

As academic standards for elementary and high school teachers rose across the nation, the Evansville school system began to urge its faculty to earn a master's degree and offered a substantial salary increase as an incentive. Since Evansville College lacked resources for graduate programs, President

Evansville College student teachers in the classroom, apparent spell-binders (1950s)

Hale entered into a cooperative arrangement with Indiana University and Purdue University to make advanced degrees available to Evansville teachers. Indiana and Purdue supplied instructors for the classes, held mainly at night, sometimes on Saturdays, and also in the summer. Professors commuted from Indiana University's Bloomington campus, while Purdue offered workshops in Evansville during the summer session. Evansville College administered the program and furnished classroom and library facilities. The degrees were conferred by Indiana University and required two summer sessions on the Bloomington campus in addition to work taken in Evansville.

In 1948, nearly 400 students were enrolled in the Evansville College Center for Advanced Study, as it was officially known. The number increased beyond that after 1963, when the Evansville school board decreed that all faculty must earn a master's degree within seven years of receiving their teacher's license.

In 1958, following a thorough examination by its inspection team, the National Council for Accreditation of Teacher Education (NCATE) granted full accreditation to Evansville College's undergraduate program. At the time only three other schools in Indiana were accredited.

Encouraged by this stamp of approval and responding to the Evansville school board's ruling, the College set about to develop its own master's degree program in education. In 1965, the North Central Association of Colleges accredited this program and, within a year, 286 persons were enrolled. The first master's degree under this program was conferred on Ann L. Humphrey in 1966. A year after that, with enrollment more than doubled, the program with the state universities was gradually phased out.

Additional education programs included a curriculum for nursing education, approved in 1962 by the Indiana State Board of Education, enabling nurse-teachers to meet Indiana's license requirements, and two programs, approved by the state in

99

School of Education Faculty

Seated, left to right Rexel E. Brown, Leland W. Moon, Wilma C. Shafer, Harry E. Whitesell, Earl M. Tapley (dean); *Standing, left to right* Robert F. Garnett, William C. Wesley (assistant dean), Ralph R. Royster, Clifford W. Kraft

1967, for training reading specialists and school counselors. Also, a high percentage of high school athletic coaches in the Tri-State area were trained at Evansville College.

Leadership in the education department has been consistently strong. For eighteen years, from 1942 to 1960, the department was headed by **Lucille Jones**, who had joined the Evansville Col-

lege faculty in 1928. A graduate of Columbia University and an experienced public school teacher, she was especially successful in building rapport between the College and the Evansville schools and principals. When she retired in 1960, she had served the College for thirty-two years.

She was followed as department head by **Earl Tapley** (Ph.D., University of Chicago), who came to Evansville College in 1957 after many years in education, including service as a high school principal.

Engineering

In 1944, with construction of an engineering and science building awaiting only the conclusion of World War II, President Hale engaged **John Needy**, an experienced engineering educator then fifty-five years old, to supervise plans for the building and to develop a new engineering curriculum. During his four-year tenure, the building was completed and the co-op engineering program, begun in 1920 but discontinued in 1931, was reac-

---

EDUCATION FACULTY

Also joining the department during this time were:

Leland Moon
(Ed.D., Columbia University) 1945-72
Director of Supervised Teaching, Director of Secondary Education

Wilma Shafer
(Ed.D., Indiana University) 1960-81
Director of Elementary Education

ENGINEERING FACULTY

Also joining the department during this period were:

Max Casler
(Ph.D., University of Illinois)
Physics 1952-58, Electrical Engineering 1958-86 (part time 1977-86)

Harold Houston
(M.S., Indiana University) 1954-71
Mechanical Engineering

Joseph Kushner
(Ph.D., Lehigh University) 1958-75
Metallurgy
(Kushner received two National Science Foundation research grants and the American Electroplating Society's Scientific Achievement Award. He was also a senior visiting fellow at the University of Birmingham, England.)

Clarence Winternheimer
(Ph.D., University of Illinois) 1959-98
Electrical Engineering
(He was an honors graduate of Evansville College.)

Bung-Chung Lee
(Ph.D., Michigan State University) 1960-96
Mechanical Engineering

Ronald Devaisher
(M.S., University of Illinois) 1960-2001
Mechanical Engineering
Director of Auto CAD (Computer Assisted Drafting) Training Center and Engineering Graphics/CAD Laboratory

tivated (1947). About one half of the school's engineering majors participated in this five-year program, which combined classroom instruction with practical experience, while the remaining students enrolled in the standard four-year program.

At first, the degree offered by Evansville College was called a Bachelor of Science in Industrial Technology, with majors in refrigeration, industrial chemistry, electronics, and machine design. After only two years, however, it was decided to change the name of the degree to Bachelor of Science in Engineering, with the major fields being electrical engineering and mechanical engineering. Graduates who had been granted the industrial technology degree could return their diploma and receive the new engineering degree in its place.

In 1948, **John Kronsbein** was appointed head of engineering. A native of Germany, his doctoral degree was from the University of Leipzig; he had received much of his education in Germany and France and had also worked in England. Kronsbein was a demanding and highly respected teacher who directed the Evansville College engineering program for ten years.

101

Engineering and science building near completion (1946)

Engineering Faculty

Front row, left to right Joseph Kushner, William Hartsaw, Max Casler, Clarence Winternheimer; *Back row, left to right* Paul Funk, Bung-Chung Lee, Harold Houston, Syama Chaudhuri, Edward Susat

His successor, **William Hartsaw** (Ph.D., University of Illinois), had started as an instructor in 1946 and by the time of his retirement in 1992 had served forty-six years, longer than any faculty member in the institution's history!

In 1954, **Edward Susat** became director of the co-op program. He was charged with placing students in their work positions and maintaining good relations with employers. Later, Susat assumed direction of the school's entire placement program. He retired in 1977.

102   ARTS AND SCIENCES

Art

Until 1940, the only art courses taught at Evansville College were those required for the elementary teacher's license, and these were taught on a part-time basis by teachers from the Evansville public schools. In 1940, the College engaged its first full-time art teacher, **Charlotte Dutch**, with part of her salary being paid by the Evansville Museum, which also made its art studio available for classes.

In 1947, art became a separate department and, with the coming of **Florence Keve** the following year, art began its rapid expansion in the College curriculum. Keve, who held a master's degree from Columbia University, turned three rooms in one of the temporary war surplus buildings into an all-purpose art center. She engaged part-time instructors from the community, such as noted artist **Fred Eilers** (who had been teaching in the Evening College since 1944), and later she played an important role in planning the facilities in the new Krannert Hall of Fine Arts. Sadly, Keve died in 1961, only a year before the building became a reality.

Krannert Hall of Fine Arts provided excellent facilities and equipment for ceramics, metal work, painting, sculpture, and commercial art; soon, faculty members with expertise in these areas were hired. **Robert Osborne**, a painter, came to the College in 1961 and succeeded Keve as department head. He resigned in 1969.

Leslie Miley Jr., who also came to the faculty at this time, was primarily a ceramic artist. In 1966, Miley was instrumental in establishing the New Harmony Ceramics Workshop as a joint venture

Les Miley at work

between Evansville College, Jane Owen, and the Robert Lee Blaffer Trust. Miley was appointed director of the summer workshop program, which concludes each year with a workshop pottery sale. He also introduced watercolor and printmaking classes into the College curriculum and served as department head during the 1965-66 academic year.

Howard Oagley (M.A., Case Western Reserve University), appointed in 1965, specialized in sculpture, printmaking, and art history and also served as the first curator of the University art collection. He retired in 1984.

Donald Dunham with students

Biology

Floyd Beghtel, who had come to the biology department in 1931, resigned in 1943 and was replaced with an acting head, **Donald Dunham** (Ph.D., Ohio State University), who had come to Evansville College two years before. In 1945, he was made head of the department and remained in this position until 1974. A highly respected teacher, he was especially noted for his success with pre-medical students, who received excellent scientific training under his guidance.

BIOLOGY FACULTY

Also joining the department during this period were:

Charles Robertson
(Ph.D., New York University) 1950-72
Zoology

P. Louis Winternheimer
(Ph.D., Indiana University) 1957-98
Botany (also University Marshal)

Wayne Mueller
(Ph.D., Indiana University) 1962-96
Zoology, Director of Environmental Studies, Department Chair

Jo Frohbieter-Mueller
(M.S., Indiana University) 1963-72
Research Biologist

103

Chemistry

Alvin Strickler, who had been head of the Evansville College chemistry department since 1921, volunteered for military service in 1942 and was soon appointed as chief of the Chemical Warfare Section at San Bernardino Airforce Command. Following his discharge in 1946 as a lieutenant colonel, he returned to Evansville College until his retirement in 1954, having served the College for thirty-three years.

His successor as department head was **Norman Long** (Ph.D., University of Buffalo), who remained until 1957; he was followed by **Lowell Weller** (Ph.D., Michigan State University), who served until his retirement in 1989. Thus, in nearly seventy years, the chemistry department had

---

CHEMISTRY FACULTY

Also joining the department during this period were:

Karl Schaaf
1932-37

Philip Hatfield
1937-42
(Both Schaaf and Hatfield were laboratory assistants as students at Evansville College who later returned to teach.)

Wyatt Powell
(M.A., Wittenberg University) 1955-61

Philip Kinsey
(Ph.D., Purdue University) 1956-95
Physical Chemistry

Clifford Shultz
(Ph.D., University of New Mexico) 1960-66
Analytical Chemistry

Eula Megli
(M.S., Pennsylvania State University) 1962-86
(Megli began as a sabbatical replacement and remained for twenty-four years, primarily teaching introductory chemistry either part time or full time.)

---

only three heads, contributing to its success as a stable and effective department.

It is also noteworthy that in 1962, when Evansville College was approved for membership in the American Chemical Society, fewer than one-quarter of Indiana colleges had been admitted to the society up to that time.

English and Journalism

When Ernst van Keuren, who had headed the Evansville College English department since 1931, resigned in 1946 to become chairman of the Division of Humanities at the new Chicago branch of the University of Illinois, his successor was **Martin Shockley** (Ph.D., University of North Carolina). He remained only a short time because of his strong disagreement with the president and trustees over the George Parker case (see page 119) and he was succeeded for eight years by Wahnita DeLong.

DeLong, in turn, was followed by **Virgil Logan** (Ph.D., University of Wisconsin), whose major field was speech, which was part of the English department at this time. Logan and his wife, Lillian, were the authors of several textbooks. In 1962, the two areas were separated and Logan was appointed head of the new speech department, but he chose to resign to accept a position at Findlay College in Ohio.

The new head of the English department was **Paul Grabill**, who had come to Evansville College in 1957 with his wife, **Virginia Lowell Grabill**; both held doctorates from the University of Illinois. Although physically handicapped by severe rheumatoid arthritis, Paul Grabill was a dynamic lecturer especially noted for his dramatic readings of Shakespeare and was a creative writer as well. He inspired many students to major in the liberal arts program in English and American literature and then to pursue graduate studies.

Virginia Grabill, also director of women's counseling from 1958 to 1965, specialized in teaching composition and creative writing. Between 1959 and 1971, thirty-eight entries by Evansville College and University of Evansville students in the annual *Atlantic Monthly* creative writing contest won honorable mention or certificates of merit. Most of these were from classes taught by Grabill.

The English department member most noted for his scholarship during this period was **Daniel Boughner** (Ph.D., Princeton University), who came to the faculty in 1950. While at Evansville College, his book *The Braggart in Renaissance Comedy* was published. In 1956, he was granted a leave to study at the Folger Shakespeare Library in Washington, D.C. When this honor was followed

ENGLISH FACULTY

Also joining the department during this period were:

Jane Olmsted
(B.A., University of Evansville) 1945-68

Charlotte Stephens
(B.A., DePauw University) 1946-59

Arthur Spence
(M.S., University of Illinois) 1946-60

Sarah Lee Snepp
(M.A., Columbia University) 1953-63

Virginia McCutchan
(B.A., Indiana State University) 1955-74

Ann (Carlson) Stuart
(Ph.D., Southern Illinois University) 1962-89

Mary Ellingson
(Ph.D., Johns Hopkins University) 1963-74
(She also taught Latin and special courses in Greek and Latin derivatives.)

George Klinger
(Ph.D., Columbia University) 1963-89

Galen Clough
(Ph.D., Indiana University) 1963-95

Joyce Clough
(M.S., Indiana University) 1963-88
(She also taught in the Department of Communication, School of Education, and International Institute.)

by a Fulbright fellowship for study in Rome and Florence, he resigned his position in Evansville to pursue his scholarly interests.

Journalism was traditionally included in the English department curriculum at Evansville College, but only one or two courses were offered each semester, often taught by a member of the English faculty, such as Professors Franklin or van Keuren.

When **James G. Johnson** was brought to the College in 1944, he was the first person to teach this subject whose education and background had been entirely in journalism; he also served as director of public relations and supervisor of publications. Although he remained only three years, he expanded the journalism offerings to six courses.

Two instructors, both named John Boyd, served as teachers of journalism and faculty supervisors for the *Crescent*. **John Allen Boyd** held the position from 1947 to 1952 and **John H. Boyd Jr.** from 1962 to 1965. Other instructors of journalism held only brief tenure.

Foreign Languages

As President Hale's tenure began, both French and German were taught by **Fritz Neumann**, a native of Germany and a summa cum laude doctoral graduate of the University of Hamburg. After leaving Germany because of his opposition to the Hitler regime, he taught in France, England, and Italy before coming to America. After the United States entered World War II, questions were raised about Neumann's loyalties, despite his anti-Nazi record, probably contributing to his decision to leave Evansville and settle in Chicago.

In 1941, Spanish returned to the curriculum after an absence of fourteen years. The instructor was **Gertrude Leich**, who remained on the Evansville College faculty until 1957 and then returned five years later to continue teaching until her retirement in 1966.

The most versatile foreign language teacher at Evansville College during this period was **F. Woody Werking**, (Ph.D., Ohio State University). A Posey County native, he exemplified Chaucer's description of a scholar: "Gladly would he learn and

105

gladly teach." Werking studied at nine colleges and universities, including three in foreign countries, many of these after he began his teaching career. Although his major language was German, he also taught Spanish, Italian, French, and Russian. Werking possessed an encyclopedic knowledge encompassing many areas of learning. (If the game of Trivial Pursuit had been invented a few years earlier, he would have proved a formidable opponent!)

Werking served as department head for twenty years, during which time the College received a gift from the Lilly Endowment to establish an electronic language laboratory.

Werking's wife, **Mary Werking**, also a graduate of Ohio State University, served as an instructor in the foreign languages department during much of this period, concentrating on Spanish.

F. Woody Werking

History and Political Science

For twenty-five years, from 1946 to 1970, the history department benefited greatly from the leadership of **Wade David**, a gifted and skillful teacher. A native of the Middle East, he earned a doctorate at the University of Illinois. Before he came to Evansville, the College offered only three courses in history; when he retired, the catalog listed thirty courses in history and fifteen in political science (most offered in alternate years). Since many of his students in his early years of teaching at Evansville College were veterans of World War II, David developed a new course dealing specifically with that war, one which would give GIs a better under-

Wade David

standing of the historic significance of their recent personal experiences.

From 1946 to 1952, history was also taught by **Cyrus Gunn**, who had previously been superintendent of schools in Mt. Vernon, Indiana. When he returned to public school administration, his successor was **Orville Jaebker**, a graduate of Concordia Theological Seminary in St. Louis. In 1954, he received a Doctor of Philosophy from Indiana University, and ten years later was named chair of the department, a position he held until 1985. Jaebker specialized in American history and developed a course on the history of Indiana, designed for students planning to teach social studies in Indiana high schools. He is also particularly remembered

Orville Jaebker

for his inspiring classes on the Civil War and Reconstruction and on Latin American history.

In 1958, **Arthur Aarstad** was appointed to teach both history and political science. Born in Norway, Aarstad was educated in the United States, earning a doctorate at Indiana University. In 1970, political science was separated from the history department with Aarstad at its head. For many years he taught all courses in political science, including comparative government, local politics, political parties, constitutional law, political theory, and international relations. When he retired in 1996, he had taught twenty-seven different courses (including some in history), both undergraduate and graduate.

Aarstad was also notable for bringing his academic expertise into the world of practical politics. Although four Evansville College faculty members had previously run for public office, none was elected until 1970, when Aarstad became the first, winning the race for Vanderburgh County councilman-at-large by a wide margin. Later he was elected to the Evansville-Vanderburgh school board and was appointed to several commissions.

Mathematics

Mathematics had been part of the physics department since the College began, but in 1946 it became a separate and autonomous department, with Guy Marchant as its head. At this time two mathematics specialists were added to the faculty.

Ralph Coleman, who would receive a Doctor of Philosophy from Indiana University in 1956, was widely regarded as an outstanding teacher and served as department head from 1957 until he retired in 1977. In addition, he chaired many important faculty committees, including the athletics board, and served as faculty representative to the Indiana Collegiate Conference.

Virgil C. Bailey, who also came to Evansville College in 1946, earned a master's degree in mathematics from the University of Kentucky. In addition, he had a strong background in athletics, having coached basketball and track before coming to Evansville. Bailey retired in 1972.

Thomas Fiddick as member of the Marching Mizzou

Thomas Fiddick (Ph.D., Indiana University) devoted his entire teaching career to the institution, a span of nearly forty years (1963-2001). His areas of special interest included diplomatic history, psychohistory, Eastern Europe, and the John F. Kennedy assassination. When the Vietnam War escalated in the mid 1960s, Fiddick often took the lead in organizing campus teach-ins, protests, and demonstrations.

MATHEMATICS FACULTY

Also joining the department during this period were:

Clarence Buesking
(M.S., Purdue University) 1957-84

Gene Bennett '61
(Ph.D., Indiana University) 1963-2001
Department Chair

Donald Curlovic
(Ph.D., Indiana University) 1964-68

Roy Meadows
(M.S., St. Louis University) 1965-69

Robert Brooks '51
(M.S., University of Illinois) 1966-89

107

THE COMPUTER AGE

The decade of the sixties is widely known as a time of dramatic change, which certainly holds true for Evansville College. Thanks to a substantial discount from the manufacturer, the College was able to purchase an IBM 1620, its first computer and the first of its kind in the Tri-State area. Some viewed it as "a science fiction monster," while others saw it as a "mechanical marvel." The necessary peripheral equipment, priced separately, totaled as much as or more than the computer itself, and no textbooks were yet available; nevertheless, a computer center was established to administer use of the 1620, and mathematics professor Clarence Buesking was named director. He wrote his own textbook suitable for undergraduates and, even though much time, care, and patience were required to operate the "new toy" properly, Evansville College mathematics students soon learned to respect the exactness of problem-solving by computer.

Beginning in 1965, Evansville College, under Buesking's direction, offered a major in computing science which could also be combined with other related majors. As the demand for computer instruction grew, three full-time faculty instructors were needed. The computer age had dawned, and the world would never be the same again!

The Cluthe School of Music was located at 1133 Lincoln Avenue from 1942 to 1962

Music

In 1941, Evansville College became affiliated with the Cluthe School of Music, an institution directed by Ora Mae Cluthe Eades; the following year the Cluthe School of Music merged with the College, becoming the Preparatory Music School, geared primarily to providing music instruction for students from kindergarten through high school.

Eades generously donated all of her school's equipment to Evansville College, and the program continued to operate from her home. It was direct-

ed by **Margaret Taylor Shepard**, who had joined the faculty only the year before.

Enrollment in the Preparatory Music School increased from 342 in 1942 to a peak of 619 in 1950, the average being about 550. Many of the teachers were Evansville College junior and senior music majors. Several "graduates" of the school went on to become Evansville College students.

For twenty years (1944 to 1964) **Alice Berger** served first as its secretary and later as its registrar. In 1966, **Eulalie (Wilson) Blesch '51**, who earned a master's degree and later a doctorate from

Music Department Faculty 1956

Seated, left to right Sylvia Olmstead, Betty Kanable, Margaret Taylor Shepard, Wesley Shepard, Mrs. Vernon Williams, Allene Herron; *Standing, left to right* Ralph W. Waterman, Cecil B. Selfridge, Mrs. Ray T. Dufford, Mrs. Clarence Fehn, William Nation, Norman Heim

Columbia University, was appointed director. In time, related subjects, such as art, drama, dance, and baton, were added to the program, leading in 1969 to a new name: the Preparatory School of the Creative Arts.

In 1942, **Gaylord Browne**, music department head since 1934 as well as conductor of the Evansville Philharmonic Orchestra, resigned his position to work in a war industry. He was succeeded as department head by Margaret Shepard, director of the Preparatory Music School.

His successor as conductor of the Evansville Philharmonic Orchestra was **George Dasch** of Chicago, who also served on the College faculty, with the College and the orchestra each paying one-half of his salary. Dasch had taught for seventeen years at Northwestern University and had conducted the Chicago Businessmen's Orchestra and the Chicago Civic Orchestra for several years. He was sixty-nine years old when he came to Evansville and retired after a decade of service.

Dasch was followed by **Minas Christian**, conductor of the University of Arkansas Orchestra. In 1954, the College and the orchestra decided to go their separate ways, although close ties have continued throughout the years.

Following World War II, **O. Wesley Shepard**, husband of department head Margaret Shepard, returned from military service and joined the music faculty as professor and co-head of the department. Already an experienced band director, he also served for seven years as associate conductor of the Evansville Philharmonic Orchestra and organized marching and symphonic bands to perform at College functions. He remained as conductor of the Evansville Symphonic Band for twenty-two years, and the Shepards continued as co-heads of the music department until Mrs. Shepard's death in 1968. Her husband continued as department head until his retirement in 1972.

A number of other fine musicians have contributed to the high quality of instruction and performance at Evansville College. Those whose tenure began during this period include:

Pauline Fehn ▪ 1942-59 ▪ Flute
Jean Bridges ▪ 1945-57 ▪ Piano
Sylvia Olmstead ▪ 1946-57 ▪ Piano
Genevieve Erickson ▪ 1946-58 ▪ Voice
Ralph Waterman ▪ 1946-61 ▪ Organ
William Nation ▪ 1946-59 ▪ Violin
Cecil Selfridge ▪ 1947-69 ▪ Voice
Alleen Herron ▪ 1947-72 ▪ Piano
Mayme Dufford ▪ 1952-59 ▪ Piano
Betty Kanable ▪ 1954-63 ▪ Public School Music
Robert Rapp ▪ 1956-85 ▪ Choral Music
Paul Nolte ▪ 1957-79 ▪ French Horn
Kenneth Drake ▪ 1958-66 ▪ Piano
Carl Staplin ▪ 1961-67 ▪ Organ
Sandra Botkin ▪ 1964-88 ▪ Piano

For many years, facilities for music instruction were just barely adequate. In 1946, a portion of the old gymnasium (erected as a temporary building in 1922) was remodeled to provide eight small studios, a large band rehearsal room, a classroom, the department office, and storage area. Because of aging and the ravages of termites, floors and ceilings were in shaky condition, especially during heavy rainfall.

Five years later, accommodations in the "old farmhouse" (see page 74) just west of the gymnasium became available, providing additional space and more security. Meanwhile, the Preparatory Music School continued to operate from the Cluthe residence. With the completion of the Krannert Hall of Fine Arts in 1962, the music department and the Preparatory Music School finally enjoyed the physical facility they had long desired and deserved.

Philosophy, Religion, and Religious Life

Edgar McKown had been appointed head of the philosophy and religion department in 1936, but in 1941, he became dean of the College (see page 116) and most courses were then taught by other instructors. Except for **Harris Erickson** (Ph.D., University of Washington), who ably served the College from 1947 to 1969, most faculty members remained only a short time.

Since Catholic parents were often uncomfortable with having all religion courses taught by Methodist clergymen, a Catholic priest and a Jewish rabbi were added to the teaching staff. One of these, **Rev. Charles Schoettlekotte**, taught scholasticism and related subjects from 1948 to 1967.

Among the directors of religious life during this period were **Mearl Culver** (1950-57) and **Arthur Mansure** (1957-62). In 1962, McKown resigned as dean of the College but continued as head of the philosophy and religion department and director of religious life for another four years; he also continued to teach on a part-time basis for another three years.

His successor as department chair and director of religious life was **R. Wayne Perkins** (Ph.D., Boston University). Perkins was fortunate to have the beautiful and well-equipped Neu Chapel as headquarters for his program, and he was quick to experiment with innovative formats in search of a style that students would find relevant and meaningful. He served as chaplain and director of religious life until 1972 and as department head until 2001.

Philosophy and Religion Faculty

Left to right Harris Erickson, Edgar McKown, Arthur Mansure

Physics Faculty

Left to right Ray Dufford, Kelly Miles

Physics

During the post-war period, the physics program was headed by **James Sears** (M.S., Purdue University), who had acquired extensive experience in electronics while serving in the Marine Corps. He was invaluable to the College in securing large amounts of war surplus electronic equipment, much needed for the opening of the engineering science building, at virtually no cost. He also aided in reestablishing the engineering department (a two-year program since 1931) as a degree-granting entity of the College. He was such a successful teacher that when he left in 1952 to do highly classified work for the armed forces and to serve as an industrial consultant, the school granted him a leave of absence for six successive years, hoping that he would return. Unfortunately, this was not to be.

Shortly after Sears' departure, **Ray Dufford**, a Phi Beta Kappa graduate of Northwestern University with a doctorate from the University of Missouri, joined the faculty. With many years of college teaching already to his credit and considerable expertise in the new areas of nuclear and atomic physics, he gave his department fifteen

years of dedicated service. Dufford was particularly fascinated by astronomy and was instrumental in organizing an astronomy society under the sponsorship of the Evansville Museum. His regular lectures for the society attracted a devoted following in the community. Dufford retired in 1967.

His able successor, **Kelly Miles** (M.S., North Carolina State University), joined the faculty in 1955. Before coming to Evansville, he held positions in the Naval Research Laboratory and the Bureau of Standards in Washington, D.C., and at Johns Hopkins University. In addition to his teaching and administrative duties, he was also technical advisor to the campus radio station, WEVC-FM. Miles retired in 1974.

Psychology

When the College began, psychology was taught as part of the education program, but in 1946, became a separate department. Its first head, **Francis Buller** (Ph.D., Yale University), had come two years earlier not only to teach psychology but also to be the school's first director of testing and counseling. He served as department head for ten years.

His successor, **H. Donnell Miller** (Ph.D., Louisiana State University), remained for five years,

Psychology Faculty

Left to right Clarence Brooks, Charles Johnson, Vivien Maves, Delbert Sampson

111

to be followed in 1962 by **Delbert Sampson** (Ph.D., University of Denver), a clinical psychologist.

In 1964, Sampson founded the University of Evansville chapter of Psi Chi, the national psychology honorary society. His tenure saw great expansion in the department's curriculum, especially in experimental and laboratory psychology. After retiring from the University in 1977, he and his wife, Mary, funded the Delbert Sampson Scholarship to be awarded annually to the outstanding junior psychology major active in Psi Chi.

Also joining the psychology department during this period were **Vivien Maves** (Ph.D., George Peabody), who served for twenty-four years, and **Charles Johnson** (Ph.D., University of Nebraska), who specialized in educational and social psychology until his retirement in 1995.

Sociology

James Morlock continued his leadership of the sociology program, becoming department head in 1947 and continuing in the position until 1970. Morlock was also an authority on local history,

publishing a widely-read volume on the subject, *The Evansville Story*, in 1956 (revised 1965).

SOCIOLOGY FACULTY

Also joining the department during this period were:

Ludwig "Bruzz" Petkovsek
(M.S., Purdue University) 1958-2000
(He was also active in community organizations, such as the Vanderburgh County Department of Welfare.)

Birk Harl
(M.S., Indiana University) 1962-76
(After retiring from the Evansville police force after twenty years of service, fifteen as a captain, he vastly expanded the Evansville College program in law enforcement. He also established Lambda Alpha Epsilon fraternity for students in this field.)

112

Sociology class, with Professor James Morlock (left) looking on, visits the police station

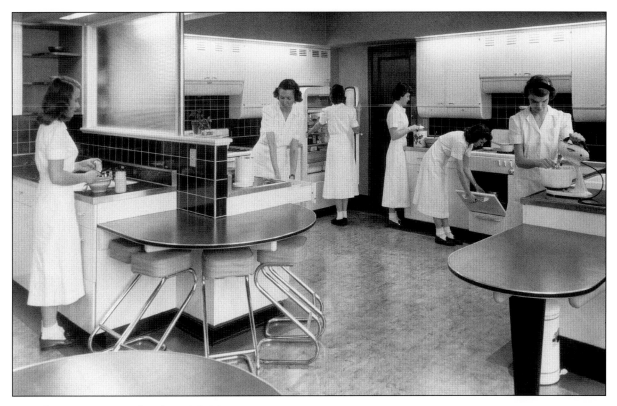

New home economics kitchen (1947)

Speech and Drama

Pearl LeCompte's tenure as director of theatre ended, after twenty years, in 1947. For the next decade several persons assumed that responsibility, but each stayed only a short time. In 1957, however, Sam Smiley (Ph.D., Indiana University) arrived and quickly rejuvenated the program, adding courses leading to a major in theatre. In 1964, two years after speech was separated from the English department, it assumed the name Department of Speech and Drama. Plays were performed in the Administration Hall auditorium and in the temporary East Classroom Building. Much ingenuity and imagination were required to give successful productions in spaces never intended for such a purpose. Nevertheless, in addition to numerous theatre classics, Evansville College was able, in 1964, to present the world premiere of *Banners of Steel* by Barrie Stavis, with Smiley himself in the leading role and the playwright coming to campus to assist with the production.

Finally, in 1967, Shanklin Theatre was completed (as described previously). Thanks to its thrust stage (with revolving capabilities as needed), its professional quality lighting and sound, and its comfortable seating for an audience of 486, Shanklin Theatre provided an excellent facility, attracting talented and dedicated students from all over the nation.

Other Areas

Other academic areas offered during this period include geology and geography, home economics, and Reserve Officer Training Corps.

▪ From 1947 to 1951, in response to the growing oil industry in the Tri-State, Evansville College developed a geology and geography department headed by **Franklin MacKnight**. The program proving less successful than expected, it was subsequently dropped. However, occasional courses in these areas continued to be offered, utilizing part-time instructors from the community.

▪ Although a number of classes in home economics were offered in the earlier years of the College, interest lagged as more women entered careers in business and the professions. **Corian**

113

Lundquist, who served in the United States Navy from 1942 to 1949 and held a master's degree from Columbia University, headed the home economics department for twenty years (1951-71), but upon her retirement the entire program was disbanded.

- A U.S. Air Force ROTC unit began on the Evansville College campus in 1951 with 194 students enrolled. The following year an all-time high of 327 students registered. Average participation after that was about 230. Each spring the ROTC sponsored a military ball, and an annual parade review was part of May Day activities. The Donald Wright chapter of the Arnold Air Force Society functioned as an honorary fraternity, with an auxiliary to the unit, Angel Flight, established for young women. ROTC cadets were also active in campus athletics.

United States Air Force officers provided instruction in aerospace studies, and students who completed the junior and senior years of the program were commissioned as second lieutenants; many later rose to the ranks of captain, major and lieutenant colonel. Some were pilots or navigators, while others filled administrative positions. In the first twenty years of the program, well over 300 men became officers.

Three graduates of the ROTC lost their lives during the Vietnam War:

Captain William Canup '64
First Lieutenant Steve Bosse '63
Captain Charles E. Shelton '54

Major Jean A. Kearby, an instructor in the Evansville College ROTC unit (1963-67), and Marine Lieutenant Tom Keppen, a 1963 graduate of Evansville College but not of the ROTC program, were also killed in action.

Over forty commissioned officers and sergeants served the institution's ROTC detachment as instructors or staff.

EVENING COLLEGE

As a private institution, Evansville College enjoyed the flexibility of initiating new academic programs whenever a need developed. For example, in September 1940 a new and important division was introduced, the Evening College, located on the second floor of Administration Hall. A separate Evening College bulletin was issued and widely distributed, with newspaper articles and radio announcements also spreading the word. Leading

114

ROTC faculty

businessmen, industrialists, and bankers lent their support and often taught courses, their practical experience proving an invaluable resource.

Evansville College was among the first in the nation to develop a program tailored to working students unable to attend during the day, including workers in factories, offices, and stores who wished to qualify for advancement. In addition, it attracted students who had started college, withdrawn, but now wished to return. It also served adults simply looking for intellectual stimulation and self-fulfillment.

When it opened, the Evening College (renamed the Community College in 1961) listed about 125 offerings, many vocational in nature, but a substantial number in the liberal arts as well. About half of the Evening College faculty came from full-time day staff; the other half were drawn from business, industry, and the community at large. All degree classes were considered the full equivalent of day courses. In addition, certificate courses in engineering and business were offered, requiring one to one-and-a-half years of study. In time, these certificate programs gave way to two-year associate's degrees in eleven fields.

In 1940, the Evening College enrolled about 850 students, this at a time when full-time day enrollment was only 530. (Throughout the years, many full-time day students elected to take some classes at night.) Attendance dropped substantially during World War II, but by 1949, it exceeded 1,000. After dipping again during the Korean War, Evening College enrollment rose steadily after 1956 and was never below 1,000 during this period. Indeed, by 1970, it had more than doubled that number.

The Evening College program was structured to enable students to complete their degrees by attending school only at night. In 1947, Mary Lou Kiefer, a retired teacher in the Evansville-Vanderburgh School Corporation, was recognized for attending the Evening College every semester since its opening in 1940. The next year, Price A. Phillips became the first student to receive a degree completed entirely in the Evening College. Twenty years later, nearly seventy persons had received degrees from Evansville College by taking all their work in the evening division.

During the division's early years, President Hale also assumed the title of director of the Evening College, but in 1943, Dean Long became assistant director, then director, and later vice president for adult education. In 1948, **Marvin Hartig**, a recent graduate of the College, was appointed assistant direc-  tor. He became director in 1953 and was appointed dean of the Evening College in 1967.

In addition to developing a broad curriculum to meet the needs of evening students, Hartig also

Marvin Hartig

assisted Long in administering the Center for Advanced Study, through which master's degree programs were provided by Indiana and Purdue Universities. Also, beginning in 1953, the Evansville chapter of the American Institute of Banking (AIB), an educational program of the American Bankers Association, moved its previously independent courses, taught by Long, into the Evening College. Classes were applicable to AIB certificates, recognized within the banking industry, or carried college credit for those wishing to earn a degree.

Later, when Evansville College offered its own master's degree program in education, registration and advising were carried out through the Evening College office. In addition, Hartig was international student advisor (some years the College had as many as 300 students from abroad); he also was in charge of veterans' affairs and services for the handicapped. (Hartig himself suffered from the effects of polio.) In 1974, he was appointed dean of academic services. Ten years later, when he left the University of Evansville, he had served his alma mater for thirty-five years.

ADMINISTRATION

Dean Long's outstanding contributions to the business administration program, the Evening College, and the Center for Advanced Study have already been noted. In addition, he organized a co-op engineering scholarship program and participated in the formation of the Evansville College School of Nursing.

Long's involvement with Evansville College athletics included fifteen years as chairman of the Athletic Board of Control. For eighteen years he was also the faculty representative to the Indiana Intercollegiate Athletics Association, the Ohio Valley Conference (and a member of its Judiciary Committee for four years and chairman for two) and the Indiana Collegiate Conference (also its vice president and then president of its Alumni Association).

Dean Long

Finally, Long was an active member of numerous professional and community organizations, most notably a charter member of the Indiana Academy of Social Science, organized in 1929, and later its president (1943-44). He was also elected treasurer of the National League of Nursing in 1968.

In all, Long served Evansville College as a teacher and administrator for thirty-eight years, filling ten different positions. (When he was appointed vice president in 1949, he became the first person to hold that title.) He retired in 1967.

- From 1941 to 1962, the important position of dean of the College was filled with great distinction by Edgar McKown, a 1922 graduate of Evansville College who had gone on to earn a Bachelor of Social Theology and then a Doctor of Philosophy at Boston University. Before he began teaching philosophy and religion at his alma mater in 1936, he served the Methodist Church as a pastor.

In 1941, President Hale invited him to be dean, posing a dilemma for McKown, since he preferred teaching to administrative work. However, he accepted the appointment provided that he could continue to teach, and with the request that the position of registrar, part of the dean's responsibility since the College began, become a separate office. Although his schedule severely limited him, McKown never lost his enthusiasm for the classroom. Among his accomplishments as dean were overseeing the establishment of a School of Nursing and the Preparatory Music School and restoring the degree-granting program in engineering. Despite his administrative duties, he contributed over twenty articles to professional journals and co-authored a textbook called *Understanding Christianity*. During his twenty-one years as dean, McKown called 4,025 seniors to the commencement platform to receive their degrees. When he retired in 1968, he had served his alma mater in various capacities for thirty-two years.

After McKown's retirement, **Nicholas Brown** (Ph.D., Yale University) was selected as dean of the College. For several years preceding his appointment, he was a staff associate of the American Council on Education in Washington, D.C. Brown's ability, integrity and tact won him many friends, and, during his seven year tenure at the College, graduate programs in education and business administration were approved by the North Central Association of Colleges, St. Mary's Hospital joined the School of Nursing program, a new sabbatical leave plan was instituted, the Richard E. Meier Foundation Lecture Series was established, computer equipment was installed, and courses in computer technology were offered.

- Other administrative positions assumed increasing importance as the College expanded from only a few hundred students to over two thousand. In 1944, **George McCoy**, who three years earlier had been named director of admission, began a fourteen-year tenure as registrar. McCoy also served as secretary of the faculty.

116

Four years of turnover in the registrar's office followed McCoy's retirement. Then **Kenneth Jones**, an Evansville College graduate with a Master of Business Administration from Bradley University and assistant business manager of the College since 1960, was appointed registrar, a position he held for 30 years. His tenure saw periods of peak enrollment and the introduction of computer technology for registration and grade reporting. Like his predecessors, Jones served as secretary of the faculty.

Kenneth Jones

- After the late 1940s, as more and more buildings were added, the position of superintendent of buildings and grounds became increasingly complex. In 1950, when A. C. Biggs came to Evansville College, a large staff – custodians, groundskeepers, carpenters, electricians, plumbers, and mechanics – was needed also. In the twenty years from 1950 to 1970, boiler capacity for steam production increased fourteen-fold, and new heating, ventilating, and air conditioning systems using sophisticated equipment were installed. Although considerable skill was needed to keep them properly maintained, Biggs proved equal to this demanding job. He retired in 1973.

During this time, W. A. (Joe) Miner, superintendent of building services, was responsible for keeping the campus clean and well maintained. He retired in 1971.

- Public relations, of great importance to a growing institution, was only part of a larger department or office for most of this period. Then, following considerable turnover, this area stabilized in 1955 under Robert Rowland. However, he was expected to serve not only as director of public relations, but also as director of development and assistant to the president. Only after Evansville College became the University of Evansville was public relations separated from other administrative functions.

- A final administrative post requiring recognition is that of bookstore manager, then in the capable hands of Emma Schreiber, who assumed the post in 1946 when the large influx of veterans began. Although she had no previous business or retail store experience, she quickly gained the expertise needed for this position. In 1959, a new bookstore was constructed just north of the McCurdy Alumni Memorial Union. When Schreiber retired in 1969, she had served the College for twenty-three years. In her final year alone, the bookstore enjoyed sales of $334,000.

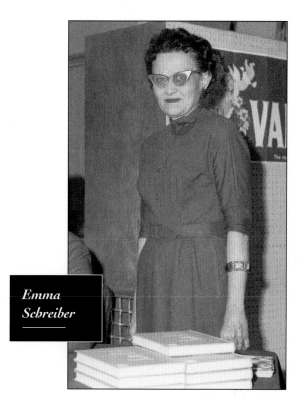

Emma Schreiber

BOARD OF TRUSTEES

117

In 1957, at the suggestion of President Hyde, the composition of the Board of Trustees was substantially altered to include members from the North and Northwest Conference of the Methodist Church as well as from the Indiana Conference (which serves the state from Indianapolis south) and also to include members of the school's Alumni Association. This revision, the first in thirty-six years, was approved by the Indiana General Assembly and raised board membership to forty-eight.

| MEMBERSHIP REVISIONS – BOARD OF TRUSTEES 1919-1957 | | | |
Appointed by	Original Charter (1919)	Revision 1 (1921)	Revision 2 (1957)
Indiana Conference	14	18	18
North Indiana and Northwest Indiana Conference	–	–	6
Evansville Chamber of Commerce	7	9	9
Alumni Association	–	–	3
Trustees At-Large	–	9	12
Total	21	36	48

(In addition, the president of the College is an ex-officio member of the board.)

The 1957 revision marked the first time that alumni were granted the right to elect trustees, the fruit of a sixteen-year effort to gain representation on the board. Alma Vaughn '34, who was among the first group of three elected by the Alumni Association, has served as secretary of the board and is a lifetime trustee.

Members are elected to a three-year term, but there is no limit to the number of successive terms they may serve. The record for tenure on the Evansville College Board of Trustees is held by Samuel Orr, who served for fifty-nine years (1936-95). Not far behind was Richard Rosencranz, a charter member, elected secretary of the board in 1919. Rosencranz held the position for forty-two years, during which time he personally signed every diploma awarded by the College, a total of 4,726. When he died in 1971 at the age of ninety-three, his term of service had reached fifty-two years.

Other trustees who served lengthy terms include:

Leland M. Feigel ▪ *33 years*
Willard C. Patrick ▪ *30 years*
William T. Jones ▪ *29 years*
Albert C. Wedeking ▪ *29 years*
Morton T. McDonald ▪ *28 years*
F. Bayard Culley ▪ *22 years*

Evansville College had nine father and son trustees and nine women. Besides Vaughn, the women include Emily Orr Clifford (see page 47), Amanta Maier (1945-62) and Mabel Nenneker (1953-62).

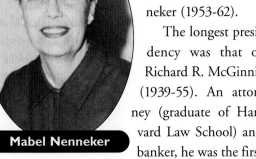

Mabel Nenneker

The longest presidency was that of Richard R. McGinnis (1939-55). An attorney (graduate of Harvard Law School) and banker, he was the first layman to be president of the board. (While McGinnis served in the navy during World War II, the duties of the president were assumed by the vice president.) Records of longevity are no longer possible since, in 1963, the board adopted a resolution limiting the term of officers of the board to five one-year terms.

Evansville College trustees have traditionally led the school's major fund-raising efforts. The 1943 campaign to raise funds for the engineering building and the student union was led by trustees Robert D. Mathias (chairman) and W. A. Carson (associate chairman). In 1955, Leland M. Feigel (an Evansville College alumnus) led the $650,000 Clifford Memorial Library building campaign, which was oversubscribed. And Kenneth C. Kent chaired the 1961 campaign for the fine arts building and the physical education center. It, too, was oversubscribed, with more than $1,650,000 pledged.

OTHER ACADEMIC MATTERS

Evansville College received national media attention in 1948 regarding an academic freedom controversy. The controversy centered around **George Parker**, assistant professor of philosophy and religion, who was summarily dismissed by President Hale for accepting the chairmanship of Vanderburgh County Citizens for Wallace.

Henry A. Wallace, secretary of agriculture in President Franklin D. Roosevelt's cabinet and Roosevelt's vice president from 1941 to 1945, ran for the office of president under the auspices of the Progressive Party. Wallace, a liberal candidate sometimes accused of communist sympathies, was strongly opposed by conservative elements, such as veterans' organizations.

When a rally of Wallace supporters was held at the Evansville Coliseum, chaired by Parker with Wallace as the main speaker, a mob of 1,500 protesters attempted to break up the meeting. Two days later, Hale, with the support of the Executive Committee of the Board of Trustees, recommended that Parker be dismissed because "he had failed to show good judgment, and because his actions had seriously jeopardized the College, indicating that his usefulness to the College was at an end." Hale also charged Parker with political activity in the classroom, although these allegations were never proved.

Parker appealed his case to the American Association of University Professors, which sent its associate secretary, George Hope Shannon, and Frederick S. Deibler of Indiana University to investigate. After extensive interviews and meetings, the AAUP concluded that Evansville College was guilty of a clear violation of academic freedom. It pointed out that at the time of his dismissal, Parker had been awarded a grant for doctoral study the following summer and that he had received a contract to teach for the coming academic year. This served to

indicate that the College was satisfied with Parker's teaching and that his dismissal resulted from exercising his rights as a private citizen in a democratic society. The AAUP further accused the College of succumbing to pressure from conservative elements who disagreed with Wallace's political ideas and argued that a college should offer an open forum for all shades of opinion.

When the College refused to reconsider its position, it was censured by the AAUP and placed on its black list, where it remained for eight years. Since the censure was not on the College itself but rather on its administrative officers and trustees, the stigma of being on the black list was removed when President Hale resigned and was replaced by President Hyde.

In 1957, the Lilly Endowment granted Evansville College $19,500 to support a thorough study of its general education requirements. Ralph Coleman chaired the faculty committee which carried out this effort. Committee members visited other campuses to observe their programs, a qualified consultant visited the Evansville campus, and a workshop was held to assist Evansville College faculty members.

As a result of this study, four new interdepartmental general education courses were created: Fundamentals of Physical Science, Modern Society, Comparative Arts, and Critical Intellectual Issues. Gradually, all of these courses were dropped from the curriculum. Nonetheless, the careful thinking that went into this study proved invaluable when the general education program was examined again in later years.

STUDENT LIFE

Campus life underwent a dramatic transformation between 1940 and 1966, a reflection of both quantitative and qualitative changes in the student body.

Before 1947, enrollment reached a peak of 500 in 1925 and fell to the lowest since the earliest days of the College in 1944, when wartime conditions caused a decline to 280. The usual average, however, fell in the neighborhood of 450 until the influx of veterans in 1947 skyrocketed enrollment to 1,722. But five years later, the figure fell to a postwar low of 861, only to rebound two years later to 969. During President Hyde's twelve-year tenure, the College recorded remarkable growth, from 1,091 full-time students in 1954 to 2,859 in 1966, an increase of more than 160 percent! During this same period, the Evening College (as noted on page 115) also more than doubled, growing from 963 to 2,210. By 1967, Evansville College was the second largest private college in Indiana, exceeded only by Notre Dame University. It was also first among America's eighty-three Methodist-related colleges in total enrollment.

With the construction of residence halls, the complexion of the student body changed significantly. Enrollment from outside the Tri-State grew from no more than fifteen percent to more than forty percent of the total, with thirty-five states represented. Also, having residence halls for women and adding a highly successful nursing program to the curriculum increased the percentage of women from thirty-three percent in 1954 to forty percent in 1966.

As the College became a residential as well as a commuter school, campus life took on a new direction. Numerous events were scheduled in the evenings and on weekends, whereas in the past – except for Evening College classes – the campus had been nearly deserted at night.

Also giving the campus a more cosmopolitan flavor was the enrollment of many international students. As far back as 1943, a program was instituted to attract students from Latin America. By 1953, there were nineteen international students on campus from Israel, Lithuania, Germany, South America, and Asian countries. After that, the number of students and the nations represented grew steadily.

"CHARLIE BROWN"

An international student from India, the late Suresh Sakaria, affectionately known as Charlie Brown, was in northern Indiana in 1965, intending to study engineering in another school when he met a stranger from a place called Evansville who advised "Charlie" to attend Evansville College instead. Sakaria considered his suggestion and accordingly boarded a bus, reaching the Evansville College registrar's office the day classes began. He enrolled, attended classes, and returned to the registrar's office after 5:00 p.m. – too late to find a place to stay. Elsie Schweikart, an employee in the office, invited him home for the night; he stayed with her four years! Hospitality such as this led to a continuing infusion of young people from all over the world.

The religious make-up of the College also shifted dramatically. In 1919, less than four percent of the enrollment was Catholic, as Catholic students were sternly warned by the bishop of the Evansville diocese not to attend Protestant-controlled Evansville College. By the late 1950s, however, almost seventeen percent of the student body was Catholic, the highest percentage of any single denomination.

For years, much to the displeasure of many students, chapel attendance was compulsory. With the influx of veterans following World War II, enrollment increased until the auditorium could no longer seat the entire student body, even when it was divided into two sections for chapel on different days. Consequently, required chapel attendance was dropped.

CAMPUS ORGANIZATIONS

Social organizations, especially fraternities and sororities, continued to play an important role in campus life. Chapters of national honorary fraternities established on the Evansville College campus include:

Pi Delta Epsilon	Journalism	Phi Kappa Phi	Scholarship and leadership
Sigma Alpha Iota (women)	Music	Pi Sigma Epsilon	Marketing and sales management
Phi Mu Alpha Sinfonia (men)	Music		
Sigma Pi Sigma	Physics	Psi Chi	Psychology
Alpha Phi Mu (women)	Scholastic achievement	Alpha Tau Delta	Nursing
(Replaced in 1962 by Alpha Lambda Delta)		Eta Kappa Nu	Electrical engineering
Alpha Psi Omega	Drama	Donald W. Wright Chapter, Arnold Air Society	Air Force ROTC honorary
Kappa Pi	Art	*(The chapter name honors an Evansville College student killed in World War II.)*	
Kappa Mu Epsilon	Mathematics		
Blue Key	Honor fraternity for leadership and community service	Angel Flight	Sister organization of the Arnold Air Society
		Cap and Gown	Senior women's honorary

Pi Sigma Epsilon 1965

121

CAMPUS ORGANIZATIONS

Local chapters of national social fraternities and sororities active on the
Evansville College campus for an extended period of time include:

Organization	Year of Formation
Alpha Omicron Pi	1951

(Originally Castalian Literary Society; continued from Moores Hill College)

Chi Omega	1951

(Formerly Gamma Epsilon Sigma; originally Sigournean Society; continued from Moores Hill College)

Phi Mu	1952

(Originally Theta Sigma)

Sigma Phi Epsilon	1955
Tau Kappa Epsilon	1956
Lambda Chi Alpha	1956

(Formerly Phi Zeta; originally Photozetean Literary Society; continued from Moores Hill College)

Sigma Alpha Epsilon	1957

(Formerly Pi Epsilon Phi; originally Philoneikean Literary Society; continued from Moores Hill College)

Zeta Tau Alpha	1964

(Formerly Beta Sigma Omicron)

Kappa Alpha Psi	1965
Phi Kappa Tau	1968

Fraternities and sororities of shorter duration include:

Alpha Phi Delta	1944-53
Alpha Phi Omega	1944-53
Pi Kappa	1946-52

(Became Delta Kappa, 1952-54)

Acacia	1949-58
Alpha Kappa Alpha	1951-58
Vauphines (A local society)	1951-59

Special mention should be made of Pi Kappa, as it was the first fraternity on campus to require pledges to perform useful work as part of their initiation instead of subjecting them to physical harassment. In addition, because its constitution forbade racial or religious discrimination, it was the first fraternity on the Evansville College campus to admit African Americans.

Also, in 1958, the American Association of University Women admitted Evansville College into membership.

Students gather in the lounge of the cafeteria 1940s

SAY NO TO CARDS

In the early 1950s, the College enacted a ban on playing cards on campus before 2:00 p.m. Many students were outraged, but college officials argued that the policy was necessary because too many students were found playing cards during the day when they were supposed to be in class.

Testing and Counseling Services

As noted in Chapter Three, Evansville College had had a dean of women since 1920 (Lucy Franklin and Wahnita DeLong) and a dean of men since 1936 (James Morlock). Their role was to enforce the rules of student conduct and to offer counseling and guidance services as needed. Like other colleges of its kind, Evansville College assigned these functions to full-time faculty members who either took on the position as an additional duty or were given released time to serve in this capacity. As fraternities and sororities were established, these organizations, the Interfraternity Council, and the Panhellenic Council were also generally supervised by these deans.

With the influx of veterans after World War II and the dramatic increase in overall enrollment, new services were offered in the areas of student affairs, health, counseling, and personnel records. For example, the College negotiated a contract in 1945 to test veterans applying for GI educational benefits. This service assisted students in finding a college or other training program suited to their

V(I)P

In October 1956, Vice President Richard Nixon spoke to Evansville College students, urging them to become involved in the political process and encouraging everyone to vote. This was the first campus visit by a United States president or vice president.

needs and talents. It was directed by Francis Buller of the psychology department.

In 1946, **Everette Walker** was appointed assistant to the dean of the College and student counselor. The next year his title changed to director of student personnel. In 1951, under **Gordon Stein**, Evansville College expanded its services beyond the campus to provide remedial instruction, testing, and counseling services to the public school system and others in the community. After Stein's death, the position was filled by his assistant, **Gordon Rettke**, who remained with the College until 1962.

Four years later, a new position, dean of students, was established, with **Robert Thompson** (Ed.D., Indiana University) appointed to this office. At first, his major responsibility covered student placement, health services, and foreign student advisement. However, as the various residence halls opened in the late 1950s and the 1960s, his chief function became appointment and supervision of student resident assistants. These upperclassmen helped plan social and recreational activities for residents and develop rules for self-government.

As the number of residence halls grew from two to five in the mid 1960s, it was decided to appoint professional residence hall directors who were trained to work with resident students and provide for their special needs. An internship program was set up with Indiana University to allow graduate students, usually doctoral candidates in higher education administration with a specialty in student personnel services, to staff these new positions. Students filling these positions usually rotated annually.

123

Students and faculty closely involved with student affairs

Seated, left to right
Marie Childers, Robert Wilson, James Voorhees;
Standing Wayne Perkins (center), Cliff Kraft (right)

In 1951, the title dean of women was dropped in favor of director of women's counseling. This position was filled by **Charlotte Stephens**, daughter of Walter M. Wheeler Sr., a trustee and treasurer of the board for several years and the College attorney from 1919 until 1930. After Stephens resigned in 1957, Virginia Grabill assumed the position, but also continued to teach in the English department. Seven years later, she returned to her first love, classroom teaching.

Although the position of dean of men was continued until 1968, the new position of director of

men's counseling was added in 1962. It was filled by **Clifford Kraft '47**, a former alumni secretary and admission counselor.

An additional community service was a reading and study center for elementary and secondary students with learning disabilities. Instruction was provided by Evansville College education majors, who were thus able to gain invaluable hands-on experience. The center also offered specialized tutoring by licensed teachers; for this service, a fee was charged.

In the early 1960s, the name of the office was changed to the Guidance Center, and its focus shift-

"PSYCHO"

Also available to students was a counseling center co-directed by persons from the psychology and education departments. Unfortunately, the name chosen for this effort was the Psycho Educational Clinic. Since students had no wish to be identified as "psycho," most refused to use the center.

Early radio broadcast from campus

ed from community service to personal and vocational counseling for Evansville College students. Its director was **Robert Wilson '52** (Ed.D., Indiana University); when he was appointed dean of students, he was succeeded by his assistant, **Robert Garnett** (Ph.D., Purdue University). Both men later held important administrative posts after Evansville College became the University of Evansville.

Radio

Finally, mention should be made of an activity involving both students and faculty.

In 1941, an elaborate radio studio was built in Administration Hall and dedicated the following February with a program featuring music, drama, and a talk by President Hale. The music department supplied much of the programming during the ensuing months, and various members of the speech department were placed in charge of other

radio programs. These broadcasts were carried by stations WGBF and WEOA, which received them from the campus studio via telephone lines.

In 1951, Evansville College opened its own radio station, WEVC-FM, using broadcast equipment donated to the College in exchange for war surplus equipment the school no longer needed.

Originally, WEVC broadcast only two hours each evening five days a week, but in the 1960s, this ten hours increased, eventually reaching seventy-two hours per week. The program format was that associated with National Public Radio today, including classical music (such as live broadcasts of the Metropolitan Opera), jazz, and educational features ranging from Shakespeare to current public affairs.

125

ATHLETICS

With the return of war veterans in 1946, the Evansville College athletic program was expanded, new coaches were appointed, and the Board of Control was reorganized to consist of four faculty members and an alumnus, with the College president and the director of physical education as ex-officio non-voting members. The first faculty members of the new board were Dean Long, E. C. VanKeuren, D. W. Dunham, and James Morlock; Joseph T. Theby represented the alumni.

Also added to the College staff was a full-time business manager for athletics. This position was held by Russell C. Goebel (1946-47), Eugene C. Robinson (1947-54), Rolland M. Eckels (1954-55), and Robert W. Hudson (1955-77).

The athletic program continued to develop so that, by 1964, thirty acres at the north end of campus, leased to the city since 1934 as a public park for $2,000 a year, were returned to the College to provide additional space for physical education and sports. A football field had already been developed on the property, and in 1966, the entire tract was fenced and an eight-lane track plus eight hard surface tennis courts were constructed.

Football

America's entry into World War II reduced the 1942 football season to five games, after which the sport was disbanded for the duration. But in 1946, **Don Ping**, the highly successful coach for sixteen seasons at Memorial High School, was appointed the football coach and director of athletics. Coach Ping's first year was a tremendous success, with seven wins, one loss, and two ties. Attendance was high all season, with 11,000 people present when the Aces defeated Murray State 20-0 at Bosse Field.

The following year the record was 4-4-1; in 1948, it was 6-3; and in 1949, 8-2-1. During these years Evansville College also participated in a post-season bowl game sponsored by the Evansville Junior Chamber of Commerce known as the Refrigerator Bowl, in recognition of Evansville's

Don Ping

preeminence in the production of refrigerators. In 1948, the Aces ended the Missouri Valley College Vikings' unbroken record of 41 wins, witnessed by more than 8,200 persons at Reitz Field. The following year the Aces defeated Hillsdale (Michigan) College 22-7.

In 1951, the College joined the Indiana Collegiate Conference, consisting of Ball State, Butler, Indiana State, St. Joseph's, and Valparaiso. In the fifties, however, success on the football field declined. Whereas Ping's record for his eight seasons (1946-53) was 38-35-5, Evansville College was able to win only four of fourteen games played with Ohio Valley Conference schools from 1953 to 1958. In 1954, Ping resigned to run for sheriff and was replaced by **Paul Beck**, his assistant since 1947. In twelve seasons, Beck's teams won forty-seven and lost fifty-eight games.

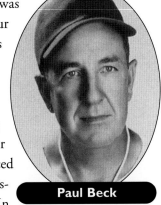
Paul Beck

Basketball

Continuing a long-standing tradition, basketball retained its supremacy as Evansville's major sport.

126

Despite the resignation of Coach Bill Slyker in 1943 to take a position in a war industry, basketball continued through those turbulent years, although with a reduced schedule, coached by **Emerson Henke**, a member of the business administration faculty and one of Slyker's players during

Emerson Henke

the mid 1930s. During his three years as coach, Henke compiled a 29-22 record.

After the war, the College signed **Arad McCutchan '34**, as head coach; he had served in the U.S. Navy and before that was Bosse High School coach for seven years. During his years as a student at Evansville College, McCutchan was Slyker's leading scorer for three years, but his first two seasons as coach were not promising, as the Aces lost thirty-three games and won only fifteen. However, steady improvement followed.

ARAD McCUTCHAN

As a college student, Arad McCutchan decided to major in both mathematics and physical education, hoping to increase his chances of getting a teaching job. With his Evansville College education complete and a splendid basketball career behind him, McCutchan had done all he could to get just the right job. However, offers did not pour in. The Great Depression sent him packing.

"I had lived in Evansville all my life and wanted to stay, but I had to go to Alabama and teach high school for two years for a salary of $80 a month," he recalled in a 1991 magazine story. "Twenty-five years later, I went back there to teach a two-day basketball clinic and made $500!"

McCutchan's value skyrocketed because of his accomplishments. Described as a "hard-nosed nice guy," he coached Evansville to five NCAA College Division championships. His record of 514-314 covered thirty-one years, from 1947 through 1977.

"He was a fierce competitor, but you never saw him screaming at anyone and you never heard a cuss word come out of his mouth," said Don Buse, an All-American at Evansville and a member of Evansville's 1971 national championship team. "He won all those games and all

Basketball Team 1950-51

Front Row, left to right Bob Sakel, Coach Arad McCutchan, Bob Barnett; *Back Row, left to right* Jim Barnett, Larry Holder, Harry Oxford

those championships, but without all the noise that so many coaches make today. He was a class guy."

He was the first College Division coach inducted into the National Basketball Hall of Fame (1981). Only John Wooden (UCLA) won more national titles in college basketball.

By the way, McCutchan's double major of mathematics and physical education paid off. In addition to coaching basketball, he taught math for twenty-five years at his alma mater.

127

When Roberts Municipal Stadium was completed in 1956, the Aces finally had a place they could call home, giving both the players and the spectators a considerable and much appreciated psychological boost. Crowds of 10,000 or more became common. The largest single game attendance was 13,913 (Evansville College vs. Kentucky Wesleyan, 1960). Such was the extent of "Hoosier Hysteria" that at one time more than 3,300 persons were on the waiting list for season tickets.

JERRY SLOAN

Jerry Sloan, later a mainstay of the Chicago Bulls and coach of the Utah Jazz, was an outstanding Evansville player during the early 1960s.

As successful as Sloan has been in the NBA, his friends will tell you he is happiest riding his tractor on his farm. His rural roots helped guide Sloan to Evansville College. After two months on the too-big, too-much-limelight University of Illinois campus, Sloan returned home to work in an oil field. After three months, he got up the courage to leave home and play for Arad McCutchan at Evansville.

"Coach McCutchan was really a unique guy with me. I just had a great feeling when I was around him and he made me feel comfortable around other people," Sloan told the *Indianapolis Star's* David Benner in a 1990 interview.

"Jerry had an intense desire to win," said McCutchan, who housed Sloan with a family instead of in a campus residence hall to help him overcome his shyness and homesickness. "There are a great number of people, when you start analyzing how fast he is, how well he can shoot, how high he can jump, who can probably outdo him. But I don't think anybody tried any harder than Jerry."

Sloan was never better than third highest scorer for the Aces, but his defense, passing, and rebounding made him an All-American in 1964 and 1965, both national championship years at Evansville. He and Dale Wise are still the only two players in Aces history to total 1,000 points and 1,000 rebounds.

A relentless defensive player in the NBA for the Chicago Bulls, Sloan made the all-star team twice and the NBA all-defensive team six times.

A knee injury ended his career at about the

same time McCutchan was preparing to retire. Sloan became the obvious choice to succeed the legendary McCutchan and become the Purple Aces' first Division I coach. He took the job in January 1977 but five days later stunned Evansville fans by resigning and returning to Chicago to become an assistant coach for the Bulls. (Bobby Watson, Sloan's successor, coached just four games before he was killed along with the Evansville team in the December 13, 1977, airplane crash near Dress Regional Airport.)

Sloan eventually became the Bulls' head coach in 1979, but was fired two seasons later. In 1988, he returned to the head coaching ranks with the Utah Jazz.

A replica of Sloan's 1965 Evansville jersey hangs high in the rafters at Roberts Stadium.

Evansville plays Franklin College

McCutchan brought national recognition to the Evansville Aces. Beginning in 1956, Big Ten and other highly-rated teams frequently played Evansville College. The Aces were able to win three out of seven games with Purdue and also beat the University of Iowa in 1961 and 1964.

In 1957, Evansville College was chosen as the host school for the first NCAA College Division National Tournament, and Roberts Stadium was the site of every College Division tournament from 1958 to 1977. McCutchan led his team to a then-record five national championships in the NCAA College Division (in 1959, 1960, 1964, 1965, and 1971). In the Indiana Collegiate Conference, the Aces won nine championships and tied twice for first place.

Evansville's first two NCAA College Division championships came in 1959 and 1960, in large part because of one of the Aces' first African Amer-

ican players, Ed Smallwood. He was a first team College Division All-American both years, and his 1,898 career points are still the third best in Aces' history. Dale Wise (the school's career leader in rebounds with an amazing 14.6 per game), Harold Cox, and Hugh Ahlering also earned All-American status in the late 1950s.

McCutchan was named Coach of the Year in the ICC seven times and twice shared the honor with other coaches. In both 1964 and 1965, he was NCAA Coach of the Year. During his long career as head basketball coach, McCutchan also carried a full-time teaching load in physical education and mathematics and participated in many civic activities. In addition, he began the custom of wearing red socks to Aces games "for luck," a custom later extended to sporting red shirts, caps, ties, coats, and jackets as a symbol of support for the team.

129

Memorable highlights during this period include:

- **A 1958 game against Kentucky Wesleyan, in which Larry Erwin tossed in the winning goal from thirty feet out with a second to go. The lead changed three times in the last thirty seconds.**

- **A 1962 game against Notre Dame University in which Harold "Buster" Briley made an eighty-five-foot basket in the final second. Even though Notre Dame won the game, the place where Briley stood when he started the ball on its long journey was marked by a gold nail in the stadium floor.**

- **A 1965 game against Southern Illinois University in which Larry Humes scored the winning points, with less than five seconds remaining, with a layup that hung for several agonizing moments on the backboard.**

The 1964-65 season was especially significant for the Aces. Not only was McCutchan NCAA Coach of the Year, but his team went undefeated in twenty-nine games and won the NCAA championship. Attendance for the season reached 149,713, third highest in the nation. The team members who made basketball history that year, in addition to All-Americans Larry Humes and Jerry Sloan, were Sam Watkins, Herb Williams, Larry Denton, James Forman, Ron Johnson, Ron Eberhard, Russ Grieger, Terry Atwater, Don Jordan, Rick Kingston, James Rubush, and Earl McCurdy. Humes still holds the Evansville scoring record with 2,236 career points.

Baseball

Baseball had no place in the College athletic program from 1928 until 1946, when Emerson Henke coached the team. The next year Don Ping, who had spent some years as a professional player, took over. Despite less than ideal playing facilities, his team won the ICC championship in 1951 with seven wins and only one loss.

Swimming

Completion of Carson Center in 1962, with its Olympic-sized swimming pool, enabled Evansville College to add swimming to its varsity athletics. **James Voorhees**, an experienced swimming coach with a master's degree in physical education from the University of Illinois, led the program in intercollegiate swimming starting in 1963. His team took second place in the ICC their first year and first place for five years thereafter.

IDA STIELER

In the twenty-first century, coaches of women's college teams are concentrating on just one sport, making good money, and gaining increased recognition from the media. In the mid twentieth century, people such as Ida Stieler did it all for less pay in almost total obscurity.

From 1935 to 1972, Stieler directed the women's sports programs and women's physical education program at Evansville College. For thirty of those years, she was the only woman in the physical education department, teaching all courses for women and supervising women's intramurals and the women's intercollegiate sports program. No varsity teams for women existed until 1969.

Born in Evanston, Illinois, Stieler moved to Evansville at an early age. She graduated from Central High School in 1923, earned a bachelor's degree from Battle Creek (Michigan) College in 1930, and began her long tenure at Evansville College five years later. By the time she retired, Stieler had groomed many of the area's high school coaches including Mary Dannatel, Karen Dawson, Linda Youngblood, and Louise Owen. At one time, approximately half of the female physical education teachers in the Evansville school system were former Stieler students.

FINANCES

Deficits plagued the institution's athletic program for many years. By the late 1940s, it was running $12,000 to $15,000 per year, leading to serious consideration of dropping football (not actually done until 1997). However, in 1951, a scholastic society was formed to raise funds from Evansville business and industry to support college football. This group was able to make annual contributions of $10,000 to the school.

Then, in 1957, at the time of the move to Roberts Stadium, trustee Kenneth Kent organized the Tip-off Club to support Aces basketball. The following year saw the formation of the College Tourney Corporation, an organization which sponsored the NCAA college basketball tournament. It proved so successful that it was able to make substantial gifts to the College athletic program. For example, in 1966, it gave $10,000 to assist in the construction of tennis courts, and three years later it contributed an additional $15,000 for portable bleacher seats. Finally, in 1962, Aqua Aids was organized to support intercollegiate swimming.

Funds from all the above-mentioned groups were especially valuable in enabling the College to offer athletic scholarships, thus keeping the Aces competitive with both private and state-supported colleges. By 1957-58, basketball gate receipts had grown to the point that the College athletic program was self-sufficient, but within a decade mounting expenses and declining attendance again spread red ink over the school's athletic budgets.

A NEW ERA: FROM ONE COLLEGE TO TWO UNIVERSITIES

The mid 1960s saw significant changes in the complexion of higher education in Evansville. Traditionally, southwestern Indiana had relied on Evansville College to meet its needs without benefit of the state educational network, which reached no closer than Terre Haute, 110 miles from Evansville. Until this time, Evansville was the largest community in the state without a tax-supported institution. A widely held viewpoint, however, maintained that since tax dollars flowed into the state government from Evansville, one of its major cities, the area should receive educational services comparable to those provided to other parts of the state. And while Evansville College tuition was moderate for a private college, it was considerably higher than fees charged by state tax-supported institutions.

The opposing viewpoint held that, although Evansville College was private, it effectively served the function of a public institution by offering programs that fulfilled the community's needs. In the words of President Hyde, then chairman of the Indiana Conference on Higher Education: "As long as Evansville College continues to meet the needs of the area – and we are continuing our expansion – there is no need for a four-year state college here." To establish a competing state institution in Evansville, Hyde argued, would be a needless duplication of services and hence a waste of taxpayers' money. To narrow the gap between private tuition and state tuition, an editorial in the *Evansville Courier* (January 27, 1965) suggested a plan utilizing federal loans as subsidies for college students instead of the more burdensome tax increases building a new school would entail.

Despite Hyde's insistence that a new institution of higher learning in the Tri-State would be superfluous, the Indiana General Assembly passed a resolution in February 1965, introduced by the Evansville representatives, directing the Boards of Trustees of Indiana University and Purdue Univer-

131

sity "to do all things necessary to select and procure a site in the Evansville metropolitan area and thereafter proceed to construct, equip, and maintain a four-year college thereon." The resolution was not well received by either state institution. Purdue was far removed from Evansville geographically, and Indiana University felt it still had a gentleman's agreement with Evansville College, dating back to the merger talks of the late 1930s, when it pledged cooperation and collaboration as long as Evansville College was satisfactorily meeting the area's educational needs.

The Evansville delegation then approached Indiana State University in Terre Haute to determine its interest in establishing a branch campus in Evansville, but President R. W. Holmstedt of ISU was reluctant to "interfere in any way with the Evansville community support of Evansville College." However, the branch campus plan was endorsed by Mayor Frank McDonald of Evansville, the Evansville Chamber of Commerce, Evansville Future, the AFL-CIO, and various political leaders. Holmstedt then assured Hyde that if a center is established, the welfare of Evansville College "will be taken into account," and he hoped there would be "full cooperation between the center and Evansville College … to the mutual benefit of all concerned." (It should be noted that Holmstedt was at this time serving his last weeks at ISU and that his successor, Alan C. Rankin, felt no obligation to continue the policies of the previous administration.)

In the fall of 1965, Indiana State University, using the name Indiana State University-Evansville (ISU-E), began offering courses for freshmen in Evansville, utilizing the former Centennial Elementary School building. Evansville College offered its library resources and initially there was talk of avoiding duplication of course offerings. However, the Evansville College curriculum already included a wide choice of programs in the liberal arts, business, education, engineering, music, and nursing, many available in the evening as well as in the day. Indeed, advanced professional programs such as medicine, law, and architec-

ture were the only major areas not covered by Evansville College, and these could not be offered by a branch campus of a state institution either. In all other areas, since nearly the entire curriculum of ISU-E was already being offered by Evansville College, duplication was inevitable and aggressive competition between the two institutions could no longer be avoided.

In December 1966, 293 acres of land lying between the West Side Expressway and Burdette Park were purchased for a permanent campus for ISU-E. It was the gift of Southern Indiana Higher Education Inc. (SIHE), a corporation established by Evansville businessmen which, by the summer of 1967, had successfully raised $1,000,000 to assist the new university. At the same time, Indiana State University requested $8.5 million from the Indiana General Assembly to begin construction at the newly donated site.

Meanwhile, Evansville College was taking significant steps to solidify and expand its contribution to higher education in the Tri-State. To do so, it was deemed advisable to change the name and organization of the institution from College to University.

The first suggestion of such a change was made by President Hyde as early as 1960, and the following year he further specified that the change should occur when full-time day enrollment reached 2,200 to 2,500.

Five years later, with full-time enrollment at 2,800 and 2,200 part-time students as well, the Board of Trustees judged that the time had indeed arrived, and it initiated the steps necessary for the Indiana General Assembly to amend the 1919 charter, making the name change official.

Four local members of the legislature – Representatives Charles Abshier and Thomas Toon and Senators Elmo Holder and Sidney Kramer – sponsored the measure (HB 1037), which passed the House of Representatives unanimously on January 25, 1967, and passed the Senate unanimously on February 13. It was signed by Governor Roger D. Branigan on February 17, exactly forty-eight years after Governor James P. Goodrich had approved the Evansville College charter in 1919.

Attending the signing, together with the Vanderburgh County legislators who had sponsored the bill, were trustees Samuel Orr and Leland Feigel and President Melvin Hyde. On that occasion, Hyde noted that "this action gives statewide and nationwide recognition of the years of educational service by a private school and encourages the board, administration, community, alumni, and friends to move confidently ahead."

The newly named institution, despite its years of substantial growth and impressive accomplishments, now faced a daunting challenge it had never known before: a competing publicly supported school equipped to offer virtually the same curriculum to Tri-State students, but at a far lower cost. It is little wonder that many perceived the state university as a threat and as a rejection of Evansville College's effort to faithfully serve its constituency for nearly fifty years. Reportedly, Hyde was personally disappointed in the community's ingratitude, leading to his decision, communicated to the Board of Trustees on June 22, 1966, to resign his position.

In his letter to the board, Hyde stated:

"After over eleven years of the most challenging and rewarding years of my life as president of Evansville College, I wish to submit my resignation ... effective September 1, 1967 ... In the field of higher education the president of a growing dynamic institution should set a time for turning over the responsibilities of leadership to capable younger minds, hearts, and hands if the institution is to maintain vigorous growth and progress."

The board asked Hyde to reconsider his decision, but he persisted in his belief that the time had come for a younger person to lead the institution in the new era symbolized by the name change.

For the new University of Evansville under fresh leadership, there would be the challenge of developing unique and distinctive programs which could attract students from a broad geographical area. We shall now turn our attention to how the University of Evansville sought to improve the quality of its curriculum and differentiate its programs from those of traditional, state-supported institutions.

133

The institution gets its fourth (and final?) name (1967)

Olmsted Administration Hall

CHAPTER FIVE

University of Evansville: 1967 to 1987

University rose garden, with Igleheart building in background

BACKGROUND

President Hyde's firm resolution to resign his position was accepted – though only with great reluctance – by the Board of Trustees, which then set about the difficult task of finding a qualified successor. A search committee of six trustees was appointed, aided by a non-voting five-member faculty advisory committee. After investigating all possible candidates, five were selected for in-depth interviews.

1967-1986

Twentieth President
WALLACE B. GRAVES

By January 1967, one candidate, Wallace B. Graves, was deemed most suitable and invited to visit campus. On January 20, following a special meeting of the Board of Trustees, it was

135

announced that Graves, then academic vice president of the University of the Pacific in Stockton, California, had been selected as the first president of the new University of Evansville.

The forty-five-year-old Graves came to UE with a rich and varied background. A native of Fort Worth, Texas, he received his undergraduate degree in political science from the University of Oklahoma in 1943. Following military service in Europe during World War II, including five months as a prisoner of war before escaping, Graves returned to pursue graduate work and an academic career.

After earning a master's degree from Texas Christian University and a doctorate from the University of Texas, he taught political science at DePauw University in Greencastle, Indiana, for eight years (1950-58), receiving the best teacher award in 1954. He then moved to Texas Wesleyan College, where he was not only professor of government, but also dean of men and, beginning in 1963, assistant to the president. Two years later, he went to the University of the Pacific, where he was responsible for academic personnel and the programs of four undergraduate colleges and six professional schools. In addition, he was involved with admission, student life, planning, and administration of the school's $9 million annual budget. His extensive experience in every aspect of academic life – teaching, student affairs, academic administration, and financial planning – made him a particularly attractive choice to be the University of Evansville's new president. Also attractive was his vision for the new University which, he declared, "not only has the opportunity, but the obligation to be experimental and altogether flexible in meeting the intellectual requirements of students who will succeed us in the twenty-first century."

NEW CHALLENGES

Two distinct challenges faced President Graves and his emerging new university, one external and the other from within.

A NEW STATE UNIVERSITY IN EVANSVILLE

The external challenge, as described in the previous chapter, came from the new state-supported university just across town. The opening of an Evansville branch of Indiana State University, a state-supported institution offering students a college degree at a greatly reduced cost, left the University of Evansville with three options:

- **Ignore the newcomer and proceed on its own way**

- **Collaborate with the newcomer to offer cooperative or joint programs**

- **Merge with the newcomer to form a single institution**

The first two options were chosen. The University of Evansville continued its traditional degree programs, whether or not similar programs were being offered by Indiana State University-Evansville. However, ISU-E students were also able to take courses, such as foreign languages, which were not yet offered by the state university, on the University of Evansville campus.

The two universities participated in joint studies to assess the educational needs of students, especially adult learners, in the Tri-State area. The most significant of these was a 1974 study supported by a $50,000 grant from the Lilly Endowment and carried out by the Battelle Center for Improved Education of Columbus, Ohio, one of the most highly respected research institutions in its field.

Its objective was to "explore alternative structural relationships for the two universities in the interest of identifying that structure which assures the most comprehensive, effective, and economic delivery of high educational services to the people in the region of service."

After reviewing and analyzing all available data, the Battelle Center team concluded, in a report issued on December 31, 1974, that the Tri-State's educational objectives would best be met by merging the two universities into a single public insti-

136

tution. This, it felt, would provide access to a greater range of resources than a private school could command. In recognition of the University of Evansville's long history of service to the area, the new institution should bear its name (or, as an alternative, be called Evansville University).

Should this recommendation prove unacceptable, the Battelle Center study suggested that both universities appoint steering committees charged with implementing a high level of collaboration between the two universities.

While the University of Evansville wholeheartedly embraced the Battelle Center's call for cooperation with Indiana State University-Evansville, the Executive Committee of the Board of Trustees, in late 1975, "unanimously reaffirmed its preference for an independent and autonomous University of Evansville, exploiting its greater potential for flexibility, quality, and distinctiveness in educational services." As in 1939, the intense sentimental attachment to the University of Evansville felt by many thousands of supporters in the Tri-State and alumni across the nation seemed to argue against a merger in which the identity of the University would be submerged or lost altogether.

NEW INTERNAL STRUCTURE

The second challenge confronting the University of Evansville after the official change from Evansville College was to establish an appropriate internal organizational framework for the institution. Changes occurred in three major areas: the Board of Trustees, faculty governance, and administrative structure.

The Board of Trustees

Because of the reorganization of the United Methodist Church in Indiana into two conferences – the South Indiana Conference and the North Indiana Conference – instead of the previous three, it became necessary in 1969 to amend the University's charter. The number of church trustees was reduced from twenty-four to twenty-one and the number of at-large trustees increased from twelve to fifteen.

The major significance of this change was that, for the first time in the history of the institution, the Methodist Church had less than a majority of the board. The reason for the shift was the possibility that the United States Constitution might be interpreted to exclude institutions controlled by religious bodies from receiving the assistance of the federal government. If that happened, construction grants and student financial aid would be eliminated, causing irreparable damage to the institution. At the same time, however, the board expressed its wish to preserve "the cherished and essential relationship of the University of Evansville to the United Methodist Church."

In 1970, the board voted to include in its membership three student representatives, one elected at the end of each University year by the senior class to serve a three-year term. The new composition of the board was as follows:

South Indiana Conference	15
North Indiana Conference	6
Evansville Chamber of Commerce	9
At-Large	15
Alumni Association	3
Student-Elected	3
University President (ex officio)	1
Total	52

It is noteworthy that of the twenty-one persons appointed at this time by the United Methodist Church, only nine were ministers, the others being prominent Methodist business and professional men.

Four years later, a further and drastic restructuring occurred, reducing the total membership of the board from fifty-two to thirty-five. They were apportioned as follows:

South Indiana Conference	6
North Indiana Conference	3
Alumni Association	3
Student-Elected	3
At-Large	18
University President (ex officio)	1
Bishop of the Indiana Area (ex officio)	1

137

This arrangement excluded – for the first time since the institution came to Evansville – any official representation from the Evansville Chamber of Commerce.

Faculty Governance

With the shift to a university structure came a significant change in the area of faculty governance. Formerly, the faculty had no official organizational structure, powers, or responsibilities. There were no faculty bylaws, which meant that only custom, precedent, and presidential rulings determined faculty power and responsibilities.

In 1968, the faculty adopted new bylaws which defined exactly who would be recognized as a faculty member, who could attend faculty meetings, who could vote, and what powers and responsibilities such a person would have. Under these bylaws, "faculty" was defined as all full-time teachers, the president, vice presidents, deans, the registrar, professional librarians, and the director of admission.

The new bylaws also created an Academic Senate (after 1970 known as the University Senate), a body empowered to act for the entire faculty and serve as its official decision-making body. However, an additional provision enabled a petition signed by at least twenty-five members of the faculty to bring any issue to the entire faculty for a decision. Membership in the senate included the vice president for academic affairs, the registrar, one faculty member representing each academic division of the University, twelve faculty members elected at-large, two persons appointed by the president, and the immediate past chairman of the senate.

138

The Academic Senate held its first meeting on June 5, 1968, and elected the following officers:

Chairman	Lowell Weller
Vice Chairman	Sam Smiley
Corresponding Secretary	Mabel Nenneker
Recording Secretary	Kenneth Jones, *University Registrar, ex officio*

In addition, several standing committees were established, some responsible to the senate and some responsible to the faculty at large. Beginning in 1973, however, it was decided that all standing committees and any new committees that might be formed would report to the senate. Moreover, the bylaws provided for the appointment of students to several of these committees. Overall, the new structure enabled the faculty and student body to influence academic and administrative policy to a much greater extent than before.

Lowell Weller

Administrative Structure

With the change from a college to a university structure, four former departments became schools, each with a dean rather than a department head. Effective July 1, 1968, the University established the following:

School of Business Administration
Ray Arensman, *Dean*
> (Followed by Thomas Lee, Gary Lynch, and Dale Hockstra)

School of Education
Earl M. Tapley, *Dean*
> (Followed by William Powell, Robert Garnett, Ronald Goldenberg, and Robert Dana)

School of Engineering
William O. Hartsaw, *Dean*
> (Followed by Jack Tooley)

School of Nursing
Helen C. Smith, *Dean*
> (Followed by Lois Merrill and Nadine Coudret)

At the same time two new colleges were created:

College of Fine Arts
Sam Smiley, *Dean*

Sam Smiley

(Followed by Joseph Wilson, Robert Malone, Patrick McDonough, and Vincent Angotti)

College of Arts and Sciences
George English, *Dean*

(English was the only new dean not already at the institution. He was followed by Charles Evans, Samuel Longmire, and Martin Jones.)

A final major administrative change was the addition of several positions at the vice presidential level, although in some cases the change involved name rather than function. Thus the title of the chief academic officer (Nicholas C. Brown), previously dean of Evansville College, became vice president for academic affairs.

In 1969, Brown was succeeded by **Fred Harris**. For twelve years Harris had held a similar position at Baldwin-Wallace College in Ohio, where he directed a faculty development program in Middle Eastern countries and contributed to international educational activities in Egypt, Pakistan, Afghanistan, and Vietnam. Harris was followed by Charles E.P. Simmons and Malcolm Forbes.

The chief financial officer (Carl Gardner) became vice president for financial affairs. An honor graduate of Eastern New Mexico University and a certified public accountant, Gardner began his work at Evansville College as chief accountant. Following his resignation two years later to become comptroller of the University of Denver, Gardner was succeeded by Larry Jackson. In 1974, the title of this position was changed to vice president for administration, in 1982 to vice president for administration and planning, but in 1985 it went back to vice president for administration. Jackson was followed by Frank McKenna, Robert Garnett, and Robert Gallman.

In the area of student affairs, the dean of students (Robert L. Wilson) became vice president for student affairs. Wilson was followed by Thornton Patberg. The titles of director of women's counseling and director of men's counseling were dropped, and the titles of dean of women and dean of men were restored. These deans were responsible for working with student organizations, such as fraternities, sororities, and student government. They also administered the student code of conduct. In 1984, the title vice president for student affairs was changed to vice president of the University and the office was expanded to include athletics and admission. The following year, the title was changed again, this time to vice president for student development.

In later years, several other positions at the vice presidential level were created:

1981 *Vice President for University Planning*
(Robert Garnett)
(In 1985, this title was expanded to vice president for planning and strategic services.)

1985 *Vice President for University Relations*
(James Ladd, formerly vice president for development)

1985 *Vice President for Student Development*
(James Dawson, formerly dean of student development)

In addition, two associate vice presidents and two assistant vice presidents were appointed.

Other administrative changes:

139

1965 Responsibility for student financial aid, formerly shared by the director of admission and the business manager, was assigned to an autonomous department under the direction of C. Arthur Tyler. (In 1968, he was succeeded by Thomas Zminkowski.)

1965 The position of assistant business manager was renamed director of purchasing and personnel.

1970 The work of the above-named office nearly doubled in only five years so it was divided into two separate departments. **Paul Estep**, a retired air force purchasing officer, was named director of personnel, and **J. Donald Widick '59**, then director of alumni affairs, was appointed director of purchasing.

1970 The position of chief accountant was changed to controller. **Charles Shike**, who had previously worked as a supervisor of accounting in the higher education system of South Dakota, held this position until he was tragically killed in the 1977 airplane crash while accompanying the basketball team to Memphis.

Many other persons in administrative and staff positions made valuable contributions to the University's success during this period. These include:

Mary Louise Bell, *Manager of Duplicating and Supply Services*

Louise Land, *Director of the Student Union*

John Oberhelman, *Director of Admission*

Harry Loveridge, *Director of Physical Plant*

Keith Shelton, *Director of Safety*

L. Ray Lynn, Emerson Abts, *University Chaplain*

William Perry, *Director of the Bookstore*

Mary Louise Bell

Louise Land

David Brownlie, *Director of the Guidance Center*

Thomas Mehaffey, *Assistant Director of the Guidance Center*

Thomas Stone, *Director of Financial Aid*

Peggy Jack, *Director of the Institute for the Fine and Performing Arts*

Doris Scheller, *Nurse, Health and Wellness Center*

Dee Kalena, *Director of University Relations*

Deryl Blackburn, *Assistant Dean of the University Evening College*

Susan Fox, *Assistant to the Dean of the University Evening College*

Richard Hansen, *Assistant Dean of Continuing Education and Community Service*

Charles Dunn, Martin McAuliffe, *Associate Director of Development*

Jerry Linzy, Stephen Mooney, Richard DuPree, *Director of Alumni Affairs*

Lois Unfried, *Assistant Registrar*
Mabel Nenneker, Sherman Tite, Jean Kleindorfer, Keith Kutzler, *Associate Registrar*

Gregory Bordfeld, *Director of Personnel*

Jean Kleindorfer

Ralph Hanna, *Director of Placement (Career Services)*

Bessie LaBudde, *Director of External Studies Program*

Robert Pollock, *Dean of Men*

Luise Schnakenburg, Marie Childers, *Dean of Women (Women's Counseling)*

Paul Novak, *Director of Center for Instructional Services*

Sylvia Moore, *Director of Student Life Center*

INSTITUTIONAL PLANNING

As noted before, little or no long-range institutional planning took place in the early years since, understandably, energies were fully engaged in the struggle to survive. After World War II, however, continued existence seemed assured, and living from crisis to crisis was no longer the order of the

THE UNIVERSITY SEAL

With the change to University status, a new seal was called for. This time its design was assigned to professional artists. At the base of a flame are the letters U and E, which together form a lamp from which a flame arises. The E is in the shape of a stack of books. The design, simple and uncluttered, was judged appropriate to its purpose.

day. The school could then turn its attention to such heretofore neglected matters as a building program. Later, perhaps inspired by the arrival of Indiana State University-Evansville, interest in institutional planning grew as the University of Evansville sought to better understand its role and mission and to formulate specific plans for fulfilling its objectives.

Thus, in 1969, an academic blueprint was formulated to project the needs of the institution for the coming decade. The plan further specified a goal of 5,000 full-time undergraduate students by 1980, plus 1,200 graduate students and about 2,800 part-time students, for a total enrollment of 9,000. A student body of this size would require a part-time faculty of 150 and a full-time faculty of 250, of whom sixty-five to seventy-five percent should hold a doctorate. To recruit a high quality faculty, salaries would have to be increased to compare favorably with national norms.

The first task in planning for such an institution was to develop a statement of mission which would become the basis of future planning efforts. President Graves asserted that no institution can be successful unless its governing body "understands, believes in, and works hard for the achieve-

ment of the mission of the institution for which they are responsible." After considerable discussion, a mission statement emerged containing six basic educational goals and objectives:

■ **To offer an academic curriculum centered about the liberal arts and sciences and a comprehensive array of programs in other areas, while maintaining the highest possible academic quality throughout the University**

■ **To maintain strong ties with the United Methodist Church and to be value-oriented in all the University undertakes; learning is not an end in itself, but the most reliable means to the end of individual and social worthiness**

■ **To be world-minded, recognizing that students must prepare to function in an increasingly interconnected global society**

■ **To view education as a lifelong process and commit the University's resources to the continuing education of all people**

■ **To preserve the independent nature and intermediate size of the University in order to assure continuing distinction, academic excellence, and a favorable student-faculty ratio**

■ **To share educational and cultural resources with the community at large and to utilize the community to create learning opportunities for students at the University**

In addition, the University would endeavor to create "an electric excitement of learning that permeates the atmosphere and that can be detected even by a complete stranger." To achieve this, regular classroom instruction should be supplemented and enhanced by independent study, advanced

141

placement, an honors research program, study abroad, and attendance at lectures, plays, films, exhibits, and concerts.

Using this document as a foundation, a task force was established in 1971 by Fred Harris, academic vice president. Its objective was to develop specific proposals that would implement the concepts stated in general terms in the mission statement. From June to August of 1971, fifty-six faculty members and administrators met regularly and frequently to examine and debate a variety of proposals. The group consisted of a central task force and several auxiliary groups, each dealing with a particular area, such as general education, fiscal matters, and student recruitment. Auxiliary units presented their findings to the central task force, which then made several recommendations to the University Senate.

First was the suggestion that the University develop "an instructional resources support team and an instructional resources laboratory" to propose new courses and revise existing ones, and that every course start with a clear statement of course objectives, followed by a syllabus elaborating the content and requirements.

Particular attention was given to a proposal made earlier in the year by Harris, a new and innovative learning system which he called the "Individualization of Learning." The goal of this system was to modify the traditional pattern by placing more responsibility on the student, with the faculty member's function being primarily that of a facilitator. In this model the institution provides basic learning supports in the form of books, syllabi, program materials, audio visual materials, and self-testing materials. Students are free to use all of these in order to proceed as rapidly as their capabilities allow. After students feel they have mastered a body of material, they are tested on it and if they

Fred Harris

pass, they advance to the next stage. If not, they return to the prior stage for further study. Student and teacher share in the learning process and engage in a dialogue concerning the meaning and implications of the subject matter. The library and the professor's office replace the lecture hall as the center of learning activities.

Although this model and many other task force recommendations were never implemented, the project succeeded in encouraging the institution to reconsider some of its traditional procedures and to attempt to develop better alternatives.

In addition, the task force report suggested that the University improve the quality of instruction on the campus by investing funds in faculty development and support. This could include loans for advanced study, attendance at professional meetings, international travel and exchange, and assistance with equipment needed for research, especially projects that might result in publication in regional and national journals.

Finally, the task force report encouraged the University to further its efforts in long-range institutional planning. A major step in this direction occurred in 1978 when the University applied for a grant from the Kellogg Foundation to hire a consultant with expertise in this area. Upon receipt of the grant, John Millett, executive vice president of the Academy for Educational Development, was brought to the campus for advice and recommendations. Soon afterwards Robert Garnett, the dean of the School of Education, was appointed to the new position of executive assistant to the president for institutional planning.

In 1980, the University Senate adopted a five-year institutional plan. This plan, which was revised the following year, provided budgeting guidelines to maintain financial stability and sought to improve projections of the University's image, maintain enrollment and increase retention of undergraduate students, continue recruitment of outstanding faculty, and ensure that the faculty would have access to necessary support services, physical facilities, and instructional resources.

BUILDINGS

The active building program already underway during the Hyde administration continued during President Graves' tenure. The University expanded its academic programs, increased its enrollment, and attracted an increasing number of students from outside the Tri-State area who needed to live on or near campus.

In October 1967, work began on a new women's residence hall, which opened for occupancy the following fall. Built for $700,000, it was first named simply New Unit, but four years later was more distinctively renamed Morton Hall, in honor of the late Ruth Wertz Morton of Newburgh, a generous benefactor of the University. The new building adjoined Brentano Hall and duplicated it in size and appearance but faced the opposite direction.

With Morton Hall, the University's need for residential housing was adequately met. Beginning in the fall of 1983, however, the four student apartment buildings at the corner of Walnut Street and Weinbach Avenue were razed. They were replaced with a complex of four fraternity houses (Phi Gamma Delta, Phi Kappa Tau, Sigma Phi Epsilon, and Tau Kappa Epsilon). The fraternities paid for construction of these new houses, built on University-owned land leased to them for ninety-nine years.

On the academic side, the School of Nursing needed a proper home. Although founded in 1953, it had no permanent base until 1967, when it took over the farmhouse which had been moved to campus in 1921 and previously had been used as a cafeteria, men's lounge, and office building for the music and business administration departments (see photo on p. 74). Because of increased enrollment, though, a new facility designed specifically for nursing students was called for.

Sigma Phi Epsilon fraternity members cheer as ground is broken for their new fraternity house

In 1970, the University applied for funds for this purpose through the United States Department of Health, Education, and Welfare and received approximately one-half of the $3 million cost. The remainder was to be raised from private sources. Ground was broken in 1972, with the official dedication ceremonies occurring three years later. The new structure featured more than a dozen classrooms and conference rooms, a lecture-demonstration room, and offices for the dean, administrative staff, and faculty. The top floor housed the Evansville Center for Medical Education, a branch campus of the Indiana University School of Medicine, which had been occupying quarters in the McCurdy Alumni Memorial Union since coming to Evansville in 1971 (see page 186).

143

Training professionals for an increasingly high-tech society required up-to-date equipment and facilities for the natural and applied sciences. After over thirty years of service, the original engineering and science building was antiquated and expansion was urgently needed. A $1 million gift from the Krannert Charitable Trust in 1976, one of the largest ever received by the University from a private source, spurred a campaign to raise the additional $2.7 million needed to expand the existing building.

Groundbreaking ceremonies occurred in 1977, with the dedication of the 30,000 square foot addition taking place the following year. The new facility brought the total space in the building to 90,000 square feet, housing completely remodeled classrooms and laboratories for engineering, chemistry, physics, biology, and computer science, an advanced solar laboratory, a specially equipped psychology laboratory, faculty offices, and general classrooms. In 1984, the structure was renamed for Robert L. Koch and family, who had donated $4.1 million to the University's New Century Capital Campaign.

A NEW NAME

Ralph Olmsted

In 1981, that central and historic landmark, Administration Hall, was renamed. The new name honored a man who had spent nearly all his working life – more than fifty years – in the service of the institution as assistant to the president, business manager, instructor in journalism, and University archivist. Upon his retirement as business manager, President Hyde conferred on him the honorary degree of Doctor of Humanities.

President Graves, at the ceremony officially marking the change to the new name of Olmsted Administration Hall, stated that Ralph Olmsted "like Administration Hall, has served our institution with great effectiveness, both in good and troubled times, for over half a century. Today they are joined as one, now and for all time to come."

In his eloquent and heartfelt response, Olmsted said:

"I have had a sixty-year love affair with this grand old building. In May 1921, I helped to pull the plow that broke the ground. A little later, I saw the cornerstone laid.

As a sophomore, I climbed over the building as it assumed its majestic form. In it, I received my diploma from President Alfred Hughes. For forty-two years, my office was there. In it, I worked with and for six presidents – all of them great men in their different ways.

In 1925, I was the youngest person on the staff. Now I am the oldest. How fortunate I have been to see a frail little college, which many thought had only a fifty-fifty chance of surviving, grow into a truly great university.

For nearly sixty years, this building has been the symbol of the University. For twenty-five years, it stood alone, and even when the other buildings sprang up around it, it still dominated the campus. The other buildings have only enhanced its beauty and dignity.

To know that this hall will bear our family name in the years to come fills me with gratitude. It makes me humble indeed but, as I am sure you have observed, not quite humble enough to refuse the honor.

My sincere thanks."

The final structure built during these years was a new football stadium. Periodic suggestions had been made that the institution construct a stadium on campus so the team would not have to play in various high school facilities. Another suggestion called for a facility near Roberts Municipal Stadium to be used both by the University and by area high schools. The University proceeded to acquire land from the state of Indiana by exchanging land the institution had purchased in 1967 from the state hospital at Lincoln and Vann Avenues. However, the plan was abandoned, both because of cost and also because of difficulty in coordinating the project with the local school corporation. In addition, the off-campus site ignored the primary reason for building the stadium in the first place.

The problem was resolved in 1984, when the University began a $2 million fund drive to upgrade the athletic facilities at Carson Center, the first phase of which included the construction of the long-awaited football stadium. An anonymous donor contributed $300,000, requesting only that the new facility be named in honor of long-time basketball coach Arad McCutchan.

Renovation of existing campus buildings also received high priority. The union building, for example, was remodeled several times: in 1971 and 1972 to remodel the Wooden Indian (multi-purpose student center) and to house the Evansville Center for Medical Education; in 1974 to house the Guidance Center, Reading and Study Skills Laboratory, Student Publications, and the Student Association; and in 1984 to further modernize the Wooden Indian.

In 1981, trustee Guthrie May donated his residence on Lombard Avenue as a new home for the University president. The former home (given by the Iglehearts) was then turned over to the Offices of Development and Alumni Relations.

Finally, periodic changes were made in Administration Hall. With the dedication of Hyde Hall in 1967, more of Administration Hall could be converted from classrooms and laboratories to administrative use. For example, in 1970 two classrooms, each large enough to seat ninety students, became

offices and the president's office was moved from the first floor to the second. And in the 1980s, the entire building was refurbished, made possible by a gift from the class of 1985 and funds provided by C. Wayne and Betty Worthington.

Wayne Mueller

TREES

In 1970, Wayne Mueller and Louis Winternheimer of the biology department published a booklet, *Trees of the University of Evansville.* Their study showed that the front forty acres contained more than 550 trees of over 80 species, including common varieties such as oak, maple, pine, ash, tulip, and dogwood, as well as persimmon, sassafras, butternut, mimosa, ironwood, yellowwood, and black tulip.

The heart of a university's academic program is its library. With the rapid growth in student enrollment, the University of Evansville's book and periodical collections outgrew the 1957 library structure in only a few years. In 1965, the total number of volumes housed by the library was 66,593, but four years later this had grown to 94,000 and by the following year the total reached 108,000, an increase of 41,407 or 62.2 percent in five years. Moreover, books were being added to the library at the rate of 12,000 or more per year, approximately twice that of previous years.

145

OLD STONE HOUSE

146

Old Stone House, located on a high hill with a panoramic view of the Ohio River in Newburgh, Indiana, was a gift to the University of Evansville from trustee Thomas Morton and his wife, Ruth. Saying, "We want it to fall into good hands and the University can use it to great advantage," the Mortons donated not only the house, but also the seventeen acres surrounding it.

The house, constructed in 1834, has a fascinating history. Its first owner, Gaines Head Roberts, had the stones with which it was built brought in on river barges and then hauled to the building site by oxcarts. Ironically, Roberts made the fortune which enabled him to build the house through the lumber industry.

A native of North Carolina, Roberts left his father's plantation at the age of eighteen to seek his fortune in the West. Traveling first to Henderson, Kentucky, he soon found his way to Indiana, where he built a log cabin on the grounds of the present house. (Today, a plaque marks the exact location of that rough, unfinished cabin.) In time, Roberts became a rich, successful, and powerful businessman, a Warrick County probate judge, and a member of the Indiana Senate, riding on horseback to Indianapolis for legislative sessions.

At the time of its completion, Roberts' home – with its stone walls that were three feet thick in the basement, two feet thick on the first floor, and eighteen inches thick on the second, and with at least five fireplaces throughout the house – was regarded as the finest residence to be found in southern Indiana.

But hard times followed. After Roberts died in 1863 at the age of 70, the property went to his son, Rufus, only to be lost to a New York trust company when the younger Roberts defaulted on a $17,000 mortgage debt.

For several years the house stood empty, and before long the legend grew among area residents that the building was haunted by a variety of ghosts and spirits. Reportedly, Indians, tall and gaunt, were seen stalking over the hill, forms clad in misty white were seen to appear and disappear, and weird sounds were heard breaking the stillness of the night. For years no one wanted to go near the place. Indeed, in the late nineteenth century, when Wesley Wilson bought the property and hoped to make it livable again, he experienced great difficulty finding live-in help because its reputation for being haunted still lingered.

In 1919, Isaac Hollinger purchased the house, using it as a sanitarium for the treatment of drug addicts. Supposedly, many sinister events, such as suicides, murders, mysterious deaths, and the sheltering of criminals, occurred within the walls of the house. There are elderly people living today in the area who say that when they were children they heard the screams of Hollinger's patients coming from the house. A magazine article, likely sensationalized, stated that it "harbored degenerates, drug addicts, criminals, desperadoes, and other characters so low that there is no adequate word with which to describe them."

In 1931, the property was purchased by Thomas and Ruth Morton. Since the house had remained a sanitarium until that time, extensive work was required to bring the house back to its original splendor. The new owners also had a horse farm on the property, but sadly a fire razed the stables in 1951, killing eight horses, including their champion stallion, Mountain Song.

In 1975, the Old Stone House was placed on the National Register of Historic Places. The grounds also featured Indiana's largest Chinquapin Oak, eighty-eight feet tall with a girth of forty-nine inches; it was estimated to be at least 100 years old when it collapsed during a thunderstorm in 1993.

Since 1969, when the Mortons donated this historic edifice to the University, the University has been faithful to the Mortons' wish that it "be used to good advantage." It has served as a guest house as well as the site of numerous conferences, seminars, and receptions.

A goal of 300,000 volumes was set for 1980, which meant adding over 21,000 volumes each year. In addition, periodical holdings would have to be doubled, 1,100 study seats would need to be added, and the number of professional librarians tripled. Also essential were group study and seminar rooms, faculty research areas, typing facilities, and equipment for computer-assisted instruction. Indeed, with the computer becoming a major learning tool, a center for computer instruction would soon be required.

It is little wonder that the library, which had seemed so spacious in 1957, now seemed hopelessly inadequate. In 1975-76, a $290,000 renovation provided additional space but proved to be only a stopgap measure. A thorough study of anticipated needs revealed that the present facility, although it housed 250,000 books, 1,200 periodicals, and over 40,000 microformats, was only about one-third as large as it should be for the size of the student body. For example, available seats in the study areas were less than one chair for every twenty (full-time equivalent) students. The recommended standard for an institution such as the University of Evansville was one chair for every five students.

Accordingly, in November 1983, a $5 million fund-raising campaign was initiated to finance a major library addition of 56,000 square feet, thus tripling the size of the library and bringing its total space to 74,000 square feet. Jack H. Kinkel '62, of Jack R. Kinkel and Sons of Evansville, was selected to design the building, and Sallie Rowland, of Rowland Associates Inc. in Indianapolis, was responsible for the interior design. The ground-breaking ceremony took place on October 20, 1984, with the dedication ceremony occurring almost exactly two years later (October 16).

The major dedicatory address was delivered by internationally renowned author Kurt Vonnegut, who saw in this library "a sacred meeting place for those who wish to celebrate life and reason." In recognition of a $1 million gift from Dallas Suhrheinrich, the new structure was named the Bower-Suhrheinrich Library to honor her family and her husband, the late William Suhrheinrich, a

147

Construction of the Bower-Suhrheinrich Library was started in October 1984 and was completed in October 1986

148

Bower-Suhrheinrich Library 1986

former Mead Johnson executive and past vice chairman and treasurer of the University's Board of Trustees.

The Clifford Memorial Library was preserved and joined to the Bower-Suhrheinrich facility by a connecting corridor on each floor. To promote a feeling of openness, glass partitioning separates the book stacks in the new portion of the library, with carpeted walls and fabric-covered end panels on each row of stacks. Thanks to this beautifully designed, spacious, and functional addition, with a seating capacity of 600, the University of Evansville at last enjoyed a library worthy of its ambitious educational mission.

Thomas Harding, the man most responsible for building Clifford Memorial Library, was succeeded in 1966 by **James O'Leary**. During O'Leary's administration, professional librarians were granted faculty rank and status and were appointed to tenure track positions.

O'Leary was followed in 1974 by **Dwight Burlingame**, who began a coordinated library instruction program in which librarians and instructors collaborated to provide students with research skills especially crucial for success in their major fields. Following a pilot program in 1975-76, a five-year grant was awarded to the University by the National Endowment for the Humanities to employ an additional librarian for bibliographic instruction.

When the NEH grant expired in 1981, library director **P. Grady Morein** continued to assign a staff librarian to coordinate and advance the library instruction program. Morein also played a major role in the planning and building of the new Bower-Suhrheinrich Library.

Other important contributions to the development of the University Libraries during this period were made by librarians in the following areas:

Ruth Miller, *Acquisitions*

Elinore Zeta, *Cataloguing*

Marvin Guilfoyle, *Periodicals*

Jonette Aarstad, *Reference*

Kathryn Bartelt, *Circulation*

THE COMPUTER REVOLUTION

Since the late 1960s, the world has witnessed a revolution in the delivery of library services. The groundwork was laid when the Library of Congress developed a means for groups of libraries to share bibliographic data through computer networks. The Ohio College Library Computer Center (OCLC) soon developed such a network and when, in 1977, libraries outside of Ohio were invited to participate, the University of Evansville became one of the first institutions in Indiana to join.

At first, libraries used OCLC to produce computer-generated catalog cards but, by 1985, in the next great technological leap, card catalogs were eliminated altogether, as well as the labor-intensive manual procedures traditionally involved in purchasing, cataloging, and circulating library materials. In its place, the University of Evansville installed NOTIS (Northwestern Online Total Integrated System), the leading automation system for academic libraries, providing an online catalog and computerizing circulation and acquisition functions. Moreover, the University's participation in OCLC's automated interlibrary loan service made the resources of thousands of other libraries available to University of Evansville students and faculty.

149

⌗

THE CLIFFORD COLLECTION

In 1980, the scholarly library of James L. Clifford was donated to the University of Evansville library by his widow, Virginia. Clifford was a distinguished professor of eighteenth century English literature at Columbia University and the son of Evansville College founder George Clifford and Emily Orr Clifford, its first woman trustee. The bulk of the more than 600 books, pamphlets, and articles which comprised his library concerns eighteenth century critic and writer Samuel Johnson and his circle of associates.

The formal dedication of the Clifford collection in 1982 was attended by Governor and Mrs. Robert Orr. The James L. Clifford Research Collection, available for scholarly research, is housed in a handsome reading room in the Clifford Memorial Library, named in honor of James Clifford's parents. Since 1982, additions have been generated from an enrichment fund, to which arts patron Frances Hanson was a major contributor.

A noteworthy consequence of the James L. Clifford research collection was the formation of the Samuel Johnson Society of the University of Evansville under the guidance of Samuel Longmire, then English department chair. The society, dedicated to the study and celebration of eighteenth century life, is comprised of faculty, students, and interested members of the community.

Among its activities is an annual spring banquet featuring a presentation by a nationally recognized scholar. This event is made possible by the society's endowment fund, established under the leadership of Alma Vaughn and Melvin Peterson.

The Samuel Johnson Society has attracted a dedicated corps of longtime members whose commitment to the organization keeps it alive to the present day.

⌗

ACADEMICS

FACULTY MATTERS

An early priority of the Graves administration was to bring the faculty teaching load into line with other institutions of higher learning. Before 1967, the standard load was sixteen credit hours per quarter, about thirty percent higher than at most comparable schools; over a three-year period, this number was reduced to twelve credit hours.

With a lighter teaching load, many faculty were able to continue and complete their work for terminal degrees and the University was able to attract more professors already holding terminal degrees.

The reduction in teaching load also provided expanded opportunities for research and publication. Believing that students are best taught by persons who are themselves still learning from their work in the library and laboratory, the Alumni Association established the Alumni Research and Scholarly Activity Fellowship in 1971 to encourage and support faculty research in a variety of areas.

	Number of full-time faculty members	Percentage holding terminal degrees
1967	148	43
1974	188	59
1980	200	74
1986	169	85

In 1968, to recognize and reward academic excellence, the Alumni Association established an annual Outstanding Teacher of the Year Award of $1,000 (later increased to $2,000). Selections were made by a committee composed of two students, two faculty members, an administrator appointed by the president, the director of alumni relations, and an alumnus. The first recipient was P. Louis Winternheimer of the biology department. (Later recipients are listed in the appendix.)

150

P. Louis Winternheimer, 1968 Outstanding Teacher of the Year, reviews an experiment in his biology lab

Faculty salaries increased dramatically during this period. In 1969-70, salaries increased one letter grade in each of the four academic ranks, according to the rating scale used by the American Association of University Professors. Although the levels of improvement dropped off somewhat in succeeding years, faculty compensation remained comparable to that of similar institutions. Fringe benefits for faculty and staff and support given to emeriti professors also increased.

Yet, despite improvements in teaching load, support for research and good teaching, and faculty compensation, several factors led to a decline in faculty morale. In the fall of 1976, the University Senate appointed a four-member ad hoc committee concerning faculty morale. After investigating general faculty concerns and formulating a questionnaire returned by 153 out of 204 faculty members (a seventy-five percent rate of return), the committee reached three major conclusions:

First, the faculty perceived the University to be administration centered, with an organizational climate which pitted managers and bosses against the managed and the bossed, as opposed to a supportive organization. The faculty and senate were viewed as powerless, while committees were considered rubber stamps for administrative decisions. The University's hierarchical structure seemed to put less value and importance on teaching and more on administrative procedures and values.

Second, there was a perception of a lack of faculty trust in the administration, a sense that rewards and promotions were based on personal likes and dislikes rather than on merit, and a feeling that administrative reprisals in terms of salary, tenure, and promotion were being imposed on those who spoke negatively.

Third, there was a perception of inequitable distribution of resources. Respondents believed that disproportionately more was spent on administration than on teaching, and that there was inadequate disclosure of University finances.

151

In an effort to remedy the situation, the ad hoc committee made three recommendations. The first called for the creation of a permanent Faculty Morale Committee, appointed by and responsible solely to the University Senate, charged with a continual ongoing assessment of faculty morale. Second, it recommended a systematic and regular faculty evaluation of the administration, including the president, assuring greater accountability as well as providing better insight into faculty problems and perceptions. Third, it recommended the appointment of the president and vice president of the University Senate as ex officio members of the University's Board of Trustees, thus improving morale by involving faculty more directly in decision-making and providing them fuller access to financial data.

In February 1977, the senate approved the first two recommendations in principle and amended the third so that the president and vice president of the senate would be non-voting participants on the Board of Trustees Executive Committee. In addition, the senate recommended that an ombudsman be appointed to chair the Faculty Morale Committee and be responsible for conducting an annual survey concerning faculty morale, reporting its findings to the senate and to the president, and investigating other faculty-related issues.

Although these recommendations indicated an awareness of problems regarding faculty morale and proposed strategies for improvement, morale continued to be a major problem, prompting some faculty to advocate formation of a collective bargaining unit. In 1979, the Faculty Association was organized as a chapter of the National Education Association; the NEA would become the faculty's collective bargaining agent if a majority of the faculty approved. After a year of discussion, the faculty rejected unionization in November 1979 by a vote of 104-63, with ninety percent of the eligible faculty members and librarians participating.

The Faculty Association hoped that the campaign, though unsuccessful, would have a positive result by bringing the faculty and administration together to do "some constructive things about bettering the University." For Graves, the faculty vote represented "a renewal of its faith in the cooperative pursuit of the University's educational mission."

Although some faculty members remained critical of certain administrative policies, perhaps a reflection of the restless spirit of the times, professors consistently gave their best to provide their students with high quality education. Indeed, the achievement record of the University's various schools, colleges, and departments reached impressive heights.

General Education

The University's general education curriculum came under close scrutiny twice during the Graves administration. The underlying principle – that certain fields of learning should be required in every well-rounded educational program – has traditionally been agreed upon by faculties across the nation. Achieving consensus on how many courses should be required and how they should be distributed was another matter, particularly during an era when students were demanding greater flexibility in selecting courses they regarded as relevant.

The task force of 1971 dealt with this issue and proposed a new plan, officially adopted by the University Senate the following year. The twenty hours of English formerly required of all students would be reduced to four hours of composition, and fifty-six hours of additional courses could be selected, distributed as follows:

Health and Physical Education	4 hours
Humanities and Fine Arts	12 hours
Natural Sciences	12 hours
Social and Behavioral Sciences	12 hours
Electives from the above categories	16 hours

Thus, about one-third of the hours required for graduation (60 out of 186 quarter hours) would fall into the category of general education and, except for English composition, no specific course was mandatory. The total number of general education hours, under this plan, would remain approximately the same as in the past.

Students took sixty-four hours of general education requirements beginning in Fall 1982

A little over a decade later, general education was reexamined when a national symposium attended by representatives of twenty-one institutions met in Colorado under the sponsorship of the Lilly Endowment. The purpose of the summer-long session was to share ideas and to develop a new plan for each of the participating institutions.

After considerable discussion and some modifications, the University adopted a new program, effective in the fall of 1982. This plan, somewhat more restrictive than its predecessor, raised the general education requirement to sixty-four hours. It was constructed as follows:

Communication Skills	12 hours
Critical Issues	4 hours

Global Perspectives	4 hours
Health and Physical Education	4 hours
Historical, Philosophical, and Religious Perspectives	8 hours
Literary and Artistic Achievement	8 hours
Mathematics or Computer Science	4 hours
Natural Sciences	8 hours
Social and Behavioral Sciences	12 hours

153

The Global Perspectives component, intended to emphasize the University's mission of world-mindedness, could be fulfilled either by taking a four-hour course in some aspect of the non-Western tradition, by studying at the University's Harlaxton College campus in England for one semester, or by attending another foreign study center.

The goal of the Critical Issues area was to expose students to some of the contemporary problems facing the individual and society, such as the environment, energy, health care, crime, and ethical dilemmas.

While not satisfactory to all, this plan met with the approval of the majority of the faculty and student body.

PROFESSIONAL PROGRAMS

Engineering

In 1968, William Hartsaw was named the first dean of the newly formed School of Engineering. He dedicated his major efforts to gaining national accreditation for the school from the Engineers Council for Professional Development. Two years later this goal was achieved.

In 1975, Hartsaw was succeeded by **John Tooley**. Tooley's appointment was unique in that, while he had earned a doctorate, he had no previous academic experience, his background being entirely in industry. Specifically, for over fifteen years, he worked at Texas Instruments in Dallas, where his responsibilities included the design of telecommunications for the Mars-Venus Voyager NASA spacecraft.

At the University of Evansville, Tooley instituted the annual Tri-State Regional Science and Engineering Fair, providing an opportunity for middle and high school students to exhibit projects they have researched or devised.

During Tooley's tenure, the University's physics and computer science programs were moved from the College of Arts and Sciences to the School of Engineering (1976). While physics quickly returned to its former home, computer science remained in engineering. Indeed, in 1976, the division's name was changed to the College of Engineering and Applied Sciences, and in 1984 to the College of Engineering and Computer Science (its current name).

Jack Tooley advises a student

WHAT GOES AROUND COMES AROUND

Over the years, the institution has see-sawed between the quarter system and the semester system.

President Hughes preferred quarters, but his successor, President Harper, promptly changed the College to semesters. After World War II, President Hale switched back to quarters, and that system remained in effect for thirty-seven years.

President Graves, however, felt that quarters put the University out of step with the majority of other colleges and universities and vigorously urged a return to semesters. The transition was achieved in 1985 and is expected to be permanent – but perhaps it is too early to be sure!

Other developments during this period include:

- In 1969, a single Bachelor of Science in Engineering degree replaced the three specialized degree programs in electrical, industrial, and mechanical engineering. But in 1972, specialized degrees in engineering were restored, and three new degrees were added: civil engineering, computer engineering, and engineering management (the latter offered in conjunction with the School of Business Administration).

- In 1971, Eta Kappa Nu, national electrical engineering honor fraternity, was chartered, with Max Casler as its faculty sponsor.

- In 1986, the UE Technical Assistance Center (UETAC) was established in connection with the Mead Johnson Company to offer Fortran for engineering and scientific professionals in the quality assurance area. The center also offered seminars in Auto CAD (computer assisted drafting) and computerized maintenance management for mid-level managers and engineers.

ENGINEERING FACULTY

Faculty members in the major areas of engineering during this period include:

Electrical Engineering
 Syama Chaudhuri
 Dick Blandford
 David Mitchell
 Mohsen Lotfalian
 James Reising
 William Thayer

Mechanical Engineering
 Paul Funk
 R. Dale White
 Philip Gerhart

Civil Engineering
 Harvey Kagan
 Hooshang Nezafati
 James Lott

Computer Science
 Bruce Mabis
 William Mitchell
 James Westfall
 William Herrin

155

Engineering Faculty 1979

Left to right Ron Devaisher, Clarence Winternheimer, Bung-Chung Lee, Jack Tooley, Dick Blandford, David Mitchell, Paul Funk, Darrell Megli, William Mitchell, Max Casler, Bruce Mabis

Business Administration Faculty 1969

Left to right front row Michael Groomer, James Julian, Tom Henrion, Ted Latz, Michael Taylor; *Middle row* Robert Martin, Dell Nussmeier, Ann Katterhenry, Ray Arensman, Miles Taylor, Maurice Tsai; *Back row* Lewis Howell, David Reeder, Royce Lorentz, Ron Faust, Allen Bess, Clifford Stone, Wen Chow

Business

In 1980, the Sigma Iota chapter of Delta Sigma Pi business fraternity was chartered. It became the umbrella organization for several student professional clubs in the School of Business Administration, including a chapter of the American Marketing Association, a chapter of the Society for Human Resources Management, an accounting club linked with the National Association of Accountants, and the International Students Club for global business majors.

156

BUSINESS ADMINISTRATION FACULTY

Economics
John Ficks
Richard Farrar
Michael Zimmer
M. Gale Blalock

Finance
Theodore Latz
Frank Gile
Paiboon Sareewewatthana

Marketing
Donald Bates
John Lennon
Robert Eckles

Management
David Eldredge
James Wilterding

Accounting
S. Michael Groomer
Allen Bess
David Reeder
Christine McKeag

Office Administration/
Business Education
Dell (Hartman) Nussmeier
Robert Martin

Computer Science (Business)
Molly Zimmer
(later transferred to the College of Engineering and Computer Science)

Education

A major movement in education during the 1960s was an increased emphasis on reading skills, beginning with the primary grades. Recognizing that children with reading deficiencies were seriously handicapped throughout their academic careers, the federal government supported training programs for reading teachers. This funding made it possible for schools to establish reading clinics, during school hours, after school, and in the summer months as well.

The University of Evansville, especially after the arrival of **Rexel Brown** (Ed.D., Indiana University) in 1968, took an active role in encouraging student teachers to earn an endorsement as a reading specialist. Advanced programs were also established at the graduate level. Brown was the first reading consultant appointed by the Indiana Department of Education. He also directed the Newspaper in Education (NIE) summer workshops, sponsored by the Evansville Printing Corporation, which provided scholarships, expertise, and materials.

Over the ten years that the University held the workshops, the project involved more than 1,000 Tri-State teachers. Brown retired from the University in 1995.

A further asset to the University's education program was the Curriculum Center, which housed a tremendous array of books, games, and audiovisuals. Under the direction of Margaret Wallace, this center also stored NASA educational materials and the Indiana Reading Association Regional Library. After Wallace retired, the Multimedia Center, directed by Linda Wulf and located in Graves Hall, was established.

Before 1970, education majors had no actual classroom experience until they began student teaching during their senior year. As a consequence, many students wasted three years before discovering that they were either ill-suited to or did not enjoy teaching.

Elementary school pupil enjoys individual attention from her UE student teacher

157

In 1970, the Career Decisions Program, developed by the School of Education, put students in the classroom as early as their freshman year, participating in tasks with which they felt comfortable. Later, as part of the ABLE (Activities Based Learning Experiences) program developed by **Carmen Andrew** and **Rosemary Schiavi**, education majors were in the classroom at each level, preparing them for student teaching well before it occurred. Having University students in the classroom all four years has proved highly beneficial.

The involvement of Evansville area schools in planning and implementing teacher preparation programs has also been invaluable. Supervising classroom teachers are considered part-time University faculty and in this capacity meet periodically with the director of student teachers to make student teaching a meaningful and valuable experience.

The School of Education, like other education departments across the nation, experimented with such trial balloons as new math, linguistic and phonetic approaches to teaching reading, artificial alphabets (ITA), programmed books, and teaching machines, but gradually most of these techniques fell out of favor. In general, the School of Education curriculum has focused on the teacher-child interaction and on developing teachers who understand the processes by which children and adolescents learn.

In the late 1970s, the University of Evansville became one of the first schools in the nation to offer dual credit or "bridge classes," courses carrying both high school and college credit. These courses, serving as a bridge between high school and college, were taught in the high school by teachers with credentials appropriate for college teaching as well. Hours earned by high school juniors or seniors could be used toward a University of Evansville degree or could be transferred to another college or university. The program began at Memorial High School in Evansville and was later extended to Bosse, Reitz, Castle, and Forest Park High Schools, and the Signature Learning Center.

158

School of Education Faculty

Left to right, front row Sylvia Kolb Moore, Janet Hartman, Wilma Schafer; *Back row* Dean Ron Goldenberg, Dewey Moore, Joel Dill, Ivan Ward, Stan Rachelson, Ralph Templeton, Rexel Brown

EDUCATION FACULTY

Also joining the School of Education during this period were:

Elementary Education
Janet Hartman

Secondary Education
Clifford Kraft
William Wesley
Carol Brennfleck
Kenneth Pool

Special Education
Sylvia Kolb Moore
Marlaine Chase
Dewey Moore
Nealon Gaskey

School Administration
Herbert Erdmann
(Former superintendent of the Evansville-Vanderburgh School Corporation)
Ivan Ward

UPHOLDING NURSING STANDARDS

Dean Helen Smith recalls an incident from her tenure which strengthened her faith in the caliber of the University's student body:

A nursing student was summarily dismissed for an entire year because she used alcohol and drugs prior to going on duty at the hospital. Her parents intervened with President Graves and he came with them to see me. He thought we should relent. I explained the gravity of allowing a student to distribute medications and use complicated equipment with critically ill patients or to make judgments about their care, and I suggested the potential liability suits that might befall the University and criminal liability that might destroy her career. The faculty resolved the problem by reducing her withdrawal to one semester and ruled that she must then return for evaluation. She returned and gave a stellar performance right through graduation. Students and faculty alike applauded her accomplishments.

Nursing

At its height, the School of Nursing offered associate's, bachelor's, and master's degrees in nursing; associate's, bachelor's and master's degrees in physical therapy; an associate's degree in radiological technology; and a master's degree in health services administration. It also supported the Gerontology Center, which offered educational programs specific to the aging, not only for students but also for the Evansville community. Health screening was provided to the elderly by nurse practitioners who traveled a multi-county region. Continuing education for health professionals was also a focus for the school.

Faculty felt a heavy responsibility to ensure that no student would fail State Board Examinations and only rarely did failure occur.

New Degree Programs

1969 Three-year **associate's degree in nursing** directed by Helen Shrode, assistant to the dean

To earn the degree, students were required to attend classes for one year full time on campus and two years alternating periods of study on campus with work experience in area hospitals. Twenty-two freshmen enrolled in 1969, and fifty-one in 1971. Graduates of the program qualified to take the registered nurse (RN) examination.

1970 **Radiologic Technology –** **associate's degree**

1970 **Respiratory Therapy –** **associate's degree**

(Continued on next page)

159

NURSING FACULTY

Faculty members in the major areas of nursing during this period include:

Medical and Surgical Nursing
Helen Broyles
Joyce Suhrheinrich
Cynthia Sublett
Leva Lessure
Roma Leach
Ann Furr Knox
Brenda Nichols
Susan Dye
Ann Clark
Sue Atkinson
Deborah Marshall
Joan Alexander
Cleo Hayden
Marcia Ashley
Joyce Dungan
Charlotte Niksch
Jean Falls
Harriet Pickett
Leigh DeNoon
Mary Titzer
Joan Kiely
Lois Latshaw

Obstetric Nursing
Dorothy Stephens
H. Mae Arensman
Pamela Enlow

Pediatric Nursing
Melissa Vandeveer
Thelma Brittingham
(also director of continu-
ing education in nursing)
Helen Shrode
Diane Siewart
Kathleen Sheller

Psychiatric Nursing
Mary Rode Petkovsek
Rosemary Brune
Vivian Davenport
Rosemarie Miutilla
Eleanor Dimmett

Public Health Nursing
Dorothy Hausman
Bernice King
Erica Janzen

Critical Care Nursing
Mary Kay Hermann
(Kittinger)

Gerontology
Kay Roberts Rudd
Mary Jo Boeglin

Nutrition
Madelaine Burns
Nancy Burzminski

1978 Physical Therapy – bachelor's degree

1978 Gerontology – bachelor's degree,
multidisciplinary

1984 Dietetic Technology –
associate's degree

Left to right, front row Wilma Winternheimer, Harriet Pickett; *Middle row* Joan Kiely, H. Mae Arensman; *Back row* Dorothy Hausmann, Jane Nelson, Kay Roberts

Nursing Faculty 1974

DAN SNIVELY, M.D.

Medical doctor, teacher, researcher, author, explorer, water sportsman, gentleman farmer, antiquarian, and expert on early American history and the history of the English language.

Author or co-author of eighty-two articles and nine textbooks, with chapters in five others, as well as several books for the general reading public.

This gives only a cross section of the accomplishments of the multi-talented Dan Snively. After his retirement from Mead Johnson, Snively joined the faculty of the School of Nursing at the University of Evansville, where he taught life sciences and pathophysiology.

On the side, he offered a popular course, the West in American History. His book, *The Pageantry of the English Language*, was published by the University of Evansville Press. His professional reputation, however, rested more on *Mind, Body, and You* (psychosomatic medicine), and *Sea of Life* (body fluid disturbances). His textbook, *The Sea Within*, went to five printings. Snively was held in the highest regard by colleagues and students alike.

The physical therapy program began at the University in 1975 with the establishment of the Physical Therapist Assistant Program within the School of Nursing. Accreditation by the Commission of Accreditation in Physical Therapy Education was achieved the following year.

In 1979, the University established a professional entry-level program, a Bachelor of Science degree in physical therapy. The program was developed by **Cheryl Griffith** (M.A., University of Evansville) and initially enrolled twelve students. In 1982 and 1986, class sizes for the program increased to twenty-two and twenty-four respectively.

Cheryl Griffith

PHYSICAL THERAPY FACULTY

The physical therapy programs became a separate department in 1989. Full-time faculty, in addition to Griffith, included:

Barbara Hahn, *Director of Physical Therapist Assistant Program*

Tink Martin

Mary Bennett

161

COLLEGE OF FINE ARTS

Art

During this period, the University's art curriculum expanded in many areas:

Undergraduate

1969   **Bachelor of Fine Arts in art** (ceramics, painting, sculpture, graphic design)

1976   **Bachelor of Science in art and associated studies** (combined studio art with a second area of study such as commercial art or business)

1976   **Bachelor of Science in art therapy**

1980   **Bachelor of Science in commercial art**

1984   **Associate of Arts**

Graduate

1976   **Master of Arts in art**

Courses in studio art, art history, art education, printmaking, and weaving were also offered for graduate credit as part of the master's program in education, and available as a major field in this program.

In 1972, a student art competition and exhibition, organized by Dorothea Schlechte and Elizabeth Geiss-Pitt ten years earlier using exhibition space at the Washington Square Branch of Old National Bank, was moved to Krannert Gallery on the University campus.

In 1969, Les Miley was appointed acting chair of the art department and the following year he became chair, a position he held until 1987 and again from 1990 to 1999. Miley was selected for *Who's Who in American Art* each year beginning in 1976; he received the Alumni Association's Certificate of Excellence in 1980; and in 1986, both the Phi Kappa Phi Outstanding Faculty Scholar Award and the Sydney and Sadelle Berger Award. A 1986 exhibition, "The Clay Connection," included Miley's work together with that of seventeen former students.

Art Faculty

Left to right Nanene Jacobson Engle, William Richmond, Les Miley, John Begley, Caroline Roth

ART FACULTY

Also joining the department during this time were:

Jerry Points
(M.F.A., Southern Illinois University) 1968-74
Printmaking

Nanene Jacobson Engle
(M.A.T., Indiana University) 1971-86
Weaving, Metal Work and Jewelry, Art Education, Art Therapy

William Richmond
(M.F.A., Southern Illinois University) 1974-97
Drawing, Metal Work and Jewelry, Sculpture

William Brown
(M.F.A., School of the Art Institute of Chicago) 1982-present
Drawing, Painting, Photography, Art Education
Later Department Chair

Fred Eilers (Drawing, Painting), **John Begley** (Drawing, Printmaking), and **Larry Barnfield** (Art Education, Art Therapy) served as longtime adjunct instructors.

In New Harmony, in addition to the ceramics workshop established in 1966 (see page 102), a weaving workshop was begun in 1972. It was co-sponsored by the University of Evansville (represented by University weaving instructor Nanene Engle) and Robert Menke. Julia Lindsay, professor of art at Wright State University, was the first workshop instructor. It continued until 1981. In 1976, a lithography workshop was initiated under the leadership of John Begley, director of the New Harmony Gallery of Contemporary Art. It continued until 1987. Finally, a new ceramics studio designed by internationally recognized architect Richard Meier was dedicated in New Harmony in 1978.

Music

The University of Evansville choir achieved particular distinction during this period. Under the direction of Robert M. Rapp, it was selected through audition in 1968 to perform for the conference at which the Methodist and Evangelical United Brethren Churches merged to form the United Methodist Church.

Four years later, it was one of six college and university choirs to represent the United States at the Symposium of Choral Music in Vienna. Together with **Robert Luther**, University organist, and **Dennis Sheppard** of the voice faculty, the choir visited Venice and Vienna and gave concerts in several other European cities. Their programs featured not only traditional masterworks by Handel and Brahms but also choral music by American composers Charles Ives, Aaron Copland, and William Schuman. To help raise the $32,000 needed for the three-week trip, the choir prepared a souvenir long-playing stereo recording including many of the selections they performed abroad. The choir also gave several performances with the Evansville Philharmonic Orchestra, as well as making a multi-state tour each spring.

In 1971, **Armand Kitto** directed the University's first opera production, *Susannah* by Carlisle Floyd. After producing Kurt Weill's *Down in the Valley,* Kitto searched for a formal home for the new opera program and successfully prevailed upon Frederick Kiechle, owner of the Alhambra Theater near downtown Evansville, to make the building available. Despite a shallow stage and no room offstage, acoustics were excellent and, after some necessary maintenance work, performances continued with *The Telephone* by Menotti, *The Secret Marriage* by Cimarosa, *Hansel and Gretel* by Humperdinck, *Cosi fan Tutte* by Mozart, and *Sleeping Beauty* by Evansville native Richard Faith.

Enthusiasm for opera continued into the late 1970s with performances of Benjamin Britten's *Albert Herring* and all the operettas of Gilbert and Sullivan, directed by English conductor Brian Daubney with President Wallace Graves playing the title role in *The Mikado.*

Also in the area of vocal music, tenor Sir Peter Pears, one of Europe's most outstanding performers and associate and champion of well-known English composer Benjamin Britten, visited the UE campus for a recital and master class. In the field of instrumental music, the University hosted the sixth annual conference of the International Double Reed Society, attended by approximately 175 persons representing 35 states and several foreign nations. Edwin Lacy of the UE music faculty chaired the 1977 event.

Through the years, several student performers have gone on to influential careers in music. Examples include David Girton, owner of Show-Biz International; William Morneweg, creator of the role of Joseph in the Broadway musical *Joseph and the Amazing Technicolor Dreamcoat;* and Tyrone Bragg, praised for his work in *Jesus Christ Superstar.* Other University of Evansville singers have performed with the Chicago Lyric Opera, Memphis Opera, Fort Worth Opera, Kentucky Opera, and several European companies.

Suzuki violin students

Music Faculty 1976

Left to right, front row Mark Simcox, Douglas Reed, Dennis Sheppard, John Koehler, Donald Colton; *Middle row* Sandra Botkin, David Wright, Paul Nolte, Carol Dallinger, Cheryl Dileo, Carolyn Colton, Eulalie Wilson; *Back row* Gregory Davis, Robert Rapp, William Bootz, Joel Lipton, Paul Dove, Laurence Shapiro, James Bursen, Edwin Lacy

MUSIC FACULTY

Also joining the department during this period were:

Voice

Paul Dove
Department Chair
Roberta Veazey
Department Chair

Violin

Carol Dallinger
Director of Suzuki Violin Program
Gerald Fischbach
Delmar Pettys

Guitar

Renato Butturi

Piano

Gregory Davis
Anne Hastings Fiedler
Mona Boyd (Whinrey)

Organ

Douglas Reed

Wind Instruments

Edwin Lacy
Bassoon, Jazz
Department Chair
William Knapp
Clarinet
David Wright
Clarinet, Band

Trumpet

James Bursen

Band

John Koehler

Musicology/Music Theory

Donald Colton
Department Chair

Theatre

Two University of Evansville Theatre graduates from this period achieved national recognition.

RON GLASS

Evansville theatre standout Ron Glass '68 is best known nationally for his portrayal of the suave and dynamic Detective Harris on the television sitcom *Barney Miller*.

Glass launched his career with an acclaimed performance in the University's 1968 production of *Slow Dance on the Killing Ground*. Using material from this role for national theatre auditions resulted in eighteen offers from leading professional drama companies. Glass accepted an offer from the prestigious Tyrone Guthrie Theater in Minneapolis, where he remained four years.

In the early 1970s, he went to Hollywood, quickly getting roles on such shows as *All in the Family*, *Maude*, *Hawaii Five-O*, and the *New Perry Mason Show*. In 1975, he joined *Barney Miller*, remaining with it for eight years.

165

In 1979, Ron Glass returned to his native Evansville to receive the University's Medal of Honor. At that time, he also was presented a key to the city of Evansville by Mayor Mike Vandeveer. He returned again in 1990 to help dedicate the newly renovated Shanklin Theatre, reprising an excerpt from *Slow Dance on the Killing Ground.*

Theatre major Dave Emge starred with Ron Glass in the acclaimed 1968 production of Slow Dance on the Killing Ground

MATT WILLIAMS

Matt Williams visits his alma mater and meets with theatre students

Matt Williams '73, an Evansville native, served as writer and producer of the first three seasons of *The Cosby Show* in the mid 1980s. He went on to create and produce television sitcoms such as *Roseanne*, *Home Improvement*, and *A Different World*.

In 1989, Williams, with David McFadzean '73 (his UE roommate) and Carmen Finestra, founded Wind Dancer Productions, which has since produced numerous TV plays and commissioned fifteen original plays. Williams has received Emmy and Humanitas nominations as well as a Peabody Award.

In 2001, he returned to his alma mater to deliver the commencement address and to receive an honorary doctorate.

In a production of Matt Williams' Between Daylight and Boonville, *Bradley Horstman (left) played the role of Bobby and Christia Stinson Ward the role of Marlene.*

Williams attributes much of his success to the strong foundation he gained at the University.

"The basics, the fundamentals, that I learned in the basement of Shanklin Theatre, I continue to use today." Williams especially values the concept stressed at the University of Evansville of "doing total theatre. Even to this day, people are shocked that I can build scenery. I can build a four by eight platform. I can scumble paint. I can handle lights. I can sew sequins on costumes. I'm not a master at any of those things, but I understand how they all work together for the total production."

ARTS AND SCIENCES

Communication (Speech)

Speech was originally part of the Evansville College English department (indeed, courses were generally labeled "oral English"). It was later teamed with theatre, when it was known as the Department of Speech and Drama with **Dudley Thomas** as its head.

In 1973, however, the program was reorganized. Speech was separated from theatre; journalism was removed from its former home in the English department; and courses were added in radio-television, film, photography, public relations, interpersonal and group communication, and advertising. The expanded program, originally called the Center for the Study of Communication, was funded by a $287,420 grant from the Lilly Endowment. **Alan Labowitz** headed the center and was followed by **Thomas Bohn**, **Jennings Bryant**, and **Joseph Webb**.

COMMUNICATION FACULTY

Also joining the department during this period were:

Dean Thomlison
(Ph.D., Southern Illinois University) 1977-present
Interpersonal and Intercultural Communication
Department Chair

Hope Bock
(Ph.D., Southern Illinois University) 1983-present
Speech, Interpersonal Communication
Department Chair

Robert West
(Ph.D., Southern Illinois University) 1984-95
Telecommunication, Advertising

Also serving the communication department for briefer periods were **Gilbert Clardy**, **John Blair**, **Laura Hubbell**, **Thomas Harris**, **Paul Sullivan**, and **Robert Field**.

167

Communication Faculty

Left to right Robert Field, Paul Sullivan, Laura Hubbell, Thomas Bohn, Gilbert Clardy

168

Student DJ at University-owned WUEV-FM

English and Journalism

Two lecture series sponsored by the English department have stimulated campus and community interest in literature and the humanities. The monthly English Coffee Hour offers readings of poetry and fiction by nationally noted literary figures. In addition, a program each spring features the best creative writing by University of Evansville students, held in conjunction with an annual writing contest and the publication of selected works by student authors. The Andiron Lectures series, more scholarly in nature, presents papers by faculty and community speakers highlighting their current research interests.

Until the early 1970s, courses in journalism were part of the English department curriculum. In 1968, **Robert Byler Jr.** (M.A., University of Missouri) was appointed to head the program. Byler had considerable experience in television and, under his direction, monthly programs were prepared by University of Evansville students and shown on Channel 14. Byler expanded the number of journalism courses to thirteen, including photo journalism, feature writing, editing, communication law, supervision of school publications, public

Sam Longmire

opinion, and history of communication. In addition, the *Crescent* was changed to tabloid size, with issues running from eight to sixteen pages.

English Faculty 1968

Left to right, front row George Klinger, Virginia Grabill, Paul Grabill; ***Back row*** Herman McGregor, Paul Schlueter, Robert Byler

169

ENGLISH FACULTY

Also joining the department during this period were:

Michael Carson
(Ph.D., Ohio State University) 1969-present
English Literature,
 Creative Writing
Department Chair,
Melvin M. Peterson Endowed
 Chair in English Literature

Ralph St. Louis
(Ph.D., University of Nebraska)
1969-94
Romantic and Victorian
 Literature

Ralph St. Louis

Donald Richardson
(Ph.D., University of Minnesota)
1969-2000
Mythology and Scandinavian
 Literature
Department Chair

Samuel Longmire
(Ph.D., Indiana University)
1974-1999
Eighteenth Century English
 Literature
Department Chair,
Fulbright Fellowship in
 Romania 1989-90

Don Richardson

John Haegert
(Ph.D., University of Chicago)
1979-present
Twentieth Century Literature
Visiting Professor at University
 of Paris, Sorbonne 1989-90

John Haegert

Laura Weaver
(Ph.D., University of Kansas)
1980-2000
Research Writing and Technical
 Writing

Laura Weaver

Also serving the English department for briefer periods were **Herman McGregor, Walter Wangerin Jr., Peter Scholl, James Gallant,** and **Jo Willa Zausch.**

Mike Carson meeting with a student

Geography

In 1970, **Jerry Kendall** (Ed.D., Indiana University), a full-time professional geographer, was appointed to the faculty, the first in nearly twenty years. Within three years, the geography program expanded from two to five courses, and a new position was added, filled by **Larry Smith** (Ph.D., University of Tennessee). Eventually ten courses in this and related areas (such as meteorology) were offered, and by 1975 a minor in geography became available. Five years later, geography was incorporated into a new administrative unit, the Department of History and Geography.

Geography Faculty 1979

Left to right Larry Smith, Jerry Kendall

Mathematics

During this period, most mathematics majors were enrolled either in the Bachelor of Arts program leading to certification to teach in high school or, beginning in 1978, in a Bachelor of Science program in applied mathematics, which included computer science and business. Also, from the early 1960s to the mid 1970s, the department offered graduate-level courses and National Science Foundation workshops for area teachers wishing to earn a master's degree in education or to professionalize their teaching certification in secondary mathematics.

Fueled by increased enrollment in engineering and by federal funds supporting the training of mathematics teachers, the mathematics department grew rapidly. From only three full-time faculty members in 1967, the department increased in just a few years to a complement of eight.

Melba Patberg, 1985

Mathematics Faculty 1968

Left to right, front row V. C. Bailey, Melba Patberg, Clarence Buesking; *Back row* J. Robert Knott, Roy Meadows, Ralph Coleman, Robert Brooks

171

MATHEMATICS FACULTY

Also joining the department during this period were:

Melba Patberg
(M.A, University of Evansville) 1967-94

J. Robert Knott
(Ph.D., Indiana University) 1968-2001
Department Chair

Kenneth Stofflet
(Ph.D., University of Wisconsin) 1969-76

Clark Kimberling
(Ph.D., Illinois Institute of Technology) 1970-present

Duane Broline
(Ph.D., University of Wisconsin) 1979-86

Mohammad Azarian
(Ph.D., St. Louis University) 1985-present

THE COMPUTER AGE

By the late 1960s, computers had swept the nation and the University of Evansville made sure it was in tune with the times. In 1969, the original IBM model 1620 was updated to an IBM 365, model 25, a computer suitable for both instruction and administrative work. **Manfred Schauss**, formerly with Bristol-Myers Squibb, was engaged as director of administrative data processing, and Professor Clarence Buesking gave up teaching mathematics to become head of the newly-formed computer science department.

A two-year associate's degree in computer science was quickly expanded to a four-year degree. In its first year (1970), thirty majors enrolled and more than 300 students participated in a variety of computer-oriented classes. Use of computers within the University also greatly speeded the enrollment and registration process, as well as billing, payroll, preparation of grade reports, financial aid

Students working on computers

work, mass mailings for student recruiting, and alumni information services.

Within three years, the capacity of the new machine was exhausted, but with support from trustee Kenny Kent, a new machine with four to five times the capacity of the previous model was ordered. Instead of the anticipated ten-year life of this new system, however, it lasted only seven years.

A few years later, when it became necessary to replace the existing computer system, two machines were purchased, one for academics, the other for administration. After about five years, when still greater capacity was needed, one larger machine was acquired to replace the two smaller ones.

172

CLARK KIMBERLING

Mathematics professor Clark Kimberling is an avid researcher and prolific writer – of both words and music. He has contributed more than seventy articles to professional and scholarly journals, and nearly forty more which focus on techniques of teaching mathematics.

During the 1980s, Kimberling developed software programs for mathematics teachers which were marketed by the University of Evansville Press. Later, this work was continued by a company of his own, Mathematics Software.

His web site, entitled "Encyclopedia of Triangle Centers" (the equivalent of 450 printed pages), has achieved wide recognition and use. Pulitzer Prize winner Douglas Hofstadter described Kimberling's work on theorem discovery in geometry as "the most interesting use I have ever seen of computers for the purpose of exploration of mathematics."

In addition, Kimberling has written extensively on the life and work of Emmy Noether, who is generally regarded as the greatest woman mathematician.

When not teaching, writing, or developing software, Kimberling collects and plays Renaissance and baroque musical instruments and composes church music for voice and instrumental accompaniment. Altogether, about twenty pieces have been issued by the University of Evansville Press and GIA Publications of Chicago. In addition, he composed the music for the wedding reception of Sir John and Lady Wedgwood, which occurred during his semester at Harlaxton in 1982.

Physics

Thanks to several additions to the faculty, the physics department could offer advanced courses in electronics, optics, solid state, and atomic and nuclear physics, as well as new classes in classical mechanics, mathematical physics, advanced electricity and magnetism, quantum mechanics, and statistical mechanics.

In 1976, former Evansville College physics professor James S. Sears (see page 111) and his wife, Anna, established a scholarship fund to support an outstanding physics or engineering major. Taking the form of a challenge grant and matched by the

Lilly Endowment, it became a significant addition to the University's academic program. Students who have won this award two years or more during this period are Steve Maier, Stephen Berry, Stephen Gravelle, and Kent Scheller.

A second major gift for the physics department was the Olaf Hovda and Richard Berger Hovda Physics Scholarship Fund, established in 1982. Scholarships from this source became available in 2002.

Physics Faculty 1976

Left to right Darrell Megli, Paul Funk, Charles Mathieu, Kerry Driggers, Benny Riley

PHYSICS FACULTY

Joining the department during this period were:

Darrell Megli
(Ph.D., Kansas State University) 1962-65, 1969-2003
Nuclear Physics, Optics, Acoustics

Benny Riley
(Ph.D., Carnegie Mellon University) 1970-present
Nuclear Physics
Department Chair

Gifford Brown
(Ph.D., Cornell University) 1979-present
Solid State Physics

Jeffrey Braun
(Ph.D., Oklahoma State University) 1984-present
Statistical Physics, Relativistic Quantum Theory

Political Science

In 1967, the Center for Urban Affairs was established, endowed by Austin S. Igleheart with a gift of $450,000 given as a memorial to his parents, Mr. and Mrs. John L. Igleheart. (John L. Igleheart, as previously noted, was an Evansville College trustee from 1922 to 1933. He gave the College its president's house in 1928 and donated $25,000 for library endowment, and made generous donations to several College campaigns between 1917 and 1933.) The center is dedicated to the study and improvement of municipal government. Its first director, **Richard Hall**, was succeeded in 1971 by **David Gugin** (Ph.D., University of Wisconsin). A four-year Bachelor of Science degree in urban affairs was first offered in 1972.

POLITICAL SCIENCE FACULTY

Also joining the department during this period were:

Ronald Adamson
(Ph.D., University of Missouri) 1971-2001
Comparative Politics, Asian Studies
Department Chair

Donald Freeman
Ph.D., University of North Carolina) 1978-96
American Politics
Department Chair
Fulbright Scholar in Singapore (1986) and the
Philippines (1993)

David Gugin often engages students in lively conversation on campus

Psychology

In 1972, when Delbert Sampson resigned as chair of the department, he was succeeded by **Clarence Brooks '63** (M.S., Indiana University), the first psychology department chair who was also a graduate of the University. Brooks made a major contribution to the department by structuring its first graduate program, initiated in 1976. He was a man of firm convictions and a strong advocate for the faculty, described as one who "displayed extraordinary integrity and the courage to voice unpopular opinions." He retired in 1985. After his death the following year, his wife, Betty, set up the Clarence Brooks Award to be given annually to an outstanding psychology major.

Brooks was followed as department chair by **William Weiss** (Ph.D., University of Maryland), a clinical psychologist with a secondary area in industrial psychology. Weiss continued the development of the University's graduate programs in clinical and school psychology.

In 1973, with the coming of experimental physiological psychologist **John Lakey** (Ph.D., University of Texas), the department added a strong science-oriented undergraduate major: psychobiology.

John Felton

175

PSYCHOLOGY FACULTY

Also joining the department during this period were:

John Felton
(Ph.D., Hofstra University)
School and Clinical Psychologist

John Ireland
(Ph.D., University of Arizona)
Clinical Psychologist

In 1983, **Barbara Jessen** (Ph.D., University of Illinois), then a ten-year member of the department, succeeded Weiss as department chair. The first woman to head the department, she continued the emphasis on graduate studies during her five-year tenure.

During the late 1970s and early 1980s, psychology and communication were the two top departments in generating credit hours. Several graduates of the program went on to careers in clinical psychology, medicine, and neuroscience, while many master's graduates made their mark as outstanding practitioners in the Tri-State community.

Sociology

Under the Federal Law Enforcement Act of the late 1960s, college tuition became available to police officers wishing to upgrade their formal education. In response, the University of Evansville offered an associate's degree in law enforcement in 1968, and two years later added a four-year baccalaureate degree program. In the fall of 1970, enrollment in the two programs reached sixty-seven. (In 1978, the name of this area was changed to criminal justice.)

A volunteer probation counseling program was also supported by a federal grant. This cooperative effort between the University of Evansville and Judge William H. Miller of the Vanderburgh County Circuit Court was directed by Patricia Becker '79. University of Evansville faculty members provided training sessions, with volunteers working on a one-on-one basis with probationers.

In 1973, a Bachelor of Science degree program in social work was established, headed by **Richard Earl**; it was discontinued in 1981.

Anthropology was added to the University's sociology program in 1974 by **Russell Lewis**, who offered classes in physical and cultural anthropology and prehistoric archaeology. Interested students

Sociology Faculty 1974

Left to right Charles Halbrook, Herb Stockman, Ludwig "Bruzz" Petkovsek, Don Magel, Alan Fliegle, William Tonso, C. Edward Marske, Russell Lewis

could either major in sociology with a concentration in anthropology or take a minor in the subject. When Lewis resigned in 1978, responsibility for the anthropology program was assumed by **James Berry** (Ph.D., Indiana University). In 1982, cultural anthropology was added to the University's general educational curriculum as a social science option.

James Berry

SOCIOLOGY FACULTY

Also joining the department during this period were:

William Tonso
(Ph.D., Southern Illinois University) 1969-99
Ethnic Studies, Deviant Behavior, Gun Control

Hanns Pieper
(Ph.D., University of Georgia) 1977-present
Medical Sociology, Gerontology
Department Chair

Dennis Wichman
(Ph.D., University of Southern Mississippi) 1977-99
Law Enforcement (Criminal Justice)

Also serving the sociology department for briefer periods were **Robert Stallings, Christopher Prendergast, C. Edward Marske**, and **Charles Halbrook.**

Hanns Pieper writes a weekly newspaper column on the problems of aging in addition to teaching sociology

177

OTHER AREAS

New faculty in other areas during this period include:

BIOLOGY FACULTY

Charles Taylor
(Ph.D., Purdue University) 1966-69
Botany, Conservation

Karen Ott
(Ph.D., Rutgers State University) 1969-96
Parasitology, Immunology, Bioethics
Department Chair

James Brenneman
(Ph.D., Louisiana State University)
   1970-present
Botany, Environmental Science,
   Genetics

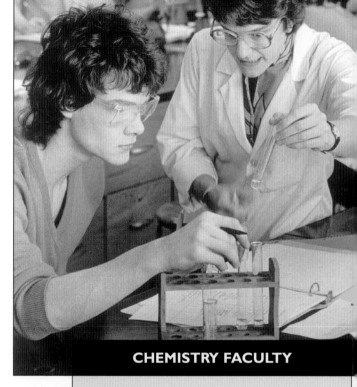

**James
Brenneman**

Eugene Schroeder
(Ph.D., University of Missouri)
   1974-2002
Zoology
Department Chair

Jerry Seng
(Ph.D., Indiana University) 1976-2003
Zoology, Genetics

Jerry Seng

CHEMISTRY FACULTY

James Manning
(Ph.D., University of Kansas) 1966-72
Analytical Chemistry

James Kroneman
(M.S., University of Wisconsin) 1963, 1968-73
Analytical Chemistry

Warren Hankins
(Ph.D., University of Virginia) 1969-77
Organic Chemistry

Vernon Shaw
(Ph.D., University of Illinois) 1973-97
Analytical Chemistry
(With Philip Kinsey, Shaw introduced computers to
   the department, including the very earliest PCs.)

William Morrison
(Ph.D., University of Kansas) 1975-present
Inorganic Chemistry

Jean Beckman
(Ph.D., Indiana University) 1978-present
Organic Chemistry
Department Chair

FOREIGN LANGUAGES FACULTY

James Talbert
(Ph.D., Indiana University)
1968-2003
Spanish
Department Chair

James Talbert

William Felsher
(Ph.D., University of Louisiana)
1969-90
French
Department Chair

Henry Miner
(Ph.D., University of Utah)
1971-present
German

Henry Miner

*Jean Beckman working
with a student on a
chemistry experiment*

HISTORY FACULTY

Philip Ensley
(Ph.D., Indiana University) *1968-present*
American History, African American History,
    Popular Culture
Department Chair

Vivian Taylor
(M.A., Indiana University) *1974-83*
Ancient and Medieval History

Daniel Gahan
(Ph.D., University of Kansas) *1986-present*
American History, Immigration, Agrarian History
Department Chair

PHILOSOPHY AND RELIGION FACULTY

Philip Ott
(Ph.D., University of Pennsylvania) *1968-96*
Bioethics, Religion in Literature
Department Chair

Robert Godbout
(Ph.D., University of Kansas) *1969-74*
Philosophy of History, Greek Philosophy,
    Aesthetics

W. Richard Connolly
(Ph.D., Michigan State University)
1971-present
Philosophy of Law, Bioethics

W. Richard Connolly

Robert Kress
*(Ph.D., University of Innsbruck,
    Austria)* *1973-79*
Contemporary Catholic
    Theology

Bruce Paternoster
(Ph.D., Yale University) *1975-87*
Philosophy of Science, Logic

*The language laboratory in the early 1960s was located
on the fourth floor of Olmsted Administration Hall*

179

ROTC

In the fall of 1971, women were admitted to the University's ROTC unit. Fifteen female students joined. Upon being commissioned, they were eligible for any air force position except pilot.

OTHER ACADEMIC PROGRAMS

With the change to university status, the unit established in 1940 as the Evening College became known as the University Evening College. Later the name was changed again to the College of Alternative Programs in 1974, directed by Larraine Matusak, and then to the College of Graduate and Continuing Studies in 1984, directed by Earl Tapley. These units offered both a rich diversity of non-credit classes and degree programs for part-time students, especially non-traditional adults whose jobs or other duties prevented them from taking regular daytime classes. In either case, this division was experimental and responsive to new ideas, opportunities, and community needs.

Bachelor of Liberal Studies

For example, in 1973, an innovative degree program designed specifically for adults, the Bachelor of Liberal Studies (B.L.S.), was first offered. It was implemented by Marvin Hartig, dean of the University Evening College.

Prior to this time, adults returning to school were enrolled in the same courses as traditional students, and their degrees were identical to those earned by full-time students. The B.L.S. program was significantly different in that special courses were designed specifically for them, and all those enrolling in a given year took exactly the same courses at exactly the same time, thus fostering a spirit of camaraderie within each group. The program was available only to persons 25 or older. Earning a degree required three years of concentrated evening course work plus the completion of an independent study project directed by a faculty member with expertise in the thesis topic. Most instructors were full-time faculty, supplemented by qualified persons from area schools and businesses. Classes focused on the liberal arts and sciences and prepared adults to deal with contemporary interests, problems, and concerns.

Originally, classes were graded pass/fail, but later this changed to letter grades at the request of area businesses, who encouraged employees to participate in the program by offering them tuition reimbursement if they performed successfully.

Each year-long sequence of Bachelor of Liberal Studies courses is divided into five-week segments and concentrates on a specific theme.

First year	Second year	Third year
Man Within	*Man and Society*	*Creative Man*
How people grow and develop as individuals	How people relate to other individuals and to social institutions	How people express thoughts and feelings
Classes deal with psychology, philosophy, religion, and mental health.	Classes deal with sociology, anthropology, history, government, ecology, economics, and business.	Classes deal with music, art, drama, and literature.

180

External Studies

A year after introducing the Bachelor of Liberal Studies option, the University offered a second non-traditional degree for adult students, the External Studies Program. The program was quite different from the B.L.S. program. It allowed participants to design an individual curriculum uniquely suited to their specific needs by utilizing past educational and job experience and then adding carefully selected course work combined with independent study. In many cases, students were able to create a major not available in traditional degree offerings at the University of Evansville or elsewhere.

Alpha Sigma Lambda

To recognize the achievements of adult students, the University applied to the adult student honorary association, Alpha Sigma Lambda, for a charter to form a local chapter. In 1976, the first group of adult students was initiated. Roger Sublett served as national counselor until 1989, when Lynn Penland assumed the position.

Paralegal Program

Another new area of study originating in the evening division was the paralegal program, available at either the associate's or bachelor's level. (Paralegals are specially trained to assist attorneys in legal research and in a variety of office procedures.) Begun in 1975, the program was administered by Dean Matusak and Roger Sublett, director of special programs. Certification by the American Bar Association was achieved in 1977.

The roster of Evansville area attorneys serving on the advisory board or teaching in the program reads like a "Who's Who" of the profession. They include Charles Berger, John Carroll, James Schwentker, Lawrence Daly, Wesley Bowers, Edward Johnson, Paul Black, Sheila Corcoran, and Jeffery Lantz. Several Evansville area paralegals also served on the advisory board.

Sublett directed the paralegal program until 1982 when it was transferred to the School of Business Administration, and renamed the Legal Para-

professional Program; **Charles Wooding** then became the program director, serving until 1986. The following year the current director, **Deborah Howard**, assumed the position.

Minerals and Land Management

In 1983, a credit program was initiated, leading to an associate's degree and then a Bachelor of Science in minerals land management. Directed by Eulalie Wilson and developed in cooperation with the American Association of Landmen, it was designed for students seeking careers in the energy and natural resources industry. Because of major changes in the energy market, the minerals land management program was phased out five years later.

Certificate Programs

The College of Alternative Programs also offered numerous certificates in such areas as transportation management, real estate, and interior design. In far less time than that required for an associate's degree, students could earn credentials documenting their proficiency in a specific area of work. Nearly all the certificate programs were phased out during the late 1980s.

Non-credit Courses

Non-credit classes, workshops, and seminars were also important offerings sponsored by the evening division and College of Alternative Programs. Most were designed to enhance personal growth and enrichment, but others were intended for professional groups and businesses. Short courses dealt with such topics as foreign languages, literature, exercise, computer skills, investing, financial planning, and hobbies. Many focused on issues of special interest to women; these were coordinated by Janet Walker and later by Marjorie Zion and Elaine Hopkins.

181

WEDNESDAY MORNING LITERATURE

The University's Wednesday Morning Literature class (now called Wednesday Mornings at UE) often enrolls more than 100 students, but its beginnings were far more modest. Barbara Graves (wife of President Graves) is a founding member and recalls some of its early history:

In the early 1970s, Barbara McKenna (wife of then Vice President Frank McKenna) and I attended a national meeting of the American Council of Education in Washington, D.C., with our husbands. This group always planned special activities for the wives of the delegates. One particular day the meetings were dedicated to the women's movement, a new idea on campuses intended to meet women's special interests. These sessions were not about belligerent women marching in the streets demanding their rights. They were, instead, slanted toward stimulating and thought-provoking programs such as book discussions and creative activities.

We returned to our campus full of enthusiasm and eager to get something of this nature started at the University of Evansville. In 1973, a group of interested ladies, including Alma Vaughn, Mary Lou Shane, Isabella Fine, Bettie Mathews, and a little later Jeanne Ellenstein, volunteered their services, guided by the director of continuing education and a young English instructor, Diane Scholl.

At first, meetings were held in our living rooms, but the idea turned out to be so successful that before long we had outgrown the private home setting and were able to move our operation to the campus. Several professors, such as Sam Longmire, Mike Carson, Phil Ott, Larry Caldwell, and Tom Fiddick, generously agreed to recycle some of their courses for our benefit.

As time went on, several men, mostly retired, joined the group (my husband, after his retirement, being one), and George Klinger, after his retirement from full-time teaching, agreed to serve as course coordinator. Also, the subject matter was expanded to include not only literature but also art, music, film, theatre, religion, history, archaeology, and even politics. Another outgrowth of our initial modest effort was the establishment of credit courses and an academic program in women's studies at the University of Evansville.

Judging by the number of people who now attend, I am not the only one who hopes that the Wednesday morning series will long continue and prosper.

Institute for the Fine and Performing Arts

In 1975, the Preparatory Music School, formerly part of the College of Fine Arts, was transferred to the College of Alternative Programs and renamed the Institute for the Fine and Performing Arts. Its mission was broadened to include classes and programs in art, drama, and dance, as well as music, and was expanded to reach people of all ages.

University of Evansville Press

An additional service to the community was the University of Evansville Press, established in 1977. The press' objective was to publish books by regional writers and works of particular interest to Tri-State readers. An advisory board, which included Elinore Zeta, George Klinger, and library director Dwight Burlingame, was responsible for manuscript selection and book distribution.

Volumes published by the University of Evansville Press during this period include:

- Ralph Olmsted *Evansville's Great Flood of 1937* (Evansville history)

- Philip Ensley *The World of Karl Kae Knecht Through His Cartoons* (cultural history)

- Margaret McKinney *Footloose and Duty Free* (travel)

- James Morlock *Was It Yesterday?* (Evansville history)

- LaVyrne Brown *I Am Glad I Have Had My Flight* (poetry)

- W. D. Snively *The Pageantry of the English Language* (linguistics)

- Clark Kimberling's church music and mathematics software (see p. 173).

Following a period of inactivity, the University of Evansville Press has recently published the Richard Wilbur Poetry Series. Under the direction of William Baer of the English department, these annual volumes are devoted to the works of poets who have received the Richard Wilbur Award, named for the Pulitzer Prize winning poet.

Books Between Bites

Started in 1979 and held monthly during the academic year, a lunchtime book review session featured faculty and community leaders and was free to the public. Over the years, Books Between Bites speakers included UE presidents Wallace Graves, James Vinson, and Stephen Jennings; numerous vice presidents, deans and department chairs; as well as Alfred Savia, conductor of the Evansville Philharmonic Orchestra; Bishop Gerald Gettelfinger, Diocese of Evansville; Mayor Russell Lloyd Jr.; Sheriff Brad Ellsworth; Prosecutor Stan Levco; Tom Tuley, editor of the *Evansville Press*; and numerous physicians, local radio and television personalities, clergy, and authors. Speakers chose the books they reviewed, and the lively sessions ranged from classics to best sellers, from professional books to trade books. The series ended in 2002.

Spring Festival

A notably successful project of the College of Alternative Programs, the annual Spring Festival, began in 1984. The day-long event highlighted arts and humanities topics related to particular persons, historical periods, or geographic areas. Examples of themes include the Orient, Evansville history, the age of Victoria, Van Gogh, Italy, Thoreau, the American West, and the 1940s.

183

The University's role in adult education received special recognition in 1984 when the University of Evansville was selected as the national headquarters for the Association for Continuing Higher Education, an organization representing 510 institutions. Roger Sublett, dean of UE's College of Graduate and Continuing Studies, was appointed its executive vice president. The association served the University well by bringing it into contact with leading educators here and abroad.

Ralph Templeton

Graduate Education

As noted in Chapter Four, Evansville College offered two graduate programs. The first, beginning in 1948 in cooperation with Indiana University, was administered by the Center for Advanced Study. The second, was an independent Master of Arts degree for elementary and secondary teachers.

With the change to university status, graduate education became a priority. For example, during the 1960s and 1970s, in response to increased demand for school counselors both in the Tri-State and nationally, the University of Evansville joined many other institutions in establishing graduate programs in counselor education.

As late as 1965, only two counseling courses were available in the Evansville area, both taught through Indiana University by a professor commuting to Evansville from Bloomington one evening a week. But in 1967, Robert Garnett, then director of special educational services, joined the faculty of the School of Education with the specif-

ic goal of coordinating a new counselor education program and developing an endorsement for school counselors. In 1970, professional certification in counseling was also offered, and new counseling courses were added to the curriculum, as well as a new faculty member, **Joel Dill** (Ph.D., Ball State University).

In 1974, when Garnett became dean of the School of Education, Dill was appointed director of counseling programs. Two years later, counseling specialist **Ralph Templeton** (Ph.D., Indiana State University) joined the School of Education faculty and in 1982 was named director of counseling programs.

During the late 1970s and 1980s, the school counselor education curriculum was revised to meet new Indiana Department of Education licensure requirements. Also, a growing number of students enrolled in the community counseling program (human services), while the number of students preparing to be school counselors

184

declined. Accordingly, the prefix "education" was removed from all counseling courses and was replaced with the prefix "counseling."

DAVIES BELLAMY

Davies Bellamy

In 1978, Davies Bellamy was recruited from Trinidad to play soccer at the University of Evansville. He was a leading scorer on the University's first Division I soccer team in 1978, he ran cross-country for the University, and he coached little league soccer camps. He viewed it as a golden opportunity to get a fine education, but could hardly have imagined the path his life at the University would take after that.

After completing a bachelor's degree in accounting, Bellamy realized that his major interests lay elsewhere, so he enrolled in the University's community counseling program, earning a master's degree in 1984. This led Bellamy to an appointment by the University as an administrator in the student life office, where he served as director of residence life and co-director of minority affairs.

He then left the University of Evansville to pursue doctoral studies at Indiana State University, completing his doctoral student internship at the University of Florida's counseling center. In 1991, he returned to the University of Evansville as a member of the faculty in the School of Education, specializing in counseling. The following year he was named director of counseling programs.

Bellamy, now a professor of education, has consistently received high evaluations from students, faculty, and administrators. As a result, in 1999, he received the Exemplary Teacher Award from the United Methodist Church. He also served as faculty athletic representative, a position which draws on his counseling skills, his deep-seated concern for people, and his lifelong dedication to athletics.

In 1968, the new University began to offer a Master of Business Administration degree and four years later two additional graduate degrees, one in humanities and another in nursing.

The Master of Arts in humanities, allowed the student to choose courses in literature, history, philosophy, and religion and also to choose from two fields, European or American studies. This degree was useful to teachers and to other adults desiring a diversified enrichment program in the liberal arts.

The Master of Science in nursing stressed preparation for leadership positions at the policy-making level of health care delivery.

In 1970, the first Master of Business Administration degree was granted, and by the fall of that year approximately 175 students enrolled in the program. Therefore, the following year, a separate School of Graduate Studies was established with Earl E. Tapley as dean. Tapley had been involved in graduate education since 1964, and since 1968 had been dean of the School of Education. (When Tapley became dean of graduate studies, William C. Wesley was appointed acting dean of the School of Education.) Supporting Tapley was the Graduate Counsel with Ralph Coleman as chairman. In 1969, its title was changed to Graduate Programs Committee.

In 1973, a Master of Science degree in engineering was added, and the following year a Master of Arts degree in continuing studies was introduced. The latter was an individualized degree allowing students to choose advanced courses in various disciplines which would best meet their objectives and needs. By 1984, the University of Evansville was offering master's degrees in fifteen subjects, including art, music, civil engineering, electrical engineering, mechanical engineering, engineering management, psychology, counseling, and computer science education, as well as a certificate in gerontology.

In time, however, enrollment in the University's graduate offerings declined steeply. In

185

1972, the Master of Arts program in education enrolled 760 students, but by 1985 enrollment in all graduate programs combined was only 508. Consequently, many graduate programs were discontinued, and the School of Graduate Studies merged with the College of Alternative Programs to form the College of Graduate and Continuing Studies.

Although a Master of Business Administration program had been offered by the University for nearly fifteen years and was accredited by – indeed, had been commended by – the North Central Association of Colleges, a serious problem arose in 1985 when the Indiana Commission for Higher Education ruled that students in all parts of the state must have access to such a program at state university tuition rates. Accordingly, if the University of Evansville was to preserve its program, it was necessary to establish some connection with a public institution.

At first, the University of Evansville sought to establish a cooperative program with the Indiana University School of Business, but Indiana University refused. The following year, negotiations began with Indiana State University in Terre Haute for cooperative master's degrees in both business administration and teacher education. ISU proposed a degree that would be available to Evansville area students at state tuition prices, but only twenty-five percent of the instruction would come from University of Evansville faculty and the degree would bear the name of Indiana State University. This arrangement was rejected by the University of Evansville.

At this point, the University of Southern Indiana (the former Indiana State University-Evansville) – after proposing a Master of Business Administration program of its own to the Indiana Commission for Higher Education (which was rejected) and then suggesting a cooperative program with Indiana University (which Indiana University refused) – offered to share a program with the University of Evansville. This degree would carry the University of Evansville name but would be financed by public funds and would thus be offered at state tuition rates. This proposal was

accepted by all parties, but when USI officials pressed for permission to offer their own program, the commission reversed its position in 1991 and decided to turn total control of the master's program over to the University of Southern Indiana, leading the University of Evansville to discontinue its graduate program in business.

In 1985, the University of Evansville and Indiana University developed a cooperative program bringing graduate work in library science to Evansville. The courses, taught at the University of Evansville, were available at Indiana University's lower rates. Under this plan, one half of the work needed to earn the Master of Library Science degree could be taken at the University of Evansville.

By the late 1960s, it was apparent that Indiana needed a second medical school. Several cities in the state, including Evansville, competed fiercely to be the site of the new school. In 1970, however, the Indiana Commission for Higher Education decided on a different approach. It resolved to develop multiple medical education centers across the state rather than building a single new medical school. Evansville was to be one of seven areas designated as a medical education center. Each center would provide freshman medical instruction. The second and third years of study would take place at Indiana University School of Medicine in Indianapolis, after which seniors would return to a regional center for the final year, consisting mainly of clinical work in hospitals.

The basic question for the Evansville community was which institution – UE or ISU-E – should administer the program. A collaborative approach was agreed on with the University of Evansville directing the first year of the program and Indiana State University-Evansville the fourth. Patrick J. V. Corcoran was appointed director of the Evansville center. The first-year program was housed in McCurdy Alumni Memorial Union until 1975 when it moved to the new nursing building. The University of Evansville participated in this program until the University of Southern Indiana erected a larger facility on its campus.

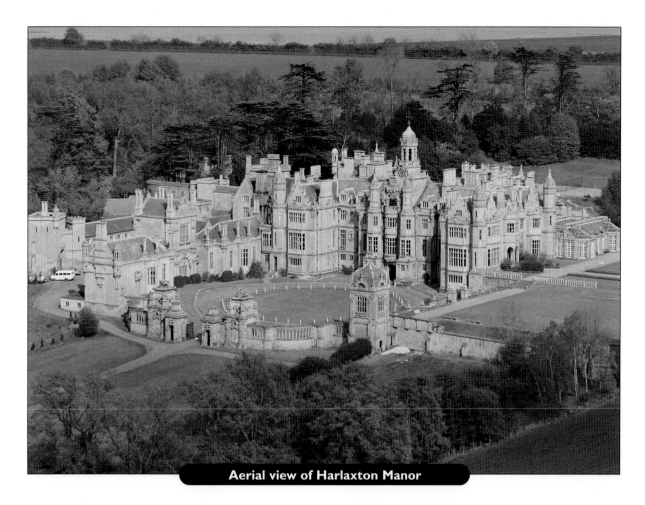

Aerial view of Harlaxton Manor

INTERNATIONAL PROGRAMS

HARLAXTON COLLEGE

It is almost universally agreed that Harlaxton College is the University of Evansville's single most significant and distinctive feature. Students and faculty unfailingly regard their stay at Harlaxton College as a highlight of their association with the University. Moreover, there is unanimous agreement that without the vision and determination of President Graves, Harlaxton College would not have been possible.

Background

When Graves came to the University of Evansville from the University of the Pacific, he was eager to establish here what had been a major and successful component of the school in California, a cluster college. A cluster college, while related to the parent institution, has its own faculty, students, and campus. According to its proponents, it provides "an intimate learning community with an opportunity to experiment with new curriculum and teaching techniques and therefore attracts creative and intellectually demanding students and instructors."

Although Mr. and Mrs. Thomas J. Morton of Newburgh generously offered to donate seventy acres of land to the University to establish the proposed cluster college, it was determined that $5 million would be required to construct and operate such a school. Even though the University of Evansville brought in Larry Jackson, provost of the cluster college at the University of the Pacific, to direct the project, the conclusion was reached that this sort of experiment might become a burden, draining funds and other resources more urgently needed for the main campus. Therefore, the administration decided to seek another and more economical means of achieving similar goals.

187

Town square in Grantham, with statue of native son Sir Isaac Newton

With an academic background in political science and a strong personal interest in international studies, Graves was convinced that an overseas study program would offer a reasonable alternative to a cluster college and would broaden and enrich the educational experience the University could offer its students. Thus, in the fall of 1969, when an advertisement in *Country Life* magazine caught the president's eye, a chain of events was set in motion which led to the establishment of Harlaxton College.

The advertisement described an English country estate in Lincolnshire in the English Midlands near the town of Grantham, in the vicinity of Leicester and about 110 miles north of London. (Isaac Newton and Margaret Thatcher were born in this area.) Known as Harlaxton, the estate was owned by the Society of Jesus (Jesuits), who had used it as a seminary. When enrollment declined sharply, the Jesuits decided to lease the manor to Stanford University for its British campus, but halfway through its lease Stanford wished to terminate the agreement, preferring to be nearer to London. Indeed, most American study programs abroad are located in capital cities (London, Paris, Rome) or university towns (Heidelberg, Cambridge). Graves, however, viewed the location as an asset rather than a liability. Being near the center of England and within easy commuting distance of all parts of the British Isles, it provided a better opportunity than any urban setting for students to learn more about the English people and their culture.

Graves quickly consulted with Jackson, who strongly favored an international studies program; indeed, prior to coming to the University of Evansville, Jackson's background included considerable time in India and Chile. Within a few weeks, Graves and Jackson were on their way to England to explore possible ways such a structure might serve the new educational needs of the University.

The Building

Harlaxton Manor is situated just off the highway linking Grantham to Leicester. Except on foggy days, a visitor, turning onto the long stately driveway leading to the manor, has a stunning view of the majestic structure. The building itself has more than one hundred rooms spread over four floors. Particularly noteworthy is a crystal chandelier hanging from the vaulted ceiling of the manor's Great Hall.

The building has a fascinating history. The central structure, built for the estate's owner, Gregory Williams, dates from the years 1831-1844. When he acquired the property in 1822, Williams dropped his surname and was henceforth known as Gregory Gregory. After several years of planning and travel, collecting ideas and fittings for his new house, he commissioned architect Anthony Salvin to design a building for him in Jacobean style.

Approach to Harlaxton Manor

Salvin's proposal was ingenious and extraordinary. He suggested that the manor house be literally dug into the hillside, with the ground sloping up behind it. The main rooms were to be on the first floor and would open straight onto the garden on two sides.

However, during construction, Gregory changed his mind about the style of house he wanted. After becoming intrigued with baroque architecture, he decided to switch architects, replacing Salvin with William Burn and David Bryce, who agreed to incorporate baroque elements into the existing neo-Elizabethan/Jacobean plans. Thus, the entrance retained its Elizabethan centerpiece but was framed by gigantic piers and pavilions characteristic of baroque style.

Inside, the Great Hall and a dining room were traditional Elizabethan, while the drawing room, anteroom, and gallery reflect the baroque manner. The conservatory is a mixture of the two.

The cedar staircase is generally regarded as the glory of the manor's interior. It has been described as "baroque in conveying an impression of power, exuberance, and abundance through struggling human figures, swarming cherubs, and tasseled festoons of drapery, with a figure of Time seen unrolling a plan of Harlaxton."

Gregory moved into the house in 1851 but died three years later. The manor remained in the family until 1937, at which time it might have been demolished had it not been for the intervention of Violet Van der Elst, a wealthy eccentric who not only rescued it but also refurbished it, adding the massive chandelier in the Great Hall, the bronze lions on the front circle, and the marble lions near the foundation on the rear terrace. Unfortunately, after using up most of her fortune to lead a vigorous campaign against capital punishment, she was forced to sell the manor at a loss in 1948.

The new owners, the Jesuits, were the first to use the property as a school, and it has served this function ever since.

Throughout its existence, Harlaxton Manor has been held in high regard by architectural experts. Mark Girouard, in his volume *The Victorian*

Both UK and US flags grace the front of the manor

Country House, wrote: "Harlaxton is so amazing it must be seen to be believed and even when one has seen it, it is not always easy to believe it."

The First Year

In 1971, after negotiating with the Jesuits to take over the unexpired portion of the Stanford University lease, the University of Evansville made immediate plans to open its Harlaxton Study Center starting with the fall semester. About fifty acres of land and the buildings erected on them were included in the lease. An appropriate curriculum was needed for the new venture and, through the efforts of the University's Undergraduate Programs Committee and the Non-Western Studies Committee, a specific proposal was presented to and approved by the University Senate.

The proposal called for two semesters of classes each year, with five weeks in between for travel, field experiences, and independent study. Tuition for Harlaxton was only $200 more per year than that of the main campus, so cost would not pose a major deterrent for those wishing to study overseas.

English tutors, together with guest lecturers from Leicester, Nottingham, and other nearby English universities, were engaged to teach most of the classes, which centered mainly in the humanities and social sciences. In addition, one faculty member from the Evansville campus was to be in residence at Harlaxton each semester. Finally, an academic director was appointed to direct the entire program.

For the initial year (1971-72), the two faculty members chosen from the home campus were Bruce Bauman (history) and Michael Carson (English). The academic director was **Jeremy Rusk**, who had taught philosophy and religion at the University of Evansville for two years before being appointed to the Harlaxton position. His strong interest in

Jeremy Rusk

international education was evident in his own career; he had recently spent two years at Oxford University doing research for his doctoral dissertation at Harvard University. He was appointed for two years but remained an additional two, before returning to Harvard to complete his degree.

Rusk's first assistant, Alexandra Leich of Evansville, had recently lived and worked in London and thereby had firsthand knowledge of England and its people.

An effective academic program, however, met only part of the new center's needs. For example, various furnishings were required to accommodate students who would be living thousands of miles from their homes. Happily, a series of fortuitous circumstances solved the problem not only quickly but also inexpensively.

A hotel in nearby Leicester had recently gone out of business and was eager to sell its beds, chinaware, kitchen equipment, and silverware. Wardrobes were purchased from a dealer in Grantham who had intended to use them in residential housing, only to find that the newer flats and apartments in the area had lower ceilings than anticipated. Thus, while the wardrobes no longer

191

Students enjoying the Harlaxton Experience

fit his needs, they met Harlaxton standards perfectly. Finally, the recent closing of a nearby school enabled the University to purchase materials and books at reasonable prices.

The entering class of September 1971 numbered about eighty, even higher than anticipated and sufficient to make the program academically viable and financially self-sustaining.

The official dedication of the Harlaxton Study Center as part of the University of Evansville took place on November 27, 1971, featuring an address by Representative Edith Green of Oregon, chairman of the House Subcommittee on Education and an ardent and powerful supporter of legislation related to education. Students from the United States and Great Britain, as well as numerous officials and dignitaries, attended the ceremony.

Even during its first year, the Harlaxton Study Center experimented with innovative teaching formats. Formal class sessions were broken into small group discussions, seminars, and tutorials. Each student received individual and personal attention, and independent study was encouraged. In addition, the faculty took pride in developing interdisciplinary courses. The first of these, The Age of Enlightenment: 1650-1800, viewed the period from the perspectives of history, literature, art, economics, sociology, and philosophy. It became the model for other creative approaches to the educational process.

A library is central to a strong academic program, but building an adequate one requires considerable time. Fortunately, both Leicester and Nottingham Universities extended library privileges to Harlaxton students (as, indeed, they had to Stanford's), with free bus service provided every Friday. In addition, with the closing of a nearby teacher-training college, Stoke-Rochford, a library of several thousand volumes became available at a low cost. Finally, many individuals from Evansville contributed books from their private collections.

From the beginning, students developed a strong spirit of camaraderie with one another and with their English tutors. All gave high marks to what came to be called the Harlaxton Experience, and when the ten-year reunion was held, fifty-five members of the historic first class attended. The satisfaction of the English tutors is perhaps best indicated by the fact that all of them decided to return for a second year in 1972.

Expansion

The first year class at Harlaxton was made up entirely of University of Evansville students, there being insufficient time between February and August of 1971 to recruit from other schools. Before long, however, the University established contact with various American colleges, especially those in the United Methodist Consortium. Among schools responding during the coming years were:

Morningside College, Sioux City, Iowa
Willamette University, Salem, Oregon
William Jewell College, Liberty, Missouri
University of Wisconsin-Eau Claire
Florida Southern University,
  Lakeland, Florida
Bradley University, Peoria, Illinois

In addition to students from America, children of parents living in Europe, such as military personnel stationed in England and staff of the United States Embassy in London, attended Harlaxton. Also, the Harlaxton director of admission (which became a full-time position) visited American secondary schools in Spain, France, Germany, Austria, and Greece to spread the Harlaxton message. Students from North Africa, the Middle East, and other parts of Asia also enrolled, although, in order to keep the student population well balanced, a quota was established, limiting the number of non-American students to no more than twenty-five percent of the total.

As a result, enrollment at Harlaxton – which had dipped to seventy for the second semester – increased significantly. The fall of 1973 brought 116 students to Harlaxton. The average enrollment for the first sixteen years of the program was 125 students per semester, with the average reaching 151 toward the end of the period.

Many American institutions with students at

Archaeology dig near Harlaxton

Harlaxton were also invited to send one or more visiting faculty and their families. The participating school generally paid their salaries (as they would if the professors were teaching on the home campus), while the University of Evansville provided room and board. Children of faculty could attend the school in Grantham and thus experience the British system of elementary and secondary education. Also, from time to time, British faculty members have spent a semester teaching at the University of Evansville or another American college, sometimes replacing the professor from the home campus who was serving at Harlaxton. The end result of having visiting professors was to effectively broaden the range of choices available to Harlaxton students.

Despite the lack of laboratory facilities, courses in biology, physics, and astronomy were offered beginning with the 1973-74 academic year. Physics laboratory work was deferred until the student's return and field studies replaced laboratory work in biology.

Also beginning in 1973, a course called History and Archaeology of Roman Britain was introduced in association with the Carr Dyke Research Group (an English archaeological society) and, with the support and advice of the archaeology department at the University of Leicester, an archaeological excavation was opened at a site about ten miles from the manor. The British government's Department of the Environment also agreed to contribute financially to the project. Students in this course received classroom instruction in history and archaeological techniques, and conducted field work which required surveying, pottery recognition and dating, and conserving metal and fragile objects. The project was particularly significant because the site, which had never been excavated before, at first appeared to be the remains of a fourth century villa but later turned out to be part of an entire town, including Roman England's chief minting headquarters. Harlaxton archaeologist Brian Simmons and his student staff discovered a number of Roman

193

artifacts including coins, jewelry, pottery, and tools, many of which are on display at the manor.

Overall, the range of courses offered at Harlaxton, while not sufficient for a four-year degree program, was adequate for a two-year associate's degree, readily transferable to most colleges and universities in America. Accordingly, in 1974, when the Associate of Arts degree was first offered, it was deemed appropriate to change the name Harlaxton Study Center to Harlaxton College.

In 1975, a new lease was negotiated with the Jesuits, but three years later, University of Evansville trustee William Ridgway purchased the Harlaxton estate, with the intention of leasing it to the University and eventually making it an outright gift. A sale price of $180,000 was negotiated for the manor with its more than one hundred rooms, a stable block, a principal's cottage, an additional two-story brick house, tennis courts, and over one hundred acres. In 1987, Ridgway officially transferred ownership of Harlaxton to the University of Evansville. Although he no longer owned the property, he remained affectionately known as "the lord of the manor."

Ridgway also sponsored a scholarship for a British student to spend a year at the University of Evansville. In addition, the Wallace B. and Barbara A. Graves Scholarship was established in 1987 (at the time of Graves' retirement), providing for a semester at Harlaxton for a University of Evansville undergraduate.

Special Programs

In addition to traditional academic offerings, a special program was developed for University of Evansville nursing students in cooperation with Grantham Hospital. The experience was especially valuable in providing American student nurses with an understanding of nursing practices in Britain's government-operated health care system. This program proved so successful that subsequently Duke University, the University of Wisconsin-Eau Claire, and Indiana University sent students to Harlaxton to share this experience. (It should also be noted that for several years Indiana

University provided a graduate student to serve as Harlaxton's student life director.)

A favorite use of the Harlaxton facility involved short-term courses such as seminars and workshops during summer months. For example, in the summer of 1973 Harlaxton hosted:

- A two-week string workshop, sponsored jointly by the American String Teachers Association and the music department of the University of Evansville

- An Anglo-American choral symposium culminating in two concert performances at Grantham Parish Church

- A study of film techniques attended by students from Britain's National Film School, including the making of the film *Matushka*

- A three-week seminar for teachers sponsored by the University of Evansville School of Graduate Studies

In addition, conferences, receptions, and banquets were frequently held during the summer months. In 1986, for example, the manor was the site of the Belvoir Hunt banquet, attended by several hundred guests, including Charles, the Prince of Wales. At the same time, the famous British auction house, Christies, presented a display of materials and artifacts donated by Belvoir patrons. (Incidentally, this event yielded a profit of £1,500. Proceeds from this and similar programs aided immeasurably in ensuring that Harlaxton College remain a self-sustaining part of the University of Evansville. Indeed, revenue generated by Harlaxton has often helped to support programs on the main campus.)

Whenever possible, opportunities for Harlaxton students to become better acquainted with the Grantham community were cultivated. One

194

*Prince Charles
(third from left)
visiting
Harlaxton in
1986; shown here
with President
and Mrs. Graves,
Dr. and Mrs.
Rowlands,
and the Duke
of Rutland*

means of achieving this was a lecture and recital series, Tuesday Evenings at the Manor, open to the general public as well as to Harlaxton students and faculty. Topics ranged over a wide variety of subjects (literature, economics, etc.), and concerts offered programs not only on current instruments such as the guitar but also on instruments associated with English history such as the lute, recorder, and harpsichord. These programs took on both educational and social significance.

Travel Programs

Since its inception, Harlaxton has emphasized opportunities for foreign travel, both in the British Isles and on the continent. Among places of special interest in Great Britain were Lincoln, Cambridge, Oxford, York, Coventry, Stonehenge, Chester, Nottingham, Leicester, Edinburgh, Stratford-upon-Avon and, of course, London. The latter two offered a particularly rich variety of theatrical and musical produc-

tions. On long weekends, visits to Ireland, Paris, Florence, Rome, or Athens were arranged, and at the end of each semester, before returning home, students had the option of a longer stay in Italy, France, or Germany, or a trip to Russia which included both Moscow and Leningrad.

*Waiting for the London-
Grantham train*

195

In the early 1980s, the emphasis on travel became a source of friction between the English campus and some faculty at the home institution. To allow students ample time for travel, Harlaxton classes were held on Monday through Thursday only; but this arrangement was sometimes abused, leading to fears that academic standards would be lowered. In response, a strict attendance policy was put into effect with severe penalties for excessive absences, thus reinforcing Harlaxton's commitment to quality education.

In addition to the student travel program, an annual two-week trustees tour to the British Isles was instituted. Generally thirty to forty persons visited Harlaxton for two to three days before taking excursions to other places of interest. A tour of another country – Italy, France, or the Scandinavian nations – was often added. For several years, Isabella Fine, director of special programs for the University of Evansville, took responsibility for organizing these tours, which often attracted people from the community as well as University trustees.

Support Groups

Harlaxton College has received enthusiastic support on both sides of the Atlantic Ocean. During Harlaxton's first year, Evansville businessman and former congressman Edward Mitchell had occasion to visit the manor. As a result of this visit, he offered to sponsor a benefit at Evansville's 4-H center, with proceeds used for such purposes as augmenting Harlaxton's library. Similar benefit parties, such as receptions and auctions at New Harmony and Louisville, have continued to the present day.

Later, a support group was organized in Evansville called the Harlaxton Society. Beginning with a handful of individuals, membership soon numbered in the hundreds, with Margaret Thatcher, then prime minister, accepting honorary membership. The University's director of special projects, Isabella Fine, administered the project. The society continues to raise money for scholarships so more students can attend Harlaxton College, and it has donated substantial funds to build library resources and to pay for various Harlaxton refur-

bishments. In addition, it sponsors several annual events to raise funds for these purposes.

In 1975, **Paul Bulger**, a past president of the State University College of Education at Buffalo, New York, and a former State Department consultant on overseas education, became Harlaxton's principal (the first to hold that title). Although already retired, he agreed to devote two years to being Harlaxton's chief administrator. Probably his most significant contribution was the formation of a British Advisory Council, originally consisting of three members but eventually increasing to nearly twenty. It came to include members of the aristocracy (Sir Simon and Lady Margaret Benton-Jones, the Duke of Rutland, and Princess Diana's sister, Sarah McCourquodale), business, professional, religious, and civic leaders from Grantham and other nearby towns and villages, and academicians from Cambridge, Leicester, and Nottingham Universities. The British Advisory Council functioned as an informal board of trustees for Harlaxton College, with standing committees on academic affairs, student life, estate management and maintenance, and long-range planning. The council also assisted the University of Evansville in diverse ways, helping it to qualify for restoration funds from various British boards, locating host families for students, advising the principal concerning estate management and new construction, and recruiting staff. The chair of the advisory council since 1981 has been Lady Margaret Benton-Jones.

Renovation and New Building

Graddon Rowlands

Since it became Harlaxton College, significant renovations and new building activity have taken place at the manor. In 1977, **Graddon Rowlands**, an Englishman with a doctorate from Duke University, became Harlaxton College's principal. Rowlands and his wife, Pamela, took particular interest in restoring

A welcome source of revenue for Harlaxton came from film producers who found the manor to be a suitable backdrop for several television and movie productions. Indeed, between July 5 and August 5, 1971, even before the first students arrived, the manor was used to film *The Ruling Class* starring Peter O'Toole. In addition to the $10,000 fee, the publicity brought the Harlaxton name before the public. Fifteen years later, the campus was used again as the setting for Paramount Pictures' *The Last Days of Patton* (pictured here), which starred George C. Scott. In addition, part of the BBC series *The Fall of the Eagles*, the American mini-series *Spaces*, and some scenes from *Dangerous Love* and *The Dark Angel* were filmed at Harlaxton Manor.

the manor to its original state of elegance, starting with the great Victorian conservatory. It now serves as both a reception area for formal occasions and a quiet place for study.

Later, several other rooms – the Long Gallery, the Blue Room, the Family Dining Room, the Stable Block, the Red Room, and Great Hall (with its walk-in fireplace) – were redecorated, and a lounge was fashioned from a former billiard room, all accomplished through generous gifts from trustees and friends of the University, especially William L. Ridgway, Mr. and Mrs. John H. Schroeder, Dr. and Mrs. Charles H. Klamer, Mr. and Mrs. R.O. Clutter, Mr. and Mrs. George E. Powell Jr., and Mrs. Norman Shane Jr.

Two significant structures have been added to the Harlaxton College estate. The first followed the introduction of physical education to the Col-

lege curriculum. In 1976-77, a program in equestrian studies was introduced; this soon expanded to include individual sports (badminton, fencing, squash, cross country, yoga, and tennis), as well as team sports (basketball, soccer, and rugby), and even dance. As these activities increased in popularity, the University constructed a separate athletic facility, Sports Hall, built at a cost of $150,000. Located near the cottage area, it houses all sports and recreation activities, and includes a large gym, a weight room, ping-pong tables, plus facilities for yoga and aerobic instruction.

The proliferation of courses at Harlaxton College also required additional library facilities. Accordingly, in 1985, a new library opened, with 15,000 volumes, besides slides, music tapes, and other materials. Later, an elaborate computer complex became part of the library operation.

197

Harlaxton College library

Conclusions

In nearly every respect, Harlaxton College's contribution has been impressive. The program is important to the cultural, social, and economic life of the East Midlands (for example, it adds some £2 million annually to the local economy), making the University of Evansville even better known in England than it is in the United States. In America too, Harlaxton has made new friends for the University through the many students from other institutions who have attended.

Nevertheless, there has been criticism of some aspects of the Harlaxton College program. Between 1971 and 1986, only about one-third of the students attending Harlaxton College came from the University of Evansville, and in only four of those years did University of Evansville students constitute a majority of the student body. More-

IN MEMORY

Most events at Harlaxton College have been happy ones; but note must be taken of a 1982 automobile accident on the estate in which six Harlaxton students were killed. Six poplar trees were planted in their memory along the main drive by the side of the soccer field, and two benches in the Carriage House courtyard have plaques attached to the seats bearing their names.

One of several lions that guard the grounds of the manor

over, since only 2.2 percent of the total number of day students enrolled at the University of Evansville spent time at Harlaxton, it was labeled by a few as a mere service facility for other colleges rather than as a vital service to its own students.

Overall, however, the Harlaxton venture is generally rated by the University community as a resounding success. Its impact cannot be measured simply in terms of enrollment or revenue generated. Rather, through the Harlaxton Experience, students have broadened their perspectives, and the reputation of the University of Evansville as a worldwide institution has been enhanced. Harlaxton College has also exerted a positive influence on the intellectual climate of the Evansville campus, aiding recruitment by attracting students seeking a college which offers distinctive programs. Indeed, the Graves administration will probably be best remembered for Harlaxton. In every possible way, it has proved an invaluable asset to the University of Evansville.

OTHER INTERNATIONAL PROGRAMS

In 1982, the Saudi Arabian Project for employees of the Saudi Arabian Agricultural Bank was established at the University of Evansville. Fully funded by the Saudi Ministry of Finance, the pro-

gram offered classes in English, management, agriculture, and computer software. After completing their classes, the students trained in area banks or on farms for three months. This project continued until 1989.

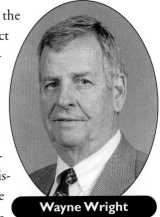

Wayne Wright

The success of the Saudi Arabian project led to the establishment of the International Institute which facilitated bringing students from other nations to the Evansville campus. Administered by UE's College of Alternative Programs, it was directed by Wayne Wright, who served in this position until his death in 2003.

An important service of the International Institute was its Intensive English Center. It offered both credit and non-credit courses enabling students from abroad to develop the level of English proficiency required for college work.

The program proved immediately valuable. Between 1983 and 1986, over ninety Malaysian students entered University of Evansville degree programs under the sponsorship of their government, which was eager for the students to learn methods of western technology. As late as 1990, over fifty students from Malaysia were enrolled in engineering and computer classes at UE.

Beginning in 1985, the International Institute negotiated several short-term contracts with schools and businesses in Japan. The first of these was with Niijima Gakuen Women's Junior College in Takasaki. It sent fourteen students to the Evansville campus for three weeks of study, with increasing numbers in succeeding years. Later, programs with Japanese institutions have included Anabuki College (eight-week English study), Nissho Foundation (eight-week English study and one-week business program), and Hiroshima Jogakuin and Takoha Gakuen Universities. Students came to participate in short cross-cultural programs and one-year academic and English study.

199

STUDENT LIFE

In 1967, when Evansville College became the University of Evansville, student life was much as it had been for many years. But within a short time, dramatic changes took place. For example, in 1967, a campus-wide dress code explicitly spelled out what students should wear and strict rules dealt with campus housing, automobiles, and student conduct.

The 1967 Student Handbook specified dress for both men and women in various areas of the campus, including the dining center, the union building, the library, and Administration Hall. Women could wear slacks only when the temperature was below zero and in Harper Dining Center during final examinations. Women could wear "Bermuda (knee-length) shorts or slacks, and sandals or shoes" on Saturdays and in the library during evenings and on weekends. Either campus dress or sportswear could be worn at all times in the union. Men had considerably fewer restrictions.

In 1969, campus residents circulated a petition suggesting that "college students should have the right to choose their dress according to personal good taste as long as it is not a health hazard to their fellow students." The following year the Student Senate recommended a self-regulatory dress code. The University agreed, and since 1973 there has been no formal dress code for students.

Another major change at the University involved campus housing. In 1967, the University required all students to live in University housing, except for those living at home and upper classmen living in fraternity houses. A year later, the Uni-

200

A tree in the south oval has cradled hundreds of scholars

versity allowed students twenty-one years of age or older to live in housing of their own choice. By 1974, only incoming freshmen (except those living at home) were required to live in University housing their first year. After the freshman year, all students could live in housing of their own choice.

In addition, there were fewer restrictions for those living on campus. One area of change concerned hours for women students in residence halls, along with the issue of visitation by male students in women's rooms. In 1967, regulations required women to sign out of their residence hall, giving their destination and time of return (no later than 11:00 p.m. on week nights and Sundays). Failure to meet this requirement brought disciplinary action from the dean of women or dean of students. Male resident students did not have a corollary rule.

Many women were indignant, asking "If our parents trust us, why doesn't the University?" And the *Crescent* declared, "Let's consider women as morally sound and responsible as men."

By the end of the 1968-69 academic year, hours had been changed to allow sophomores to return one hour later than freshmen; juniors and seniors were allowed to set their own hours, but if they were under 21, their parents had to give permission before extended hours could take effect. Within a few years all women students were free to choose

Just one light load, with many more to follow

201

their own hours, with the exception of freshmen, whose hours were restricted and set by their parents.

In accepting this liberalization of women's hours, President Graves stated to the Board of Trustees that the social code of a campus "must reflect the views and collaboration of parents as well as those of students and administrators." He also indicated how grateful he was that students here "are not clamoring for so-called visitation rights in dormitories, and I want the board to understand that I deplore such practices on other campuses and will resist any effort to establish them here."

But almost as soon as he had said it, students began "clamoring" for such rights. In February 1970, the Student Affairs Committee of the Student Government Association asked the University to approve visitation rights in all campus housing units on Friday nights and Sunday afternoons. The Administrative Board approved it in March and sent it to Graves, who delayed a decision by turning it over to the recently established Student Affairs Committee of the Board of Trustees. In June 1970, the board approved a motion which required each residence hall to vote on whether to have a visitation policy and if so what hours to establish. Any student not wishing to participate, even if her hall decided to do so, would have the right to make her room "off-limits for guests at any time." Although some parents and alumni might have been upset by these changes, the *Crescent* declared: "These decisions show the administration is approachable and receptive to the student voice and not totally aloof and unreasonable, reflecting the University's potential for change without bitterness and repression."

In 1972, the University initiated its first experiment with "proximity housing." Eighty women moved into formerly all-male Hughes Hall, to make it the first coed residence hall on the campus. The plan was implemented in response to students who believed that those choosing the arrangement were mature enough to cope with any problems that might arise.

Other areas of student behavior were also reexamined. The 1967 Student Handbook included only three brief paragraphs on the subject of student conduct. These suggested that students were expected to show "the character and maturity of responsible students in a university community," giving the University the right to expel any student whose "conduct or attitude the University believes to be detrimental to the welfare of the institution." The only activities specifically prohibited were "gambling and the use or possession of alcoholic beverages (including beer), whether on campus or in fraternity houses." The following year the "illegal use or possession of narcotics" was also strictly prohibited. In all other areas, the administration enjoyed a great deal of latitude in determining which activities were "detrimental to the welfare of the institution."

However, both students and administration felt the need for more detailed guidelines governing student conduct and for greater involvement by the students in the daily life of the institution. In addition to the Student Affairs Committee of the Board of Trustees, chaired by Leroy Hodapp '44, each year the senior class elected a classmate to serve a three-year term on the Board of Trustees.

The 1970 Student Handbook included a statement on "Rights, Freedoms, and Responsibilities." Approved by the Student Senate, the Academic Senate, and the Board of Trustees, this document listed fifteen major offenses which might result in disciplinary action. In addition to the prohibition on gambling and the use of alcohol and drugs, the list included:

Dishonesty, such as cheating and plagiarism

Damage to University property and alteration or misuse of University documents or records

Obstruction or disruption of teaching

Disorderly conduct, vandalism, or lewd or immoral conduct or expression

Unauthorized possession of firearms, explosives, dangerous chemicals, or other weapons

Violation of any state, federal, or local law or ordinance on or off campus (added in 1973)

Student catching up on her reading

dent Graves, however, reversed their decision and ordered White to resign his position. "The possession or use of narcotics is contrary to University regulations and condemned by faculty, administration, alumni, and trustees," said Graves, who added: "I also believe that the majority of our students do not take pride in the arrest and conviction of their president on a narcotics charge. When members of student government assume the responsibilities of leadership, they forego the freedom to act solely in accord with their personal values and desires."

Many students protested Graves' decision, claiming that White had been treated arbitrarily and unfairly, and asking Graves to reverse his decision. Graves refused, but White retained his office because of a "textual flaw" in the Administrative Board rules.

The 1970 statement documenting student rights, freedoms and responsibilities also guaranteed an uncensored student press, the right of "recognized student organizations" to freely select guest speakers for their programs, and protection against improper academic evaluation.

Specifically, University rules assured students that their grade "must be determined by testing and/or performance of work" and could no longer be lowered solely for being absent from class. Also, students could take some classes on a pass-fail basis without affecting their grade point average. Many did.

In turn, students pledged that any demonstrations they wished to hold would be orderly and not jeopardize the University's programs. Also, student editors agreed to act responsibly and observe "the canons of good journalism." (However, no definition of this term was ever stated.) Symbolic of the changing times, beer ads were accepted by the *Crescent* for the first time in 1970, and an advertisement for a New York abortion service appeared as well.

Next, the handbook specified the due process procedure to which each student was entitled. Although the process was complex and perhaps cumbersome, its purpose was to protect the rights of all students. A major test of the process involved the 1971 arrest of the Student Government Association president, Joe White, for possession of marijuana. After White received a thirty-day suspended sentence, the question arose as to whether he should be removed from his office as SGA president. The personnel committee of the student affairs office recommended that White be placed on disciplinary probation but later suspended the probation. Presi-

203

UE students exercise their free speech rights, early 1970s

Also, in keeping with the times, protests similar to those being held on other college campuses were held on the University of Evansville campus. A major issue was the undeclared war then raging in Vietnam. On October 15, 1969, the campus observed National Moratorium Day in protest of the Vietnam War, including a class boycott, silent meditation, prayer, and folk singing; a follow-up anti-war demonstration was staged one-and-a-half years later.

In an altogether different political mood, a group of students expressed support for the U.S. government on election day in 1980 by setting fire to an Iranian flag in response to Iran's holding of American citizens as hostages.

204

CAMPUS PROTEST

Although the University of Evansville campus was peaceful compared to many others across the nation, there were tense moments nonetheless. President Graves recalled one example:

For a number of years, the University of Evansville sponsored a U.S. Air Force ROTC program. Until the war in Vietnam began, this program was quite popular.

The culmination of the year's ROTC activities was a military review shortly before the University's commencement ceremony. It was quite an event, with graduates in full military regalia and a reviewing stand draped in patriotic bunting and populated by faculty, guests from the military reserve, the city mayor, and me. A marching band often was included and always a color guard adding its special flair.

On the occasion I have in mind, a group of our students, dressed as babies (diapers and all), decided to cavort around the marching cadets, yelling silly epithets. Their idea was to demonstrate how juvenile it is to dress in military uniforms and parade about, actually how juvenile warfare is. Theirs was an anti-Vietnam War statement.

I was greatly embarrassed sitting on the reviewing stand, with the harassers coming dangerously close to disrupting the cadence of the marching cadets. Of course, the whole scene was abhorrent to our guests. I was about to break up the demonstration, like the Lone Ranger, when the ROTC commandant suggested: "Let's wait a minute to see if we can get through the review without seeming to be upset." Grudgingly, I agreed, and although the visiting major general had some nasty remarks to share with me, we lived through the demonstration.

But I couldn't let it go at that. The demonstrators had denied the ROTC its special moment, and I thought that was unfair. So, on Monday I called three or four of the student demonstrators whom I knew into my office. I told them that, while I did not intend to take any action against them, I thought they had taken unfair advantage of the cadets by ridiculing the parade. After all, the ROTC had never tried to break up any of their anti-war meetings or activities, and I thought each ought to respect the rights of the other. The young men left the office looking as if they had narrowly missed being executed by the lord high chancellor, and I felt better having expressed my feelings to the demonstrators.

And what do you know? A year later at commencement time, a graduate's father came up to me to say that his son had told him about our meeting. The young man told his father he appreciated my courtesy and the trouble I had taken to explain my position in this matter. The father dittoed those remarks, and I deeply appreciated his message.

Perhaps we should never despair about the future of our younger generation!

205

The Wooden Indian, c. 1985

Another series of protests similar to those on other campuses involved race. Unquestionably, there were racial problems on campus. In October 1966, a Ku Klux Klan symbol appeared on the second floor of Hughes Hall; the house mother said it was done "absentmindedly." Black students disagreed, however, claiming that since the symbol was displayed in the only predominantly black section of the residence hall, it was premeditated. In response to their concerns, the University agreed in 1968 to establish a course in African American history, agreeing also to attempt to recruit an additional seventy-five black students for the fall of 1968 and to raise this number to 300 the following year. In addition, the University promised to provide a maximum of five scholarships to qualified Evansville-area black students and to investigate possible discrimination by University fraternities and sororities. In 1969, black students also asked Graves to recruit black instructors, to inaugurate a black social studies program, and to recognize a separate campus organization for black students. Accordingly, the formation of the Black Student Union was approved later that year.

Overall, during these years, the University of Evansville campus was, in the words of Graves,

206

"blessed by order and constructive harmony in a period of unprecedented strife and destruction on campuses coast to coast." He attributed this to the fact that the University's student body was comprised of men and women "anxious to learn and prepare themselves for useful professions and fruit-

Considerable controversy also arose regarding the University's drinking policy. In 1984, the Student Association formulated a policy allowing alcohol in certain areas during supervised events. President Graves refused to accept it because of the value orientation of the University, and because most students were under twenty-one. Then, the University changed its policy for non-student groups using campus facilities, but when several students protested the double standard, Graves acknowledged the validity of their complaint. From then on alcohol on campus was banned altogether.

ful lives." In addition, he noted, "the tradition of the University has discouraged extremist students and faculty members from coming here, while faculty and administration have doubled their efforts to maintain an atmosphere which is open, intimate, and humane."

Enrollment

Between 1965 and 1980, full-time day enrollment remained steady at around 3,000, with total registration around 5,000. The fall of 1980 saw an all-time high of 856 new freshmen. But after this peak, a significant decline occurred with day attendance dipping to 2,458 in 1985, total enrollment falling to 4,033, and the number of entering students reaching only 451. These figures were the lowest in twenty-two years.

During the early 1970s, the number of students from outside the immediate area significantly increased, so that by 1974 campus residence halls were filled to capacity. By 1981, however, occupancy began to decline, dropping to only seventy-one percent of capacity in 1986.

Financial Aid

It has long been known that state universities cannot operate any more cheaply than private institutions. Indeed, well-managed private institutions often do better than their publicly-supported counterparts. Only generous subsidies from taxpayers' money enable state institutions to charge lower tuition. It is the constant hope of the private sector that various forms of financial aid (work-study programs, loans, etc.) from state and federal sources will successfully bridge the gap, thus allowing students to lessen the issue of cost as a factor in choosing a school.

In 1919, Evansville College offered its students only six $50 scholarships. Additionally, students could borrow from the Methodist Student Loan Fund up to a maximum of $2,000. Eleven years later, twenty-five scholarship of one hundred dollars per year for four years (one-half of tuition) were authorized for freshmen from Evansville-area high schools. By 1970, however, the Office of Financial

Aid was dispersing more than $2 million annually, with fifty-nine percent of the student body receiving some kind of student aid. Aid took the form of scholarships, national defense loans, the Federal Nursing Loan, and the federal work-study program. Within a decade, the total financial aid awarded each year had increased to over $6 million, with the average amount per student equaling the total amount given in scholarships fifty years earlier.

During the 1960s, the University successfully and fully met the financial needs of its student body. Then, severe cuts were made in funds for education, both at the state and federal levels, so that by the fall of 1981, the University could meet only eighty percent of the freshman class need and only sixty-five percent of the needs of returning students. This reduction in governmental financial assistance imposed a severe hardship upon the University for several years to come.

Religious Activity

Religious activity continued to be an important part of campus life. During the late 1960s and the 1970s, services at Neu Chapel varied, some being traditional (organ, choir, sermon) while others used a non-traditional (jazz, contemporary Christian music, drama) format. As now, students, especially pre-theology majors, often arranged and conducted the services.

In the early and mid 1980s, the University's religious life program shifted its emphasis to service projects in the Evansville area, such as Habitat for Humanity and Patchwork Central, and to missions. Over the Christmas break of

Wayne Perkins

1984-85, an international dimension was added when Wayne Perkins and Philip Ott led a group of about ten students to Haiti to do construction work and improve sanitation. Visiting Haiti, where eighty percent of the population is illiterate,

SPEAKERS

A further outgrowth of the task force project of 1970 was the Informal Learning Sequence (ILS). The University already had the Richard E. Meier Foundation Lecture Series, which had brought in such speakers as John Kenneth Galbraith, Vance Packard, Art Buchwald, and Arthur Schlesinger Jr. However, Vice President Harris believed that some less formal presentations by speakers interacting with students in relaxed and intimate settings would be beneficial. Presenters met with students, often in the classroom, for discussion and exchange of viewpoints. Such speakers were highly qualified but less celebrated and therefore more affordable than those previously brought to campus. ILS speakers often spent a day or two on campus rather than the usual two to three hours.

FILMS

A film series emphasizing movies dealing with social issues, hence called Cinema Sociology, began in 1981. (In 1987, it became known as the UE Fine Film Society.) Each film was followed by a discussion. The entire series was open to the community at no charge.

sixty percent is unemployed, and the infant mortality rate is fifty percent, provided an eye-opening opportunity for middle-class American students to learn firsthand about the difficulties facing millions of people in developing countries.

A year later they returned to Haiti with eleven students and four leaders: Perkins, Father Carl Roos (director of the Newman Center), Sister Kimberly Lorey (Holy Spirit Catholic Church), and Charles Klamer (a medical doctor and University of Evansville trustee).

They organized an even more ambitious mission trip to Zimbabwe in 1986-87. First, $28,000 had to be raised for travel, lodging, meals, and materials to achieve the group's major goal, renovating the kitchen for the Nyadire Methodist Hospital Compound. In addition to Perkins, Ott, and Klamer, the mission's leaders included James Dawson, vice president for student affairs (later president of Tennessee Wesleyan College and Coker College in South Carolina).

After graduation, many University of Evansville students who participated in these mission trips were inspired to continue their efforts to help the poor and needy.

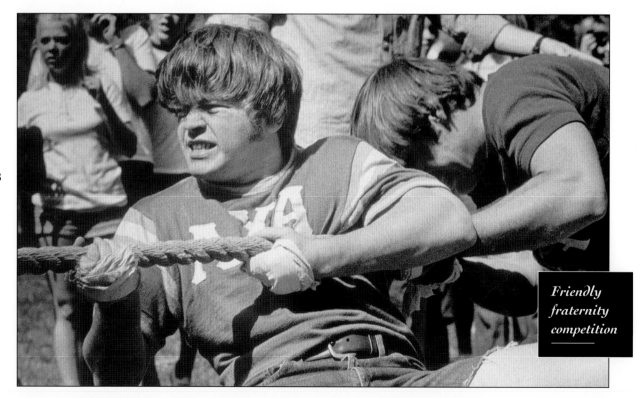

Friendly fraternity competition

ATHLETICS

Football

In 1966, Coach Paul Beck asked to be relieved of his responsibilities. He was replaced by his assistant coach, Jim Byers, an Evansville native who had gone on to football fame at the University of Michigan. During his eleven years as head coach, Byers' record was fifty-one wins, fifty losses, and three ties, making him the most successful coach in the history of Evansville football. Byers led his teams to four conference championships in his final six years as head coach. The highlight of his tenure was the 1974 season, when the team won eight games, lost two, and received a bid to play in the NCAA Division III play-offs, which they lost to Central Iowa, 17-16. Byers resigned after the 1976 season to become the University's athletics director.

An important question of these years regarded the level of competition at which the football team should play. Previously, all teams had played at the College Division level, which included most of the smaller colleges in the country. But when the NCAA established three divisions, the University had to decide on the future direction of its athletic programs. Basketball, so successful at the College Division or Division II level, might compete in Division I, while the football program would have much greater success if it could play at the Division III level, as it had in the successful season of 1974. Although the NCAA would allow the football program to compete at a different level than the basketball program, and even though the decision to change divisions was related more directly to basketball, it nonetheless had an effect on the football program.

The original decision was to keep football at the Division III level, which according to new NCAA regulations meant phasing out the University's football scholarships. That decision coincided with the appointment of a new head coach, John Moses, who served during the 1977-79 seasons. His record of 6-25 led to his dismissal and the appointment of Randy Rodgers as his successor at the beginning of the 1980 season. It was also decided at that time to move the program to Division II in association with the long-awaited decision to

Football practice

construct a football facility on campus. By the time the fund-raising effort for the new stadium was underway in 1984, questions were still being raised about the future of football. Coach Rodgers' four-year record of 17-32-3 led to his dismissal after the 1984 season, but the University decided to stay at the Division II level. After a 2-8 record in the 1985 season under the new coach, Dave Moore, the University decided to drop to Division III, a decision which saved the University $100,000 by discontinuing its football scholarships.

Soccer

On January 24, 1974, William Vieth, a former All-American soccer player at St. Louis University and an official at Citizens National Bank in Evansville, made a report to the Athletics Committee at the University of Evansville, seeking varsity status for men's soccer. The report presented a prospective schedule for the fall of 1974 which included Ball State, DePauw, Earlham, Wabash, Southern Illinois, Indiana State, and Butler. As the program improved, other Midwestern schools with nationally ranked programs, such as Eastern Illinois, Indiana, St. Louis, Quincy, and Southern Illinois-Edwardsville, could be added. The team, with Vieth as its first volunteer coach, would play its home games behind Carson Center, north of the baseball diamond. The first players would be current students with previous soccer experience.

The following month, soccer was granted varsity status, particularly because, as President Graves stated, "Interest has been stimulated by our involvement in international studies, both at the Harlaxton Study Center in England and through foreign students here at the University." Arad McCutchan, director of athletics, commented that "While other colleges and universities are looking for a chance to eliminate some sports, we are able to adopt a new varsity sport."

The first year, the team won three and lost eight, followed by seasons of 6-6 and 3-8 under Coach Vieth. In 1977, the University hired Bob Gaudin, former soccer coach at Evansville Day School, who led the team to its first winning record, 9-2. Gaudin concluded, "We have accomplished what we set out to do this year and that was to build a solid Division I soccer program."

Average attendance was 300 per game, with the final game drawing 1,000. The program really took off in 1978 with a record of 13-6, finishing the season ranked twentieth in the nation. The Aces played top-rated Indiana and St. Louis at Bosse Field; the Indiana game drew 5,200 fans. After the game Vieth said, "This one did it for sure; ... it proved that the University of Evansville belongs with the best in college soccer. It simply proved what we've known all along ... that Bob Gaudin has done the finest job in the country." Indiana coach Jerry Yeagley agreed when he observed that "on a given day the Aces could defeat any team."

Jon Halliwill (left) and head coach Fred Schmalz get ready for the start of soccer practice; Halliwill was the goalkeeper on UE's 1985 NCAA Final Four team, and later served as an assistant coach

Soccer team captains Joe Kofron (left) and Mick Lyon (right) celebrate UE's first league tournament championship, 1987

Unfortunately, Gaudin's success was a factor in his dismissal when the University decided the program needed a full-time coach who could also teach physical education. Gaudin did not have a master's degree and therefore could not be hired in the physical education department. Nevertheless, he had been responsible for establishing a solid Division I program, which his successor, Fred Schmalz, former coach at Wyoming University and at Davis and Elkins (West Virginia), would continue.

The highlight of Schmalz's first season, 1979, in which the final record was 9-5-6, was a victory over number-one ranked Alabama A&M, 1-0. During his first four seasons, the team averaged about 1,000 fans per game and had a combined record of 32-19-12. The program reached extraor-

dinary heights in the 1982 season when the Aces had a record of 15-3-4, tying Indiana University 1-1. The Aces finished fourteenth in the nation and received a bid to the NCAA post-season tournament, losing a hard-fought first-round game to Indiana in Bloomington, 1-0.

From 1982 to 1991, the team continued to build its already strong reputation. It had a record of 172-40-19, received nine bids to the NCAA tournament, reached the NCAA Final Four in 1985 and 1990, and held a number-one ranking in the country for part of two seasons. Throughout that time, the Aces were in the top twenty during part of every season. Schmalz was Soccer America's Coach of the Year in 1985 and a finalist for the National Soccer Coaches Association of America Coach of the Year award.

Among the best Soccer players for the Aces during this period were:

- Papa Jobe, third leading scorer, even though he played for only two years (1977-78)

- Second team All-Americans Just Jensen and John Nunes (1982)

- Third team All-Americans Dan McHugh, Mike Mikes, and Andrew Norton (1985)

- Senior Bowl participants (in addition to Jobe and Nunes) Frank D'Amelio, Dan Jenkerson, Gerard Homer, Scott Westbrook, and Rob Schoenstein (1978)

The development of soccer at the University of Evansville is a remarkable story of progress from its beginnings in 1974 to becoming one of the best soccer programs in the nation. Not only did the team achieve an impressive win-loss record, but attendance at Aces games remained in the top ten among all college soccer programs in the country. This accomplishment more than fulfilled Bill Vieth's hope that soccer "would be a credit to the University, the students, and the city."

211

Richie Johnson grabs a rebound against Butler. Johnson helped lead the 1982 Purple Aces to their first Division I NCAA Tournament appearance

Men's Basketball

After its successful season of 1970-71, concluding with a fifth national championship (more than any other college in Division II), many began to wonder if it might be time to move the basketball program to Division I. Some impetus for that move had occurred in 1968 when the two state-supported members of the Indiana Collegiate Conference, Indiana State University and Ball State University, decided to leave the conference and change their status to Division I. That situation, added to the fact that Butler University was already in Division I, caused some members of the Athletics Committee to press for a change in status. The immediate decision, however, was to remain in Division II but to attempt to add new members to keep the conference strong. The two new schools added were Wabash College and Indiana Central College, institutions similar in size and type to the remaining members.

That situation might have continued except for a decision by the NCAA to separate the former small-college category into two separate divisions, Division II and Division III. Division II comprised schools that, while not strong enough to compete at the highest level, still wanted to award athletic scholarships, while Division III was designed for those wanting to compete without providing athletic scholarships. Wabash and DePauw chose Division III; the remaining schools – Valparaiso, St. Joseph, Indiana Central, and Evansville – chose Division II.

In choosing Division II, the football program, which was becoming competitive at the Division III level as indicated by its successful season of 1974, would have to become Division II also. Increased costs of competing at that level, along with lower attendance associated with less competitive teams, could create financial problems for the football program. Whereas, if the basketball program became Division I, the football program could remain at Division III. That factor, as well as the feeling that membership in the ICC was no longer attractive to local basketball teams, led to serious consideration of a change in status.

Attendance statistics suggested a major problem:

1964-65	149,713	(A record)
1970-71	93,743	(A significant decline, despite being a championship season)
1972-73	68,773	
1974-75	63,066	

Declining attendance was serious because the subsequent loss of revenue would impact the entire athletic program. This situation led the Athletics Committee to consider three options. The first was to move slowly, trying to keep the ICC in operation, encouraging Butler, Wabash, and DePauw to seek Division II status, continuing the Division II finals in Evansville, and making every effort to bolster the basketball schedule by securing "name" schools to supplement the basketball schedule. Remaining in Division II would keep the NCAA tournament here as well as raising hopes for a sixth national championship. However, name schools that could boost attendance might not play here because of a rule restricting them to only six games against Division II schools.

The second option was to actively seek a new conference affiliation, thereby gaining Division I status. Possible conference affiliates included Butler, Valparaiso, St. Louis, Bradley, Louisville, Drake, Detroit, Cincinnati, Marquette, DePaul, Xavier, Loyola, and Indiana State. The proposed conference would be for basketball only, with the hope that the ICC would remain in existence for all other sports. The new basketball conference would allow the University to compete against similar schools with the hope that the conference might achieve a strong enough status to give the winner an automatic berth in the NCAA Division I basketball tournament. Unfortunately, this option would place other sports in a tenuous position, for there was no guarantee other ICC schools would consent to continuing a conference without basketball. That would create serious scheduling difficulties. Moreover, it might cost the University

some $50,000 in additional funds for recruiting, scouting, and basketball assistants.

The third option was to commit to Division I immediately so that by the 1976-77 season, seventy-five percent of the schools on the UE schedule would be Division I, as required by the NCAA. This option might be the only way to upgrade the schedule to Division I status, but it could be disastrous to other less competitive sports by forcing them to compete at the Division I level. The costs of this option would be the same as those of option two, except for additional guarantees of at least $15,000 per team to get established Division I schools to come to Evansville.

After considering these alternatives, the Athletics Committee decided on option three, to announce its intention to petition the NCAA for Division II status in football by June 1, 1978, and to Division I basketball as soon as scheduling could be arranged. In March 1976, the Board of Trustees approved the University's admission to a new conference "efficiently located geographically and comprised of intermediate-size private universities of good quality like the University of Evansville." Such a conference would give the University "greater stimulation and challenge than teams at the Division II level are likely to provide" and at a cost of no more than $17,000 more than current expenditures, costs which should be more than offset by improved receipts.

In September 1976, the NCAA approved the University's petition to become Division I in basketball during the 1977-78 season. On January 8, 1977, a night he was being honored for his recent 500th basketball victory, Arad McCutchan, believing that a new coach should lead the team in its first season in Division I, announced his retirement at the end of the season.

A search for a successor led to the decision to hire Jerry Sloan, former All-American during the championship seasons of 1964-65. He accepted, but six days later decided to decline the offer. A month later Bobby Watson, assistant coach at Oral Roberts, was named the new head coach. He asserted that "winning Division I basketball will

213

come in time. The University is a Division I school from the administration right down through the student body. I will do whatever it takes to generate a winning program." With that objective in mind and with considerable enthusiasm and optimism within the Evansville community, the University embarked on what it hoped would be a new athletic era. Soon after, however, these hopes and dreams would be shattered in a most agonizing and tragic way.

THE CRASH AND ITS AFTERMATH

Evansville Aces Basketball 1977-78

214   *Left to right, front row* Associate Coach Mark Sandy, Associate Coach Stafford Stephenson, Head Coach Bobby Watson, Associate Coach Ernie Simpson, Student Coach Scott Doerner

Middle row Tony Winburn, Kevin Kingston, Mike Joyner, John Ed Washington, Kraig Heckendorn, Greg Smith, Mark Siegel

Back row Bryan Taylor, Barney Lewis, Steve Miller, Ray Comandella, Keith Moon, Mike Duff, Warren Alston

The months of anticipation of a new era for UE basketball came to a close on December 3, 1977, when the new Purple Aces, clad in white and purple rather than the old orange uniforms of the McCutchan era, took the floor to host an old rival, Western Kentucky University. Enthusiasm and excitement ran high as the fans eagerly awaited the beginning of Division I basketball under new coach Bobby Watson. The coach spent the previous eight months recruiting players as well as speaking at least 115 times to community groups, hoping to instill spirit and support for his team. Although the Aces lost that game 82-72, the fervor appeared to be back among the famous Red Shirts of the glory years, and it appeared to be only a matter of time until a winning Division I program would be a reality. After a second defeat at DePaul, the Aces returned to Roberts Stadium to win its first Division I game over Pittsburgh, 90-83. After a road defeat against a strong Indiana State team, led by Larry Bird, the Aces were ready to embark on a road trip to play Middle Tennessee State University in Murfreesboro on December 14, 1977.

But the hopes and dreams of this new era in Aces basketball were shattered on the evening of December 13 when the DC-3 airplane carrying the team to the game crashed shortly after take-off from Evansville's Dress Regional Airport, killing all on board.

Following the tragedy, the most immediate task of University leaders was to respond quickly and compassionately to the grief consuming the University community. Although other institutions had faced similar tragedies – including the loss of California Polytechnic's football team in 1960, Wichita State's football team in 1970, and Marshall University's football team the same year – no institution is prepared for such a tragedy, and each has to search for the most appropriate ways to respond. Indeed, Marshall's president, Robert B. Hayes, called Graves to offer whatever help he and his staff could provide.

Another immediate need was to inform the families of the victims and to console them in whatever way possible. Members of the University staff, including President Graves, athletics director Jim Byers, vice president for student affairs Thornton Patberg, and former coach Arad McCutchan, spent the evening at the community center identifying bodies of the victims and trying to comfort their families and friends. All of those involved agreed with McCutchan's observation that "I've never had to face anything like this before."

It was also decided to open Neu Chapel to the campus community and to conduct a brief memorial service there the next day. At that service an estimated 1,000 people crowded into Neu Chapel, into classrooms in the basement, into stairways,

IN MEMORIAM

Coach
Bobby Watson

Players
Warren Alston
Ray Comendella
Mike Duff
Kraig Heckendorn
Michael Joyner
Kevin Kingston
Barney Lewis
Stephen Miller
Keith Moon
Mark Siegel
Greg Smith
Bryan Taylor
John Ed Washington
Tony Winburn

Student Managers
Jeff Bohnert
Mark Kirkpatrick
Mark Kniese

UE Athletic Business Manager
Bob Hudson

UE Controller
Chuck Shike

UE Sports Information Director
Greg Knipping

Sportscaster
Marv Bates

Aces supporters
Charles Goad
Maurice King

Five members of the crew

215

and outside to hear a 35-minute tribute to those who died. On this occasion President Graves stated, "We should not forget this tragedy, but we must do our best in the days ahead to develop our potentialities, to love God, and to carry on for them."

The chapel, available for private meditation and prayer as well as for a public memorial service, served as both a rallying point for the University

BOB HUDSON

Picture a big old bulldog with a twinkle in his eye. That is how one of his many friends remembers Bob Hudson. From 1955 until he died in the 1977 airplane crash, Hudson was business manager for athletics.

But Bob Hudson did much more than pay bills. He was a marketing, publicity, and promotions whiz before anyone used those job titles in college athletics. He knew more people in Evansville than the mayor. He was ticket manager and fund-raiser. His day in the office started at 6:00 a.m. "I can get more done between six and eight than I can the rest of the day," Hudson explained.

For twenty years, he directed the NCAA Division National Finals at Roberts Stadium. After his death, it took years to update records because Hudson kept files in his head, not in his desk.

Three months after Hudson's death, Don White in the *Evansville Sunday Courier & Press* noted, "Doesn't it look like the late Bob Hudson left behind the biggest pair of shoes ever? At last count, there were three men – an athletics director, a director of athletic development, and an athletic business manager – assigned to the duties which were Hudson's alone through a couple of decades."

community and a quiet refuge to help assuage the overwhelming pain and grief. William K. Stephens, reporting in the *New York Times*, described Neu Chapel as "an English Gothic chapel of Indiana marble that seemed to say, 'Here is comfort.'" A study of student reaction to the tragedy undertaken three months later by four University of Evansville professors, John Ireland, William Weiss, Hanns Pieper, and Jerry Kendall, concluded that "the memorial service was listed by most students as being the single most helpful activity." The service provided therapeutic value for many who could see hundreds of other students "who felt much the same grief, thus allowing one to feel a sense of community and to put one's own losses and feelings in perspective."

Because of the intimate nature of the University, many students knew one or more members of the team personally. The above mentioned study concluded that the majority of students interviewed knew at least one member of the team, and

many considered one or more to be a friend. William Stephens described the institution well as a "small, intimate university where human tragedy touches almost everyone personally."

Following the memorial service, University administrators had to decide whether to continue to hold classes. Because the tragedy occurred so close to the Christmas break, some believed it would be appropriate to call off classes until after the holidays. Others believed that to do so would only delay, not avoid, the painful process of accepting the reality of the event, in that the sooner that reality was accepted, the better the University community would be. The final decision was to cancel classes for two days, Wednesday and Thursday, a decision accepted as appropriate by most students. Only seventeen percent of those polled believed that classes should not have reconvened until after Christmas.

Most students felt there were better ways to honor the dead than by calling off classes. One way was to participate in the American Red Cross blood drive at the University, already scheduled for that week. During the two-day drive, the number of units contributed set a record for the local Red Cross blood center.

Since the team was almost as much a part of the local community as it was of the University itself, another way to honor those who had died was to hold a community-wide memorial service. That service was held on Sunday, December 18, at Roberts Municipal Stadium, a site Graves believed to be most fitting because it had been "created by the citizens of Evansville who loved basketball and who have supported the Purple Aces through thick and thin for many, many years."

The governor of Indiana, an Indiana United States senator, the Eighth District congressman, the mayor of Evansville, representatives of the Methodist, Catholic, and Jewish faiths, and representatives of the National Collegiate Athletic Association attended the service.

In his address, Graves thanked all those who had sent notes of concern and sorrow, for through the expression of such thoughts "we are consoled, restored, made whole again, by the knowledge of your high regard for the integrity and worth of the University of Evansville." The community will never overcome the loss of "these wonderful men, who are precious and irreplaceable, for they have enriched our lives beyond description and they have given new strength and an unconquerable sense of purpose to their university."

Graves concluded:

"Out of the agony of this hour, we shall rise. Out of the ashes of a desiccated dream, we shall build a new basketball team, stronger, more valiant than ever before. That was the mission of our fallen brothers. Their dream will be fulfilled. Their supreme sacrifice will be vindicated. Out of the brokenness and despair which now grips this institution will burst a new University of Evansville more sensitive to human needs, more resolute in purpose than ever before. That is our tradition. That is our destiny."

217

Commemorative fountain in Memorial Plaza, sometimes called the "weeping basketball"

In addition to organizing these two memorial services, the University tried to help bereaved families by assigning University personnel to be with each one when they arrived in Evansville to arrange for the transportation of bodies to home towns, to have staff members in attendance at every funeral, to organize and present personal effects of victims to family members, and to give counsel about funeral expenses and arrangements as well as other matters involving the victims' families. Personal letters of sympathy were written to the families by President and Mrs. Graves, by the wife of the chairman of the Board of Trustees, and by many faculty and staff members. In addition, families received several mailings of memorabilia – including memorial service programs, newspaper articles, and photographs.

Before long, an extraordinarily large number of financial gifts began pouring in to the University. Such overwhelming generosity was unexpected.

For example, the Pittsburgh Steelers staged a benefit basketball game raising $25,000, and a Henry Mancini-Rich Little benefit show netted $12,000. An additional $10,000 came from the Tournament of Roses and the Pacific Ten and Big Ten Conferences, and $8,000 from the Big Eight Conference. In all, the University received over 2,000 separate gifts, each one acknowledged by a member of the University staff.

These donations were used for three purposes: constructing a memorial for those who perished, rebuilding the University's basketball program, and funding scholarships in the name of those killed in the crash. Almost $300,000 was donated within four months, and eventually, nearly $40,000 more was given. Of that amount, $175,416 was designated for a memorial, $135,855 for rebuilding the team, and $27,753 for scholarships. The money was put into restricted accounts so that all donors would know that their gifts were being used for the specific purpose they had indicated.

Despite the University's efforts, controversy arose concerning the nature of an appropriate campus memorial. The original decision by Graves was to construct a plaza immediately and a monument later. Some donors questioned the decision to construct a plaza with memorial funds because the University had been considering such a structure even before the crash. Nonetheless, the plan went forward with a groundbreaking ceremony on March 30, 1978. The University decided, however, to delay construction of the memorial until all of those involved – especially parents and relatives of those who had died – could be consulted. With that in mind, Graves invited members of the victims' families to meet with members of the Board of Trustees.

At that meeting, the board approved plans for constructing a memorial located on the recently completed Memorial Plaza at an estimated cost of $57,000. It would consist of a pair of triangular stone walls spaced ten feet apart and a fountain centered on a disk-shaped cobblestone basin sloping gently to the fountain's center. The backdrop to the fountain would be a stone wall six and a half feet high and approximately sixteen feet long. Part of Graves' statement at the memorial service of December 19, 1977, would be cut into the wall. In addition, there would be a bronze tablet listing the names of the twenty-four University-affiliated people who perished in the tragedy.

Six families, feeling they had not been sufficiently consulted about the expenditure of funds, hired a lawyer to demand that the University provide full financial accountability of all memorial donations. Their action led to an editorial in the *Evansville Courier* questioning whether money was being spent appropriately and questioning the attitude of the University as well.

The University had maintained that, as a private institution, it was not required to provide a public accounting of its expenditures. The *Evansville Courier* writer, however, argued that because of the tremendous outpouring of funds, largely from the community, the University did indeed "owe the community a complete accounting of funds." Furthermore, the article stated that the University "could have avoided the current unpleasantness by providing full information earlier. It's that simple." It concluded that "although the

University is a private institution, it is an important and quite visible part of this community, and that fact can't be ignored."

In his reply, Graves stated that the financial management of the fund was "correct in every respect. We believe every expenditure falls well within the spirit and intentions of donors, and that the great majority of the University's friends and supporters are entirely satisfied with the University's policy decisions." No financial improprieties were found and after the University released an official report detailing its expenditures, the case was apparently closed.

During the months following the crash, the National Transportation Safety Board investigated its causes, holding extensive hearings in Evansville and analyzing the remnants of the airplane. In August 1978, the NTSB reported that the pilot faced two problems as he began lift-off: The airplane's rudder and part of its wing were locked, and the airplane was not climbing properly. This combination made it impossible for the pilot to avoid a crash. The report speculated that the locked controls completely occupied the pilot's attention to the point that he failed to perceive a more dangerous emergency, the continued upward pitching of his aircraft. Locks had been placed on the rudder and a part of the right wing to prevent wind damage to the plane while it was on the ground. For some reason, the locks were not removed before takeoff. Adding to the problem was that too much baggage had been loaded into the rear of the plane. As a result, it could not climb properly at takeoff. Also, the airplane had been three hours late arriving and had spent only seven minutes on the ground. In its conclusion, the report neither blamed any individual nor questioned the qualifications of the flight crew.

Lawsuits naming the University were filed on behalf of three of the dead students. Insurance companies agreed to represent the University in the legal proceedings which ensued. These suits lasted until February 1983, when they were settled out of court. The end result was that the University paid $12,000 in settlement money.

OFFICIAL REPORT DETAILING EXPENDITURES OF MEMORIAL CONTRIBUTIONS

Total Fund – $334,259

$66,259	Funeral expenses for team, staff, and University friends who died in the crash
$57,847	Memorial Plaza construction
$55,000	Memorial structure to be located in the center of the plaza
$25,878	Scholarships
$ 17,315	Bus for transportation of University athletic teams
$ 7,865	Partial salary for one year of a full-time trainer for student athletes
$ 7,068	Replacement of University property destroyed in the crash
$ 5,650	Increased travel expense incurred by the team in switching to its Division I schedule
$ 5,573	Refurbishing dressing rooms at Roberts Stadium
$ 4,971	Recruiting expenses for a new team and staff
$ 2,664	Payment of bill incurred before the accident but due afterward
$ 633	Thank-you reception for Pittsburgh Steelers following benefit game
$ 500	Costume for team's new Ace Purple mascot
$ 500	New seven-foot long beds for basketball players
$76,536	Reserve for payment of additional legal fees and cost overrun for the memorial structure (any funds remaining to be placed in the endowed scholarship program)

219

Dick Walters
1979

The University decided to cancel the rest of the Aces basketball season because no makeshift team could possibly compete at a Division I level. Southern Illinois University substituted for the Aces in the Holiday Basketball Tournament, and applications for a new head basketball coach were opened through January 31, 1978. After considering all available candidates, the University appointed Dick Walters, head coach of DuPage Junior College in Illinois for nine years, to be new head coach beginning on March 2.

Walters immediately began the awesome task of recruiting an entire basketball team. Walters patched together a team made up of eight transfer students and a large number of freshmen. He also made a determined effort to sell the program to the community by speaking at 157 different gatherings. As a result, more than 450 fans showed up to watch the first practice in October 1978, and the first home games in December were sellouts.

During his first season, Walters led the team 13-16 record, a most impressive showing for an entirely new team playing a challenging Division I schedule. Equally impressive was the season attendance of 112,214, the largest attendance since 1972. By March 1982, the rebuilding process was complete. Evansville was champion of the Midwestern City Conference and lost by just five points to Marquette in its first NCAA Tournament game at the Division I level.

OTHER SPORTS

Swimming

The University of Evansville swimming program, launched successfully in 1962 by head coach Jim Voorhees, continued to win conference championships, placing first in five of its first eight years in the league.

In 1970, Bob Lodato won the NCAA College Division 200-yard backstroke and placed second in the 100-yard backstroke, as the team finished twelfth out of seventy-three schools competing in the finals. Lodato was also an excellent student, receiving a $1,000 NCAA scholarship for graduate study, one of three swimmers chosen and one of thirty-two from around the country.

Another outstanding competitor was Ed Hooker, an All-America diver for four years. Ranked in the top twelve nationally, he was a runner-up in the Division II National Championship in one-meter diving in 1975, and was a qualifier for the national finals in both one-meter and three-meter diving for four years in a row.

Under Coach Dave Enzler the Aces continued their success with Midwestern Collegiate Conference championships by Andy Haas in three events, Brad Szurgot and Lance Musgrave in one each, Coach of the Year honors for Enzler, and team first-place finishes in 1984 and 1985, and a second-place in 1986.

Baseball

In 1980, under its new coach, Jim Brownlee, the baseball team began to play a Division I schedule. In 1984, the team won thirty-three games, going on to a school record of thirty-eight wins the following year, an impressive record considering the amount of scholarship aid available and the caliber of the competition the team played since becoming Division I.

Tennis

The campus had no tennis courts until 1966, but since then the tennis team has won over fifty percent of its matches. Several players, including

Volleyball became one of the first women's sports at UE to reach varsity status

Jim Unverzagt, Dean Hall, Mark Hord, and Dan Flanigan, won the conference championship at number one singles.

Golf

In 1986, the golf team won the Midwestern Collegiate Conference championship for the first time.

Track

A new track was constructed in 1965 but in 1981 outdoor track was discontinued, although cross-country continued.

Wrestling

Wrestling did not begin until 1969 when space was made available for the team in Carson Center. Although some progress was made in the development of a competitive wrestling program, the program was dropped in 1981 in order to reduce athletic budget deficits. At the time of that decision, seven wrestlers had qualified for and participated in the Division I regionals.

Women's Sports

Women's basketball, dropped in 1928 after eight seasons, was reactivated on a limited scale with the team playing against neighboring colleges. In 1969-70, the sport was played under new rules, with five on a team instead of six and with all five permitted to play anywhere on the court instead of only half the court.

During the 1970s, the program expanded considerably, both in backing for existing sports and the addition of other sports. Part of the reason for

Linda Wambach-Crick is one of the most influential people in the history of UE women's athletics. She was an outstanding athlete for the Aces in the '70s, became the first full-time women's basketball and volleyball coach at UE, and later served as assistant athletics director

Linda Wambach-Crick

221

this expansion was governmental pressure under Title IX of the Education Amendments of 1972 which required institutions to provide equal opportunity for both men and women in athletic competition. Accordingly, the University established varsity competition for women in eight sports: basketball, cross-country, golf, softball, swimming and diving, tennis, track and field, and volleyball.

As the institution moved to Division I basketball in 1977, other sports, including women's athletics, were required to move to that division as well. Although that created problems in scheduling and in the ability to compete, most women's programs did well, particularly after joining the Division I North Star Conference in 1983, which included Loyola, Notre Dame, DePaul, Butler, Detroit, Dayton, and Xavier. From the inception of the conference, Evansville was the only member to participate in all six of the conference sports.

LOIS PATTON

Ida Stieler (see page 130) paved the road for women in varsity athletics at Evansville College; Lois Patton made sure the road stayed open.

A professor in health and physical education for thirty-two years beginning in 1966, Patton also directed the women's sports program at UE from 1970 to 1982. Her leadership brought women's athletics from the intramural to the varsity level. Funding increased, opportunities increased, and Patton coached everything. For eight years, she never coached fewer than two sports. In 1973-74, she was head coach of all four women's sports: basketball, softball, tennis, and volleyball. By the time she retired from coaching in 1981, eight women's sports had been established at the varsity level.

Patton was more than a women's sports advocate, however. In 1978, she became head of the University of Evansville physical education department. It is a rarity, and was almost unheard of then, for a woman to chair a university's physical education department. Among Patton's initiatives was convincing the administration to add athletic training to the curriculum. Today, in large part because of Patton, students at UE can major in athletic training, movement science, or exercise science.

Her efforts and integrity were recognized in 1994 when she was inducted into the University of Evansville Athletics Hall of Fame. After her retirement in 1998, her talent with her camera kept her involved in Aces sports as a photographer for the UE athletics department.

FINANCES

As might be expected when dealing with a nearly twenty-year period, the Graves administration saw many fluctuations in the University's financial condition. At the beginning of the Graves administration (fiscal year 1967), the University's annual budget was $5.2 million, with a net income of $29,820 and an endowment of $2,028,905. At the end of the 1985 fiscal year, the budget was $27,345,021, which translates to an increase of 517 percent. There was a budget deficit of $108,127, but the endowment had increased to $7,322,262, an increase of 360 percent.

When Evansville College became the University of Evansville, a new position, that of vice president for development, was created. Robert Rowland, formerly assistant to the president and director of public relations and development, was appointed to this office. He was followed by Jesse Kent, Steven Camp, James Ladd, and Thornton Patberg. All worked successfully to bring organization and consistency to the school's fund-raising efforts.

The first major campaign of the Graves administration was part of the University's observance of fifty years in Evansville (1919-69). Its goal was $40 million: $18 million for construction, $19 million for endowment, and the remainder for support funds.

Major contributors during this period, in addition to those previously noted, include:

- **1969 Bequest to the endowment fund of $862,500 from the estate of Mrs. Edward J. Fehn**

- **1969 Phi Mu Alpha Sinfonia fraternity – $98,000 to endow the addition of a permanent faculty position in stringed instruments**

- **$50,000 from the estate of Mrs. Phelps Darby**

- **$76,000 from the estate of Gardner C. Johnson**

- **$50,000 from the estate of Tina Skora and her son Isadore for nursing scholarships**

- **$40,000 from the Lilly Endowment to develop a comprehensive campus-wide academic skills center, stressing effective reading, note-taking, and test-taking**

Despite such generous gifts and years of high enrollment, the institution ran at a deficit several times during this period, the largest single cause being the athletic program which incurred a deficit every year, reaching a peak of $775,000 in fiscal 1985 and totaling $5.1 million for the period.

An additional source of financial stress arose from a dramatic increase in the number of administrative positions (associate and assistant vice presidents, and deans), positions which typically paid significantly higher salaries than faculty appointments.

Thornton Patberg served his alma mater as admission director, vice president for student affairs, and vice president for development

Unfortunately, the University's recruiting efforts also proved markedly less successful, resulting in a 1985 freshman enrollment of only 451, fifty less than had been projected. Since indicators failed to show the shortfall until too late, the trustees were obliged to choose between making radical changes in University programs or approving a loan to cover the anticipated deficit.

The latter course was chosen, with $1.6 million to be borrowed and then repaid in three years. Meanwhile, the budget for 1986-87 was cut to $2 million below that of the preceding year. A significant decrease came from salaries (forty percent from teaching faculty, sixty percent from administration) and $1 million was cut from maintenance, renovation, publications, travel, supplies, and contractual services. There was an increase in tuition and room and board, but it was kept as low as possible.

Fortunately, the actual deficit turned out to be less than anticipated (only $1.37 million because of Harlaxton College's $400,000 surplus for the year), and freshman enrollment for 1986 showed a gratifying increase to nearly 550, with full-time enrollment reaching approximately 2,500.

These improved numbers, however, came after the accreditation team from the North Central Association of Colleges made its ten-year inspection of the University's operation. Although the association renewed its accreditation of the University of Evansville for another ten years, its report contained two major criticisms of the institution.

The first concerned the persistent issue of faculty morale. The association noted that the increase in the number of administrators when major cuts were being made in faculty and support personnel had left the academic programs underfunded, thus causing "a major morale problem." These problems, combined with the University's declining financial resources, resulted – in the words of the North Central Association of Colleges – in the faculty's "lack of confidence in the University's administrative leadership."

The University's financial problems also disturbed the North Central Association of Colleges evaluation team in 1985. Its report described the situation as a "crisis," pointing out that current operating expenses surpassed current revenues by an anticipated $1.7 million, almost as large as the total budget deficits over the preceding eighteen years. The association, citing the institution's long history of successfully overcoming financial difficulties, was optimistic about the University's survival, but in October 1986, the Board of Trustees decided that, after almost twenty years of "distinguished leadership," the time had come once again (in the words used previously by President Hyde) to "turn over the responsibilities of leadership to capable younger minds, hearts, and hands."

At the same time, however, the Board of Trustees appointed President Graves to the position of chancellor for a term of three years. His chief responsibility would be to continue the $40 million "Facing the Future" campaign, designed to expand the institution's endowment. Pending the appointment of the next president, a new office was created, executive vice president and chief operations officer, a post to be filled by the vice president of administration, Robert F. Garnett.

Wallace B. Graves' term of nearly twenty years as president far exceeded the tenure of any of his predecessors. It was a time of economic difficulty, marked by inflation, recession, and a reduction in governmental support for education. Many small private institutions experienced severe financial crises during this period, many failing to survive at all. It was also a time of student unrest, protest, and even violence on some college campuses. Finally, the University had to weather what was by far the most catastrophic, heartbreaking tragedy in its long history. With assurance and skill, President Graves rose to the many challenges set before him. Harlaxton College, for which he is best remembered, is but one of many impressive accomplishments.

CHAPTER SIX

University of Evansville: 1987 to 2004

BACKGROUND

During this period, the University of Evansville was led by two presidents, each facing formidable challenges and both providing the quality and style of leadership the situation required.

In 1986, a thirteen-member presidential search committee, headed by H. Lee Cooper III, was charged with finding a suitable successor to President Graves. The committee included members of the Board of Trustees, faculty, students, alumni, and church and community leaders. In addition, the Presidential Search Consultation Service, a branch of the Association of Governing Boards of Universities and Colleges, was tapped for advice concerning effective recruiting procedures and techniques.

1987-2001

Twenty-first President
JAMES S. VINSON

After the committee sorted through more than 150 applications, the field was gradually narrowed down, and in time the committee determined that the person "whose experience and skills will best help the University of Evansville meet its needs and fulfill its dreams" was Dr. James S. Vinson, vice president for academic affairs and professor of physics since 1983 at Trinity University in San Antonio, Texas. At the end of April 1987, after an official visit to meet with the entire University community, his appointment was formally announced.

Born and raised in Chambersburg, Pennsylvania, the new president was a Phi Beta Kappa graduate of Gettysburg College (1963) and received both a Master of Science (1965) and a Doctor of Philosophy (1967) in physics from the University

225

of Virginia. His teaching career began at MacMurray College (1967) in Jacksonville, Illinois, and continued at the University of North Carolina at Asheville (1972-78) where he was a professor of physics, chairman of the department, and director of the computing center and computer network. After serving as dean of the College of Arts and Sciences at the University of Hartford (1978-83), he went to Trinity.

In addition to these impressive academic credentials, Vinson brought to the position a great interest and particular expertise in fiscal affairs as related to university administration. Since the University of Evansville was struggling with a very substantial deficit as well as dwindling student enrollment, his knowledge and skill in this field were especially needed.

When President Vinson came to the University, it had, in his words, "some temporary problems with finances," but had a sound foundation which would enable him to move on with little difficulty to the next level. To do so, he stated, would require "clarifying the focus of the University at that particular point in its history" by revising the general education program and by making the University "more residential, more national, and more international." He summarized his goal as helping the University "get better, not necessarily bigger."

Notwithstanding this goal, Vinson succeeded in increasing enrollment for several years. At the same time, SAT scores increased by more than 100 points. In addition, Vinson streamlined the University's academic and administrative structure. The number of deans was reduced from eight to four; vice presidents from five to four; and faculty committees from twenty-three to eight. Also, several unprofitable units were scaled back, especially graduate degree and community outreach programs. As a result of these and similar measures, the University's cumulative deficit was quickly erased.

During President Vinson's tenure, the University's academic program made solid advances, several new buildings were added, and the quality of student life was enhanced. Despite fluctuating enrollment, from some of the highest to the lowest

226

THE UNIVERSITY MACE

On September 16, 1988, James S. Vinson was formally inaugurated as University president. This occasion provided the first opportunity to use the new University mace, a gift of Betty and Wayne Worthington. The staff of the mace is constructed of cherry wood and encircled with four sterling silver sleeves. The first sleeve is hand engraved with seven Greek letters which are the initials of words describing the elements of a well-rounded life (see page 67). The second and third sleeves are engraved with the names of the new president and the donors. The fourth names the designer (Nicholas Logsdon) and the manufacturer (J. C. Boardman and Co.).

The staff is surmounted by a sterling silver orb with two medallions impressed in it. One is the seal of the University while the other depicts a cross. Atop the orb are two griffins, symbols of vigilance and strength.

THE UNIVERSITY MEDAL

On the occasion of President Vinson's inauguration, a University medal became part of the University president's academic regalia for all ceremonial events. President and Mrs. Vinson and their families donated the medal in memory of their fathers, Wilbur S. Vinson and Samuel L. Alexander.

numbers in the University's history, a balanced budget was maintained each year.

After fourteen years, Vinson believed he had successfully achieved his mission at the University of Evansville and that fresh leadership might be helpful in meeting the challenges that lay ahead in the new century. To allow sufficient time to find the best possible successor and to provide a smooth transition to the next administration, he agreed to

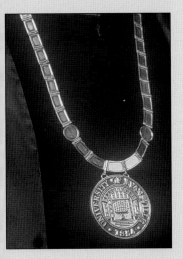

Made of sterling silver, the medal is attached to a chain which is linked together by bars of silver, with the engraved names of every president of the University and the years they served. Also, one silver bar is engraved with each of the four different names of the University since its origin in 1854.

THE UNIVERSITY SEAL

In the late 1980s, a new University seal was devised. Its design resembled the one used earlier by Evansville College. In this way, the University hoped to connect more closely with its origins and to emphasize that all its broad and varied academic programs shared the common ideals symbolized by the seal's seven-branched candlestick.

continue in office for an additional year after announcing his resignation.

Following his term at the University of Evansville, Vinson was appointed president and chief executive officer of the National Science Center Foundation, a nonprofit organization headquartered in Augusta, Georgia, devoted to improving student academic achievement in mathematics and the sciences.

2001-

Twenty-second President
STEPHEN G. JENNINGS

A search committee for a new president, headed by Robert Koch II and with members drawn from the entire University community, was appointed. Heidrick Struggles International, an executive search firm, assisted with the task. The committee reviewed more than 100 applicants, inviting nine finalists to campus before choosing Dr. Stephen G. Jennings, president of Oklahoma City University and former president of the College of the Ozarks and Simpson College. Interestingly, Jennings was not among the original applicants, but was nominated for the position by R. Kevin LaGree, who had succeeded Jennings as president of Simpson College.

The fifty-four-year-old Jennings was chosen especially for his leadership in educational circles, fund-raising skills, collaborative management style, and forward thinking. Born a Hoosier and son of a Presbyterian minister, his bachelor's degree in sociology was from Trinity University in San Antonio (the same institution James Vinson had served prior to coming to Evansville). Jennings' graduate work was done at Miami University in Ohio (a master's in personnel counseling), the University of Georgia (a doctorate in human development and higher education administration), and Harvard University (a diploma from the Institute for Educational Management). Jennings also holds honorary doctorates from two schools of

227

which he was formerly president, Simpson College and the College of the Ozarks.

The new president had held administrative positions at several universities since 1970, including three presidencies since 1983. He served as an evaluator for the North Central Association for Colleges and Schools, as well as a consultant on such topics as motivation, leadership training, and management in higher education. He made more than fifty presentations at national and regional meetings and published eight articles in juried journals. He was included in six editions of *Who's Who in America* and also received the Distinguished Alumni Award from the School of Education at the University of Georgia and the Alumni Achievement Award from the College of Education at Miami University.

As the major goals of his administration, Jennings stated three priorities:

- **To improve the University of Evansville's image**

- **To develop a strategic plan for the University, including a substantial increase in enrollment**

- **To complete Widening the Circle, the major fund-raising campaign started by President Vinson**

On April 9, 2002, Stephen Jennings was formally inaugurated as the twenty-second president of the University of Evansville. His message to an audience of about 600 centered on his philosophy of servant leadership. "Great leaders anywhere are to be seen as servants first – on every level," Jennings said. "When one is a servant, one is always searching, listening, expecting and willing to serve. Servants serve first and make a conscious choice to lead later."

Jennings came to the University at a time when the institution had developed what some described as a chasm between the school and the community and when enrollment was at its lowest in a decade. He worked quickly to reverse these trends.

Early in his tenure, Jennings established a strate-

228

A Gallery of First Ladies

Claudia Hyde

Claudia Bray Hyde, a native of Sioux Falls, South Dakota, began piano lessons when she was eight years old and later studied music at Carlton College and the Cincinnati Conservatory of Music. Returning home to Sioux Falls to teach high school, she soon met and married Melvin Hyde, also a teacher.

As first lady of Evansville College, she worked hard to build strong bonds among the College family, entertaining faculty, staff, and students on a regular basis.

Mrs. Hyde was gentle, gracious, and kind. An associate recalls that at a meeting of the College women's organization, she said to the lady beside her, "If I speak, pinch me." The person asked, "Why?" and she replied, "My husband is afraid that if I voice my opinions, the group might feel obligated to do what I say."

At the age of 98, Mrs. Hyde was still very alert. When told she was being included in the University's history, she responded, "Please keep it short or people will be bored."

Barbara Graves

Barbara Graves met her future husband when both were children in Texas. Their parents played bridge together; Barbara, Wally, and brother George Graves played children's games together. Wally and Barbara dated in high school and college, married, and by the time they arrived in Evansville, were parents of four children, the youngest only four years old.

As first lady, Mrs. Graves hosted a variety of faculty and University social activities, including many benefit affairs. A notable annual fall event was the Texas Roundup, complete with barbecue on spits, checkered tablecloths, paper lanterns in the trees, and square dancing in the union parking lot. It became a cherished tradition.

Equally at home with trustees and their wives, friends and supporters of the University, the British gentry and royalty, and ordinary citizens in whatever country she happened to be in, Mrs. Graves represented the University with distinction and, building on her southern heritage, honed Hoosier hospitality to perfection.

Claudia Hyde

Barbara Graves

Susan Vinson

Sally Jennings

Susan Vinson

Susan Vinson, in addition to experience in "administrative spousing," came to Evansville with academic degrees in nursing and counseling with a professional background in both nursing education and substance abuse prevention and treatment.

A native of Virginia, Mrs. Vinson first met her future husband on a blind date with "a cocky Yankee." She decided "to give him a chance – just in case."

As first lady of the University of Evansville, she hosted the freshman class annually during orientation and she was responsible for welcoming the approximately 5,000 guests who visited the May House each year. The culmination of Mrs. Vinson's service to the University, however, was her appointment as the first full-time coordinator of health education and wellness programs. Focusing on such issues as stress management, date rape, unwanted pregnancy, HIV-AIDS risks, and alcohol and drug abuse, Vinson counseled fraternities, sororities, clubs, and individuals, bringing equal doses of genuine concern and "tough love" to her work.

The highlight of her time as the University's health educator, she later reflected, was receiving the Interfraternity Council's Award as Administrator of the Year. There is little doubt that without her efforts, serious consequences would have marred the future lives of many UE students.

Sally Jennings

Unlike her predecessors, Sally Jennings had plenty of practice as first lady before coming to the University of Evansville – nearly two decades, in fact, since her husband had been a college president since 1983.

Mrs. Jennings grew up in Missouri but earned a Bachelor of Science degree in sociology at Trinity University in San Antonio, Texas. There she met Steve Jennings who, as junior class president, was responsible for the concession stand during Homecoming. In need of an assistant, Jennings called her roommate. Upon discovering that she was out, he asked Sally instead. She later recalled, "I thought he was nice, so I said okay."

In her professional career, Mrs. Jennings worked as a social worker in Ohio, Texas, and Georgia, and taught sociology in New Orleans. After 1983, however, she chose to devote herself fully to the responsibilities of raising her children and being the wife of a college president.

Nevertheless, she found time to actively volunteer for groups such as Habitat for Humanity, the Child Abuse Prevention Council, United Way, and the Girl Scouts of America, holding significant offices in several of these organizations and receiving awards for distinguished service.

Since coming to Evansville, Mrs. Jennings has served on the board of the YWCA and the UE Theatre Society, and has been active with the Friends of UE Music and the sesquicentennial celebration committee. In addition, she was instrumental in orchestrating the first WISE (Women Inspiring Success and Excellence) Forum.

With her enthusiasm and sincerity, Mrs. Jennings exemplifies the openness and warmth that characterizes the Jennings administration.

229

gic planning committee, a broad-based group including students, faculty, staff, trustees, alumni, and community members, assisted by the Indianapolis-based consulting firm Baird, Kurtz, and Dobson. The committee was to examine all aspects of the institution to ensure that the University met its mission of providing the best possible environment for all students in the most economical fashion. Six specific goals were targeted:

- **Retain and enhance academic quality, utilizing modern technology whenever possible**

- **Increase overall enrollment**

- **Improve student life and alumni relations**

- **Increase financial resources**

- **Enhance public relations and University involvement in the community**

- **Better define the role of athletics**

AN OPEN DOOR POLICY

Soon after coming to the University of Evansville, Jennings requested that the solid door leading to his office in Olmsted Administration Hall be replaced by a glass one. This minor cosmetic change was quickly noticed; it symbolized a new level of accessibility to the president. Jennings also demonstrated his approachability by hosting weekly open houses in his office during his first year.

Dave Johnson wrote in the *Evansville Courier & Press*:

"Jennings is a people's president: whether he's around a group of professors, fans, students, coaches, or custodians, he acts as if he's one of them. But it's no act. That's really the way Jennings feels. He comes across as friendly, outgoing, and approachable – someone who cares what others think, someone who loves to get out and mingle."

230

BUILDINGS

Building activity during President Vinson's tenure focused on two areas: residential housing and a major addition to the Koch Center for Engineering and Science.

The need for expanded residential housing arose not only because of higher enrollment during the early and mid 1990s but also because of increased student interest in living "where the action is" – on campus.

For several consecutive years, residence halls filled to capacity at the start of the school year. Faculty members with homes near campus offered rooms to incoming students on a temporary basis. Meanwhile, conference and game rooms in the residence halls were converted into living quarters, with students also housed in the Fehn House, a University guest house on Rotherwood Avenue.

In an effort to eliminate the annual housing crunch and also to give students lifestyle options other than residence hall living, the University purchased new property comprising:

- **University Villages (the former Armory Heights Apartments), accommodating eighty-six students, located off Rotherwood Avenue**

- **The Ramona Apartments, accommodating twenty-four students, located on Lincoln Avenue**

- **Two houses on Weinbach Avenue, reserved for students enrolled in the University's Honors Program (residents were required to have a minimum GPA of 3.25, and the facilities carried the designation ACE – Academics Conducive Environment)**

- **Ten other houses and four duplexes, to be used as needed**

Generally, in order to create more space in the residence halls for freshmen, upperclassmen occupied off-campus facilities.

Even with these additions, the need for new on-campus housing became increasingly evident. In 1993, the building now known as Mary Kuehn Powell Residence Hall was constructed, the first new residence hall built on campus in twenty-five years. It houses about 120 students. The following year, Schroeder Residence Hall, housing about 160 students, was added. Architect Jack Kinkel '62 designed both halls. Powell Hall was named for Mary Kuehn Powell, a member of the UE Board of Trustees since 1986 and its treasurer from 1991 to 1995. Schroeder Hall honored John H. Schroeder, founder of Crescent-Cresline-Wabash Plastics, a member of the Board of Trustees and its chairman from 1978 to 1981.

By combining these new structures with other purchased property, the institution, within the space of seven years (1987-94), nearly doubled the number of students it could accommodate in University-owned housing.

Student lounge in Schroeder Hall

231

MARY KUEHN POWELL RESIDENCE HALL (1993)

*Early and later
construction of
Powell Hall*
———

232

*Residence hall
completed in
record time
for student
occupancy as
classes start in
1993*
———

On the academic side, the major building achievement of this period was the $16.9 million Koch Center for Engineering and Science renovation project. The 1977 addition to the 1945 engineering science building had been renamed in 1984 to honor University trustee Robert L. Koch, whose $1 million pledge in the New Century Capital Campaign (the University's first million dollar gift) made the original expansion possible. Koch Center, home to the College of Engineering and Computer Science and the biology, chemistry, mathematics, and physics departments, soon became the most heavily used academic building on campus.

Although Koch Center greatly enhanced facilities for instruction and research, it became apparent well before the century's end that further expansion would be needed to prepare students for the challenging technology, constant innovation, and growing complexity of the new millennium.

Accordingly, in January 2000, ground was broken for an extensive addition to Koch Center, and the facility was ready for use by August 2001. At the same time, the 1977 addition was renovated so that faculty offices of the College of Engineering and Computer Science, previously scattered in various locations, could be unified in one central area.

The 2001 Koch Center addition, joined to the south end of the older part of the building through a three-story sky-lit atrium, featured a 100-seat auditorium, state-of-the-art technology, and much needed office and classroom space. Laboratory space was increased by about fifty percent and possibilities were expanded for interactive learning, interdisciplinary collaboration, and joint student-faculty research. Majors in engineering, mathematics, and

Students socialize and study in the atrium of the 2001 Koch Center addition

science could work together in analyzing and solving problems, thus gaining valuable skills sure to serve them well when they entered the working world.

The final phase of the renovation project, remodeling the 1945 building, was completed in 2002. Funds for the extensive work involved in modernizing, expanding, and constructing these facilities came from three sources: (1) a variable rate bond issue, (2) the University's reserve funds, and (3) the Widening the Circle capital campaign.

233

New labs in Koch Center are stocked with state-of-the-art equipment

ROBOT HELPS WITH UE GROUNDBREAKING

An article by Patricia Swanson in the *Evansville Courier & Press* on January 13, 2000, began with the headline above and continued:

University of Evansville officials staged a traditional groundbreaking Wednesday with the aid of a most untraditional helper – a robot.

UE President James Vinson said it seemed appropriate to use a robot considering that the ceremony was for a $16.9 million renovation of the Koch Center for Engineering and Science, where robots share space with students.

A small box-like robot, called Pioneer 1, crawled up the ramp to the platform where various officials were seated.

The robot had gloves for the eight officials who would be wielding the actual shovels.

Pioneer stopped near Vinson, who walked over and commented that it really would be nice if the robot let him have the gloves.

Pioneer 1 performed perfectly, offering up the gloves and then lowering the holding container and moving a few feet away. "Thank you very much," Vinson said. "I appreciate it."

At the August 30, 2001, dedication ceremony for the new addition, a time capsule inserted in the cornerstone of the 1945 building was opened and replaced with a new time capsule. The 1945 capsule contained printed materials and various artifacts pertaining to that period.

Eight University of Evansville students, representing the disciplines most closely associated with the new facility, participated in the ceremony. They were:

Lindzy Friend	*Senior Biology Major*
Kimberly Scott	*Junior Physics Major*
Brigitte Robinson	*Junior Chemistry Major*
Jennifer Legeay	*Student Government Association President*
Nicholas Armstrong	*Sophomore Physics Major*
William Eddings	*Senior Civil Engineering Major*
Anne Kitchens	*Junior Mathematics Major*
Katherine Achim	*Junior Computer Engineering Major*

Mary and Delbert Sampson

OTHER BUILDING ACTIVITIES 1990-2000

Shanklin Theatre (Renovation) 1990

Carson Center and **Student Fitness Center** (Renovation and expansion; also made handicapped accessible, with ramp added to east entrance of Carson Center) 1991

Krannert Hall of Fine Arts (Made handicapped accessible – senior gift) 1991-92

Harper Dining Center (Elevator installed) 1991-92

Neu Chapel (Ramp and new sidewalk at south entrance to provide handicapped access and new accessible restrooms on first floor – senior gift) 1993

University Bookstore (Relocated from campus to a former pharmacy on the corner of Weinbach and Lincoln Avenues, providing more space for clothing, textbooks, and general interest books) 1994

Koch Center for Engineering and Science (Entrance renovated to provide handicapped access and enhance landscaping – senior gift) 1995

Sampson Hall (Formerly the University Bookstore; renovated; now houses the Crayton E. and Ellen Mann Health Center and the Offices of University Relations and Publications; name honors Delbert Sampson, former psychology department chair) 1995

Wallace B. Graves Hall (Renovations) 1995, 2000

Central area of **South Oval** (Three flag poles displaying United States, Indiana, and University of Evansville flags installed; also enhanced lighting and new landscaping – senior gift) 1997

McCurdy Alumni Memorial Union (Renovated and elevator added for handicapped accessibility) 1997

Panhellenic Center (Renovation of an office building at 2032 Lincoln Avenue, providing 1,000 square feet for each of the University's four sororities) 1998

235

ADMINISTRATORS

Administrative appointments during this period include:

1988 **Erik Nielsen,**
 Vice President for Academic Affairs

1989 **Will Thielman,** *Bookstore Manager*

1990 **Dell Nussmeier '66,** *Associate Coordinator of Academic Advising*

1993 **Terry Mullins,** *Dean, School of Business Administration*

 Verla Richardson '74, M '82
 Co-director of Financial Aid

 W. Scott Shrode '74, *Vice President for Development*

1995 **Larry Colter,**
 Dean, College of Arts and Sciences

 Philip Gerhart,
 Dean, College of Engineering and Computer Science

 Howard Rosenblatt,
 Vice President and Dean of Students

Howard Rosenblatt

1997 **Stephen Greiner,**
 Vice President for Academic Affairs

1998 **Lynn Penland,**
 Dean, College of Education and Health Sciences

Lynn Penland

2001 **Thomas Bear,**
 Dean of Admission

 John Byrd,
 Executive Vice President

John Byrd

236

 Dana Clayton,
 Dean of Students

2002 **John "Jack" Barner,**
 Vice President for Institutional Advancement

 Stuart Dorsey,
 Vice President for Academic Affairs

 Jean Beckman,
 Dean, College of Arts and Sciences

Dana Clayton

2003 **Jeffery Wolf,** *Vice President for Fiscal Affairs and Administration*

RISE TO THE TOP

Ten former University of Evansville administrators have gone on to become college presidents.

Larry Jackson
Lander College (South Carolina)

Paul Hartman
Kentucky Wesleyan College

Charles E.P. Simmons
Lake Erie College (Ohio)

Patrick McDonough
*Marietta College (Ohio);
 later University of Wisconsin - Stevens Point*

Larraine Matusak
Thomas Edison College (New Jersey)

James Dawson
*Tennessee Wesleyan College;
 later Coker College (South Carolina)*

Ann Stuart
Texas Woman's University

Roger Sublett
Union Institute and University (Ohio)

Erik Nielsen
Franklin College (Switzerland)

Stephen Greiner
Virginia Intermont College

ADMINISTRATIVE ROSTER, 2003-2004

President
Stephen G. Jennings

Vice Presidents
John W. Byrd, *Executive*
Stuart B. Dorsey, *Academic Affairs*
John C. Barner, *Institutional Advancement*
Jeffery M. Wolf, *Fiscal Affairs and Administration*

Athletics Director
William P. McGillis

Harlaxton College Principal
J. Gordon Kingsley

Assistant Vice Presidents
Jennifer L. Graban, *Academic Affairs/Grants Director and Affirmative Action Officer*
Charles H. Sparrenberger, *Technology*

Deans
Jean C. Beckman, *College of Arts and Sciences*
Robert A. Clark, *School of Business Administration*
Lynn R. Penland, *College of Education and Health Sciences*
Philip M. Gerhart, *College of Engineering and Computer Science*
Dana D. Clayton, *Students*
Thomas E. Bear, *Admission*
Michael A. Tessier, *Associate Dean of Students, Director, Residence Life*
Robert W. Pool, *Assistant Dean of Students/ Director, Student Engagement*

Directors
Academic Advisement, **Deborah A. Kassenbrock**
Administrative Services, **Mark J. Logel**
Alumni Relations, **Sylvia Y. DeVault**
Annual Giving and Development Services, **Jamie L. Elkins**
Assessment, **Christine L. McKeag**
Athletic Compliance and Student Services, **Jennifer M. Daniels**
Career Services, **Carroll E. Wells**
Center for Teaching Excellence, **Michael J. Stankey**

Continuing Education, **Lynn R. Penland**
Counseling and Health Education, **Sylvia T. Buck**
Dining Services, **Stephan O. Chavira**
Facilities Management and Planning, **Larry S. Horn**
Financial Aid, **JoAnn E. Laugel**
Honors Program, **Mary E. Pritchard**
Human Resources, **Gregory R. Bordfeld**
Intensive English Center, **Constance B. Vernon**
International Student Services and Activities, **Rhonda J. Hinkle**
International Studies, **Wesley T. Milner**
Internet Applications Laboratory, **Mark L. Shifflet**
Planned Giving and Capital Support, **Christopher L. Mueller**
Publications, **Susan M. Heathcott**
Safety and Security, **Harold P. Matthews**
Sports Information, **Robert W. Boxell**
Student Accounts, **Michael R. Bengert**
Student Fitness Center, **Jeffrey A. Chestnut**
Student Publications, **Tracy A. Maurer**
Study Abroad and Harlaxton Coordinator, **Earl D. Kirk**
Technology Services, **Keith D. Jackson**
Transfer Admission, **Cherie C. Leonhardt**
University Relations, **Marcia A. Dowell**
World Cultures, **J. Burton Kirkwood**
Writing, **Tiffany E. Griffith**

Other
Administrative Assistant to the President, **Rebecca L. Dillbeck**
Associate Athletics Director/Senior Woman Administrator, **Sarah E. Solinsky**
Bookstore Manager, **Kevin J. Collins**
Controller, **Donna J. Peak**
General Manager, WUEV-FM, **Michael J. Crowley**
Senior Associate Athletics Director, **Lawrence M. Ryan**
University Librarian, **William F. Louden**
University Physician, **Randall R. Stoltz, M.D.**
University Registrar, **Keith M. Kutzler**

ACADEMICS

Notable strides in the University's academic program during this period made it possible to attract highly effective faculty and better prepared students (as measured by test scores and class standing).

National studies conducted during the 1990s showed that approximately one-third of the faculty at four-year schools worked only part time as professors, but the percentage of part-time faculty at the University of Evansville was considerably lower. Although teaching assistants are a mainstay at most public universities, it was the policy of the University of Evansville that nearly all classes be taught by full-time faculty.

This practice played a significant role in gaining the high rating the University received annually in the ranking of America's Best Colleges by *U.S. News & World Report*. In addition to percentage of full-time faculty (the University of Evansville ranked first in the Midwest in this regard), *U.S. News & World Report* considers fifteen indicators of excellence, including:

- **Academic reputation**
- **Class size (average 20 students or less)**
- **Student selectivity**
- **Financial aid availability**
- **Retention and graduation rate**
- **Financial resources available to faculty**
- **Level of alumni giving**

238

After grouping the nation's approximately 1,400 accredited four-year colleges and universities by mission and region, the yearly study compares each school with others in its peer group. Beginning in 1993 and each year thereafter, the University of Evansville received favorable ratings in two categories, Best Regional University (Midwest) and Best Value (Midwest). In addition, on the *U.S. News & World Report's* Internet-only information for 2002, the University of Evansville was ranked

Best Regional University (Midwest)		Best Value (Midwest)
Year	Rank	Rank
1993	7	7
1994	8	1
1995	13	8
1996	11	13
1997	15	12
1998	13	6
1999	12	8
2000	11	8
2001	10	9
2002	10	7
2003	10	4

U.S.News Best Colleges 2004

in the top five schools in the Midwest for international enrollment (seven percent).

Although pleased with the University's ranking, President Jennings determined, as a principal goal of his administration, to move the institution into the top five.

Also, in 2000, the University of Evansville was ranked in a University of Florida study as one of the top 100 private schools in the nation for (1) Merit and Achievement Scholars (fourth among Indiana institutions) and (2) Median SAT scores (third among Indiana institutions).

In 1997, responding to interest expressed by many faculty in enhancing the effectiveness of their teaching, the University established Faculty Innovational Instructional Grants (FIIG). Within a year, twenty-eight proposals for pilot projects and experiments with new methods of instruction were funded. Then, supported by a $200,000 grant from the Lilly Endowment, the Center for Teaching Excellence was established to assist faculty wishing to explore new technology and innovative approaches to learning. Directed by Michael Stankey of the communication department, the project has enjoyed the active participation of over 200 faculty.

Scott Lank (right) works on some scenes with theatre students

A further validation of faculty excellence was the inclusion of eleven professors in *Who's Who Among America's Teachers* (1998). Only high school and college students who had been cited for academic excellence themselves in *Who's Who Among High School Students* or the National Dean's List are invited to participate and are restricted to only one nomination. *Who's Who Among America's Teachers* honors a select five percent of the nation's faculty. Those named from the University of Evansville were:

Tony Beavers (*philosophy and religion*)

Larry Caldwell (*English*)

Cheryl Griffith (*physical therapy*)

John Haegert (*English*)

Scott Lank (*theatre*)

Nancy Leonard (*management*)

Chris McKeag (*accounting*)

Margaret McMullan (*English*)

Les Miley (*art*)

Wayne Perkins (*philosophy and religion*)

When he was again chosen for inclusion in 2002, John Haegert joined the less than two percent of America's teachers honored more than once in the nationally distributed publication.

239

FOR THE RECORD

- Typically, seventy-nine percent of all UE pre-med students who apply to medical school are accepted. (The national average is fifty-five percent.)

- Nearly eighty percent of UE physics majors continued their studies in graduate school.

- Ninety percent of UE pre-law students were admitted to law school.

- In 2001, ninety-seven percent of UE education students who took Indiana's Teaching Proficiency Test passed, surpassing the state average of ninety-two percent. The comprehensive exam tests both basic skills and knowledge of a specialized area. UE students excelled in each category, surpassing the state average in both.

- UE's legal studies program, one of only two four-year programs in Indiana accredited by the American Bar Association, is one of only 100 accredited programs in the entire nation.

- Of the almost 1,300 colleges and universities offering teacher education programs, fewer than half receive accreditation by the National Council for Accreditation of Teacher Education. The University of Evansville has been accredited since 1958.

- The 2002-03 Missouri Valley Conference Honor Roll listed 125 UE athletes. Student athletes need a 3.2 grade point average to qualify.

- In 2003, for the sixth time in seven years, 89 percent of UE civil engineering graduates passed the Fundamentals of Engineering exam administered by the Indiana Board of Professional Registration. The national passing rate for the eight-hour-long examination is 78 percent.

THE LIBRARY

The University's academic program was greatly enhanced by the rapid development of new library technology. In the early 1990s, the wide acceptance of microcomputers and CD-ROMs helped create computerized periodical indexes. Unlike earlier computerized searching techniques, these indexes required no special training, making them readily accessible to the average library user. CD-ROMs were also cumulative in nature, thus eliminating the need to search separately by year as was formerly the case. In a short time, the standard reference indexes (the best known being the *Reader's Guide to Periodical Literature*), the mainstay of library operations for decades, all but disappeared from the shelves.

Despite their immediate popularity, CD-ROM indexes were soon eclipsed by even more powerful technology – the Internet and the World Wide Web. At the University of Evansville, this transformation began in 1995 when a local area network,

first designed and coded by collection development librarian Marvin Guilfoyle, was established across the entire campus. Almost at a stroke, it became possible for the library to deliver these indexes to students and faculty in offices, computer labs, and residence hall rooms.

As significant as this breakthrough was, a still more revolutionary change soon followed, enabling students or faculty to locate not only citations to journal articles but also the full text of the articles themselves, thus sparing the library the cumbersome and expensive task of actually acquiring the entire journal. In this way, access to over 2,500 journals effectively doubled the size of UE's subscription holdings. In fact, it was now possible to use the library without actually entering the building. In light of the shift from physical ownership of books and journals to electronic access to information, the impact of the World Wide Web on all aspects of the University Libraries would be difficult to overstate.

Much library research is now done online

In 2000, the library catalog system also changed. After fifteen years, the NOTIS library automation system was retired in favor of a new-generation online catalog and library management system called Voyager. This allowed the University of Evansville to put its entire online catalog on the World Wide Web, thus providing easy access to anyone, anywhere an Internet connection was available.

Also in 2000, the University added new network personal computers, more than doubling the previous number. The new computers, known as ACE (Automated Catalog of Evansville) terminals, could access the new Voyager online catalog. As the new millennium began, the University of Evansville boasted a beautifully housed, profession-

ally staffed, increasingly electronically sophisticated library delivering an array of full text information resources across the campus and to Harlaxton College. In addition, thanks to a $20,000 matching grant from the Clowes Fund of Indianapolis, a music listening facility was established on the top floor of Clifford Library.

In this "new age," the traditional methods of evaluating a library and its services by the number of items it holds or subscribes to or how many people walk in its doors are no longer relevant. The University of Evansville now has electronic access to more than 47 million resources from 6,700 libraries and information centers around the globe. Significantly, while the library committed forty-six percent of its 1995 materials budget to books, currently this figure is less than thirty percent.

LIBRARY FACULTY

Directors
Ravindra Sharma
(1989-94)
William Louden
(1994-present)

Cataloguing
Steven Mussett

Reference
Randy Abbott

Periodicals
Danielle Williams
Kathy Norman

Library Instruction
Margaret Atwater-Singer

William Louden

241

OTHER ACADEMIC MATTERS

■ The number of full-time faculty during this period fluctuated between 155 (1988-89) and 184 (1998-99). Approximately eighty-five percent of faculty held a terminal degree (an earned doctorate or its equivalent).

■ Beginning in 1988, student perceptions of the faculty were measured by an analysis procedure called the Instructional Development and Effectiveness Assessment (IDEA). Students were asked to evaluate their professors' teaching methods, choice of materials, and knowledge of their field. This program, intended to indicate each faculty member's effectiveness in the classroom, resulted in mean scores for University of Evansville faculty ranking in the seventy-first percentile nationally, considerably higher than the mid forty percent national average reported by participating institutions.

■ Freshmen beginning at the University of Evansville in the fall of 1990 were greeted by a new general education curriculum described by the University as "different from almost ninety percent of other schools in the country." The new program had three components:

The World Cultures Sequence

This, the cornerstone of the whole curriculum, consisted of three courses: The Ancient World; The Emergence of the West; and The Modern World. Professors from various departments planned and taught these classes, taken by all entering students at the same time. In this way, freshmen of all majors shared a common intellectual experience. The sequence introduced the student to the achievements of diverse cultures and societies throughout history and around the world. It has been directed by faculty members Philip Ott, Deborah Howard, Patricia Vilches, and Burton Kirkwood.

Integrated Distribution Requirements

To fulfill this portion of the general education package, students completed courses from two different disciplines outside their majors, selected from the following areas: humanities, fine arts, natural sciences, mathematics, social sciences, and foreign languages.

Senior Seminars

This capstone requirement, entailing independent research and a significant writing component, serves as the culmination of the general education curriculum.

Patti McCrory and her world cultures class meet outdoors on a mild spring day

242

IT'S AN HONOR

As the academic caliber of the UE student body rose (one out of seven entering freshmen in 2003 ranked at the very top of their graduating class), the need for enriched learning opportunities for exceptionally bright students became apparent.

Accordingly, the University established an honors program. It features interdisciplinary courses, small seminar-style classes, advanced independent study, a senior project, and a collaborative learning atmosphere. Honor students explore a wide range of material and work closely with faculty members who, in turn, are challenged by their contact with gifted students.

To be considered for the Honors Program, an incoming student needs high test scores (at least 1250 on the SAT or 28 on the ACT) and a high grade point average. Approximately seven percent of the freshman class enter the program each year; about 130 students participate in the program during any given year.

Students in the program play an active role in its administration through the eight-member Student Advisory Council. A Harlaxton representative is appointed each semester to serve honors students attending the British campus.

Outside of the classroom, honors students enjoy such perks as:

Use of a special honors lounge which houses computers, a scanner, and both color and black and white printers

Attendance at theatre, film, current events discussion groups, and presentations by guest speakers

Special housing, field trips, and volunteer social service activities

The Honors Program sponsors an annual game show called "Who Wants a 4.0" in which faculty pit their wits against the students.

Richard Connolly, James Reising, Judith Sebesta, and Mary Pritchard have served as coordinators of the Honors Program. Student transcripts indicate honors courses and graduation from the program, which can be cited on résumés and job or graduate school applications. In addition to brightening the college experience, participation in the Honors Program can serve as a key to a brighter future.

■ In 2001, the General Education Program was revamped once more. It required forty-one semester hours from eleven general categories. The World Cultures Sequence remained the cornerstone of the program but was reduced to two courses: The Ancient World to the Reformation, and The Emergence of the Modern World. Also retained were the foreign language requirement and the senior seminar. The remaining hours are to be taken in the following areas:

American Traditions	3 hours
The Creative Dimension	3 hours
Health and Wellness	1 hour
Human Behavior and Society	3 hours
International Perspectives	3 hours
Mathematical Thought	3 hours
The Philosophical/ Spiritual Dimension	3 hours
Science and Technology	7 hours

A diverse selection of courses within each category can be selected to fulfill the requirements. The revision also provides that the interdisciplinary course taken at Harlaxton, The British Experience (see page 296), can be counted towards general education credit.

243

■ The Felsher Case

William Felsher came to the University of Evansville in 1969 as chair of the foreign languages department. In time, after a series of disagreements with various members of the administration, Felsher was replaced as department chair but continued to serve as a tenured professor. Then on October 1, 1990, new department chair David Seaman requested and received Felsher's permission to visit a class session in order to evaluate Felsher's teaching techniques. Upon discovering that a test was scheduled for that hour, Seaman attempted to leave the room, but was prevented from doing so when Felsher blocked the exit with his desk. From a classroom window, Seaman called out for help from campus security, complaining that he was being detained against his will.

Although confinement is legally a felony, the University chose not to file charges, but instead informed Felsher that there was adequate cause to show that he was "unfit to remain a tenured faculty member." Felsher disputed this contention, and presented his case to the University's Faculty Appeals Committee and to its Board of Trustees; both supported his dismissal. When the case traveled to the Vanderburgh County Superior Court and, later, the Indiana Court of Appeals, the University's position was again upheld.

In retaliation, Felsher sent e-mail messages under administrators' names and developed web sites under their names attacking the University of Evansville, causing the University once again to file a suit against him. The court upheld the injunction. However, Felsher continued to distribute derogatory pamphlets outside Roberts Municipal Stadium before commencement, and he regularly pickets the University when it hosts prospective students and their parents. Felsher persists in his vendetta against the University.

PROFESSIONAL PROGRAMS

Engineering

1991   The College of Engineering and Computer Science received over $78,000 in matching funds from the National Science Foundation for four projects requiring computers, printers, and various pieces of advanced electronic equipment.

1998   The University of Evansville was the host site for a HAZUS (Hazards of the United States) training and demonstration project. Civil engineering professor **Nasim Uddin** (Ph.D., State University of New York) and several students participated in the project, a loss-estimation software program used to assess community risk in the event of an earthquake, flood, tornado or hurricane. Vanderburgh County was the first "showcase community" to collaborate with the Institute for Business and Home Safety in developing and implementing a hazard mitigation strategy for natural disasters. HAZUS software predicts in advance which areas or buildings pose the greatest risk of loss of life or injury or severe curtailment of community services should a catastrophe occur, and it aids in developing a methodology for keeping losses to a minimum. Students gained valuable firsthand experience which could make their own community a safer place in which to live and work. They presented the results of their research at a national professional conference.

2001   A new degree program was established, the first of its kind in Indiana and available in only a few other institutions in the nation. Called the Bachelor of Science in Internet Technology, the program is interdisciplinary. To learn how to analyze and evaluate the Internet for information exchange and as a tool for commerce, stu-

Nasim Uddin

dents take courses in information theory, marketing, management, mass communication, law and ethics, psychology, computer science, and computer graphics. In addition to course work, students are required to work as interns for companies, agencies, or for the University's Internet Applications Laboratory. Graduates of the program are well-equipped to work in e-commerce, manage an Internet technology department, or serve as computer programmers or web developers. Robert Morse directs the program.

2002 The new Engineers for Indiana program at the University of Evansville allows twenty-five incoming freshmen and transfer students from other schools to enroll at the same tuition as that charged by state-supported Purdue University, a savings of approximately seventy-five percent. Eligible students can also apply for a standard financial aid package, thus further reducing their actual cost. Participants must pledge to seek their first employ-

ment within Indiana or with a company based in Indiana, thus generating more engineers to fill the state's need for highly trained professionals.

AN INGENIOUS DEVICE

In 2003, mechanical engineering senior Abdullah Ridha, a native of Kuwait, devised a mini electrical lift useful in residence halls for items too heavy for an individual to move. The lift proved invaluable to technicians repairing campus air conditioning units. Before Ridha built the small steel machine, the University had to spend $48 a day to rent a lift. This project has saved the University not only money, but time and manpower; waiting for a lift to be delivered has been eliminated, and Ridha's "ACEPower" lift can be operated by a single person.

245

Amber Duff tests out a walker designed for her by UE students Nancy East and Michael Austin

A FIRST PLACE DESIGN

In 2001, a team of University of Evansville students netted themselves $10,000, won $10,000 for the University, and received an all-expenses paid trip to Chicago for themselves and their faculty advisor for a special awards ceremony. It was their reward for providing a disabled girl with independence of movement and the opportunity to exercise her legs.

Their adaptive mobility device for Amber Duff, a four-year-old from Cynthiana, Indiana, who is blind, deaf, and has cerebral palsy, won first place in the College Division of the North American Engineering Design Contest sponsored by *Design News*.

Monica Duff, Amber's mother, met several times with a mechanical engineering class to discuss Amber's instability problems with walkers. Two seniors in the class then designed a specially adapted walker as their senior project. The following year, another team built on that idea and made a type of tricycle that allows Amber to move about an area in a semi-reclining position.

246

Doug Stamps (top, standing) consults with engineering students Ryan Ogle (left) and Dalen Zuehsow on their design for Amber's tricycle

CONCRETE CANOES!

Mark Valenzuela with one of UE's concrete canoes

Engineers love a challenge. Telling engineers that a task is impossible is often all it takes to spark their creative energies.

Civil engineering students at UE are no exception. Every year, the American Society of Civil Engineers sponsors a race for builders of concrete canoes.

Based on his own experiences with concrete canoe races at other universities, UE civil engineering professor **Mark Valenzuela** (Ph.D. Cornell University) understood the kind of excitement these events can generate and communicated his enthusiasm to his students shortly after arriving at the University in 1999.

Of course, there were obstacles to overcome (such as Koch Center being gutted in preparation for building the new addition), but before long, a twenty-one foot concrete canoe, christened *High Noon*, was ready for testing in the Carson Center swimming pool. In the actual race at the regional conference, however, UE finished eighth out of eight competing schools.

But the UE team was not discouraged. After all, their vessel did not sink (canoes from two other schools did), although it did develop severe cracks and the paddlers had to furiously bail out water with their hands until a teammate swam out to give the crew a pump.

Nevertheless, the students involved learned a lot and enjoyed themselves. So there was no hesitation about trying again the next year. The new concrete canoe was much sleeker and slimmer than its predecessor, enabling it to go much faster in the water, and it was much stronger and more durable, hence less prone to cracking. In honor of the first year's misadventures, the new vessel was christened *Bassackwards*.

The results were far from spectacular but did show improvement. UE finished fifth out of a field of ten, was given a "Wackiest Theme" fun award for the clever name, and won their bid to have the next regional competitions held on UE's campus.

247

Although a huge undertaking for a school the size of UE, Evansville successfully hosted the 2003 event. Nearly 250 participants attended. This time the UE boat was more stable and its hull design made it more maneuverable than its predecessor. Amazing everyone, even Evansville's own cheering fans, UE came in third overall.

The students' efforts garnered a lot of media attention, with reporters from the *Evansville Courier & Press* and the local ABC, NBC, and FOX affiliates covering various phases of the team's progress.

Student leader Brennan McReynolds summed it up best when he said:

"The concrete canoe project was important because it forced us to step out of our comfort zone and challenged us to do something we had never done before. It showed that even small schools can excel and earn the respect of the bigger and better-known universities."

ENGINEERING FACULTY

Also joining the college during this period were:

John Parr
(Ph.D., Auburn University) 1988-present
Electrical Engineering

Chris Gwaltney
(M.S., University of Illinois) 1990-present
Civil Engineering

Brian Swenty
(Ph.D., University of Missouri-Rolla) 1993-present
Civil and Environmental Engineering

Deborah Hwang
*(Ph.D., Massachusetts Institute of Technology)
  1995-present*
Computer Science
Program Director

Douglas Stamps
(Ph.D., University of Michigan) 1995-present
Mechanical Engineering

Virginia Tamondong
(Ph.D., University of Alabama) 1996-present
Mechanical Engineering

Wadieh Hawa
(B.S., University of Evansville) 1997-present
Computer Engineering

Colleen Gordon and Brennan McReynolds spent endless hours preparing the concrete canoe for competition

248

1998 UE MOON BUGGY TEAM IN HUNTSVILLE, ALABAMA

Each year mechanical engineering students compete in the moon buggy competition as part of their senior design project. Students design and build a human-powered vehicle that can be easily collapsed into a small storage bay, be reassembled and then navigated on a simulated lunar terrain. Schools from around the country travel to Huntsville, Alabama, to compete in this NASA-sponsored event.

Education and Health Sciences

A 1990 administrative restructuring merged the School of Education with the School of Nursing and brought the health and physical education department, until then part of the College of Arts and Sciences, into the new unit, henceforth known as the College of Education and Health Sciences. The former School of Nursing became the Department of Nursing, chaired by **Rita Behnke** and later by **Jane Allen**; the School of Education retained its name and was chaired in recent years by **Nealon Gaskey**, **Walt Lewis** and **Charles Watson**; and the health and physical education department was renamed the Department of Human Kinetics and Sport Studies in 1996. (See pages 253-254.)

John Beineke, Cathy Barlow, Stephen Greiner, and Lynn Penland have served as dean of this unit.

249

Rita Behnke

Education

Students in the School of Education engaged in several notable projects during this period, as delineated below.

1990 *LEAP (Learning Enrichment for Academic Progress)*, supported by PRIDE (People Responsible for Improving the Development of Education), a Lilly Endowment grant, and corporate funding from Alcoa and Bristol-Myers Squibb, brought 100 or more minority middle school and high school students to campus for sessions on computers, time-management, and international cultures. Seventeen University of Evansville students served as peer counselors each year and Evansville area businessmen participated as role models.

1991 *Make the Right Choice*, a joint project of the University of Evansville and the Metropolitan Evansville Chamber of Commerce, featured visits to middle schools by Evansville area workers explaining what they do on their jobs and what science, mathematics, and language classes students need to prepare them for productive careers.

1991 *Outstanding Educators of the Year,* a special awards program, recognized outstanding teachers and administrators in Vanderburgh County. It was initially a joint project of the University of Evansville and the Mead Johnson Nutritional Group; since 1997, the University's co-sponsor has been the *Evansville Courier & Press*. Four persons (a teacher in an elementary, middle, and high school, and an administrator) are selected annually, each receiving $1,000; winners are also eligible to enroll in a free course at the University of Evansville.

1992 *The middle grades reading network*, a statewide project, was funded by a $386,094 Lilly Endowment grant and headed by Jack Humphrey, former direc-

tor of reading for the Evansville-Vanderburgh School Corporation. In 1996, the Lilly Endowment granted an additional $470,362 for this project to purchase 300,000 books and teaching materials.

1994 *A cooperative program between UE and the YMCA* involved more than 100 University of Evansville students, many of them members of Alpha Omicron Pi sorority and Phi Kappa Tau fraternity. The program helped children ages 6-14 with their studies and provided seasonal recreational activities.

1994 *Professional development partnership*, a joint project of the University of Evansville and Bosse High School, enabled bridge (see page 158) and honor students to use University computer labs and receive UE library cards. Bosse teachers had access to the University's new electronic equipment. In addition, selected Bosse instructors made videotapes demonstrating their teaching techniques, valuable in training University of Evansville education majors.

UE student volunteers for America Reads

Don Rodd (left) and Dave Enzler (right), directors of the Fit Family Program

1995 *The Signature Learning Center*, a joint project of the University of Evansville, the Evansville-Vanderburgh School Corporation, the University of Southern Indiana, Ivy Tech State College, and the Catholic Diocese, was designed to meet the needs of gifted high school students. Located in the former Sonntag Hotel next to the Victory Theatre in downtown Evansville, the center emphasized mathematics, science, foreign languages, and economics. In 2002, the center became Signature School, Indiana's first charter high school.

1997 *America Reads*, supported by federal (AmeriCorps) and state funding. About thirty UE students each year tutor kindergarten through third grade pupils on a one-on-one basis at least twice a week for thirty minute sessions. Through this pro-

gram, over 1,500 children increased their reading abilities by one grade level and in many cases by two. In addition to providing reading instruction, the UE tutors assist with parent programs, book fairs, and other literacy-related projects.

1997 *Fit Family Program* was funded with a $50,000 grant from the Foundation for Community Health. Don Rodd of the human kinetics and sport studies department and Dave Enzler of the Student Fitness Center directed about fifty University of Evansville students working with 360 eighth graders and their parents on projects related to physical fitness and wellness (nutrition, substance abuse, etc.).

251

EDUCATION FACULTY

Also joining the school during this period were:

Janet Dill Waller
(M.A., Ball State University) 1988-present
Elementary Education

Paul Plath
(Ph.D., University of Illinois) 1995-2002
Secondary Education

Robert Ciscell
(Ed.D., Indiana University) 1996-present
Middle School and Secondary Education

Amy McBride Martin
(M.S.E., Drake University) 1998-present
Elementary Education, Mathematics

Nursing and Physical Therapy

Although the associate's degree in nursing was phased out in 1989 and various master's programs in the School of Nursing were also discontinued, a number of innovative changes added new vitality to the curriculum.

In 1993, the nursing faculty embarked on an extensive review of its offerings, utilizing a framework developed by Joyce Dungan. Her Model of Dynamic Integration led, three years later, to the implementation of a new curriculum, with its first students graduating in 2000.

———

A new combined master's and bachelor's degree program in health services administration began in 2000, allowing students to earn both degrees in five years. (The separate bachelor's and master's programs in this area, in place for several years, continued to be available.)

A BANNER YEAR

In 1997, the nursing department enjoyed a banner year.

Kathleen Scheller, a member of the nursing department since 1975, was certified as a pediatric nurse in 1997, earning the highest score for the year in the United States. The National Certification Board of Pediatric Nurse Practitioners and Nurses presented Scheller with a plaque in recognition of this accomplishment.

Also in 1997, the University was granted $50,000 from the Foundation for Community Health for a project titled "Smokefree Babies." The program helped pregnant mothers who wanted to stop smoking to achieve their goals. Nursing students and those with related majors performed the initial interviews. Later the students helped collect and analyze data, such as measuring carbon monoxide levels in the body. As a result of these efforts, expectant mothers learned how lifestyle changes could benefit their babies.

Kathleen Scheller (right) supervises a student's work

The health services administration curriculum combines courses in traditional clinical areas with courses in management, finance, and other aspects of health care delivery. Two internships – available at a variety of settings including hospitals, rehabilitation centers, and long-term care facilities – are required. Key faculty members who initiated the program included William Stroube, executive-in-residence and a former Bristol-Myers Squibb executive, and Rita Behnke, chair of the nursing department.

––––––

In 1989, physical therapy became an independent department. Two years later, a combined bachelor's and master's degree in physical therapy was first offered, consisting of two years of prerequisites followed by three years in the professional program. The curriculum is fully accredited, and clinical opportunities grew from fewer than fifty to more than 275 domestic sites, in addition to international clinical placements in England, the Netherlands, Switzerland, and Australia. In 2003, the physical therapy program was revised, adding a half year to the curriculum. This enabled students to earn a bachelor's degree in a chosen field, such as biology or movement science, as well as a master's degree in physical therapy.

Janet Szczepanski demonstrates physical therapy techniques with students

––––––

PHYSICAL THERAPY FACULTY

Also joining the department during this period were:

Mary Kessler
(M.H.S., University of Indianapolis) 1990-present
Department Chair

Terry Chambliss
(M.H.S., Washington University) 1991-present

Janet Szczepanski
(M.H.S., University of Indianapolis) 1993-present

Frank Underwood
(Ph.D., University of Missouri) 1997-present

Human Kinetics and Sport Studies

In 1987, **Paul Jensen** was appointed chair of the physical education department, the first in the school's history without any responsibilities in either the athletic program or intramurals. Ten years later, the unit's name was changed to the Department of Human Kinetics and Sport Studies. The department offers five majors:

Paul Jensen

253

Athletic Training

Exercise Science

Movement Science
(originally called Sports Medicine)

Physical Education

Sport Studies

In 2001, enrollment in the department peaked with over 140 majors.

HUMAN KINETICS AND SPORT STUDIES FACULTY

Current faculty members in the department are:

Paul Jensen
(M.S., University of Illinois)
1974-present

Rita Nugent
(M.S., Indiana State University)
1973-present

Donald Rodd
(Ph.D., Pennsylvania State University)
1995-present

Gregory Wilson
(P.E.D., Indiana University)
1999-present

Also serving the department as athletic trainers are **Terry Collins, Jeffrey Tilly,** and **Catherine Doremire.**

Jane Allen

Joyce, Gregg, and Bob Wilson

ALL IN THE FAMILY

The School of Education and Health Sciences boasts two second-generation members on its faculty roster.

Jane Allen, chair of the nursing department, is the daughter of Helen Smith, the University's first dean of the School of Nursing.

Both parents of Gregory Wilson, assistant professor of human kinetics and sport studies, have strong connections with the University. His mother, Joyce, served the physical education department as its secretary for sixteen years, and his father, Robert, held a variety of positions in the areas of psychology, counseling, and student affairs.

Bob Wilson graduated from Evansville College in 1954 with majors in education and psychology. Combining these interests led to his appointment as the first elementary school counselor in the Evansville-Vanderburgh School Corporation. With this pioneering program well established, Wilson returned to his alma mater, serving as director of the counseling center, dean of students, vice president for student affairs, and professor of psychology.

All three Wilson sons graduated from UE. Gregg began his academic career as a history teacher at Memorial High School in Evansville, but soon after completing a doctorate at Indiana University in kinesiology and sports psychology, he returned to UE to teach these subjects.

For Jane Allen and Gregg Wilson, the University of Evansville is truly in their blood.

254

Business Administration

Following Joseph Holt's retirement in 1989, **Elaine Hopkins** became director of the Center for Management Education and Services, serving until the center was discontinued five years later. During its more than forty years, CMES offered classes to most major Tri-State companies, including Alcoa, Atlas Van Lines, Deaconess Hospital, General Foods, Mead Johnson, Old National Bank, Whirlpool, and Zenith.

BUSINESS ADMINISTRATION FACULTY

Also joining the school during this period were:

Charles O'Neal
(D.B.A., Indiana University) 1981-93
Marketing

William Lafief
(Ph.D., Indiana University) 1985-92
Marketing, Social Psychology

Walayet Khan
(Ph.D., University of Arkansas) 1989-present
Finance

James Schaefer Jr.
(Ph.D., Southern Illinois University) 1990-present
Accounting

Laurence Steenberg
(M.B.A., University of Chicago) 1989-98
Management

Brian Engelland
(M.B.A., Columbia University) 1992-97
Marketing

Bruce Alford
(Ph.D., Louisiana State University) 1993-97
Marketing

Robert Montgomery
(D.B.A., Mississippi State University) 1998-present
Marketing

Laura Paglis
(Ph.D., Purdue University) 1999-present
Management

In keeping with the University's international emphasis, the School of Business Administration participates in Global Learning of the Business Enterprise (GLOBE), which teaches students the fundamentals of international trade through the process of negotiating business agreements with GLOBE companies in other countries. The program, sponsored by Junior Achievement of Southwest Indiana and with financial assistance from General Electric Corporation, began in 1994. It was initiated by **Michael Garlich** and later directed by **Edison Moura** and **Martin Fraering**.

For purposes of this project, UE students formed a corporation called Aces International, which then entered into negotiations with GLOBE students at the Universidad Technologica Nacional in Buenos Aires, Argentina. Under the terms of the agreement, our University exported beanie babies to the Argentine students, who in turn sent us leather goods such as belts, wallets, and key fobs. These products were sold in each country to fellow students, friends, and family. Also, a group of students from each country visited each other's university for a week. GLOBE companies are funded by the students, who purchase stock in their company. At the conclusion of each project, the company is liquidated and the proceeds are distributed to the student-shareholders.

In subsequent years, products sent to Argentina included hand-held computers, flashlights, and electronic schedule organizers. Among the items received in return was dulce de leche, a caramel candy that is an Argentine specialty.

255

Laurence Steenberg

Ralph Larmann (right) and students

ARTS AND SCIENCES

Art, Art History, and Archaeology

The University's art program underwent considerable restructuring and expansion during this period. In 1990, when the College of Fine Arts was discontinued, two separate departments – one for art, the other for archaeology and art history – were established, both administered by the College of Arts and Sciences.

In the art department, both master's degree programs for art, the Master of Arts in education and the Master of Arts in studio art, were discontinued, along with the Bachelor of Science degrees in art therapy and commercial art.

Replacing them, however, was a series of major additions to the department's offerings, such as studio classes designed specifically for non-art majors, a visiting artist series which brings in five professionals each year to lecture and demonstrate their specialty, a summer program in Amsterdam (Netherlands), new classes in both traditional and digital photography and, most notably, a greatly expanded program in graphic design.

The department's visual communication major became its most popular option. Focusing on the creative use of computers in graphic design, the major prepared students for careers requiring skills in computer-generated art, such as web design, desktop publishing, advertising, and design work for television and industry. **Ralph Larmann** (M.F.A., James Madison University) heads the program. He has also developed award-winning drawing pages on the web.

In addition, the Ceramics Workshop in New Harmony continued to receive national recognition and to attract students from all regions of the United States. Its director, Les Miley, whose work has been featured in over 170 exhibitions in America and Europe, was selected by the Arts Council of Southwestern Indiana as its Artist of the Year (1996) and as Arts Educator of the Year (2000).

The field of art history benefited from the 1985 appointment of **Shirley Schwarz**, the University's first full-time art historian. Five years later, when archaeology and art history became a separate department, both a major and a minor were offered in these areas. Art history courses at Harlaxton College supplemented those offered on the home campus with some distinctly British-oriented courses taught by **Nicholas McCann** and **Pamela Tudor-Craig** (later Lady Pamela Wedgwood).

The history of archaeology at the University of Evansville has Harlaxton connections as well. The first archaeology courses were taught by **David Wrench** and **Brian Simmons**. They concentrated on Roman Britain and included work on an actual excavation (see pages 193-194). This program continued until Simmons retired, at which time archaeology was discontinued at Harlaxton College.

On the main campus, the coming of Erik Nielsen, the University's new vice president for academic affairs, sparked interest in the field. His background in Etruscan studies, with more than twenty years of experience as director of excavations at an important site in Murlo, Italy, (continuing throughout his tenure at the University of Evansville), served well in establishing a strong program. A full-time faculty member, **Patrick Thomas** (Ph.D., University of North Carolina, Chapel Hill) was appointed in 1990. The number of archaeology majors, only five when Thomas came to campus, rose to over thirty within two years. When Nielsen left the University to become president of Franklin College in Switzerland, Thomas was appointed department chair and continues in the position.

In 2002, there were nearly seventy majors in archaeology and ten in art history. As one of the few departments in a small institution offering an archaeology major focused on the Mediterranean area, it has been able to recruit talented students nationally. Nearly all graduates participate in study-abroad programs, internships, or other forms of practical field experience.

The archaeology and art history department also collaborates with the philosophy and religion department in two joint majors and minors: classical studies and biblical studies. In addition, a considerable number of archaeology majors have elected to minor in the anthropology program offered by the sociology department (since 2001 called the Department of Law, Politics, and Society).

ARCHAEOLOGY AND ART HISTORY FACULTY

Also joining the department during this period were:

Anthony Tuck
(Ph.D., Brown University) 1996-2002
Etruscan Archaeology

Steven Tuck
(Ph.D., University of Michigan) 1997-2001
Roman Archaeology
(Not related to the above)

257

A WINNER

When Shirley Schwarz retired in 2000, the department created a prize in her honor for the best undergraduate research paper on a topic related to art history. The first Shirley J. Schwarz Prize was awarded in 2002 to Whitney Bair.

Chemistry

1992   The chemistry department was awarded computer software through Autodesk Educational Grants. The molecular modeling program HyperChem draws three-dimensional models of polymer and protein molecules, allowing the user to view them from different perspectives and to follow the change in structure occurring when molecules react. It was but one of several valuable instruments and pieces of equipment the department acquired during this period.

1998   The department received a $40,000 grant from the United States Department of Naval Surface Warfare to develop a separation system for detecting multiple biological agents. Students as well as faculty were actively involved in this research.

2001   The chemistry department expanded its biochemistry program into a major, preparing students for graduate studies, medical school, or work in industry. A new biochemistry laboratory, with over 1,500 square feet located in the Koch Center for Engineering and Science addition, enabled the University to add this important program to its curriculum.

CHEMISTRY FACULTY

Joining the department during this period were:

Donald Batema
(Ph.D., University of Missouri) 1989-present
Laboratory Supervisor
Environmental Science, Research Management

Ruthellen Miller
(Ph.D., Miami University, Ohio) 1990-96
Biochemistry

Shane Thread
(M.S., Purdue University) 1992-2000
General Chemistry
(Also coached the University's cross country team)

W. Bryan Lynch
(Ph.D., University of Pittsburgh) 1994-present
Physical Chemistry

Ray Lutgring
(Ph.D., Purdue University) 1995-present
Organic Chemistry, Biochemistry
Department Chair

Arlen Kaufman
(Ph.D., Purdue University) 1996-present
Analytical Chemistry
Director of Environmental Studies

258

Bryan Lynch

English

During much of this period, major emphasis was placed on the English department's creative writing program. (Indeed, during the 1994-95 academic year, creative writing functioned as a separate department, independent of the literary criticism program.) Many creative writing majors earned a Bachelor of Fine Arts degree rather than the traditional Bachelor of Arts, the University of Evansville being one of only seven schools in the country to offer the fine arts degree in creative writing at the undergraduate level.

On two occasions, UE students, competing with graduate students, won important creative writing contests and also participated in the Bucknell Young Poets Workshop (which accepts only fourteen students from the entire nation) and the Radcliffe Publishing Institute.

Margaret McMullan

Faculty members who were active creative writers include William Hemminger and William Baer (see next page), and **Margaret McMullan** (M.F.A., University of Arkansas), the author of three novels. The first, *When Warhol Was Alive*, was published in 1994. *In My Mother's House* and *How I Found the Strong* followed. As coordinator of the department's English Coffee Hour readings, McMullan helped recruit award-winning fiction writers, essayists, and poets to present their work to UE students and faculty. In addition, she serves as the department chair.

———

A 1998 symposium on distinguished American playwright Arthur Miller (most famous for his Pulitzer Prize-winning *Death of a Salesman*) was attended by scholars, directors, and producers from across the nation and by Miller himself, who lectured and read from his works.

———

To further encourage literary pursuits, honorary trustee Melvin M. Peterson funded an endowed chair in literature which was named in his honor. Peterson specified that the person chosen "be an acknowledged inspiring and resourceful teacher, a friend of students, and a model for his or her fellows. The recipient's character should reflect the gentility, humanity, and wisdom of the liberal arts tradition." In 2003, Michael Carson was named the first Melvin M. Peterson Endowed Chair in English Literature. In the same year, Peterson donated funds for a creative writing workshop for University of Evansville alumni, intended to foster their talents and encourage them to seek publishers for their work.

Melvin Peterson

259

A TALE OF TWO BILLS

Bill Hemminger

When it comes to versatility, it is difficult to match Bill Hemminger. He is a translator, fluent in French and Russian; a pianist of exceptional competence, having perfected his skills at the famed Juilliard School of Music in New York; and a published writer of both poetry and fiction. (His short story, "A Friend of the Family," won an award from the Syndicated Fiction Project). He is also a gourmet cook, an accomplished gardener and – in earlier days – a sheep farmer.

Hemminger earned a Bachelor of Arts degree in French and comparative literature at Columbia University, and a master's degree in international affairs and a doctorate in comparative literature at Ohio University.

He was also a student at the Sorbonne in Paris, served for two years with the Peace Corps in Senegal, and spent another two years as a Fulbright lecturer at the University of Madagascar.

At the University of Evansville, Hemminger has a joint appointment as a member of both the English and the foreign languages departments. He is also active in the world cultures program; in this area he obviously knows whereof he speaks.

Bill Baer

Shortly after joining the University of Evansville faculty, Bill Baer and his wife, Mona, launched the only journal in the United States devoted solely to metered poetry, *The Formalist*. The first issue was published in 1990. This semi-annual magazine is now found in the university libraries of Harvard, Yale, Columbia, Oxford, and Cambridge. In addition to the poetry itself, the journal offers critical essays on literature and interviews with prominent poets. Howard Nemerov, Anthony Hecht, Arthur Miller, Richard Wilbur, and John Updike are among the distinguished writers who have served on the publication's editorial board.

Baer was a winner of the Jack Nicholson Screen Writing Award and was also the recipient of a National Endowment for the Arts creative writing grant for fiction.

COLLABORATIVE EFFORTS

Two members of the English department supplied texts for art exhibits shown in the Midwest and California. In 1992, Ralph St. Louis (right in photo) collaborated with William Brown (left) of the art department in presenting a collection of photographs entitled *Expressions of Peace.* The exhibition travelled to eight galleries in Ohio, Illinois, Kentucky, and Indiana.

Four years later, Laura Weaver also collaborated with Brown, providing the text for a collection of photographs entitled *Living the Dream: Celebrating Diversity,* a Martin Luther King Jr. celebration exhibited in the Bower-Suhrheinrich Library. In 2000, Weaver's text accompanied drawings by Matt Busby in *Divided Together: Written and Visual Explorations of the Self,* and in 2003 her words joined the work of sculptress and UE instructor Nel Bannier and other artists in exhibits shown on the UE campus and also in Santa Ana, California, and St. Peters, Missouri.

ENGLISH FACULTY

Also joining the department during this period were:

Larry Caldwell
(Ph.D., University of Nebraska) 1988-present
Medieval Literature, Linguistics
Director of the University Writing Center

Arthur Brown
(Ph.D., University of California - Davis) 1995-present
American Literature

Melanie Culbertson
(M.F.A., Indiana University) 1999-present
Creative Writing

Robert Griffith
(M.F.A., University of Arkansas) 2000-present
Creative Writing

Foreign Languages

The University of Evansville offers a major and minor in French, German, and Spanish, both in liberal arts and in education, plus minors in Latin American studies, Russian studies, and Japanese studies. Classes are also offered in Greek, Hebrew, Latin, and Italian, making a total of nine languages in the University's curriculum. Foreign language majors are required to participate in a study-abroad program, towards which their financial aid applies, and they take at least two semesters of a second language. In recent years the department has successfully placed all foreign language education majors in jobs within three months of graduation; several have also been admitted to graduate programs.

261

Scholarships

The foreign languages department offers four endowed scholarships:

**Year
Started**

1987 **Hood/Hardy Scholarship,** funded by Richard and Miriam Hood and William and Lina Hardy

1994 **Rudolph and Mary Ellingson Scholarship**

1995 **The F. Woody and Mary Werking Scholarship**

1996 **DeMerode Scholarship,** established by **Louiza McCarty**

LOUIZA McCARTY

Louiza McCarty, a native French speaker, came to the United States from Belgium as a war bride after World War II. Her 1964 publication *Diction: Premiers Pas (French Diction: The First Steps)* enabled students to read and speak French correctly. Too often, after several years of study, students' mastery of French grammar and verb conjugations was nearly perfect, but their ability to pronounce and understand the language was sadly deficient. McCarty set about to remedy the situation through use of her own three-step method: First, she taught her students to recognize the characteristic sound of each letter, especially the distinctive French vowels. Second, she developed a basic vocabulary of 2,000 words, sufficient for everyday conversation. Finally, she guided her students in using these words to form sentences, first short and later more complex. McCarty shared her unique style of language mastery with University of Evansville students from 1968 until she retired in 1982.

262

Language Laboratory

In 1998, the University installed a state-of-the-art fully digitalized Sony LLC 2000 language laboratory system, with thirty computer stations for the foreign languages department and an additional twenty stations for the Intensive English Center. The system incorporated audio, video, computer graphics, and information from CD-ROMs. It boasted excellent sound quality and was extremely user-friendly, enabling students to access program material quickly on their hard drives. The laboratory also allowed students to receive newspapers, magazines, and radio and television broadcasts from the country they were studying.

Special Events and Activities

1979 **Sankt Nicholas Fest,** an annual event, attracts up to 275 middle and high school teachers and students of German. The fest features readings, sketches, and musical presentations. It was initiated by Henry Miner, who was later assisted by **Marie-Lise Charue** and **John Meredig**.

1994 **Hispanidad** was a week-long celebration of Hispanic languages and culture. Planned by foreign languages department professor **Patricia Vilches** in conjunction with the Indiana Humanities Council and the Evansville Museum, activities included lectures, dances, movies, and classes which focused on both Spanish and Latin American culture and United States business ties with Hispanic nations.

1995 **Multicultural Sketches, an Understanding of Peoples**, was sponsored by the foreign languages department, co-directed by Patricia Vilches and **Ann Baker**, and supported by the Indiana Arts Commission and the Evansville Museum. The program embraced such topics as nineteenth century German art song and chamber music, Hispanic dance, African American jazz, Native

American crafts, French Canadian folk songs, and cultures of Asia.

1998 **Foreign Language Cultural Immersion Floor,** a joint project of the foreign languages department and the Offices of Residence Life and International Student Services and Activities, featured a living/learning community in Moore Hall for twenty-five students. A variety of activities supplemented classroom learning of a foreign language, such as playing familiar board games in other languages and watching television programs shown in a variety of languages via satellite link. (In addition, the International Students Club, made up of both Americans and students from abroad, sponsors an annual banquet and bazaar.)

2000 **Epsilon Beta chapter of Phi Sigma Iota,** a national honor society for outstanding advanced students of foreign language and literature, was established at the University. Its membership included both students and faculty.

FOREIGN LANGUAGES FACULTY

Also joining the department during this period were:

Catherine Fraley
(M.A., Indiana University) 1991-present
French

Ellen Klein
(Ph.D., University of Illinois) 1992-99
German

Gerald Seaman
(Ph.D., Stanford) 1992-2000
French
Department Chair

Juan delValle
(M.S., Ohio University) 1996-present
Spanish

Yoshiko Nagaoka
(Ph.D., University of Maryland) 1997-present
Japanese

Also, Latin is taught by Patrick Thomas of the archaeology department, and Greek by James Ware of the philosophy and religion department.

Deborah Howard (right) and students

Law, Politics, and Society

In 2001, the legal studies program merged with the former political science and sociology departments to form a new entity, the Department of Law, Politics and Society with **Deborah Howard** (J.D., University of Louisville) as chair.

The legal studies program, formerly administered by the School of Business Administration, boasts over 200 graduates, many working in law offices, banks, insurance agencies, and government offices, while some have gone on to law school or other graduate programs.

263

Mathematics

1991 With a $47,290 grant from the National Science Foundation, the mathematics department made a significant move toward incorporation of computers into its curriculum. By 1993, all calculus and upper-division courses were taught in computer-equipped classrooms, putting the department in the forefront of a national trend toward increased use of computers in mathematics instruction.

1997 Mohammad Azarian published an English summary of a 570-year-old Arabic manuscript, "Meftah al-hesab," in the *Missouri Journal of Mathematical Sciences*. Originally written by Persian mathematician Jamshid Kashani, it served as a textbook for more than five centuries and as an encyclopedia for many generations of students, accountants, astronomers, architects, engineers, land surveyors, merchants, and other professionals. Original handwritten copies of the manuscript can be found in libraries throughout the world. Azarian presented topics and ideas from each of the five books considered mathematically significant.

MATHEMATICS FACULTY

Also joining the department during this period were:

Mark Gruenwald
(Ph.D., Northern Illinois University) 1989-present
Department Chair

David Dwyer
(Ph.D., Purdue University) 1990-present

Troy van Aken
(Ph.D., Bowling Green State University) 1994-99

Erin Bredensteiner
(Ph.D., Rensselaer Polytechnic Institute) 1997-present

264

Music

A variety of degree programs within the department trained students for careers in music education, music management, and music therapy, as well as performance.

As of 2003, the music therapy program had placed over 130 graduates in schools, hospitals, rehabilitation centers, and nursing homes, with some establishing their own private practice. Begun in the mid 1970s, **Alan Solomon** (Ph.D., University of Kansas) directed the program until 2000 and **Mary Ellen Wylie** (Ph.D., University of Kansas) has directed it since. (Solomon also served as department chair from 1986 to 2000.)

A recent addition to the degree available in performance is a degree with a sacred music emphasis. First offered in 2000, it prepares students for professional church music positions.

The music department places strong emphasis on public performance, both for its students and for its faculty. Students give junior and senior recitals and participate in a rigorous ensemble program, including several choruses, chamber groups, and a full symphony orchestra.

Douglas Reed , organ

Tibetan Monks of the Drepung Loseling Monastery perform in Shanklin Theatre

Several music faculty have performed widely in the United States and abroad and have made recordings which won favorable reviews. These include CDs by clarinetist David Wright, pianists Gregory Davis and Garnet Ungar, and University organist Douglas Reed. Reed's recordings high-lighted music by Indiana-born William Albright. Similarly, baritone Joseph Hopkins issued a CD of songs by Evansville-native Richard Faith, with the composer accompanying at the piano.

Special programs featuring students, faculty, and distinguished guest artists complemented these activities. A partial list includes:

1994 **William Warfield,** Bass-Baritone
Soloist with the Symphony Orchestra

Symphony Orchestra on Tour
With sixty-eight members, the largest in University history, the orchestra per-formed at Bosse High School in Evans-ville and also in Greensburg and Lawrenceburg, Indiana

1998 **Abbey Simon,** Piano
With the Symphony Orchestra

Yolanda Kondonassis, Harp

1998-2002
Bach Cantata Series
With the Neu Chapel Choir

1999 ***Beauty and the Beast***
Opera by Richard Faith
Performed by students from the University and area high schools

Awadigin Pratt, Piano

2001 **Tibetan Monks of the Drepung Loseling Monastery**
Chant and ceremonial dances

The King'singers
British vocal ensemble
Concert and master classes

2002 **Caius and Gonville Choir,**
Cambridge University, England
Concert and master classes

265

Opera.com.edy
Comic opera by Jason Charnesky and
Bruce Trinkley, commissioned by the
University of Evansville, performed on
campus and in area high schools

Preservation Hall Jazz Band

2003 **Bach's *St. Matthew Passion***
Performed by the University Choir, with
solo parts taken by UE alumni, conducted by **Johnny Poon** (D.M.A., University
of Iowa), director of choral activities

Peter Schickele, composer and pianist

Collage
Contemporary solo, ensemble, and
orchestral music
Performance included two new works
commissioned by UE, with the composers in attendance. Program arranged
by **Richard Loheyde** (D.M.A., University
of Texas), director of the University's
Symphony Orchestra.

Important musical events in other locations
included:

2000 **A Carnegie Hall Program in New
York City** in which Johnny Poon conducted a 200-member festival chorus
drawn from vocal ensembles at UE and
several area high schools, with guest
soloists and the New England Symphonic Ensemble.

2001 **A Tour of Russia** with the thirty-five-
member University Choir, performing
both a capella and with the Moscow Philharmonic Orchestra. Also gave concerts
in St. Petersburg and elsewhere in Russia.

2002 **A Summer Music Festival at
Harlaxton College**

Acquisition of new instruments greatly
enhanced UE's music program during this period.
A small mechanical-action organ built by C.B.
Fisk was installed in 1994. The instrument, situated near the front of Neu Chapel, is especially suited to early organ literature.

Johnny Poon

In 1998, the University commissioned a small
portable organ from organ builder John Schreiner,
made possible by a gift from the McGary family of
Newburgh, Indiana. Charles McGary '79 initiated
the gift as a memorial to his mother, Francile
McDonald McGary, a 1946 music graduate of
Evansville College. The organ is about three-
fourths the size of an upright piano and contains
153 pipes. The oak cabinet is decorated with carv-
ings by sculptress Morgan Pike. Its primary use is
to accompany vocal soloists, choirs, and instrumental groups. It is easily transported and, despite
its small size, can produce a considerable volume
of sound. The organ was dedicated in 2000. The
following year it was employed in *Cantata Sancta*
by Sydney Hodkinson, a piece commissioned by
the McGary family and the Friends of UE Music,
when it premiered in Neu Chapel.

Also useful in allowing music students to hear and perform seventeenth and eighteenth century compositions in an authentic manner were the University's 1974 Dowd harpsichord and an additional one given by Paul Hinrichs of Madisonville, Kentucky.

In 2002, the University shipped its 9-1/2 foot, eight octave Bösendorfer Imperial Grand piano to Harlaxton College. During its twenty-seven years in Wheeler Concert Hall, the Viennese-built instrument, donated by Arnold Habig, former chief executive officer and chairman of the board of Kimball International of Jasper, Indiana, had been used for 1,187 faculty, student, and guest recitals. At Harlaxton, where the fine instrument was urgently needed, it was placed in the Great Hall of the manor, a space suitable to its size and sound.

Schreiner organ, gift of the McGary family

Replacing it in Wheeler Concert Hall was a nine-foot Steinway concert grand piano donated anonymously along with five additional Steinways (three six-foot and two seven-foot instruments) for faculty studios and student practice rooms. The pianos, valued at $300,000, were hand-selected by members of the University's faculty. Henry Steinway, the last direct descendant of the firm's founder to have the Steinway name, personally signed the inside of each instrument.

Several musical organizations have made valuable contributions to the University's music program.

- **The UE Music Therapy Association** promotes awareness and knowledge of music therapy by hosting guest speakers and by conducting fund-raising projects to support members who wish to attend regional or national music therapy conferences.

- **Friends of UE Music,** a community-based support group with about 100 members, assists the University in promoting recital programs, raises funds for special projects, contributes to commissions of new music, and helps endow music scholarships.

- **Sigma Alpha Iota** is the largest music fraternity in the world for women. UE's Beta Epsilon chapter won the Outstanding Chapter in the Nation award in 2002. It was the fifth time Beta Epsilon received this award, a distinction no other chapter has won more than once.

- **Phi Mu Alpha** is the largest music fraternity in the world for men. UE's Epsilon Upsilon chapter collaborated with Sigma Alpha Iota to sponsor a school enrichment program in which UE students taught music to elementary and middle school children. This was funded by a Music Forte grant.

267

- **Pi Kappa Lambda,** Delta Upsilon chapter, is an honorary music fraternity for faculty and students.

- **American Guild of Organists**

- **American String Teachers Association,** Paul Rolland Memorial Student Chapter

Carol Dallinger (right) in her studio

The University of Evansville also hosted the 2001 International Trumpet Guild conference. Over 800 performers and teachers attended from across the nation and Great Britain, China, Taiwan, Italy, Germany, Russia, France, and Canada. **Timothy Zifer** (Ph.D., Louisiana State University) of the music faculty chaired the conference, which concluded with a performance by a 100-trumpet choir.

MUSIC FACULTY

Also joining the department during this period were:

Lonnie Klein
(D.M.A., University of Illinois) 1989-99
Director of the Symphony Orchestra

Elizabeth Dodd
(M.M., University of Tulsa) 1996-present
Voice

Debra Cordell
(M.M.T., Western Michigan University) 2000-present
Music Therapy

Elizabeth Dodd

Tim Zifer

Philosophy and Religion

Department member **Anthony Beavers** (Ph.D., Marquette University) played an active role in the use of computers to enhance instruction in the humanities. Collaborating with colleagues Richard Connolly (philosophy), William Hemminger (English and French), Deborah Howard (law), Arthur Brown (English), Michael Carson (English), and Soumendra De (finance), he developed the web site "Exploring Ancient World Cultures" in 1995.

It began with the invention of writing and continued with Egypt, the ancient Near East, Greece, Rome, India, China, the Islamic World, and medieval Europe, ending about 1450. Originally intended to supplement the University's World Cultures Sequence, it has also proved useful to high schools and colleges elsewhere.

Beavers' later web site, "Exploring Plato's Middle Dialogues," received favorable recognition from the *New York Times* and National Public Radio. Then, in conjunction with Peter Suber of Earlham College, Beavers created two additional search engines for philosophy: "Hippias: Limited Area Search of Philosophy on the Internet" (1997) and "Noesis: Philosophical Research Online" (1998). Both projects gained positive reviews nationally as well as in England and Australia.

Anthony Beavers

___

PHILOSOPHY AND RELIGION FACULTY

Also joining the department during this period were:

James Ware
(Ph.D., Yale University) 1995-present
Historical Theology, New Testament

Larry Colter
(Ph.D., Yale University) 2001-present
Philosophy of Mind and Language
Department Chair

Physics

By the late 1980s, research experience was encouraged, and later required, of all physics majors. In addition to many on-campus projects, off-campus research was carried out at the Argonne National Laboratory, Indiana University Cyclotron Facility, Georgia Institute of Technology, Cornell University, and the University of Notre Dame. Also, seminars were organized, enabling students to share their research data.

Faculty research resulted in publications by Gifford Brown in solid-state physics and a NASA-supported study by Ben Riley on rarified gas dynamics.

269

- In the early 1990s, due mainly to the University's active pre-physical therapy program, the service component of the physics department expanded dramatically. This program peaked in 1995 but declined after that.

■ The introduction of state-of-the-art equipment ensured consistently high quality offerings for majors and non-majors. For example, with a grant from the Alcoa Foundation, a NeXT computer was purchased and a NeXT laboratory established. The powerful Mathematica program became an integral part of this system.

Introductory physics benefited from the use of Project Kaleidoscope (PKAL), begun in 1990. Ten years later, the new physics lecture hall in the Koch Center for Engineering and Science addition provided a computer for every seat, multiple video projectors, and state-of-the-art laboratory facilities supervised by **David Fentress**.

Psychology

In 1988, **Mark Kopta** '74 (Ph.D., Northwestern University), a clinical psychologist, was appointed department chair. He had established a national reputation in psychotherapy, with significant publications in the field and wide media coverage, including the *Los Angeles Times*.

In 1989, the University discontinued its master's program in psychology in order to strengthen its undergraduate program. Kopta's strong research skills led to an emphasis on undergraduate research, with several articles in national journals co-authored by faculty members and students.

During Kopta's tenure, the number of psychology majors increased dramatically – 140 by 2001 – making the department one of the largest in the University.

The years around 1990 saw a dramatic increase nationwide in the number of women majoring in psychology. As a result, by 2000, women members of the American Psychological Association outnumbered men. As increased enrollment required additional faculty positions, the University increasingly sought women with superior credentials who might also serve as role models for women psychology majors.

Mark Kopta

PSYCHOLOGY FACULTY

Also joining the department during this period were:

Lora Becker
(Ph.D., State University of New York) 1999-present
Behavioral Neuroscience

Mary Pritchard
(Ph.D., University of Denver) 1999-present
Social Psychology

Theatre

Kennedy Center/American College Theatre Festival

The American College Theatre Festival (ACTF) provides opportunities for college and university theatre departments to showcase their best work at regional and national festivals. Through awards and scholarships, ACTF honors both excellence of overall production and individual student performance.

In 2002, more than 900 productions and 18,000 students participated in the ACTF nationwide. The University of Evansville has been selected to perform in the regional festivals more often than any other school in the nation, and has received six invitations, more than any other university, to per-

Pictured left to right Clint Corley, Megan Gleeson, Karl Kenzler, Carrie Peterson, Shelly Keiser, Matt Tripodi, Robert Miller in Chechov's *The Three Sisters*, April 1989 in Shanklin Theatre

form at the national festival at the John F. Kennedy Center for the Performing Arts in Washington, D.C. In 1988, because of its outstanding record, the University of Evansville was invited to perform a play of its own choice without entering the prior regional competition. (Only Yale University was similarly honored.)

A FIERY START

Even a fire under their bus did not keep UE theatre students from making their mark at the regional competition of the American College Theatre Festival. In 1995, the police pulled over the school bus near Sullivan, Indiana, when an officer noticed the right rear wheel was on fire.

The theatre company was transported to a nearby truck stop and they were unable to resume their trip for several hours. However, arriving in Green Bay, Wisconsin, for the regionals only minutes before registration did not deter two UE students from winning awards at the event.

271

UE'S FESTIVAL PERFORMANCES

1969	Arms and the Man		1988*	Spring Awakening
1971*	The Imaginary Invalid		1989	Roots in a Parched Ground
1973	Lysistrata		1990	The Rose Tattoo
1974	As You Like It		1991	Into the Woods
1975	House of Blue Leaves		1992	Along the Yellow Breeches
1976*	Ah, Wilderness!		1993	The View from Here
1977	Romeo and Juliet		1994	Edith Stein
1978	The Cherry Orchard		1995	O Pioneers!
1980	The Mound Builders		1996	Vinegar Tom
1981*	All the Way Home		1997	The Seagull
1982*	Between Daylight and Boonville		1998	Jack's Holiday
1983	A Streetcar Named Desire		2001	The Caucasian Chalk Circle
1984	Ladyhouse Blues		2002	Jekyll and Hyde
1985	The Tempest		2003	Street Scene
1986	Strider			
1987*	Oklahoma Rigs!			

*National festival participant at the Kennedy Center/
American College Theatre Festival

Evansville Courier & Press • www.myinky.com/ecp/news/   Sunday, January 13, 2002

UE actors make competition history

by ROGER MCBAIN
Courier & Press staff writer
464-7520 or rmcbain@evansville.net

Two University of Evansville students have helped Evansville's first American College Theatre Festival make history for a second time this week.

In an unprecedented feat, Kelli Giddish and Rob Robinson swept top individual acting honors in the regional American College Theatre Festival, which concludes today.

Another UE student, Daniel Mefford, won the Irene Ryan's Best Partner award.

It's the first time in the Irene Ryan competition's 31-year history that students from the same school have taken both acting scholarships in this region.

Giddish and Robinson were among more than 320 competing actors from scores of colleges from Indiana, Illinois, Michigan, Ohio and Wisconsin.

Fifteen UE students have won the regional Irene Ryan scholarships since 1974. Four of them went on to win the national award named after the actress best remembered as Granny Clampett in "The Beverly Hillbillies" TV series.

Reprinted with permission

Other Major Events

Two plays written by UE theatre faculty member **R. Scott Lank '78** were produced in Evansville: *Along the Yellow Breeches* as part of the 1991-92 theatre season; and *First Dance*, by the Repertory People of Evansville in 1993.

In 1995, John David Lutz, theatre department chair, was honored with an Indiana Governor's Arts Award for his leadership in arts education.

President James Vinson (left), Alice May (center), and John David Lutz (right) at the May Studio Theatre dedication (1994)

IT CAN BE ANYTHING YOU WANT IT TO BE

The 1992 campaign, called "A New Kind of Theatre," had two goals: to complete the renovation of Shanklin Theatre and to add a "black box" laboratory theatre to the present facility.

- For the main stage, needed renovations included an enlarged costume and scene shop, an acting classroom, and a dance studio. Through a $500,000 matching gift from the Lilly Endowment, a facelift to the theatre itself expanded the original 7,200 square feet to 11,000; the lobby area was remodeled; carpet, wall coverings, curtains, and seating were replaced; and equipment was updated with the installation of a computer-programmed sound and lighting system. In addition, four headset receivers for the hearing impaired and ramps for the wheelchair-bound made Shanklin Theatre handicapped accessible.

- The new theatre, popularly known as a "black box," was described by John David Lutz as "a large room where nothing is stationary, and everything is mobile so it is very fluid and very versatile. It can be anything you want it to be. It allows room for students to use their imaginations regarding the shape and size of the stage." Most productions are student-directed.

Matt Williams '73, co-creator and executive producer of *Home Improvement* and *Thunder Alley*, and Judy Steenberg, a 1990 honorary alumna, executive director of *TriAd*, and past president of the UE Theatre Society board of directors, chaired the theatre renovation campaign. The new theatre was named for Alice George May '34 who, with her late husband, Guthrie May, is a long-time supporter of her alma mater. The May Theatre was dedicated in 1994.

273

GOOD LUCK! (YOU'LL NEED IT)

Theatre is one of the University's most prestigious programs. Consequently, the number of applicants far exceeds the available spots. Currently, department faculty journey to New York, Chicago, Las Vegas, Atlanta, Seattle, Los Angeles, and Denver, as well as to cities in Florida, Kentucky, and Texas, to conduct interviews and auditions. In addition, the department schedules several on-campus audition dates each year. Typically, approximately 350 high school seniors apply for the program annually.

The 2003 freshman class numbered forty-four, exceeding the total number of majors in the entire theatre program twenty years ago. The forty-four students came from nineteen states, and six were first in their high school class. The total number of theatre students at the University was about 125.

For their auditions, students who aspire to a career in performance are asked to memorize and present a two to three minute monologue from a contemporary play, twenty to thirty lines from a play by Shakespeare, and one verse from a Broadway musical.

The department also offers preparation for work in design and technology, theatre management, and theatre education.

The application process is arduous, but every effort is made to find the most talented and best qualified students available and to select those with the highest potential for success in a theatre-related career. Thus far, the process seems to work!

THEATRE FACULTY

Other faculty teaching during this period were:

Cathy Norgren
(M.F.A., Carnegie Mellon University) 1983-88
Costume Design

Patti McCrory
(M.A., University of California-Santa Barbara) 1988-present
Costume Design

Charles Leslie
(M.F.A., University of Texas) 1992-98
Technical Director

Susan Caromel
(M.F.A., Southern Methodist University) 1995-2000
Acting

Charles Meacham
(M.F.A., University of Illinois) 1998-present
Technical Director

Christia Ward
(M.F.A., Southern Methodist University) 2000-present
Acting

274

OTHER AREAS

Joining other departments during this period were:

BIOLOGY FACULTY

Patricia Akrabawi
(M.S., University of California-Davis) 1992-present
Biology Laboratory Supervisor

Dale Edwards
(Ph.D., Wake Forest University) 1994-present
Zoology, Evolution, Ecology

Michael Cullen
(Ph.D., Case Western Reserve University) 1996-present
Developmental Neurobiology
Department Chair

Michael Cullen

Brian Ernsting
(Ph.D., University of Michigan) 1997-present
Molecular and Cellular Biology

Mark Davis
(Ph.D., University of Illinois) 1998-present
Microbiology, Biochemistry

COMMUNICATION FACULTY

Douglas Covert
(Ph.D., Michigan State University) 1987-97
Environmental Communication

Caroline Dow
(Ph.D., Michigan State University) 1987-98
Mass Media

Michael Stankey
(Ph.D., University of Illinois) 1995-present
Mass Communication, Advertising
Department Chair

Jane Brown
(Ph.D., University of Pennsylvania) 1998-2002
Public Relations

Mark Shifflet
(Ph.D., Rutgers University) 1998-present
Mass Communication, Radio and Television
Associate Director, Internet Technology

Annette Parks

HISTORY FACULTY

Burton Kirkwood
(Ph.D., Florida State University) 1995-present
American History, Latin American History,
Labor and Urban Issues

Annette Parks
(Ph.D., Emory University) 1996-present
Medieval History

James MacLeod
(Ph.D., University of Edinburgh) 1999-present
British History, Religious History, World War I

James MacLeod

275

NEW DEGREES AND PROGRAMS

This period was marked by a retreat from graduate education and renewed emphasis on high quality undergraduate liberal arts and professional training. However, two master's degree programs remained in the curriculum: one in physical therapy and the other in health services administration.

In addition, a new graduate degree, the Master of Science in public service administration, was introduced in 2002. To enter requires at least five years of work experience and a bachelor's degree. The program prepares graduates for leadership in organizations where public service is a primary goal. Students take all classes as a group for their entire two years in the program. Courses deal with social justice and diversity, ethics, marketing, information systems, finance, management theory, human resources, statistics, grant writing, and applied research.

■ A new undergraduate program in women's studies began in 1997. It was initiated by **Wioleta Polinska**, with the support of the philosophy and religion department and Dean Colter of the College of Arts and Sciences. An interdisciplinary minor, early offerings included such courses as Women and the Law, Women and Religion, Women Detective Fiction Writers, Women and Politics, and Women's Literature. Focusing on the roles and contributions of women in our culture, the program is housed in the law, politics, and society department.

Continuing Education

Despite a marked decline in regular credit courses offered in the evening, the University's Center for Continuing Education – offering a wide variety of courses and programs for all age groups – remains active and highly successful.

The *Bachelor of Liberal Studies* program (see page 180) was directed by Eulalie Wilson and, after Wilson's retirement, by Lynn Penland. B.L.S. students became eligible to graduate with honors, and over the years B.L.S. graduates have been admitted to master's degree programs throughout the country.

The *External Studies Program* (see page 181), a customized degree program directed by Bonnie Daly, assistant director of the Center for Continuing Education, also continued through this period. The program typically enrolls about thirty-five students.

The *Wednesday Morning Literature Class* (see page 182), renamed Wednesday Mornings at UE in 2003, grew from an enrollment of ten to fifteen to a high of 174 in 1996 and averages about 100 per semester. Topics for the course, coordinated by George Klinger and Patricia Colter, have included film, comedy, the Romantics, war and peace, notable women, the American spirit, free thinkers, and revolutionaries.

Children participate in the aquatics program

For children and young people, the center's *Kids College* sponsors the Evansville Children's Choir and offers driver education and recreation courses, including an extensive aquatics program, directed by Paul Jensen. As many as 1,200 to 1,400 students have enrolled.

LONG-LASTING ADJUNCT

Although the vast majority of classes at the University of Evansville are taught by regular, full-time faculty, the adjunct staff is invaluable because of their special expertise or work experience. Since their career positions generally demand most of their time, however, adjunct teachers often serve the University for only brief periods.

A happy exception is geography instructor Don Hunter, a teacher at Bosse High School in Evansville for twenty-five years, who taught his first class at the University (then Evansville College) in 1964. The roster of his courses includes: World Regional Geography, Conservation of Natural Resources, Physical Geography, Foundations of American Education, Methods of Teaching Social Science, and Earth Sciences for Youth (a summer program). In addition, he taught education at Harlaxton College, led field trips from the English campus and, since 1985, has been charged with the Bachelor of Liberal Studies cultural geography courses.

It is true that Hunter missed a year to serve as Vanderburgh County Commissioner and two years to teach geography for the State Department at the Teachers College in Kabwe, Zambia. Even so, Don Hunter is UE's most enduring adjunct professor and one of its most esteemed as well.

Evansville Children's Choir

The *Institute for Alcohol and Drug Studies,* begun in 1983 by the School of Nursing, was moved to the Center for Continuing Education in 1989. The institute is an annual, week-long on-campus conference dealing with treatment, prevention, and education. Although designed for professional development of workers in the substance abuse field, it also carries college nursing credit for UE students. The institute, bringing nationally recognized speakers to campus, has enrolled as many as 300 each year.

The *Tri-State Regional Science and Engineering Fair,* previously managed by the College of Engineering and Computer Science and then by the education department, was transferred to the Center for Continuing Education in 1999. Coordinated by Carla Doty, community education specialist, the fair encourages young people to develop expertise in the scientific method. Approximately 225 Tri-State middle and high school students participate in the science fair annually.

277

The project was divided into three parts:

- **The College Exploration Program.** Through partnerships with area high schools, secondary school students were encouraged to enroll in college-preparatory courses. Then, in the summer, juniors and seniors were invited to attend a two-week mini-college entitling them to college credit. The program, SummerStart, was designed for students wishing to get a head start on college by acquiring better study habits. Also, five credit hours could be earned by taking a regular University course, such as world history. In addition, students learned to design a web site.

- **The College Success Program.** For this part of the project, $90,000 was allocated for University faculty members to create innovative ways to teach and to serve as mentors for freshmen. A special course, UE 101 University Success, assisted high school students in their transition to college by emphasizing both academic and life skills. In addition, a new software program, the Degree Audit and Registration System, helped ensure that students stayed on track toward their degree, and specially formed Student Success Teams focused on those most at-risk.

- **The Career Advantage Program.** All UE undergraduates were offered internships related to their career interests. These and related co-op experiences approximately doubled over the five-year period EXCEL operated. Two interactive Internet-based networks were planned: AlumNet utilized e-mail to link students with alumni sharing common career interests, and UE JobLink provided an interactive Internet site matching UE students with prospective employers. The main goal was to substantially increase the number of jobs available to UE graduates in Indiana.

Kenneth Pool surrounded by science fair trophies

Excel

In the mid 1990s, the Lilly Endowment turned its attention to three major educational issues: (1) reports showing a decline in the number of Hoosiers attending college, (2) an increase in the number of students going to college but not finishing their degrees, and (3) an increasing number of college graduates leaving Indiana for employment opportunities elsewhere.

In December 1996, the University of Evansville submitted a proposal addressing these concerns and was granted $4.03 million for a five-year project named Experiential and Collaborative Environment for Learning (EXCEL). Vincent Angotti, associate vice president for academic affairs, directed the program and Tamara Wandel served as project coordinator.

278

1998 freshman class

President Stephen Jennings

280

Professor William Bootz

WUEV disc jockey

Professor Yoshiko Nagaoka

281

▲ *UE students cheer the Aces on to an 81-76 overtime victory over Western Kentucky, 2002*

◀ *Clint Cuffle (23) earned all-Missouri Valley Conference and Academic All-America honors, 2002-03*

▼ *Krista McKendree was the first women's soccer All-American at UE, 2000*

283

◀ *David Weir '92 became the first American college player to compete for a European team in the World Cup; he played for his native Scotland in 1998*

▲ *Andy Benes was the number one pick in the 1988 major league draft, a member of the 1988 Olympic Team, and then went on to play 15 years professionally*

▲ *Latasha Austin jets around an LSU defender in the 1999 NCAA Women's Basketball Division I Tournament at Baton Rouge, Louisiana*

284

Men's soccer Aces vs. Eastern Illinois, 1997

◀ *Eric Fish was a record-setting quarterback and Academic All-American in 1995*

▼ *Jen Thomson helped lead the 1997 softball team to its second 30-win season*

285

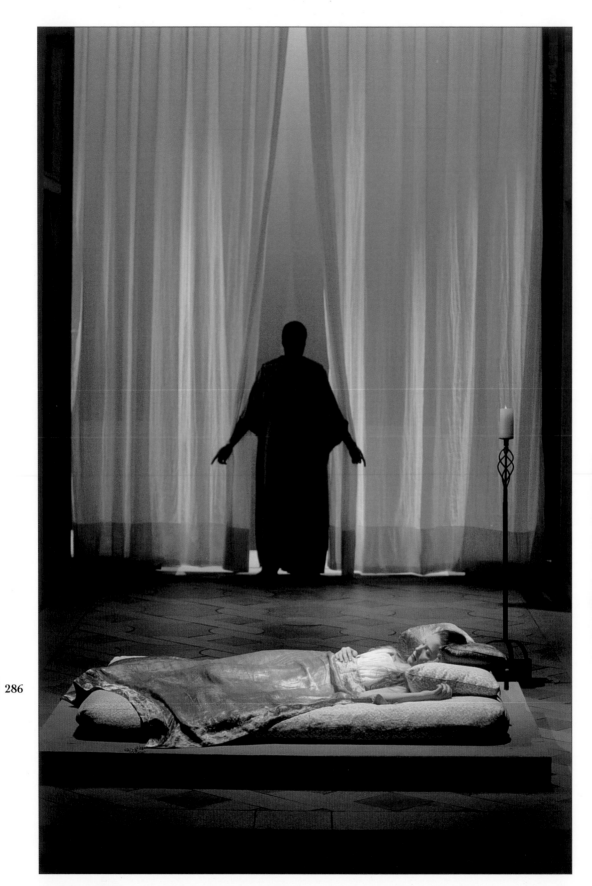

286

Othello, *2002*

▲ Much Ado
about Nothi
1982

▲ *John David Lutz (right) in the title role of* Hamlet *and Sharon Overman as* Gertrude *in the premiere production dedicating Shanklin Theratre, April 1967*

▲ *Professor John David Lutz (center)*

▼ Grapes of Wrath, *1999*

287

◄ Henry V, *1994*

▲ Jeckyl & Hyde, *2001*

288

Roots in a
Parched
Ground,
1989

▲ *Sabino Humbane,*
computer science major

◄ *Neu Chapel mirrored in the*
windows of the May Studio

▼ *Jared Welch,*
marketing major

289

▲ *Addition to Koch Center for Engineering and Science, completed in 2002*

▼ *Front row (left to right)* Pat Meunier, Craig Kerkhoff, Colleen Gordon, Noelle Wiemeier; *behind canoe* Rachel Wright, Corey Markfort, Brennan McReynolds, Julie Elpers, Cassy Wade, Jason Mathias, Mark Valenzuela, Jody Chapman, Ryan Scott, Jared Ashmore, Amy Lochmondy, Clemens Klein, April Wolf, Liz Carstens, Clint Cuffle, Chad Gibson, Jake Ziliak, Nate Mominee, Brad Kempf, Rob Huckaby, Tyler Tackett, Drew Flamion, Matt Deaton, Ben Sperry, Dana Shoup

2003 Aces Concrete Canoe Team with *Ace Purple*

Drawing class

aron Peterman, art major

291

Professor James Brenneman's botany class

▲ *Professor Burton Kirkwood (left)*

▼ *Hispanidad, sponsored by the foreign languages department and a grant from the Indiana Humanities Council, was a week-long festival that celebrated the Spanish language and culture (1994)*

◄ *Bike race (1998)*

▼ *International banquet and variety show (1992)*

293

▲ *Professor Michael Zimmer (center)*

▲ *Krinai Sullivan (right),*
physical therapy major

Professor Daniel Gahan ▶

▼ *Professor William Weiss (center)*

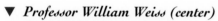

INTERNATIONAL PROGRAMS

HARLAXTON COLLEGE

The program at Harlaxton College, so successfully launched by President Graves (see pages 187-199), continued to prosper under his successors. Despite dips in enrollment following the Persian Gulf War and the September 11 attacks a decade later, the Harlaxton experience proved attractive to an increasing number of University of Evansville students (some of whose parents attended a generation earlier) as well as to students from a host of contractual colleges and universities (most sending their professors as well).

All students now attend Harlaxton College for one semester. Those who wish to spend more time abroad are encouraged to enroll elsewhere, thus receiving a more diversified international experience. As a result of this policy, each semester's class is entirely new. Currently, an average of 120 stu-

---

THEN AND NOW

Among the second generation students at Harlaxton was John Worthington (Fall 2002), whose father, Steve, was in the first UE class to attend the Harlaxton Student Center (1971-72). Steve noted that most of the pioneer group (whom he calls "guinea pigs") attended for two semesters and formed a close community. Several marriages resulted, and five, ten, and twenty-five year reunions have attracted a large number of attendees from all over the country.

In the early 1970s, the Gregory Arms (a mile from the manor) was a hangout where students mingled with the locals, played darts, and drank English beer. Today, the manor has its own bistro and the "Greg" has been turned into an upscale dining establishment.

John Worthington enjoyed easy access to computer labs (his dad could only dream of a PC), the library is well stocked with VCRs (not known to the "guinea pigs"), and e-mail and instant messaging have replaced letters and telephone calls.

As a sign of the times, the former openness of the manor and grounds has been lost to security and safety concerns. There is no longer entrance from the front, and the gates to the gardens are tightly locked. Fortunately, however, the spirit of camaraderie remains.

Steve Worthington

John Worthington

The Gregory Arms

dents enroll each semester, approximately one-half from the University of Evansville. At least thirty percent of all recent UE graduating classes have attended Harlaxton.

Four principals directed the program at Harlaxton during this period. Following the tenure of Graddon Rowlands (1978-89), **Angus Hawkins** was appointed to the position. Although he remained only two years (1990-92), he made a lasting contribution by originating a six-hour interdisciplinary class, The British Experience, which combined English literature, history, art, and political science. This cornerstone course, the core of the

Angus Hawkins

curriculum at Harlaxton, accounts for forty to fifty percent of a student's academic program. In addition, Hawkins instituted musical evenings, with interested students joining him as he played the viola. (He is also the only principal thus far to become a father while at Harlaxton!)

His successor, **Robert Stepsis** (Ph.D., Harvard University) served as principal for a full decade (1992-2002). Besides discontinuing use of Harlaxton by unaffiliated groups during the academic year (arguing that it is, after all, the students' home) and closing the campus to all overnight visitors except students' families, Stepsis developed a master plan for systematic improvements to

Robert Stepsis

the physical facility. These included greatly enhanced landscaping, a new roof on the manor and the carriage house (one semester the students never saw the front of the manor, as it was under scaffolding), and complete renovation of students' rooms in both the manor and the carriage house.

2003 CONTRACTUAL INSTITUTIONS

- **Baker University**
  Baldwin City, Kansas

- **Emory and Henry College**
  Emory, Virginia

- **George Washington University**
  Washington, District of Columbia

- **Lenoir-Rhyne College**
  Hickory, North Carolina

- **Fairfield University**
  Fairfield, Connecticut

- **Hannibal-LaGrange College**
  Hannibal, Missouri

- **Hardin Simmons University**
  Abilene, Texas

- **Marian College**
  Fond-du-Lac, Wisconsin

- **University of Southern Indiana**
  Evansville, Indiana

- **University of Wisconsin**
  Eau Claire and Stout, Wisconsin

- **William Jewell College**
  Liberty, Missouri

With its new furnishings and lounge, the carriage house can now accommodate seventy-eight students as well as summer visitors.

In addition, to provide for future physical improvements, Stepsis was instrumental in developing an endowment fund, financed through a 1995-96 campaign, Harlaxton College: The Complete Experience. Its $2 million goal was exceeded by $44,000. Also to keep Harlaxton up to date with developing technology, Stepsis encouraged greater use of e-mail, facilitated computer connections with the main campus library, and employed the web for personal data, field trip bookings, and many other functions.

Finally, during Stepsis' tenure, the student base expanded to include non-traditional adult students.

Through the University's Center for Continuing Education, summer classes such as "Comparative Issues in British and American Education" and "The British Health Care System" became available.

In 2003, a new leader, **J. Gordon Kingsley**, (Th.D., New Orleans Theological Seminary), began his tenure as principal at Harlaxton. Prior to assuming this post, Kingsley had worked in the development field for health care and had served for thirteen years as president of William Jewell College, long a major feeder school for Harlaxton College.

Harlaxton College achieved national recognition in 1996 when it was ranked among the top twenty-five American study-abroad programs in *The Student's Guide to the Best Study-Abroad Programs: Where to Go from Those Who Know!* Over 300 American students enroll annually

J. Gordon Kingsley

SUZY LANTZ

In her twenty-four year association with the University of Evansville, Suzy Lantz wore many hats. Beginning as an adjunct instructor in the English department in 1979, she went on to serve as an admission counselor, assistant and associate director of admission, and director of transfer and international admission. To the hundreds of students and parents who are her fans, friends, and admirers, however, she is best known as Harlaxton College coordinator and director of the UE study abroad program.

A highly publicized incident during Lantz's tenure as Harlaxton coordinator was the event known as the Great Pizza Caper. Distressed by the lack of "proper" pizza in England, two students – Jim Donahue and John Bruce – were designated by their fellow students to fly to New York City, pick up a quantity of pizzas to go, and

return them to Harlaxton. The students took up a collection to cover the two pizza pilgrims' airfare. Donahue, son of the noted television personality Phil, had been instructed not to leave England and thus chose to use an assumed name, Frankie Idabal. A famous pizza parlor in Greenwich Village provided the needed pies and the pair returned to Harlaxton in short order, much to the acclaim of their comrades.

One of Lantz's most popular projects (originated by her predecessor, Dan Niccum), Harlaxton Awareness Week, encouraged UE students to attend the British campus. The week promoted the Harlaxton Experience with a special British meal at Harper Dining Center (featuring roast beef and Yorkshire pudding), a British movie, a demonstration cricket match, and perhaps best of all, a British auto show in Memorial Plaza, complete with a double-decker bus, an Edinburgh taxi, a variety of MGs and Jaguars, and even a Rolls Royce – all shined up and flying British flags.

Lantz's dedication to serious academics was balanced by a unique appreciation for the lighter side of college life. Aptly described by UE President Stephen Jennings as the "most elegant lady in Evansville," it is little wonder that Suzy Lantz was greatly missed after her retirement in May 2003.

297

Harlaxton College library

Harlaxton College offers its students many opportunities for both academic and personal growth. As former Harlaxton principal Robert Stepsis once noted:

"Our premise has always been that the classroom is Britain itself. At home, American students could study art or literature, history or politics in textbooks, but here they could actually see, feel, touch, and smell many of the things they were reading about. Stonehenge, Hastings, the great Gothic cathedrals of Lincoln and York, Stratford-upon-Avon, the Lake district, Parliament, the paintings of Constable and Turner – all could... experienced directly."

Travel outside of England also serves to broaden the student's education. Even with a strictly enforced attendance policy, there is still ample time for extended weekend trips to Ireland and Paris.

Perhaps even more remarkable, Stepsis observed, was Harlaxton's impact on the individual:

"I am not sure that I can fully describe what happens to our students here or how the tremendous changes that they experience in these four months come about. I can only say that in nearly thirty years as a university faculty member and administrator, I have never seen students grow in maturity, self-confidence, and sophistication as fast as they do in the short time that they are at Harlaxton."

for courses at Harlaxton. The total number since the program began in 1971 approaches 10,000. In addition, about 600 people attend a variety of conferences, short courses, and concerts each summer, and wedding receptions are frequently held at the manor when students are not in residence.

In 2002-03, Harlaxton College added a series of internships with British parliamentary offices, committees or government ministries, either in London or Nottingham. Participants earned academic credit through Harlaxton College and gained firsthand knowledge of England's political institutions.

298

A CLUNKER

In 1999, *The Haunting*, starring Liam Neeson, was filmed at Harlaxton. Critics judged the film "incredibly dull" and labeled it a "clunker," but the audience could at least enjoy a good view of Harlaxton Manor!

Social Life at Harlaxton

- Romances flourished under Harlaxton's magic spell. Students, faculty, members of the Advisory Council, plus a dean and an assistant dean of Harlaxton (Bruce and Jane Roberts) met at Harlaxton. Some even had their wedding receptions there.

- An established tradition, just before leaving Harlaxton, is the naked mile run. Students run from the road to the manor naked, except for shoes, in the dark of night with their closest friends.

- Students meet the locals through the Meet-A-Family program, in which local families host a group of Harlaxton students in their homes approximately once a month. The students reciprocate the hospitality by inviting the families to the manor for an American Thanksgiving meal or for Spring Fest. Students also compete against and meet the locals in the Sports Hall at Harlaxton.

Harlaxton dining hall

OTHER INTERNATIONAL PROGRAMS

Until the late 1980s, Harlaxton College offered University of Evansville students their only opportunity to study abroad, but the number of available options increased dramatically after that, numbering well over 100 institutions on every continent except Antarctica.

The opportunities for study abroad came in a dazzling variety. Through its International Institute the University of Evansville established academic cooperation agreements with universities and colleges in Brazil, Japan, Korea, Malaysia, Taiwan, Argentina, Mexico, the Netherlands, and Germany. In addition, it has signed sister-university agreements with seven universities, three in Japan, three in Korea, and one in Malaysia.

Under the auspices of the Council on International Educational Exchange, University of Evansville students can study abroad for a summer, a semester, or an academic year. Included in the list of possible countries are Japan, the Dominican Republic, Czechoslovakia, Hungary, Poland, Spain, and France. The International Student Exchange Program offers programs with approximately 100 affiliated universities. Although most programs totally immerse the visitor in the language and culture of the host country, some are taught in English, such as the European Studies Program at the University of Amsterdam. Denmark's International Studies program, affiliated with the University of Copenhagen, also makes all of its courses available in English. Students can live with a Danish family or, if they prefer, with Danish students in a residence hall.

Other international programs involved an exchange between the host school and the University of Evansville. For example, University of Evansville students could exchange places with a student from the University of Osnabrück, Germany, in Evansville's sister city. American participants were required to be proficient in German.

Tokoha Gakuen University, Nagoya Gakuin University, and Hiroshima Jogakuin College in Japan operated active exchange programs with our University. Tokoha Gakuen, UE's sister university

299

in Shizuoka, sent approximately ten students each year to study in our Intensive English Center and/or in our undergraduate programs. Some attended Harlaxton College as well.

We, likewise, sent students and faculty to Tokoha each year for a summer program. University of Evansville students reasonably fluent in Japanese lived with local families and pursued intensive study of Japanese language and culture at Tokoha Gakuen. At the same time, Japanese students who were English language majors took a course in public policy taught by University of Evansville professor David Gugin. The program with Jogakuin College in Hiroshima, a prestigious four-year women's school, involved exchange of not only students and faculty, but also teaching and research materials; it began in 1991 and is ongoing. In 2001, Kwassui Women's College in Nagasaki joined the roster of Japanese schools sending students to UE for work in the Intensive English Center and also for short-term programs.

Also noteworthy is the summer field archaeology program at Murlo near Siena, Italy, site of an ancient Etruscan culture. University of Evansville students work at an active dig site with fifteen to twenty other students from various colleges and universities and a staff of professional archaeologists, a photographer, an architect, and an illustrator. The site, dating back to 600 B.C., was featured in the Time-Life Books series "Lost Civilizations," the *New York Times*, *National Geographic*, the European edition of *Newsweek*, and television specials in Italy and Germany.

University of Evansville students have also been successful in continuing their studies abroad after graduation. Nine were awarded prestigious Fulbright fellowships, at least one each year between 1999 and 2002. In 2001, forty-five-year-old Bache-

Students get hands-on experience in archaeology at Murlo

lor of Liberal Studies graduate Steve Crawford became the first non-traditional UE student to win a Fulbright fellowship; he pursued a graduate degree in Finland. The same year, Melissa Wege won an international research grant to study economics and work as an intern in Russia; her internship was with a ballet company and her research focused on Russian policies regarding funding of the arts.

The goal of international studies at the University of Evansville was best summarized by David Gugin who, as chair of the political science department and coordinator of international studies, was

Fulbright fellow Steve Crawford with his wife and son in Finland

instrumental in establishing many of the programs described above:

> **"We would like to have all students at the University begin to see themselves as participants in a society that is larger than their own state or country. We want our people to be comfortable in a multilingual, multicultural society."**

Thirty-one percent of UE's Class of 2002 studied abroad, placing the University fifth among institutions of its kind in the percentage of graduates to do so. The following year, the percentage rose to 43.4, 171 at Harlaxton and twenty-three at other sites.

At the same time that our students were encouraged to study abroad, the University's efforts to bring international students to the home campus expanded. Students from over eighty nations have attended the University (see map on page 332), and the International Students Club, formed in 1976, sponsors numerous campus events focusing on the contributions of foreign cultures to American life.

The number of students enrolled at the University of Evansville from Japan and the Near East is especially notable; many study at the University's Intensive English Center and others register as full-time students. Other nations have also made significant contributions to the University's international program:

- In 1991, the University of Evansville hosted five Bulgarian students who excelled in their academic work here, one eventually completing a doctoral degree in physics at Carnegie Mellon University.

- In 1997, about a dozen students from Washington High School, a private institution in Buenos Aires, Argentina, came to the University of Evansville for a four-week intensive English program. It was the University's first exchange program with a secondary school.

- In 2001, due to the attacks on September 11, seventeen students from the United Arab Emirates returned to their home country, mainly because of their families' concern for their safety. Happily, in the spring semester, all but one of the seventeen resumed their studies at the University of Evansville.

301

STUDENT LIFE

Enrollment

As had been the case during the previous administration, President Vinson's tenure was marked by drastic fluctuations in the University's enrollment.

In 1988, freshman enrollment was 612, but by 1990 it had dipped to 528. However, two years later it increased to 708 and in 1995 it rose to 785. After this peak, there was a steady decline, falling in 2000 – Vinson's final year – to 556 and the following year to 513.

Some attributed the decline to the decision to end football, others to the decrease in pre-physical therapy majors. Probably a combination of these together with other factors contributed to the low enrollment which marked the late 1990s. Then, in 2002, thanks to an intensified recruiting program, attendance at open houses grew to the highest level ever; one was attended by approximately 1,000 students and parents. As a result of these efforts, the 2002 freshman class reached 603, rising in 2003 to 663, the largest since 1998.

Total full-time undergraduate enrollment showed similar variations. The 1988 figure was 2,281, but steady increases brought it to a 1995 peak of 2,879. Years of decline followed, enrollment falling to 2,473 in 2000 and to 2,152 in 2002 (reflecting several years of small freshman classes.)

In contrast to the ebb and flow in enrollment, average composite SAT scores for freshmen showed a steady and gratifying increase, rising from 1,021 in 1988 to 1,147 in 2000. Most freshman classes had ten or more National Merit finalists. In the freshman class entering in 2003, one in seven students ranked first in their high school class, one in three had a high school GPA of 4.0, eight were Lilly Scholars, thirty-nine were Hoosier Scholars, and seventy-five qualified for the University's Honors Program.

Also noteworthy is the increasing number of students who lived in University-owned housing, rising to 1,909 in 1995, and the amount available for financial aid, which more than doubled between 1990 and 1995, reaching $29,173,000 by 2002.

Attrition (the number of students leaving a college or university without completing a degree) was a nationwide problem, one which the University of Evansville addressed with considerable success. For example, in the 1992-93 school year, eighty-four percent of University of Evansville freshmen returned to campus, compared to a national retention rate of seventy percent. However, a survey of ninety-four schools similar to the University of Evansville (private institutions of approximately the same size and caliber) showed that UE's attrition was six percent above the average for these institutions. Reasons for students leaving ranged from academic to financial or personal. An effective tool in combating attrition, both at the University of Evansville and elsewhere, has been tutorial programs, especially those using peer tutors.

Further efforts to lower the University's attrition rate were aided by a 2001 $10,000 Ameritech grant (the fourth Ameritech grant the University received) to help fund a virtual institutional research office. The office tracked pertinent academic and personal information, including students' majors, grade point averages, advisors, family situations, and debt load. Such data enabled the University to identify the strengths and weakness-

Admission Ambassadors are a group of student volunteers (some years as many as 80) who assist the admission office with new student recruitment. They lead campus tours, host prospective students for overnight visits, and communicate with prospects via letters, telephone calls, and e-mail. AAs are selected competitively and only after an extensive interview process. Many UE students have based their decision to attend the University on the positive impression made by an Admission Ambassador.

es of its students and guide them into programs in which they were most likely to succeed. Emphasis was on early intervention to assist students at risk.

Since the 1980s, the University has committed a department within its student life center to multicultural affairs. Currently headed by Jeffery Chestnut, the office provides support services to minority students and has played a major role in the annual Martin Luther King Jr. Day celebration. The event includes a reenactment of the march on Washington, D.C., drawing University and community participants each year, and an address by a major outside speaker. Additional programs include those for Black History Month and an annual town hall forum on race and diversity.

Martin Luther King Day reenactment march

AFRICAN AMERICANS AT UE

Zerah Carter

In 2002, the University of Evansville African American Alumni awarded its first scholarship in honor of Zerah Priestly Carter '38, the school's first black graduate.

Carter enrolled at Evansville College at the request of President Earl Harper, who reportedly asked William Best, principal of Evansville's all-black Lincoln High School, "to select a colored student who could see but not see and who could hear but not hear" because of the prejudice the student was expected to encounter. Carter became a "test case" and was asked to ignore any racism that would occur. Despite being the only black student at Evansville College, Carter fitted in and soon became very active in campus life.

When Ball State University officials learned that Evansville College was bringing a "colored girl" to a school event in Muncie, College officials were told she could attend but would have to lodge off campus. When Harper refused this condition, Carter was finally allowed to stay on the Ball State campus to avoid further controversy and embarrassment.

After graduating from Evansville College, Carter taught at Lincoln High School and Central High School. She became an ordained Methodist minister in 1974 and received the UE Pioneer Award in 1999.

The UEAAA required less than two years to raise $28,000 for the Zerah Priestly Carter scholarship fund.

Since it was College policy not to track its students by race, few accurate statistics are available concerning the number of African American students who enrolled after Carter. But it is known that in 1949 only thirty-nine African Americans – out of a total enrollment of about 1,500 – were registered. Two decades later, seventy-six – out of about 5,000 day and evening students – were attending, less than two percent of the school's total enrollment. In 2002-03, the figure remained approximately the same.

In the 1990s, the University was able to attract a number of African American faculty members through the Lilly Foundation grant to encourage hiring of minority professors in institutions of higher learning.

303

Pre-college Programs

Summer College Program for Students with Disabilities

In 1991, both the *Chronicle of Higher Education* (July 24 issue, page one plus nearly two pages inside, including photo) and *USA Today* (August 21) highlighted this unique seven-week orientation program, a joint venture of the University of Evansville and the Evansville Association for the Blind.

Initiated by Allen Woody and Frank Kern of the association, the program began in 1969 with eight students and has expanded to as many as twenty from across the nation each year. To date, about 500 have participated, most previously educated in schools for the blind, but some coping with other handicaps such as deafness, cerebral palsy, and learning disabilities.

Participants live in University residence halls and take regular UE classes. At the same time, aided by instructors in daily living skills provided by the Evansville Association for the Blind, they learn to function in the outside world, developing such skills as shopping and doing laundry, crossing a busy intersection, and ordering books on tape. The program is one-of-a-kind because it is the only one in the country operating on a college campus.

"Graduates" of the program are ready for the college or university of their choice. Approximately fifty percent choose some form of higher education.

Engineering Options

This summer program was initiated in 1992 and designed to foster interest in science, mathematics, and engineering among female high school sophomores and juniors. The program, funded by the Alcoa Foundation and the Kellogg Foundation, was directed by Dean Tuley, who noted that at the ninth grade level, equal numbers of boys and girls were interested in technical or scientific careers, but by the twelfth grade there was a two to one ratio of men over women. Current camp director Philip Gerhart, dean of the College of Engineering and Computer Science,

noted that even today "some think engineering is not an appropriate field for women." He views the program as an effort to break down the stereotype.

Participants in the program spend a week on the UE campus, living in residence halls and attending lectures and informal gatherings led by professional female engineers, who serve as role models. Field trips include time with a mentor at her work site. Options enjoys support from a variety of sources, including the American Society of Civil Engineering, Vectren, Alcoa, Whirlpool, Toyota, and a NASA Space Grant.

Health and Safety Issues

In 1993, the University of Evansville became smoke-free. Smoking was banned in all classroom buildings, recreational facilities, and dining areas. Residence halls were also made smoke-free, including student rooms, except for designated rooms in Moore and Hughes Halls, and then only with permission of the roommate.

The University also prohibits the use, possession, or sale of alcoholic beverages, and the use, possession, or distribution of narcotics and any other illegal drug. Students accused of violating these policies can request an administrative hearing. Depending upon the severity of the offense, the University reserves the right to contact local authorities for

Engineering Options participants display one of their projects

FITNESS FOR ALL

The Student Fitness Center was an idea proposed and designed by students, working with University administrators. So important was a fitness center that Student Congress voted to raise the student activity fee by $100 a semester to finance the $3.2 million project.

Opened in 1991, the facilities include:

- Two basketball courts
- Two volleyball courts
- Four badminton courts
- Four racquetball/handball courts
- One indoor running track
- One free-weight room
- One aerobics room
- One conditioning room, featuring resistance and aerobic machines as well as stationary cycles

Programming includes personal fitness assessment, individualized training, aerobics, dance (hip-hop, line, basic), yoga and pilates, kickboxing, tai chi, and self-defense. The center also sponsors an extensive intramural schedule. More than seventy-five percent of the student body participates in at least one intramural event a year, and the aerobics room – complete with balance bars and mirrors – is used by the theatre department on a regular basis.

The Student Fitness Center is strictly for the use of students, faculty, staff, and administration. No athletic teams are allowed to hold practices or schedule events there.

Thus far, a single problem has arisen. Mark Guttman, former student president, lamented: "The only thing is, we didn't realize how popular it would be. We should have made it bigger."

305

action separate from or in addition to University disciplinary action. In situations where the well-being of members of the University community is threatened or affected, the student can be suspended or expelled immediately, with an opportunity for appeal from off campus.

In 1994, in an effort to wipe out any possible drug use in the residence halls, the residence life staff and the dean of students conducted several room searches and interviews. Although these interviews were optional, some students felt intimidated and accused the questioners of employing scare tactics. However, since six incidents involving drugs had occurred within two months, a sharp increase over recent years, the University maintained that the investigation was in the best interests of the student body. The problem is ongoing, with sixteen drug violations occurring on University property between 1997 and 2002. Liquor violations are also a matter of concern since, in addition to citations by University of Evansville security officials, several arrests were made by Evansville police.

In 1993, a social awareness task force, comprised of students and administrators, developed a sexual assault policy in accordance with the 1992 Higher Education Reauthorization Act. The act specifically requires a statement of policy and the establishment of procedures if a sex offense has occurred. In the mid 1990s, the UE Sexual Misconduct Policy was issued, defining all terminology, actions, procedures, and rights of the accused and victims in all forms of sexual conduct, including assault, battery, and rape.

In 1996, a health fee was implemented in order to enhance health services to students, including a new health education program which offered information on nutrition, alcohol and drugs, as well as sexually transmitted diseases. A health educator was added to the staff to implement these services and also to counsel students who received judicial sanctions resulting from alcohol violations and other problems. The health educator also vis-

ited campus Greek organizations and residence halls. In addition, students continued to receive free medicine and the services of a nurse or physician. To provide greater visibility and also much needed space, the health center, previously housed in Moore Hall and later in a small house on Frederick Street, was moved to a central location near McCurdy Alumni Memorial Union.

When University of Evansville students attend Harlaxton College, their health fee is transferred there. Students from other colleges and universities enrolled at Harlaxton are required to pay the health fee, thus enhancing the health services they receive.

During the later 1990s, there was a renewed interest in mental health. Formerly, the testing and counseling office was primarily concerned with administering national standardized psychological tests. During summer orientation and registration of new, transfer, and international students, the office was charged with academic placement testing and with distributing test results to faculty advisors.

In an effort to provide better individual counseling services, it was felt more appropriate to move these functions to the academic advising office and to appoint two professional counselors who could devote their time entirely to students' personal needs. In addition, the health educator became part of the counseling department, with the name of the office changed to the Office of Counseling and Health Education.

Finally, greater attention was devoted to student safety. A security officer was assigned to each residence hall, fraternity houses were inspected regularly for fire hazards, and emergency telephone stations were installed in off-campus apartment areas as well as around campus.

Additional Student Services

- Career services also have expanded significantly, offering students career panels, health career fairs, and résumé writing and interviewing technique workshops. In addition, closer working relationships with alumni

new student center. Financed by a gift from William Ridgway, a long-time member of the University's Board of Trustees, the renovation cost about $500,000 and included a lounge (named the Underground), a computer lab, and a convenience store (Ace's Place). The lounge, with its pub-like ambiance featuring leather chairs and sofas, big-screen television, games, and a coffee bar (Jazzman's Cafe), proved a popular and welcome addition to the campus. Meanwhile, planning continues for a full-fledged student center.

have been established, and computer facilities more fully utilized. Going online helps students become more aware of job opportunities and ways to enhance their marketability. A connection was also made to Harlaxton College, so that students can continue their career exploration while studying abroad.

■ The need for a student recreation facility had long been recognized, and a first step was taken in 2002 with the transformation of the lower floor of Harper Dining Center into a

307

UE students take advantage of career services resources (top) and leisure activities (right)

Student Activities

As of 2003, approximately sixty-five percent of the student body lived in residence halls and apartments, each manned by a qualified residential coordinator and several resident assistants. All residential coordinators are college graduates and many hold graduate degrees. Resident assistants are upperclassmen at the University. Faculty members make regular visits to residence halls, giving special programs in their areas of interest, and administrators attend all council meetings to monitor student needs and concerns.

On designated floors, men and women are permitted to meet on a limited schedule in each other's residence hall rooms. There are also several twenty-four hour visitation floors available in each residence hall.

Greek life has also continued to flourish. In 1999, Phi Gamma Delta became the sixth fraternity on campus. In the same year, Sigma Alpha Epsilon, after razing its former home, opened a new and much larger building on Lincoln Avenue. In the new century, total membership in the University's six fraternities reached 270, with roughly the same number in the four sororities, for a total of about twenty-five percent of the student body. In addition, the UE Greek system has included several historically African American fraternities and sororities; while these are not currently active on campus, many alumni participate in city-wide chapters.

Membership in a Greek organization offers social and leadership opportunities, scholarship and spiritual support, competitive intramural sports, and a network of brothers and sisters spanning the globe.

Leadership and service opportunities open to the entire campus have dramatically increased as the number of student organizations mushroomed to over 130. An annual banquet recognizing outstanding individuals and organizations has been instituted.

Two campus organizations have commanded particular respect:

■ **The Student Alumni Association** was established in 1978 as the UE Student Foundation. It seeks to develop a sense of tradition, pride, and loyalty in UE students who will be future alumni leaders. Members play a major role in Fall Homecoming, the largest alumni event held on campus, and in preparations for alumni dinners and other alumni-related activities.

SAA also sponsors an externship program which enables UE alumni to share their profession with students who aspire to work in a similar career area. Usually held during spring break or in the summer months, the program enables externs to gain hands-on field experience or guided observation of the graduate's daily work, an invaluable aid to students in forming their own career goals. Their service often proves useful to the graduates as well.

SAA also sponsors:

• *Balloon Bouquets* delivered on holidays, birthdays, and special occasions

UE Greeks

- *School Spirit Send-offs* sent to freshmen from their parents

- *Senior Send-off* a picnic with live entertainment to congratulate graduating seniors

Faculty, administrators, or current members nominate students for membership in the Student Alumni Association. Typically, twelve to fifteen students participate in the program.

- **The University's Leadership Academy** is a student-run organization begun in 1995. Its twenty to thirty participants make a two-year commitment to take part in both individual development and group dynamic programs requiring 150 to 200 hours per semester. Members plan and host leadership conferences and community projects involving organizations such as the Boy Scouts and Impact Ministries. At commencement, each participant receives a special bronze medallion. In 2000, the Leadership Academy received the Student Award for Leadership and Training from the National Association of College and University Residence Halls.

Marjabelle Young Stewart, a manners expert, was invited by the Leadership Academy in 1995 to speak on etiquette

Social Concerns

The needs of society increasingly engaged the interests of University of Evansville students during this period, causing student volunteer activity to expand quickly.

- In 1991, a major recycling effort began on campus, led by Robert Dale, supervisor of buildings and grounds, focusing on paper and aluminum cans. The program not only made the student body environmentally aware but also yielded significant amounts of cash for campus improvement projects. Campus recycling is ongoing.

- In the mid 1990s, Amnesty International sponsored a campaign on campus, Breaking the Silence, which focused on controversial issues related to homosexuality. Also, an annual Jeans Day began. On this day, students and faculty were asked to wear jeans as a symbol of support for gays and lesbians. Its sponsors hoped the gesture would "make a statement in favor of equality for all people, regardless of sexual preference." Although the effort failed to attract widespread support, it has continued as an annual event under the auspices of PRIDE (People Respecting Individual Diversity Everywhere).

- Each University Greek organization hosts an annual philanthropic event to raise funds for a variety of local and national charities. These have included the Evansville Association for Retarded Citizens (EARC), the Evansville Rescue Mission, the YMCA, Tri-State Food Bank, American Red Cross Blood Bank, the Susan

309

Komen Research Breast Cancer Fund, the Leukemia and Lymphoma Society, Riley Hospital, the Children's Miracle Network, and Paul Newman's Hole-in-the-Wall Gang Camps. In 2002-03 the total funds raised by UE Greeks surpassed $33,000.

■ The international mission trips described in Chapter Five continued, led by **John Brittain** (D.Min., St. Mary's Seminary and University), who succeeded Wayne Perkins in 1987 as director of religious life and chaplain. As his first destination, Brittain chose a city in northeastern Brazil, one of the poorest regions in South America. Here the UE group, consisting of eight students and four leaders (Brittain, Perkins, Ott, and Brittain's wife, Eileen), constructed rooms for a nursery school and Sunday school wing at a Methodist church located on the outskirts of the city.

John Brittain, university chaplain (center)

Subsequent mission projects included:

- *1989-90 Nuevo Laredo, Mexico*
  Assignment: Assist in the construction and painting of pews for the Methodist church and completing the upper level and roof of the buildings

- *1990-91 Belize City, Belize*
  Assignment: Assist in renovating Wesley (Elementary) School, replacing windows and faulty wiring, installing ceiling fans, and painting

- *1993-94 Obninsk, Russia*
  Assignment: Assist local residents in hospitals and children's homes; UE was the second university in the nation to send a group to the former Soviet Union

- *1994-95 St. Ann's Bay, Jamaica*
  Assignment: Assist in completion of a new community building for the church's outreach program. Also to take medical supplies donated by St. Mary's Medical Center in Evansville for the St. Ann's Bay Hospital

- *1997 South Africa*
  Assignments: (1) Assist various ministries of the Central Methodist Mission in Capetown, (2) Assist an agricultural mission and an urban work project in Durban, (3) Assist with feeding and medical services for homeless persons at the Central Methodist Mission in Johannesburg

- *January 2002 Ciudad Juárez, Mexico*
  Assignment: Construct a one-room concrete block house (done in cooperation with Operación Hogar)

Beginning in the spring of 1988, the chaplain also began offering spring break mission trips. These were restricted to locations within the United States and included:

- *1988 Henderson Settlement*
  Frakes, Kentucky

- *1989 Habitat for Humanity*
  Collegiate Challenge, Cleveland, Ohio

- *1991 Haitian Refugee Center*
  Miami, Florida

- *1992 Inner City Ministries*
  Memphis, Tennessee

- *1993 Hurricane Andrew Relief*
  Redland, Florida

- *1997 Urban Ministries*
  Chicago, Illinois

- *2002-03 Methodist Mission*
  Gary, West Virginia

For several years, as many as 100 persons were involved in some form of mission work with the University.

University of Evansville students interested in volunteering their time and skills to Tri-State service projects had numerous opportunities available to them.

As early as 1988, ten members of Kappa Chi became involved with a community program for youth that soon surpassed even the most optimistic expectations. Central United Methodist Church's POWER program was first designed to provide inner-city children with after-school snacks, but the volunteer efforts of UE students and others broadened the program considerably. By 2003, more than thirty UE volunteers tutored students three days a week and provided an evening recreation and story time.

By 1994, interest in such projects led to the creation of a volunteer services office, which provided information about various non-profit agencies, such as the Evansville Rescue Mission, YMCA, Habitat for Humanity, Tri-State Food Bank, Patchwork Central, and the Humane Society, as well as nursing homes and after-school programs. As part of Welcome Week orientation, the entire freshman class visited these and similar locations.

UE students help with a Habitat for Humanity house

311

RELIGIOUS ORGANIZATIONS

University of Evansville students who wish to affiliate with a religious organization enjoy an array of options.

Kappa Chi, one of the most active student organizations on campus, is a co-ed Christian fraternity. It is also the oldest and largest religious group on campus, and is especially active in service-oriented community projects such as POWER (see page 311) and fund-raisers to fight hunger.

Newman Center houses the campus outreach program for the Roman Catholic Diocese of Evansville.

Apostles is an informal group of people exploring religious vocations. The Apostles are made up of pre-theology majors, candidates for the ministry, those considering mission work, and students employed as youth workers in local churches.

Baptist Student Union, sponsored by the Southern Baptist Convention, is open to all students interested in spiritual growth and service to others.

Neu Chapel Deacons are a select group of student volunteers who assist in planning and conducting University worship services as well as developing other aspects of the religious life program.

Chapel Choir provides music for the University worship service in Neu Chapel.

Fellowship of Christian Athletes is a campus "huddle," a local chapter of the national FCA that is open to athletes, coaches, and other Christians.

Inter-Varsity Christian Fellowship is a student-led chapter of the International Fellowship of Evangelical Students.

Hillel offers fellowship and growth opportunities for Jewish students as well as educational opportunities for the whole campus. Hillel sponsors a campus-wide Passover Seder each spring.

Islamic Student Association offers fellowship, support, and growth opportunities for Islamic students.

Upward Bound, a student-led music ministry, performs at local churches, nursing homes, and children's homes.

Student Christian Fellowship is the campus outreach of the Independent Christian Churches.

University Life is the college-age group of Christian Fellowship Church of Evansville.

In 1997, the volunteer services office instituted the first UE Makes A Difference Day in conjunction with the national program, and by century's end UE student volunteers were contributing about 10,000 hours of community service annually.

President Jennings was especially emphatic in his support of volunteerism, writing in the *Evansville Courier & Press* (April 21, 2002):

A university must instill an everyday attitude of service in its students and employees. They should be aware of the multitude of opportunities available and, depending upon their time, family commitments, interest, and abilities, encouraged to voluntarily pursue these life-expanding experiences. Soon, volunteering becomes a way of life and is incorporated into the classroom, workplace, community, and nation. Because it is a part of their lives, they realize that they are just one bit of a larger society wherever they live and that they alone can make a difference...Entire classes have developed service projects and learned how to plan a project, find funding, carry out plans, and complete the goals – all while a part of the regular learning process of the class. The fastest-growing kind of student activities at UE relates to volunteerism.

Faculty member Arlen Kaufmann (left) and student

Student-Faculty Relationships

■ The University of Evansville offers many opportunities for students and faculty members to collaborate on research and other projects. An outstanding example is the UEplore Undergraduate Research Program, begun in 1988 when the University of Evansville joined the National Conference on Undergraduate Research (NCUR) with a paper by physics major Kent Scheller (who later joined the physics faculty at the University).

With support from Scheller's mentor, Benny Riley, and also Erik Nielsen (vice president for academic affairs) and President Vinson, the University was able to secure a matching grant from the Eli Lilly Foundation for $75,000 to cover expenses for three years. Subsequently, the University has funded the program, which enables students from various disciplines to present their research to a national audience. Over ninety UE research projects have been offered thus far, in addition to numerous papers presented at regional undergraduate conferences and professional societies. A highlight of the program occurred in 1997 when chemistry major Tina Rosen-

baum was invited to present her research in Washington, D.C., before Congress.

UExplore Undergraduate Research Program was coordinated for ten years by Benny Riley (physics) and currently by Douglas Stamps (engineering).

Tina Rosenbaum

313

■ In an effort to build greater trust between students and faculty, an academic honor system, adopted by both the Student Government Association and the Faculty Senate, went into effect in 1995. All incoming students pledged: "I will neither give nor receive, nor will I tolerate an environment which condones the use of unauthorized aid." Faculty, in turn, was responsible for clarifying what aid is unauthorized. The Student Handbook published the Academic Honor Code in its entirety.

An Honor Council, composed of twelve students and seven faculty, was formed, and a judicial board comprised of five students and two randomly selected professors act on each alleged violation. Punishment for a first offense is determined on a case-by-case basis, but a second infraction results in suspension from the University, with a third violation punishable by expulsion.

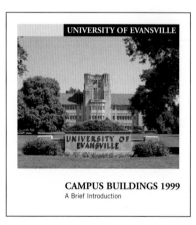

UNIVERSITY OF EVANSVILLE

CAMPUS BUILDINGS 1999
A Brief Introduction

CAMPUS BUILDINGS

In 1999, two professors, Philip Ensley and William Brown, supported by an ARSAF grant, joined with six students who received EXCEL funds to produce a book, *Campus Buildings 1999: A Brief Introduction*. In this volume, campus buildings were highlighted, with photographs, historical background, and architectural information provided on each.

314

Speakers

Several nationally known speakers have addressed UE students and the community, most under the auspices of the Patricia H. Snyder Concert and Lecture Series, named in memory of a former University trustee. Included were:

1992 **Ralph Nader**
Consumer Advocate

1994 **Leon Lederman**
Nobel Prize-Winning
Physicist

1995 **Benjamin Hooks**
Former Executive
Director of the NAACP

1996 **Richard Leakey**
Anthropologist

Benjamin Hooks

1997 **Jeanne-Marie Santraus**
French Literary Scholar

Ray Bradbury
Novelist, Short Story
Writer, Essayist,
Screen Writer, Poet

Shirley Ann Grau
Pulitzer Prize-Winning
Novelist, Short Story Writer

1998 **Mark Timmons '73**
Philosopher

Francine Childs
Professor of Afro-American
Studies at Ohio University

W. D. Snodgrass
Pulitzer Prize-Winning
Poet

Julian Bond
Civil Rights Leader

Naomi Wolf
Feminist Writer

Naomi Wolf

Harry Wu
Human Rights Activist

1999 **Mae Jemison**
Astronaut

James Reston Jr.
Author

Elie Wiesel
Nobel Peace Prize
Winner

2000 **Linda Wertheimer**
National Public Radio
Host

E. O. Wilson
Pulitzer Prize-
Winning Biologist

2001 **Ellen Goodman**
Columnist

2002 **Jules Feiffer**
Pulitzer Prize-Winning
Cartoonist, Playwright

Elie Wiesel

WUEV-FM

WUEV's professional radio staff during this period included:

Station Managers
Kay Nelson, Leonard Clark, Michael Crowley

Telecommunications Engineer
Phillip Bailey

Major achievements of the University's radio station included:

1993 Final nominee (top five) Jazz/New Age Station of the Year in the National Association of Broadcasters MARCONI Radio Awards

1994 Finalist in the National Association of College Broadcasters Third Annual National College Radio Awards in the Sports Play-by-Play category

Station manager Leonard Clark nominated for Faculty Advisor of the Year Award (sponsored by Interep Radio Store)

315

Student DJ at
WUEV-FM

1995 Received an award from the Indiana Society of Professional Journalists in its college division competition, placing first or second each year thereafter in Best College Radio Newscast, Best Radio Feature, and Best Radio Documentary categories

1996 First college radio station in Indiana and one of the first in the nation to be accessible on the Internet (made possible through a grant from Ameritech)

Clark awarded Sagamore of the Wabash Award for distinguished service to the state of Indiana

Sent first foreign correspondent to Harlaxton College. A grant allowed purchase of computers and software located on the main campus, with a duplicate set installed at Harlaxton, enabling students there to send stories back to the University via File Transfer Protocol. Through the use of digital cameras, photos to accompany each story were sent back to be archived on WUEV's web site. Among the news stories was coverage of the funeral of Diana, Princess of Wales.

1998 National Catholic Communicators Association Gabriel Award for Children's Program Rated G and a Certificate of Merit for Station of the Year

2000 Won Indiana Broadcasters Spectrum Awards: First place for Best Public Service Announcement; second place for Best Station Promotional Announcement

2001 By mayoral proclamation, April 1 designated WUEV Day in Evansville to mark the fiftieth anniversary of the station

2002 Clark named co-winner of the Indiana Sportscaster of the Year Award presented by the National Sportscasters and Sportswriters Association

ATHLETICS

Men's Basketball

One of President Graves' last, and some would say his best, decisions came in the spring of 1985 when Jim Crews was hired as the University's basketball coach. The previous coach, Dick Walters, had rebuilt the program after the 1977 airplane crash and led Evansville to its first NCAA Division I tournament appearance in 1982, but three subsequent mediocre seasons led to his resignation.

Crews was a popular replacement because fans in southwest Indiana had watched him play for Indiana University's 1976 national championship team that went undefeated and had watched him coach under Bobby Knight at IU for eight seasons. Crews set the stage for future success right away by bring-

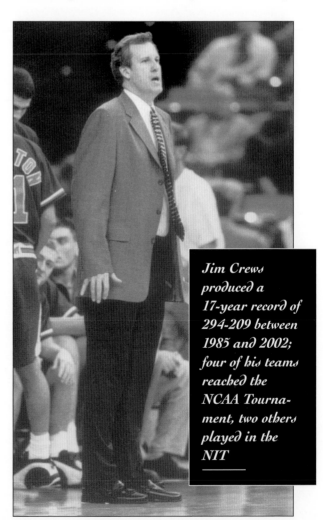

Jim Crews produced a 17-year record of 294-209 between 1985 and 2002; four of his teams reached the NCAA Tournament, two others played in the NIT

Scott Haffner (3) shooting one of his 11 three-pointers in his 65-point game February 18, 1989, at Roberts Stadium

ing in two players who were unhappy at their colleges: Marty Simmons from Indiana University and Scott Haffner from Illinois. Both became eligible in 1986-87, and Evansville immediately captured the Midwestern Collegiate Conference championship, despite being picked to finish next to last in the preseason poll. One year later, the Aces played in the National Invitation Tournament for the first time, defeating Utah at Roberts Stadium in the opening round before losing to Boston College in the second round, also at Roberts Stadium.

In 1989, despite having lost Simmons to graduation, Evansville won twenty-five games, the school's highest victory total since the 29-0 season of 1965. The final victory was the most exciting. Playing on national television in Tucson, Arizona, against Oregon State in the first round of the NCAA Tournament, eleventh-seeded Evansville dropped behind number six seed Oregon State 21-10 in the opening nine minutes. But the Aces caught up in the second half and won 94-90 in overtime after guard

65 POINTS

One minute into the game at Roberts Stadium between Evansville and the University of Dayton on February 18, 1989, UE's Scott Haffner tried to save a ball from going out of bounds and twisted his foot. "I thought to myself: This is not a very good start," Haffner recalled. It is hard to imagine what a healthy Haffner would have done that day. By the time the afternoon was over, Haffner had scored a school record 65 points in the Aces' 109-83 win over the Flyers. Those were the most points scored in a Division I men's basketball game during the decade of the 80s, and at the time it was the sixth highest scoring total in Division I history.

Haffner scored 30 points in the first half, and by late in the second half the sell-out crowd of 11,157 remained standing, few knowing his exact point total but most realizing they were watching history. At the end, Haffner's totals read: 12 of 16 two-point field goals, 11 of 13 three-point field goals, and 8 for 8 at the free throw line.

"I really didn't know how many I had until fairly late in the game," Haffner said afterward. "A Dayton player was at the free throw line and I put my hands on my hips and just happened to glance into the crowd. One of the fans held up five fingers on one hand and one on the other. It was a little like a dream toward the end. You just get into a groove where everything feels like it's going to go in, and that's what happened."

Haffner's performance that day improved Evansville's record to 20-3. It also put the Purple Aces into the national spotlight just weeks before the start of the NCAA Tournament. The national publicity no doubt helped Evansville earn a berth in the NCAA Tournament, despite losing to Xavier in the conference tournament, and four months later Haffner was chosen as the second round pick of the Miami Heat in the NBA draft.

Reed Crafton made a twenty-five foot shot with eleven seconds remaining in overtime. Crafton's heave gave Evansville the lead for good at 92-90. The victory was UE's first in the Division I men's basketball tournament.

The Aces reached the NCAA Tournament again in 1992 at Dayton against Texas-El Paso, in 1993 at Orlando against Florida State, and in 1999 at New Orleans against Kansas, and played in the NIT again in 1994, hosting Tulane. Although they did not win another post-season game under Crews, the Aces produced a fifteen-year streak in which they never finished below .500 against conference opponents. When the streak ended in 2002, only six other schools could still make the same claim: UCLA, Princeton, Syracuse, Xavier, Temple, and Arizona.

Soccer

While basketball remained the most popular sport with fans, attracting average attendance of 10,000 or more for six straight seasons beginning in 1991-92, soccer was becoming even more successful nationally. A streak of nine consecutive trips to the NCAA Division I men's soccer tournament began in 1984, and included Final Four appearances in 1985 (a 3-1 loss at home against UCLA in front of a standing-room-only crowd of 3,000) and 1990 (a 1-0 loss to Rutgers at Tampa). Evansville's Rob Paterson won the Adi Dassler Award in 1989, the soccer equivalent of football's Heisman Trophy. In 1998, Evansville graduate and Scotland native David Weir became the first former U.S. college player to compete for a European team in the World Cup. By 1996, when Evansville won its first Missouri Valley Conference championship, UE had produced twelve All-Americans in fifteen years.

The stature of men's soccer dropped slightly in the mid 1990s, but women's soccer began to play a major role. Women's soccer became UE's newest varsity sport in 1993 and quickly became competitive under the leadership of coach **Mick Lyon**, a former All-American on UE's team in the 1980s. Beginning in 1996, the Purple Aces

won the Missouri Valley Conference regular season and/or tournament titles for six consecutive years. They also qualified for three NCAA tournaments in a four-year period. The women's soccer program produced its first All-American in 2000 when defender Krista McKendree was selected.

Other Women's Programs

While soccer led the way in terms of championships, the women's programs in basketball, tennis, softball, and swimming also captured league titles. One of the most dramatic improvements came in women's basketball in the late 1990s, following a five-year period in which the Aces compiled a record of 18 wins and 113 losses. Third year

From 1996 to 2001, UE won the MVC regular season and/or MVC Tournament championship each year in women's soccer

Coach Kathi Bennett guided Evansville to its first NCAA Tournament appearance in women's basketball in 1999

coach **Kathi Bennett** led the 1999 team to a 19-11 record and the school's first NCAA Division I women's basketball tournament appearance at Baton Rouge against host Louisiana State. One year later the Aces set a school record with twenty-one victories and made their first trip to the Women's NIT, losing in overtime at Missouri.

Baseball

Evansville's total athletic program continued to grow through the 1980s and 1990s. Jim Brownlee's baseball team made NCAA Division I Tournament appearances in each decade, and in 1988 Evansville native and UE student Andy Benes was the first pick in the professional baseball draft, going to San Diego. Benes played on the 1988 U.S. Olympic team before beginning a fourteen-year career in the pros. (Evansville's second Olympian came in 2000 when swimmer Nikola Kalabić competed in the 100-meter freestyle at Sydney, Australia, for his

native Yugoslavia.) Brownlee left UE in 2002 after winning 701 games, the most by any coach in any sport in UE history.

Football

Non-scholarship football had been played since the mid 1980s, and in 1991 UE helped form the Pioneer Football League along with Butler, Dayton, Drake, Valparaiso, and San Diego. All six schools were NCAA Division I members that wanted to play non-scholarship football. While the Pioneer League gave Evansville a good home, changes in the NCAA landscape led the trustees to discontinue the University's football program in 1998. At the time, the trustees indicated that four major concerns led to their decision:

- NCAA legislation, including scheduling requirements, and the fact that the NCAA does not sponsor a national championship for Division I non-scholarship football

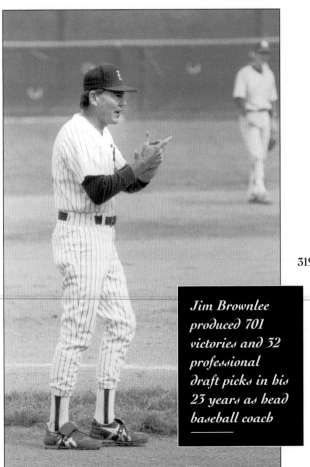

Jim Brownlee produced 701 victories and 32 professional draft picks in his 23 years as head baseball coach

319

- NCAA certification and gender equity; like many schools, UE added programs (women's soccer and women's golf, most notably) and increased emphasis on existing programs in order to meet NCAA gender equity guidelines

- National trends, which indicated that private colleges would have to spend more to remain competitive in non-scholarship football, especially when more state-supported institutions were moving from scholarship to non-scholarship status

- Need for additional athletic facilities on the UE campus for other varsity sports

Conference Affiliations

Before century's end, plans took shape to refurbish fourteen-year-old Arad McCutchan Stadium, bulldoze the surface and turn the football stadium into a soccer facility for both the men's and women's programs. Named Black Beauty Field at Arad McCutchan Stadium, it hosted its first soccer match in August 2000.

Conference affiliation changed dramatically during the 1990s. The mid 1980s version of the Midwestern Collegiate Conference included Evansville, Butler, Xavier, Detroit, Loyola, St. Louis, Oral Roberts, Oklahoma City, and associate member Notre Dame, which competed in all sports except men's basketball. The league became even stronger in 1989 when Marquette and Dayton replaced Oral Roberts and Oklahoma City. But the unraveling began in 1991 when Marquette and St. Louis withdrew from the MCC, followed by Dayton in 1993. When it became apparent that Xavier would soon follow, UE officials knew that the end had come for perhaps the best conference in the nation comprised solely of private institutions.

However, some options remained for UE. One was to stay in the new MCC, which retained Loyola, Detroit, and Butler, while trying to entice state schools such as Wright State, Cleveland State, Wisconsin-Milwaukee, Wisconsin-Green Bay, and Illinois-Chicago to fill in the ranks. Another possibility was to seek membership in the Ohio Valley Conference which included southern neighbors Murray State, Austin Peay, and others. The third and eventually most appealing choice came soon after University officials began examining their options. The Missouri Valley Conference commissioner's office and most of the presidents of MVC schools began courting UE, primarily because Evansville would enhance men's basketball in the conference.

Not everyone was excited about the Aces joining the Valley. The MVC's men's basketball coaches took a straw vote and were unanimous in their opinion that Evansville should not be added. The coaches were not eager to compete for a conference championship with one more strong program.

By the summer of 1993, it was clear that most in the MVC hierarchy wanted Evansville, and the feeling was mutual. The MVC was the most competitive league among UE's options and included longtime region rivals Indiana State and Southern Illinois. Also, men's basketball had always been the MVC's foundation, just as it was at Evansville. The only negative aspect was the cost. Membership in the MVC would require additional funding in many sports if UE expected to compete with higher budget schools such as Illinois State and Wichita State. Additional travel expenses would also be unavoidable, especially compared to a "bus league" such as the OVC.

On November 4, 1993, Evansville was voted into the MVC as the eleventh member, joining Bradley, Creighton, Drake, Illinois State, Indiana State, Northern Iowa, Southern Illinois, Southwest

320

JIM BYERS

Possibly no athletics director in NCAA history has faced a hand in his first year like the one Jim Byers was dealt. Byers gave up his successful career as football coach at UE early in 1977 to become the school's first Division I director of athletics. Nine months later, the Aces basketball team died in an airplane crash.

From that terrible low point, Byers built a Division I program in his twenty-one years that reached the NCAA tournament in soccer eleven times, basketball four times, and baseball once; won three Midwestern Collegiate Conference all-sports championships; and produced twenty-one academic All-Americans. It was Byers who hired soccer coach Fred Schmalz and baseball coach Jim Brownlee, both of whom became two of the most successful coaches in their respective sports. It was Byers who pursued Indiana University assistant coach Jim Crews and convinced him to take the head coaching position at Evansville in 1985. It was Byers who built up the women's athletics program and hired some of the most respected women's coaches in the country, including soccer coach Mick Lyon, basketball coach Kathi Bennett, and softball coach Gwen Lewis. And it was Byers who helped create three leagues: the Heartland Collegiate Conference, Pioneer League (football), and Midwestern Collegiate Conference.

"Jim was the kind of boss every coach wants," says former basketball coach Jim Crews. "First of all, his father was a coach (legendary Evansville Reitz High School football coach Herman Byers) and Jim was a coach himself, so he knew what his coaches needed to be successful. When things were going well and times were good, he stayed in the background. When times got tough, he was right there fighting for you."

Jim Byers (left) is presented a plaque by President Vinson upon his retirement in 1998

Added soccer coach Fred Schmalz, "Not many football-oriented coaches would have the faith in soccer that he did. Not many would get themselves on the NCAA Soccer Committee at a time when he didn't know if a soccer ball was filled with air or stuffed with feathers. But Jim did it because he thought it was important."

One of Byers' few disappointments as athletic director came in his final year, when UE decided to drop football. He tried to convince the administration that football was worth keeping, but in March of 1998 President Vinson announced that the sport was being cut.

In 2000, a group of Byers' former football players created the James A. Byers Athletic Student Scholarship, to be presented each spring to a junior in any of the Purple Aces' varsity sports.

"I don't expect the scholarship to be awarded to the most gifted athlete," Byers says. "This is designed to reward the athlete who gives the extra effort, who shows outstanding leadership, who tries just a little harder to make his or her team win. Those were always the traits I looked for in my players when I coached."

Missouri, Tulsa, and Wichita State. Evansville began competing officially in the new league in the fall of 1994. Although UE finished eighth or ninth each year in the MVC's all-sports standings

through 2000, it needed only four years to win conference championships in men's and women's basketball and soccer.

A New Era

An era had passed by the time Jim Byers retired as director of athletics in May 1998. The only athletics director in Evansville's Division I history at that point, Byers helped transform a department that, in 1977, put virtually all its resources into one or two men's sports into a department that, in 1998, included fifteen sports, eight of which were women's. Soccer had earned national prominence, and basketball and other sports were holding their own regionally against much tougher competition than UE ever faced in Division II.

UE's athletics program was greatly affected by the timing of the transition from the Vinson to the Jennings administration. Byers' successor, Laura Tietjen, remained for just two years, from June 1998 to August 2000. Her resignation came soon after Vinson announced he would retire the following spring. Vinson then decided to appoint an interim athletic director, allowing the future president to choose the next director. As a stopgap, UE vice president of fiscal affairs and administration Robert Gallman was appointed, while continuing to serve as the University's chief financial officer.

The plan was that Gallman would serve no more than one year. However, that plan was altered for two reasons. First was a decline in UE's enrollment. The other was a decline in UE's men's basketball attendance, from an average of more than 10,000 in 1996 to less than 6,000 in 2002. These two strains on the budget forced Jennings and the trustees to take the most serious look ever at the future of UE athletics. Consideration was even given to leaving Division I for non-scholarship Division III because of potential savings.

322

This evaluation by a special committee of trustees effectively shut down the search for a new athletics director. UE officials knew that few if any good candidates would apply for a Division I position that might evaporate within a matter of months. Consequently, Gallman was forced to remain in his dual role, leaving the athletics department with no full-time director during the most critical months in its history.

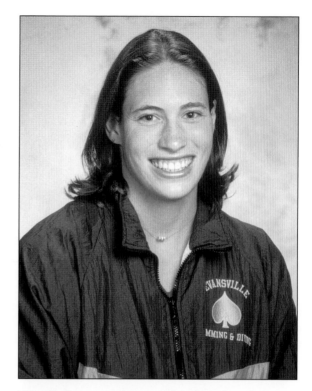

Kim Dodson was Evansville's first female to qualify for the NCAA Division I Swim and Dive Championships in 2001

The confirmation that a special committee to study athletics had been formed became public on January 23, 2002, when a story in the *Evansville Courier & Press* quoted Jennings, "Why not Division II? Or Division III? If there was a Division IV we'd look at that, too."

Nevertheless, daily newspaper and television coverage helped efforts to remain in Division I. Community reaction favoring Division I was "surprisingly strong," according to Jennings, who managed to keep a sense of humor throughout the ordeal. "Yesterday, someone flashed the 'We're #1' sign at me," he said at a meeting discussing the department's future. "But they didn't use their index finger."

More surprising than the community fervor was the overwhelming vote of confidence from UE's academic community. With budgets already squeezed by the decline in enrollment, faculty and staff were concerned that more money might be siphoned from undergraduate education in order to prop up athletics. But Jennings and the committee made it clear that additional funds from outside the University would be necessary to keep Division I athletics. At an open meeting in February, the trustees committee, faculty, and staff put aside their worries and spoke up almost unanimously in favor of retaining Division I athletics.

With local fans, business, the campus community, and alumni solidly behind Division I, Jennings announced on March 14 that the committee had unanimously voted to remain in Division I as part of its long-range plan to build enrollment and increase the school's exposure nationally.

New Faces

Spring of 2002 looked much brighter in the athletics department than the preceding winter months. New on-campus baseball and softball stadiums opened. Softball became the fifth UE team sport to win a Missouri Valley Conference championship and the sixth to compete in an NCAA Division I championship. **Bill McGillis**, formerly senior associate director of athletics at the University of New Mexico, was hired in April as the full-time director of athletics, ending Gallman's tenure of twenty-one months. Just eight days after McGillis arrived, he hired Hampton University men's basketball coach **Steve Merfeld** to replace Jim Crews, who ended a seventeen-year career in March when he took the head coaching position at Army.

Bill McGillis (left) was hired as director of athletics in April 2002; eight days later he hired Steve Merfeld (right) as basketball coach

COACHING STAFF

UE's 2003 coaching lineup included only four who were in the same position two years earlier.

Mary Pat Boarman
Women's Golf

Tricia Cullop (2000)
Women's Basketball

Dave Golan
Men's Soccer

Jim Hamilton
Men's Golf

Tomas Johansson
Men's Tennis

Gwen Lewis (1991)
Softball

Steve Merfeld
Men's Basketball

Chris Payne (1976)
Women's Tennis

Rickey Perkins
Men's and Women's Swim and Dive

Ron Raab
Women's Soccer

Dave Schrage
Baseball

Mike Swan
Volleyball

Don Walters (2000)
Men's and Women's Cross Country

CULLOP

GOLAN

LEWIS

PERKINS

RAAB

SCHRAGE

Although the 2001-02 UE athletics deficit reached about $1.8 million, through a combination of increased ticket sales, new corporate money, and vigorous fund-raising efforts, the financial picture improved by approximately $400,000 in less than a year. Average attendance for men's basketball rose from 5,822 (2001-02) to 6,671 (2002-03), and membership in the Purple Aces Club made impressive gains. Overall, the support of the Tri-State community has played a significant role in keeping the University of Evansville competitive at the NCAA Division I level.

323

FINANCES

During the Vinson era, the University consistently balanced its budget, often with a considerable surplus. (Accumulated operating surplus in 1991 – $653,000; in 1995 – $2,796,000; in 1999 – $747,000.) In 1987, operating expenditures stood at $29 million, while the comparable figure for 2000 exceeded $60 million.

During the first year of the Jennings administration, the University experienced financial difficulties caused by a lengthy period of declining enrollment. Extensive cuts in spending, no raises for faculty (for the first time in decades), and minimal new hiring, however, resulted in a balanced budget for the fifteenth consecutive year, and a substantially larger freshman class justified a brighter financial outlook for the future.

A university's endowment is a major source of scholarship funds and financial aid, enabling an institution to attract a diverse student body. Historically, however, the University of Evansville's endowment has lagged behind that of several Midwestern private institutions, such as DePauw University, Oberlin College, and Valparaiso University. However, tremendous strides were made in this area during Vinson's administration, as the following table illustrates:

1988	$11,153,000
1994	$23,668,000
1997	$37,623,000
2003	$54,000,000

Also noteworthy is the University's financial contribution to the Evansville area, aptly characterized by Vinson when he described the institution as "a smokeless industry that adds an estimated $84 million a year to the local economy."

In 1991-92, for the first time in the institution's history, annual giving exceeded $500,000. Only eight years later, this figure doubled when annual giving went well over the million dollar mark.

In 1997, Education Securities Inc. (ESI) selected the University of Evansville as the first university to be designated as a "best practice" case study. A subsidiary of the Student Loan Marketing Association (Sallie Mae), ESI is a consulting firm which provides financial and management services to colleges and universities across the nation. It cited the institution for its success in "engaging faculty in redesigning and implementing a more focused and distinctive curriculum, overhauling its academic and administrative structure, and instituting an innovative performance-assessment process." ESI's report commended Vinson's pragmatic approach to solving institutional problems, a process which could be applied to other liberal arts colleges as well.

Fund-Raising Campaigns

In October of 1985, a year before the end of his tenure, President Graves initiated a five-year, $40 million fund-raising program. Called Facing the Future, the campaign was designed to increase the endowment and provide more funds for scholarships. The effort was co-chaired by D. W. and Alma Vaughn, both UE graduates, trustees, and long-time University and community leaders. Graves, after being appointed University provost,

324

D. W. and Alma Vaughn, co-chairs of Facing the Future campaign

worked closely with a team of volunteers to bring the campaign to a successful conclusion, exceeding its goal by $8,877,066.

WIDENING THE CIRCLE
The Campaign for the University of Evansville

In 1999, President Vinson announced a $50 million campaign, Widening the Circle, the largest in the institution's history. Specifically, the campaign targeted the following areas:

Koch Center for Engineering and Science
$15 million to upgrade and add to the science and engineering facility and bring state-of-the-art technology into the classrooms

Athletic Facilities
$2.5 million for new baseball (Charles H. Braun Stadium) and softball (James N. and Dorothy M. Cooper Stadium) stadiums, more intramural athletic fields, and renovation of Black Beauty Field at Arad McCutchan Stadium (soccer)

Harlaxton College
$1 million to renovate the carriage house, which accommodates seventy-eight students

National Guard Armory
$5 million to renovate the old armory, to be named the Ridgway Center after long-time UE supporter and life trustee William Ridgway

STUDENT LOBBY

On two occasions, UE students found their financial aid threatened by budget cuts at either the federal or state levels.

A 1995 bill before Congress targeted virtually all forms of federal student aid. Both students and college officials agreed that the proposed cuts would be devastating, ending the hope of a college education for many and sending others into long-term debt for their education.

Therefore, students at UE tried their hand at lobbying against the $20 billion in cuts during a two-day onslaught of telephone calls, letter writing, faxes, and electronic mail to elected officials in Washington. Student Congress reported that the outcome of the protest was beyond what they had hoped for. Only 500 letters were expected to be written, but approximately 1,700 letters opposing the proposal were sent.

In February 2003, a delegation of UE students and administrators traveled to Indianapolis to lobby against a proposed cut in state grants for Hoosiers attending private universities. For those enrolled at UE, the reductions would amount to $714,000. If the bill passed, 628 UE students would find their financial package reduced and forty-five would lose it altogether. The Evansville group, joined by representatives of other private Indiana colleges, were cordially received by state legislators and achieved some success. The proposed cuts would have reduced the maximum amount a student could receive from $9,300 to $8,000 or less. Instead, the figure was set at $9,100, decidedly a victory for the student lobbyists.

325

*John H. Schroeder, chair of the
Widening the Circle campaign*

Student Center

$2 million to create a place for students to relax, with a game room, computer lab, meeting rooms, and other recreational areas

It was subsequently determined that the engineering costs involved in renovating the armory would be prohibitive. Therefore, Harper Dining Center was renamed William L. Ridgway Center, with the dining area continuing as Harper Dining Hall, and the lower level converted to a student lounge (see page 307).

William L. Ridgway

326

Endowment Fund

$7 million to add to the existing $53 million

(This goal was later increased nearly $18 million.)

Annual Giving

$17.5 million, more than twice the usual amount, to be used primarily for financial aid for students

(The annual fund supplements endowment income as a source of financial aid for students.)

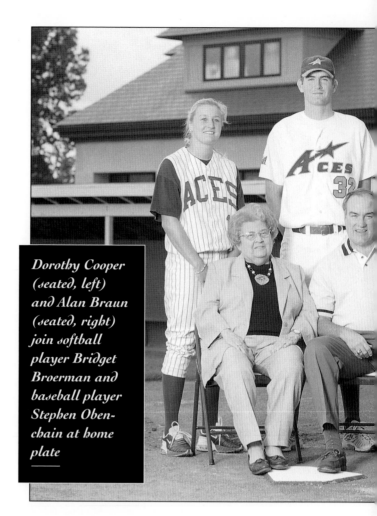

Dorothy Cooper (seated, left) and Alan Braun (seated, right) join softball player Bridget Broerman and baseball player Stephen Obenchain at home plate

Campaign leaders included trustees Michael Hinton, Wilfred C. Bussing III, Lawrence Kremer, Rita Eykamp, Wayne Davidson, John Conaway, Alan Braun, H. Lee Cooper III, Larry Dunigan, and Arthur Shoener. When the campaign was publicly announced, $32 million had already been pledged. The fifty-five-member Board of Trustees gave $15 million, including a $500,000 challenge gift from life trustee and campaign chair John H. Schroeder and his wife, Virginia.

A year later, with eighty-four percent of the objective already reached, the goal was increased to $60 million. Twelve gifts of $1 million or more were received by the end of 2000, thus enabling the University to offer fifteen new endowed scholarships. With strong alumni participation and pledges from ninety percent of full-time faculty, staff, and administrators, the campaign proved the most successful in the history of the University. Not only was the new goal of $60 million exceeded

by $422,154, but it was achieved in three years instead of five!

In 2002, the Lilly Endowment challenged the University of Evansville to raise an additional $3.5 million, offering to match, dollar-for-dollar, up to that amount raised from alumni, parents, students, faculty, and staff.

Major Gifts

■ In 2001, the University of Evansville received $2 million in honor of Elda Patton Herts '42. After earning a bachelor's degree in education at Evansville College, Patton spent two summers at the University of Mexico, becoming so proficient in Spanish that she worked in the U.S. Embassy in Argentina during World War II. After the war, she decided to embark on a medical career, but was rejected by several American universities because of her age and gender. Finally accepted by the University of Padua in Italy, she went on to become a psychotherapist in New York City, rising to prominence as senior psychiatrist, supervising psychiatrist, and head of outpatient services at several New York hospitals and clinics. In 1971, Patton received an honorary doctorate from the University of Evansville. She died in 1992.

■ In 2002, the University received more than $1.5 million from two bequests, one from the estate of Crayton E. Mann '41, a former Welborn Baptist Hospital administrator, the other from the estate of Frances E. Cokes, the first woman pilot in Indiana to be commercially licensed. The funds were to be used primarily for scholarships; one, as designated by Mann, a quadriplegic, to be awarded to a disabled student. A part of the Mann estate also supported the University health center, renamed for him and his wife.

■ Late in 2002, the University received its largest bequest ever – $2.5 million from the estate of Dorothy M. Cooper. Her husband, James, an alumnus and former trustee, and she, also a graduate, were recipients of the University's Alumni Achievement Award (1975) and shared a strong interest in their alma mater's athletic program. The softball stadium was named in their honor, and Mrs. Cooper threw out the first pitch at its dedication. The bequest specifically provided scholarships for one varsity baseball and one varsity softball player and for a student majoring in physical therapy, with additional scholarships to be awarded at the University's discretion.

327

PRESIDENT'S CLUB

In 2003, the University acquired its 1,000th President's Club member, Adele Jeffers Everett '76. She joins her father, Albert Jeffers '49, her husband, Paul '75, their son, Joel '00, and Joel's wife, Lane '00, to form a multigenerational chain of UE supporters. The President's Club recognizes alumni, parents, and friends who donate at least $1,000 annually to help students achieve a quality college education.

Special Programs

Three freshmen are designated **Fund for Educational Excellence** (FEE) scholars annually. These include the Suhrheinrich scholarship, established in 1985 by Dallas Suhrheinrich in memory of her husband, former trustee and a member of the FEE Council, William Suhrheinrich.

In 1993, approximately $4 million, again designated for scholarships, was received from the estate of life trustee Philip Drachman, a businessman and real estate investor.

Sponsor-A-Student, established in 1991, recognizes donors who make unrestricted gifts of $2,000 or more for scholarship support. This program fosters a personal relationship between donors and students. "Donors can actually get to know the students they are sponsoring and follow their progress through college," observed trustee Wayne Davidson. To encourage participation, Mr. and Mrs. Davidson offered to match all donor increases, up to $10,000 per donor, until May 2004. Within a year the number of University of Evansville students receiving scholarships through the Sponsor-A-Student program rose to 496, compared to 212 the previous year. As a result of the Davidsons' challenge, fifty-seven new donors joined the program and eighteen active donors increased their gifts.

MOVIE

A small but noteworthy donation to the University was received in 1991 when Columbia Pictures filmed part of its movie *A League of Their Own,* starring Gina Davis, Tom Hanks, and Madonna, in southern Indiana (Huntingburg and Evansville). Each day the movie was filmed at Bosse Field in Evansville, 3,500 extras were needed. One hundred forty seven University of Evansville students and staff participated, and the film company agreed to contribute one dollar to the UE scholarship fund for each UE person taking part. Although Madonna was reportedly unenthusiastic about the city of Evansville, participants in the film found it an enjoyable and unique experience.

The **John Collins Moore Society** honors the University's founder. Established in 1994 with more than 250 charter members, its roster exceeded 3,000 in six years. Its members are persons who have included the University of Evansville in their estate plans, wills, trusts, gift annuities, life insurance policies, or other deferred-giving vehicles.

Judy and Wayne Davidson

In 2002, the University inaugurated a **Trustee Scholarship** in recognition of the trustees' role in the success of the Widening the Circle campaign. Full, three-quarter, and one-half tuition scholarships are offered to high school seniors who ranked number one in their class at the time of application. All scholarships are renewable yearly for students who maintain a 3.35 grade point average. The first year, seventy-eight Trustee Scholarships were awarded; the following year the number rose to 101.

FREEDOM OF CHOICE

Dependents of UE faculty and staff traditionally receive full-tuition scholarships if they qualify for admission to the University.

Beginning in 1990, however, students could choose between attending the University of Evansville or selecting another private institution from more than 530 schools in forty-seven states participating in the Tuition Exchange program. In 2003, a new program added several hundred more schools to the list of those already available. Thus, homebodies can still follow the traditional path, while others can get far away from home if they wish to do so.

1854-2004: AN OVERVIEW

Moores Hill Male and Female Collegiate Institute, forerunner of today's University of Evansville, was founded as a civic project by residents of Moores Hill, who felt the need for a college in their own community. The college offered degrees in business and agriculture as well as classes in teacher training to serve the needs of students from the farms and small towns of southeastern Indiana. Equally important, it provided a classically-oriented liberal arts education, with preparation for the ministry a major focus.

FOUNDERS DAY

Each February, the University of Evansville observes Founders Day, a commemoration of four major events in its history:

- **February 8, 1810: John Collins Moore, founder of Moores Hill College, was born.**

- **February 10, 1854: Moores Hill Male and Female Collegiate Institute was incorporated by the state of Indiana.**

- **February 17, 1919: Evansville College was incorporated by the state of Indiana.**

- **February 17, 1967: The University of Evansville was incorporated by the state of Indiana.**

329

With the move to Evansville, the College's educational emphasis shifted to programs suited to its new urban setting. These included a cooperative program in engineering, a comprehensive array of business administration courses, classes for teachers, vocational courses, a carefully planned curriculum in the liberal arts, and continuing education programs. Even in 1919, the school's first year in Evansville, 289 persons enrolled in community courses. Alfred Hughes, the institution's first president in Evansville, emphasized his belief that the College should be not only *in* the city but *part of* the city, and that it must serve its community in every way possible.

Through the Evening College, established in 1940, the institution further bonded with the community, offering one of the most extensive continuing education programs in Indiana, making it possible for students to complete a college degree by attending classes solely at night. For thousands of individuals, the evening program has broadened horizons and opened doors, enabling job advancement and providing opportunities for personal growth and development.

Over the years, the institution has dramatically broadened its sphere of influence to include students from all fifty states and over eighty countries. At the same time, University of Evansville students, in increasing numbers, have chosen to study abroad at the University's Harlaxton College or elsewhere. (Over forty-three percent of the Class of 2003 took a portion of their course work outside the United States.) Furthermore, as the student body has become increasingly diverse and cosmopolitan, its academic caliber has increased.

As a private institution, the University of Evansville has faced many of the obstacles and enjoyed many of the advantages which characterize such schools. Heading the list of problems is the ongoing search for the financial resources needed to fulfill its mission. (During the Great Depression, some students found it necessary to pay their tuition with potatoes and carrots instead of cash.) Fortunately, a growing roster of dedicated and generous donors has enabled the University to survive periods of difficulty and to flourish and grow.

Flexibility in programs and a favorable student/faculty ratio are generally associated with smaller private colleges and universities. In contrast to large state institutions, which tend to be research-oriented, the University of Evansville has encouraged its faculty to make quality teaching and the needs of students its primary concerns. Also, professors are required to develop familiarity with a broad range of subject matter, giving them broader perspectives than those of narrowly trained specialists.

This spirit has also carried into the curriculum. The University of Evansville deliberately emphasizes the fundamental and theoretical aspects of discovery and learning, both to equip students to live in a fast-changing world and also to protect them against the obsolescence of purely vocational training.

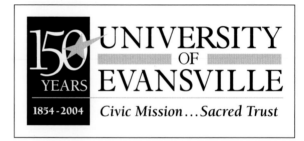

"Civic Mission…Sacred Trust" is the motto chosen by the University to mark its sesquicentennial anniversary celebration in 2004. The words reflect the institution's commitment to quality, value-based higher education and its service to its community. Many events, including musical presentations, lectures, symposiums, theatre performances, and a television documentary, together with this volume, are part of the sesquicentennial events.

In accordance with University tradition, the culminating programs take place in February of 2004 and 2005. These events will highlight the institution's determination to succeed, even when faced with adversity, and to achieve a local, regional, and national reputation for distinctive service and academic excellence.

President's Epilogue

CIVIC MISSION...SACRED TRUST

The future of the University of Evansville will continue to reflect the cycle of growth, consolidation, challenge, and renewal that has defined and strengthened the University over its 150-year history. Amidst that change, however, will be an unyielding devotion to the values embodied in the sesquicentennial theme: Civic Mission...Sacred Trust. While those words were chosen to reflect the principles and values on which the University was founded and has operated under the last 150 years, they signal much about what it will strive for in the years ahead.

A VISION FOR TOMORROW

As we embark on future chapters of the University's development, we are committed to a vision built on the core values of academic excellence, the integration of liberal and professional education, and a challenging student-centered environment. At the heart of our vision for the future is an unrelenting desire to provide life-transforming educational experiences that prepare students to engage the world as informed, ethical, and productive citizens. Major goals to be achieved over the next ten to thirty years include:

- **An academic reputation that places us among the most admired Midwestern universities of our type**

- **An endowment of $400 million by 2030**

- **Academic selectivity characterized by high numbers of well-qualified applicants seeking admission to the University**

- **State-of-the-art physical facilities complemented with state-of-the-art technology**

- **Development of the surrounding neighborhood into a major destination area for the city and as a laboratory for student involvement in the community**

- **Recognition as a world leader in international education**

THE EVANSVILLE EXPERIENCE

Looking to the future during this time of rapid technological and societal change, it is more important than ever to define the set of educational experiences that will make up the unmistakable hallmarks of a University of Evansville education. The hallmarks that will continue to guide our educational mission have recently been given significance by inclusion in the University's long-range planning document: *Strategic Choices – A Five Year Plan for the Future*. The following description from that plan forms the nucleus of those characteristics that will be fundamental to our educational efforts and ultimately our very success in the decades to come.

Academic Quality At the heart of the Evansville Experience will be an uncompromising emphasis on academic quality. This quality is derived from an outstanding faculty, the enrollment of academically well-prepared students, and the availability of excellent facilities and other resources needed to offer a rich learning environment. The University of Evansville's learning environment will strive to be collaborative, student-centered, and focused on teaching in a primarily undergraduate setting.

UE students came from or went to 74 countries between 1999 to 2003 (indicated by gray shading)

International Focus The University believes that students should be prepared to live, work, and learn in an ever more intimate global society. To this end, the University actively recruits international students to campus and encourages American students to study abroad at Harlaxton College or one of the more than 100 cooperating universities around the world. This focus is further supported by a general education curriculum that emphasizes a world view.

Strong Professional Programs Grounded in the Arts and Sciences
By focusing general education on the arts and sciences, the University seeks to prepare students for a lifetime of opportunity and successful transitions. Preparing students with superior communication, critical thinking, and problem-solving skills is fundamental to our educational philosophy. These abilities, along with the confidence to conceptualize and contextualize, are critical to rapid advancement. Our goal is to prepare students with the skills and abilities necessary to quickly assume positions of leadership in their profession and community.

Residential Collegiate Model The importance of being a residential campus is more about students being actively involved in a stimulating campus community than about where they actually reside. Our goal is to provide opportunities for students to grow in their ability to take responsibility for their own behavior, relationships, and the attainment of personal goals. The residential experience provides an important laboratory where students learn to help shape the quality of life in the community where they live. Understanding and taking responsibility for both community and self is an important step in leadership development.

Church-Related and Values-Based The University remains committed to its long-standing relationship with the United Methodist Church. The church's historic support of higher education and strong tradition of inclusiveness and open inquiry are fundamental philosophies that support the mission of the University. It is a tradition that allows students to pursue a personal faith journey on their own terms and to become servant leaders who appreciate and respond to the needs of others. This relationship reflects our strong belief in a values-based learning environment that encourages students to understand the ethical and spiritual significance of their personal and professional behavior.

FACING THE FUTURE

As we look to the future, the challenges we face are similar to those of the past 150 years. At the end of the day, we must be satisfied that we offer an education of real value, and that its value is worth the cost. The University is stronger and better prepared to meet those challenges and that makes us more confident than ever in singing the last line of our University hymn…*We face the future unafraid.*

Stephen G. Jennings
President, University of Evansville
September 2003

The Miser, *1968 theatre production*

Appendix

AWARD WINNERS AND
SELECTED ADDITIONAL NOTABLE ACHIEVERS
University of Evansville Honor Roll

**Mabel Dillingham
Nenneker/Guthrie May
Outstanding Senior Award**

1974   Susan (Gascoigne) Boyer
W. Scott Shrode

1975   Robin (Gooch) Norris
Teresa (Thomas) Farish
Eric Stein

1976   Martha (Taylor) Starkey
Robin Babbitt

1977   Nancy Schwarz
Dirk Baer

1978   Cynthia (Poti) Ortega
Christopher Weaver

1979   Nancy Croker
Steven Hipfel

1980   Karen (Hoevener) Heber
Gabriel Reising

1981   Cynthia Bumb
Vincent Mathews

1982   Marni Lemons
Joel Reynolds

1983   Judith (Allen) Seitzinger
Kameron McQuay

1984   Lisa Akers
Kirk Waiz

1985   Sylvia (Young) DeVault
Ronald Schroeder

1986   Kay Sichting
Scott Terranella

1987   Lynette Fields
Eric Schaefer

1988   M. Lynn (Hausman) Jump
Kent Scheller

1989   Mara (Fick) Springer
Kevin Carpenter

1990   Kimberly Seibert
Michael Acuna

1991   Amy Humphries
Michael Long

1992   Tina (Hooper) Brake
S. Mike Rasmussen

1993   Jennifer (Mead) Wilcox
Mark Guttman

1994   Joy Marcrum
Michael McGovern

1995   Sonya (Jenkins) Brindle
Patrick Staples

1996   Michelle Breunig
Chad Walker

1997   Alison Becker
Martin Gregorie

1998   Brandi (Doyle) Cannon
Len Devaisher

1999   Trisha (Mentek) McRoberts
Trenton Kriete

2000   Andi Hamilton
Matthew Amick

2001   Jennifer Barchet
Jove Oliver

2002   Kisha Tracy
Aaron Peterman

2003   Erica Corbin
Brennan McReynolds

Athletic Hall of Fame

1972-73
Edward Stuteville
Ralph Rea
"Bounce" Harper
Wilfred "Gus" Doerner
Ray Bawal
Ed Smallwood
Jerry Sloan
Gene Logel

1973-74
Don Ping
Hugh Ahlering
Larry Humes
Larry Gates
Bill Slyker
Joe Theby

1974-75
Clyde Cox
Lowell Galloway
Bud Johnson
Ralph Weinzapfel
John Harmon
Bob Sakel

1975-76
Bob Gerhardt
Bill Parish
Bob Barnett
Dale Wise
Bud George
Bill Russler

1976-77
Bob Scott
John Harrawood
Jim Smallins
Ken Lutterbach
Wayne Boultinghouse
"Buster" Briley
Gordon Bryant
Craig Blackford

1977-78
Walter Riggs
Paul Beck
Bob Lodato
Don Buse
Mike Woodward
Morris Riley
Sam Watkins
Allen Stremming

1978-79
Warren Alston
Marv Bates
Jeff Bohnert
Ray Comendella
Mike Duff
Charles Goad
Kraig Heckendorn
Bob Hudson

Michael Joyner
Maurice King
Kevin Kingston
Mark Kirkpatrick
Mark Kniese
Greg Knipping
Barney Lewis
Stephen Miller
Keith Moon
Chuck Shike
Mark Siegel
Greg Smith
Bryan Taylor
John Ed Washington
Bobby Watson
Tony Winburn

1979-80
Arad McCutchan
Louise Owen
Mel Lurker
Marty Amsler
Dan Scism

1980-81
Herb Williams
Pete Rupp
John Wellemeyer
Randy Mattingly
Bob Polk
Russ Grieger

1981-82
Don Watson
Bob Glaser
John MacDougal
Ken Coudret

1982-83
Virgil Bufford
Ralph Coleman
John Feigel
Emerson Henke
Ben Karasiak

1983-84
Harold Cox
Jerry Denstorff
Ted Foland
Kern McGlothlin
Roy Wyttenbach

1984-85
Cheryl Becker
   Edwardson
Gordon Jaffray
Ed Katterhenry
Dean Long
Ida Stieler

1985-86
Luther Small
Archie Owen
Bill Vieth

1986-87
Pam Hendricks-
   Zwickel
Carl Horn
Charlie Uhde
Bob Walther
Steve Welmer

1987-88
Paul Bullard
Rick Coffey
Darla Edwards
J. O. Jackson
Quentin Merkel

1988-89
Mark Freeman
Brad Leaf
John Nunes

1989-90
Jerry Canterbury
John Lidy
Mary Ellen Greaney-
   Muensterman
John Vernasco

1990-91
Shelly Brand-Adlard
Dave Gossman
Bill Harrawood
Ed Hooker

1991-92
Frank D'Amelio
Rhonda Smith
Ron Sutton
Tom Wolff

1992-93
Harold Brown
Kay Conder
Patrick Heck
Richard Schleicher

1993-94
Mark Hord
Michael Madriaga
Dan McHugh
Lois Patton

WILFRED "GUS" DOERNER

| 1994-95 | Andy Benes
Kerri Blaylock
Terry Foran
Scott Haffner | 1972 | Ronald Browning
Esther Luttrull
Raymond Miller
Paul Scheips
O. Glenn Stahl | 1976 | Wayne Davidson
Rita Eykamp
Elmer Graham
Eugene Hendershot
Minnie Magazine
Woodrow Oestreicher
Robert Statham |

1994-95 Andy Benes
         Kerri Blaylock
         Terry Foran
         Scott Haffner

1995-96 Kim Horvath
         A. J. Lachowecki
         Gerald Seid
         Jim Voorhees

1996-97 David Denny
         Rob Paterson
         Debbie Roberts-Shultz
         Marty Simmons
         Joe Unfried

1997-98 Byron Buckley
         Debbie Bajovich-
            Kliegl
         Bill Sharpe
         David Weir

1998-99 Linda Crick
         Dan Godfread
         Paul Jensen
         Rob Maurer
         D. W. Vaughn

1999-00 Jim Byers
         Al Dauble
         Christy Greis

2000-01 Quentin Hartke
         Graham Merryweather
         Laura Seib-Wyatt

2001-02 Scott Cannon
         Shannon Cook-Burger
         Meg Dettwiler
         Sal Fasano
         Eric Fish
         J. Robert Knott

2002-03 Mick Lyon
         Al Baity
         Dorothy and
            James Cooper
         Andy Elkins
         Bob Hawkins

Alumni Certificate of Excellence

1971 Wilfred Doerner
      William Miller
      Jo Frohbieter-Mueller

1972 Ronald Browning
      Esther Luttrull
      Raymond Miller
      Paul Scheips
      O. Glenn Stahl

1973 Robert DeBard
      Ronald Glass
      Robert Graper
      Emaline Bumb
         Kleinknecht
      Nancy Roser
      Charles Van Vorst

1974 Robert Carithers
      H. Joel Deckard
      Marilyn Durham
      Robert Plane
      Marguerite Roberts
      Harvey Seifert
      Jerry Sloan

1975 Robert Dunville
      Mary Ray Durry
      Kenneth Hutchinson
      Louise Owen
      Charles Thompson
      Samuel Watkins Jr.

1976 Wayne Davidson
      Rita Eykamp
      Elmer Graham
      Eugene Hendershot
      Minnie Magazine
      Woodrow Oestreicher
      Robert Statham

1977 Jack Frohbieter
      William Nation Sr.
      Robert Northerner
      Helen Passwater
      J. Robert Polk
      Edgar Williams

1978 Rod Clutter Sr.
      Jack Hahn
      Emerson Henke
      Chester Lynxwiler
      Howard Lytle
      Ferol Martin
      Frank Russell Jr.
      William Vieth
         (Special Award)
      James Vogel

337

*Tom Armstrong (above),
creator of Marvin (left)*

1979   John Conaway
        Victor Fisher
        Kenneth McCutchan
        Joel Crist Reynolds
            (Special Award)
        Harold Sander
        Helen Smith
            (Special Award)
        Marjorie Soyugenc
        Warren Wilhelm Jr.

1980   Tom Armstrong
        Joan Finch
        Abdul Kamara
        Keith Langsdale
        Frederick Silber
        Robert Silber

1981   Tom Heaton
            (Special Award)
        Jane Heneisen
        Roy House
        Ed Katterhenry
        Louise Owen
        Laurence Shapiro

1982   Jack Brenton
        Darryl Halbrooks

1983   Flossie Klein Becknell
        Arthur Fellwock
        Harold Halbrook
            (Special Award)
        Dean Long
        William Neal Jr.
        Ralph Olmsted

1984   Gustav Anguizola
        Charlotte Baldwin
        Jerry Linzy

1985   David Lawson
        Matt Williams

1986   Earl Buechler
        H. William Gilmore

1987   Virginia Adye
        Susan Mueller
        Vincent Parker

1988   Wendell Dixon
        Barbara Price
        Tom Tuley

1989   Andrew Benes
        Bernice King

Distinguished Alumnus/a Award

1990   Wayne Davidson

1991   Alma and D. W. Vaughn

1992   Arad McCutchan

1993   Matt Williams

1994   (no award given)

1995   John B. Conaway

1996   J. Allen McCutchan

1997   Richard Lyon

1998   Donald Griffin

1999   (no award given)

2000   Donald Ricketts

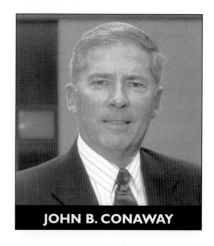

JOHN B. CONAWAY

2001   Elizabeth and
        David McFadzean

2002   Rita Eykamp

2003   Verna Fairchild

338

Bernice King

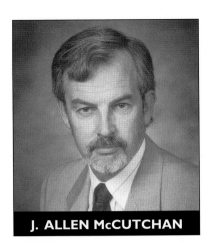

J. ALLEN McCUTCHAN

Samuel Orr
Honorary Alumnus/a Award

The highest recognition the Alumni Association bestows on non-alumni

1971   A.C. Biggs
        Robert Hudson

1972   (no award given)

1973   V.C. Bailey
        Ralph Coleman
        Carl Hottenstein

1974   Dale Campbell
        Carolyn and
            Donald Dunham
        Naomi and
            Robert Rowland
        J. Harry Whetstone

1975   William Montrastelle
        Thomas Morrison
        William Robertson

1976   Oscar Jeude
        Martha and
            Jesse Kent Jr.
        Thomas Rose

1977   Alvin Dauble
        Claudia and
            Melvin Hyde
        Dean Long
        Aubrey Ryals

1978   Annamargaret and
            Raymond Clutter
        John Cooke
        Robert Green

1979   James Byers
        John Oberhelman

1980   Barbara and
            Wallace Graves

1981   Clarence Harrison
        Clarence Pitman

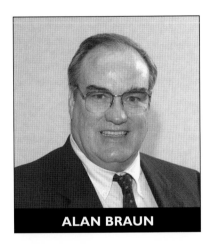

ALAN BRAUN

1982   John H. Schroeder

1983   Robert Kent
        Samuel Orr

1984   William Suhrheinrich
        C. Wayne Worthington

1985   Robert L. Koch Sr.

1986   Wahnita DeLong
        Phillip Drachman
        Dallas Suhrheinrich

1987   Orville Jaebker

1988   H. Lee Cooper III

1989   (no award given)

1990   Judy Steenberg

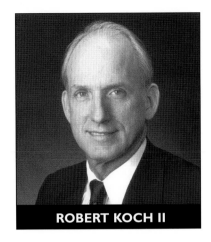

ROBERT KOCH II

1991   Melvin Peterson
        William Ridgway

1992   Barbara McKenna
        Virginia Schroeder

1993   Virginia Grabill

1994   (no award given)

1995   Dan Mitchell

1996   Robert Menke

1997   Susan and James Vinson

1998   Mary Kay Powell

1999   Larry Dunigan

2000   John C. Schroeder
        Ruth Bromm

2001   Alan Braun

2002   Richard Shymanski

2003   Robert L. Koch II

Young Alumnus Award

1997   Andrew Benes

1998   Anita Horn

1999   Joe Wallace

2000   James Purucker

2001   Michael Alden

2002   Michael Parker

2003   J. Bryan Nicol

DAN MITCHELL

MICHAEL WOODARD

Edie Bates Alumni Volunteer Service Award

1999	Edie Bates
2000	Meg Dettwiler (posthumously)
2001	Jerry Purdie
2002	Michael Woodard
2003	Wilfred Bussing III

Board of Trustees Presidents

Bishop William Anderson *1919-21*

Bishop Frederick Leete *1921-27*

Rita Eykamp

340

Tink Martin (left) and Mary Kessler

Alfred Craig *1927-28*

Bishop Edgar Blake *1928-39*

Richard McGinnis *1939-55*

F. Bayard Culley *1955-63*

Samuel Orr *1963-68*

Leland Feigel *1968-71*

Kenneth Kent *1971-75*

Raymond Clutter *1975-78*

John H. Schroeder *1978-81*

Lowell Holder *1981-84*

Raymond Clutter *1984-87*

Wayne Davidson *1987-90*

H. Lee Cooper III *1990-93*

Robert Koch II *1993-96*

Ronald Reherman *1996-99*

Rita Eykamp *1999-2002*

Alan Braun *2002-*

Sadelle and Sydney Berger Awards

Awarded to faculty for outstanding creative or scholarly work and for outstanding service to the University of Evansville or the Evansville community

Scholarship (listed first)
Service (listed second)

1985	Nadine Coudret Clark Kimberling
1986	Arthur Aarstad Les Miley
1987	John David Lutz Ludwig Petkovsek
1988	(no awards given)
1989	Charles O'Neal Samuel Longmire
1990	Tom Fiddick David Gugin
1991	Laura Weaver Robert Knott
1992	Ben Riley Hope Bock

1993   (no awards given)

1994   John Haegert
        Cheryl Griffith

1995   Douglas Reed
        Louis Winternheimer

1996   Michael Zimmer
        James Berry

1997   Shirley Schwarz
        David Reeder

1998   William Baer
        Richard Connolly

1999   Daniel Gahan
        Bernice King

2000   Mary Kessler
            and Tink Martin
        William Hemminger

2001   Johnny Poon
        Ben Riley

2002   Robert Morse
        Arthur Jensen

2003   Margaret McMullan
        Michael Carson

Exemplary Teacher Award

Sponsored by the General Board of Higher Education and Ministry, Division of Higher Education, United Methodist Church

1992   Daniel Gahan
        History

1993   Philip Gerhart
        *Engineering and
        Computer Science*

1994   Karen Ott
        Biology

KAREN OTT

1995   Mary Rode   1999   Davies Bellamy
        Nursing   *Education*

1996   Deborah Howard   2000   Ann Baker
        Law, Politics and Society   *Foreign Languages*

1997   Bruce Alford   2001   Michael Carson
        Business Administration   *English*

1998   Dick Blandford   2002   Amy McBride Martin
        Engineering and   *Education*
        Computer Science

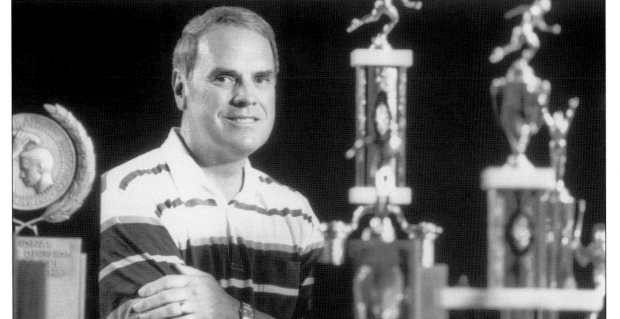

Robert Knott

*Ludwig
Petkovsek*

Outstanding
Teacher Award

1968   P. Louis Winternheimer
      Biology

1969   Paul Grabill
      English

1970   Orville Jaebker
      History

1971   Arthur Aarstad
      Political Science

1972   Ludwig Petkovsek
      Sociology

342

RAY ARENSMAN

1973   Warren Hankins
      Chemistry

1974   Donald Dunham
      Biology

1975   Ralph Coleman
      Mathematics

1976   Ray Arensman
      Economics

1977   Virginia Grabill
      English

1978   Michael Carson
      English

1979   Robert Kress
      Philosophy and Religion

1980   David Gugin
      Political Science

1981   Dorothy Hausmann
      Nursing

1982   Jean Falls
      Nursing

1983   Samuel Longmire
      English

1984   Michael Zimmer
      Economics

1985   Karen Ott
      Biology

1986   Ben Riley
      Physics

1987   David Wright
      Music

1988   Les Miley Jr.
      Art

1989   John Haegert
      English

1990   Donald Richardson
      English

1991   Larry Caldwell
      English

1992   Daniel Gahan
      History

1993   William Hemminger
      *English,
         Foreign Languages*

1994   W. Richard Connolly
      Philosophy and Religion

1995	Carol Dallinger *Music*
1996	Walayet Khan *Finance*
1997	Laurence Steenberg *Business Administration*
1998	Brian Swenty *Engineering*
1999	Jerry Seng *Biology*
2000	David Dwyer *Mathematics*
2001	Douglas Stamps *Engineering*
2002	Patrick Thomas *Archaeology and Art History*
2003	Mark Valenzuela *Engineering*

Long Time Staff

Service of twenty or more years and primary area(s) of affiliation

Don Anderson
Maintenance

Diane Ary
Athletics

Sue Baldwin
Development; Academic Affairs

Billy Betz
Maintenance

Johnny Biggers
Maintenance

Robert Bradshaw
Maintenance

John Brown
Maintenance

B. Andrew Bullock
Grounds

Byron Bullock
Maintenance

Mary Campbell
Student Services

Jeannie DePriest
Continuing Education; Music

Linda Deutsch
English; Arts and Sciences

Marjorie Dremstedt
Bookstore

Don Dunville
Maintenance

Pearl Durkee
History, Political Science, Geography

Al Eagan
Physical Plant

M. Hayward Embry
Physical Plant

Marilyn Evans
Education

Judith Fiddick
Communication; Law, Politics, and Society

Steve Fischer
Maintenance

Sylvester Geppner
Maintenance

Etta Gilford
Library

George Glover
Maintenance

SHE COULD ALWAYS FIGURE SOMETHING OUT

Although **Barbara McKenna** never held an official University position, she had a strong presence both on campus and in the community.

At the University of Evansville, Barbara was a founding member of the Samuel Johnson Society and the Wednesday Morning Literature class, president of the Theatre Society, which she helped restructure and revitalize, and chairperson of the Pearl LeCompte Assistantship Fund. After her death, the Theatre Society established the Barbara McKenna Award to honor community volunteers who have served the University's theatre program.

Off-campus, she wrote a weekly column for the *Evansville Press*, was president of the League of Women Voters, and was especially active with the YWCA, being instrumental in its fundraising efforts and the Personally Speaking lecture series. As a memorial to her, the YWCA established an annual Barbara St. Clair McKenna Tribute to Achievement award, which recognizes community leaders for outstanding service.

To this day, associates pay tribute to McKenna's special achievements and outstanding service:

"She was a mentor for everyone who knew her; everyone wanted to be like her."

"You could always call on Barbara when you were in trouble. She could always figure something out."

Betty Gray
Placement

Ruby Heseman
Engineering; Registrar

Arlen Hoffman
Maintenance

Helen Horn
Human Resources

Kathryn Huber
Athletics

Virginia Jones
Neu Chapel

Charlotte Kagel
Counseling

Joan Kappler
Physical Plant

Ann Katterhenry
Business Administration

Paul Kitzinger
Maintenance

William Kitzinger
Maintenance

Joe Lancaster
Maintenance

Tom Land
McCurdy Alumni Memorial Union

Peg Mathieu
Arts and Sciences

Robert McKinney
Maintenance

Jo Ann Meth
Human Resources

Bennett Mullins
Maintenance; Chemical Stock Room

Stephen Neff
Maintenance

Joan Perry
Neu Chapel

Anna Pitchers
Business Administration

Peg Poetker
Student Life; Admission

Employee Excellence Awards

	Staff	**Administrative**
1995	Shirley Robuck *University Relations*	Heidi Gregori-Gahan *International Student Services*
1996	Helen Horn *Human Resources*	Robert Dale *Buildings and Grounds*
1997	Janice Gunn *Financial Aid*	Sylvia (Young) DeVault *Alumni Relations*
1998	Ottis Putler *Mechanical and Civil Engineering*	Verla Richardson *Financial Aid*
1999	Judy Duncan *Student Life*	Gregory Bordfeld *Human Resources*
2000	Donald Dunville *Maintenance*	Keith Jackson *Office of Technology Services*
2001	Jo Anne Meth *Human Resources*	Angela Dawson *Financial Aid*
2002	Barb Poellein *Purchasing*	Dell Nussmeier *Academic Advising*
2003	Andy Bullock *Grounds*	JoAnn Laugel *Financial Aid*

Mary Lou Powers
Physical Plant

Barbara Purdue
Development

Mary Purdue
Financial Aid

Cecil Raymond
Housekeeping

Shirley Robuck
Academic Affairs

Doris Scheller
Health Center

Don Schneider
Maintenance

Elsie Schweikart
Bookstore

Judith Seeley
International Student Services

Connie Sherlock
Student Accounts

Betty Sitzman
Engineering

John Small
Shipping/Receiving

Esther Stephans
Library

Marzee Taylor
Nursing

Jean Brackmann Templeton
Nursing; Registrar

Andrea Tepool
Business Administration

Jean Titzer
Nursing

Barbara Walker
Instructional Services

Liz Wannemuehler
Admission

Evelyn Woosley
Development

Lucilla Wright
Center for Management Education

Alan Yancey
Grounds

Ken Zirkelbach
Maintenance

University of Evansville Scholars

Fulbright Scholars

1994-95   Ellen Zinkiewicz
          Hungary

1995-96   Sue-Je Gage
          Korea

1999-00   Hiliary Douglas
          Vietnam

2000-01   Rob Olinger
          Russia

2001-02   Steven Crawford
          Finland

          Terri Reuter
          Korea

2002-03   Kristina Johnson
          Germany

          Jean Nicole
            Matheson
          Thailand

Rhodes Scholar
David Dodds '78

Mellon Fellow
Phyllis Toy '83

Pulitzer Prize
Lisel Neumann Mueller '44

Ruth Shafer Hines

Oldest Living Graduate

At this writing, **Ruth Shafer Hines** is believed to be the oldest living graduate of the University of Evansville. It is notable that she received her baccalaureate degree at the age of sixty-one.

Born in 1902, she enrolled at Evansville College shortly after it opened its doors (downtown), taking the twelve weeks of college classes then required to get a teaching certificate. Her first job was at a one-room schoolhouse in rural Kentucky, followed by a position in Oregon. Returning to Evansville College (now with its own campus) in 1923, she took more courses but did not complete a degree, devoting herself instead to being a homemaker and mother. After 1942, Hines resumed her teaching career with positions in Warrick County schools (Chandler and Newburgh), where she remained until 1968, retiring five years after completing her bachelor's degree.

Master Builders

UE alumnus Jack H. Kinkel '62 and the architectural firm of Jack R. Kinkel and Sons are responsible for much of the newer architecture on campus:

- **Plazas in front of the McCurdy Alumni Memorial Union, Krannert Hall of Fine Arts and William L. Ridgway Center**

- **Bower-Suhrheinrich Library**

- **Handicap access to Neu Chapel, Koch Center for Engineering and Science and William L. Ridgway Center**

- **McCurdy Alumni Memorial Union renovation and addition**

- **William L. Ridgway Center renovation (the Underground)**

- **Powell Hall**

- **Schroeder Hall**

345

Selected Bibliography of Books Published by University of Evansville Faculty

Baer, William (ed.). *Conversations with Derek Walcott.* Jackson, Mississippi: University Press of Mississippi, 1996.

Baer, William. *The Unfortunates.* Kirksville, Missouri: New Odyssey Press, 1997.

Beavers, Anthony F. *Levinas Beyond Horizons of Cartesianism.* New York: Peter Lang, 1995.

Bohn, Thomas W. (and Richard L. Stromgren). *Light and Shadows: A History of Motion Pictures.* Port Washington, New York: Alfred Publishing Company, 1975.

Brittain, John N. *The Backside of God and Other Occasional Sermons.* Lima, Ohio: CSS Publishing Company, 2000.

Brittain, John N. *Living Vertically.* Lima, Ohio, CSS Publishing Company, 2000.

Burlingame, Dwight F. (ed.). *Library Development: A Future Imperative.* New York: Haworth Press, 1990.

Dwyer, David and Mark Gruenwald. *College Algebra.* Minneapolis, Minnesota: West Publishing Company, 1995.

Fiddick, Thomas C. *Russia's Retreat from Poland: 1920.* New York: St. Martin's Press, 1990.

Freeman, Donald M. (ed.). *Foundation of Political Science: Research, Methods, and Scope.* New York: Free Press, 1977.

Donald Freeman

Gahan, Daniel. *The People's Rising: Wexford 1798.* Dublin: Gill and MacMillan Ltd., 1995.

Gerhart, Philip M. (and Richard L. Gross and John I. Hockstein). *Fundamentals of Fluid Mechanics.* Reading, Massachusetts, 1992.

Grabill, Paul. *Youth's a Stuff Will Not Endure.* New York: Avon Books, 1978.

Hankins, Warren (and Marie Hankins). *Introduction to Chemistry.* St. Louis, Missouri: C.V. Mosby Company, 1974.

Harding, Thomas S. *College Literary Societies: Their Contribution to Higher Education in the United States 1815-1876.* New York: Pageant Press International Corporation, 1971.

Kimberling, Clark. *Geometry in Action.* Emeryville, California: Key College Publishing, 2003.

Kirkwood, Burton. *The History of Mexico.* Westport, Connecticut: Greenwood Press, 2000.

Kress, Robert. *Whither Womankind?* St. Meinrad, Indiana: Abbey Press, 1975.

Logan, Lillian and Virgil G. Logan. *Teaching the Elementary School Child.* Boston, Massachusetts: Houghton Mifflin Company, 1961.

MacLeod, James Lachlan. *The Second Disruption: The Free Church in Victorian Scotland and the Origins of the Free Presbyterian Church.* Great Britain: Tuckwell Press, 2000.

Martin, Suzanne "Tink" and Mary Kessler. *Neurologic Intervention for Physical Therapist Assistants.* Philadelphia, Pennsylvania: W.B. Saunders Company, 2000.

McKown, Edgar M. (and Carl Scherzer). *Understanding Christianity.* New York: Ronald Press Company, 1949.

McMullan, Margaret. *When Warhol Was Still Alive.* Freedom, California: The Crossing Press, 1994.

O'Neal, Charles (and Kate Bertrand). *Developing a Winning J.I.T. Marketing Strategy.* Englewood Cliffs, New Jersey: Prentice Hall, 1991.

Pieper, Hanns G. *The Nursing Home Primer.* White Hall, Virginia: Betterway Publications, 1981.

Richardson, Donald. *Eye-Witnesses: Dramatic Voices from the Gospels.* Wheaton, Illinois: Harold Shaw Publishers, 1988.

Richardson, Donald. *Great Zeus and All His Children.* Englewood Cliffs, New Jersey: Prentice Hall, 1984.

Richardson, Donald. *Hercules and Other Legends of Gods and Heroes.* New York: Gramercy Books: 1989.

Schlueter, Paul. *The Novels of Doris Lessing.* Carbondale, Illinois: Southern Illinois University Press, 1969.

Schwarz, Shirley J. *Greek Vases in the National Museum of Natural History, Smithsonian Institution, Washington, D.C.* Rome: L'Erna di Bretschneider, 1996.

Smiley, Sam *The Drama of Attack.* Columbia, Missouri: University of Missouri Press, 1972.

Smiley, Sam. *Playwriting: The Structure of Action.* Englewood Cliffs, New Jersey. Prentice Hall, 1971.

Snively Jr., William Daniel (and Jan Thuerbach). *Healing Beyond Medicine.* West Nyack, New York: Parker Publishing Company, 1972.

Snively Jr., William Daniel. *The Sea of Life.* New York: David McKay Company, 1969.

Snively, Jr. William Daniel (and Donna R. Beshear). *Textbook of Pathophysiology.* Philadelphia, Pennsylvania: J.R. Lippincott Company, 1972.

Strickler, Alvin (and Andrew A. Sherockman). *A Laboratory Manual for General Chemistry.* Ann Arbor, Michigan: Edward Brothers, 1953.

Thomlison, T. Dean. *Toward Interpersonal Dialogue.* New York: Longman, 1982.

Tonso, William R. *Gun and Society: The Social and Existential Roots of the American Attachment to Firearms.* Washington, D.C.: University Press of America, 1982.

Unger, David J. *Analytical Fracture Mechanics.* Mineola, New York: Dover Publications, 1995.

Wangerin Jr., Walter. *The Book of the Dun Cow.* New York: Harper and Row, 1978.

347

List of Photographs and Credits

Known credits for the photographic images which appear in this history of the University of Evansville are cited below. Principal sources of the photographic images are the University of Evansville archives and collections. Several persons graciously provided photographs for print. If a photograph is not listed below, it is part of the University collection with no known photographer. Every reasonable effort has been taken to attribute the correct source for each photographic image that appears in *We Face the Future Unafraid*.

From *From Institute to University*, by Ralph Olmsted: pages 27, 41 (both), 58, 72, 95, 98, 106 (bottom), 116, 117 (left), 118, 126 (bottom), 127 (top), 130, 142. From UE *LinC*: pages 229 (Hyde, 1967), 303 (Carter, 1938). From *The School of Nursing 1953-1974* by Mildred Boeke: page 82. By Adlard Photography: pages 195 (top), 229 (Graves). Courtesy of the Arizona Diamondbacks Baseball Club: page 284 (top left). Courtesy of Sue Baldwin: page 144. Courtesy of B'nai B'rith Speakers Bureau: page 315 (top). Courtesy of Steve Crawford: page 301 (top). By Bonnie Daly: page 277 (bottom). Courtesy of Elizabeth Dodd: page 268 (bottom right). By Wayne Doebling: pages 214, 216. By Chris Donahue: page 319 (left). By Chris Eberhard: pages 283 (bottom, left and right), 285 (bottom right), 318. By Erik Photographic: pages 165, 260 (right), 325, 336. By Marion Ettlinger, courtesy of Royce Carlton Inc.: page 314 (bottom right). Courtesy of Jo Frohbieter-Mueller: page 145. By Steve Goodrum: page 222. By Gray Photography: pages 103 (left), 227 (right), 245, 251, 258, 338 (bottom), 340 (top right). By Bob Gwaltney, *Evansville Courier & Press*: page 234 (bottom). By Susan Heathcott: pages 190, 295 (right), 298, 299. By Michael Hebert: page 284 (top right). Courtesy of Ruth Shafer Hines: page 345. Rendering courtesy of Holabird and Root: page 290 (top). Courtesy of Orville Jaebker: page 106 (right). Courtesy of George Klinger: page 235. By Dan Knight, courtesy of Studio B: pages 286, 287 (bottom right). By Raymond W. Koch: page 160. By Tanner Lee: page 290 (bottom). By Dave Lucas, courtesy of *Evansville Press*: page 287 (top left). By John David Lutz: page 167. By Eileen Martin: page 249 (top). By Mason Studio: page 65. By Mark McCoy: pages 283 (top), 284 (bottom), 285 (top left). Courtesy of J. Allen McCutchan: page 339 (top left). By Mark Miller: pages 287 (bottom left), 288 (all). By Thomas J. Mueller Studio: page 207. By Thomas O. Mueller: page 91 (bottom). By Willard H. Muensterman: page 93. Courtesy of Mystical Arts of Tibet Agency: page 265. By E.W. Newman Camera Shop: pages 40 (top), 77 (left). Courtesy of Erik Nielsen: page 300. By Paul Novak: pages 236 (bottom), 342 (top). By Lynn Penland: page 24 (bottom).

Photographs by Craig Perman: pages 134, 151, 153, 157, 168 (top), 169 (top), 170 (top right), 171 (top), 172, 175 (both), 178 (top right and bottom left), 184, 206, 209, 210, 212, 231, 239, 252, 263, 281 (top right), 285 (top right), 287 (top right), 294 (top right), 305 (top), 308.

Photographs by Photics LLC: pages 39, 47, 89, 146, 154, 166 (bottom), 170 (Haegert), 179 (bottom right), 217, 225 (right), 226, 227 (left), 229 (Jennings), 232 (bottom), 233, 236 (Rosenblatt, Penland), 246 (top right), 247, 250, 254 (top), 255, 259 (both), 260 (left), 261, 269, 270, 273, 275 (Cullen), 277 (top), 279, 281 (bottom), 289 (top, left and right), 291 (top left), 292 (top right and bottom), 293 (top and bottom right), 294 (bottom, left and right), 295 (left, both), 296 (bottom), 303 (top), 307 (top), 309, 313 (bottom), 314 (top right), 315 (bottom), 316, 326 (all), 328, 338 (top), 339 (center and bottom), 340 (bottom), 341 (both), 346, 347.

Photograph by PhotoImage: page 340 (top left). With permission from the *St. Louis Post-Dispatch*: page 107. By Tim Schermerhorn: page 204 (left). By John Schreiner: page 267. By B.J. Scott: page 83. By Sean Sharp: pages 285 (bottom left), 323 (bottom left). By Greg Smith: page 164 (top). By Mike Thomas: page 321. By David M. Turner: page 170 (top left). Courtesy of Susan Vinson: page 229 (Vinson). Courtesy of Susan Watson: page 86. By Mike White, courtesy of *Evansville Courier & Press*: page 17. By Kim Whitmore-Weber: page 276 (both). Courtesy of the Wilson family: page 254 (bottom).

Photographs by Steve Woit: pages 230, 234 (top), 236 (top left), 241 (left), 242, 248, 253 (top), 256, 266, 268 (top and bottom), 274 (both), 275 (center and bottom), 280 (both), 281 (top left), 289 (bottom), 291 (top right and bottom), 292 (top left), 293 (bottom left), 294 (top left), 297 (both), 305 (bottom), 307 (center and bottom), 310, 313 (top).

Photograph courtesy of Steve Worthington: page 191 (top).

Index

Please note that awards and names listed in the appendix are not included in this index.

354

Tooley, Jack, 128, 154, 155 (photo)
Toon, Thomas, 132
Torbet, Charles, 43, 51 (photo), 55, 61 (photo), 78, 93
Track, 72, 221
Trimble, G.A., 31
Tripodi, Matt, 271 (photo)
Tri-State Regional Science and Engineering Fair, 154, 277
Tsai, Maurice, 156 (photo)
Tuck, Anthony, 257
Tuck, Steve, 257
Tudor-Craig, Pamela, 257
Tuley, Dean, 304
Tyler, C. Arthur, 139

Uddin, Nasim, 244, 245 (photo)
UE African American Alumni, 303
UExplore, 313
Underwood, Frank, 253
Unfried, Lois, 140
Ungar, Garnet, 265
University Mace, 226
University Medal, 226-227
University of Evansville Press, 182-183
University of Southern Indiana see: Indiana State University
University Senate, 151-152

Valentine, Roy H., 42 (photo)
Valenzuela, Mark, 247, 290
van Aken, Troy, 264
Van Keuren, Ernest, 55, 126
Vandeveer, Melissa, 160
Vannest, Charles, 55
Vaughn, Alma, 118, 150
Vaughn, D.W., 49
Veazey, Roberta, 165
Vernon, Constance B., 237
Vieth, William, 210
Vilches, Patricia, 242, 262
Vinson, James S., 225-227, 231, 234, 273 (photo)
Vinson, Susan, 229
Voorhees, James, 124 (photo), 130

Wade, Cassy, 290
Walker, Everette, 123
Walker, Heber P., 55, 61 (photo)
Walker, Janet, 181
Wallace, Margaret, 157
Waller, Janet Dill, 252
Walters, Dick, 220, 316
Wambach-Crick, Linda, 221
Wandel, Tamara, 278
Wangerin Jr., Walter, 170

Ward, Christia Stinson, 167, 274
Ward, Ivan, 158 (photo), 159
Ware, James, 263, 269
Washington, John Ed, 214, 215
Waterman, Ralph, 109 (photo), 110
Watkins, John, 51
Watkins, Sam, 130
Watson, Bobby, 213-215
Watson, Charles, 249
Weaver, Laura, 170, 261
Webb, Joseph, 167
Wedeking, Albert C., 118
Wednesday Morning Literature, 182, 276
Wege, Melissa, 300
Weir, David, 282, 318
Weiss, William, 216, 294
Welch, Jared, 289
Weller, Lowell, 104, 138
Wells, Carroll E., 237
Werking, Mary, 106
Werking, F. Woody, 105-106
Wesley, William C., 100 (photo)
West, Robert, 167
Westbrook, Scott, 211
Westfall, James, 155
WGBF, 66
   see also: Radio
Wheeler Concert Hall, 87-88
Wheeler, Walton M., 48
White, J.C., 42 (photo)
White, Joe, 203
White, R. Dale, 155
Whitesell, Harry E., 100 (photo)
Whitmoyer, Irwin, 68 (photo)
Wichman, Dennis, 177
Widick, J. Donald, 140
Wiemeier, Noelle, 290
Williams, Danielle, 241
Williams, Fletcher, 68 (photo)
Williams, Herb, 130
Williams, Matt, 166-167, 273
Williams, Mrs. Vernon, 109 (photo)
Wilson, Eulalie (Blesch), 108, 181, 276
Wilson, Gregory, 254
Wilson, Joseph, 139
Wilson, Joyce, 254
Wilson, Robert, 124 (photo), 125, 139, 254
Wilterding, James, 156
Winburn, Tony, 214, 215
Winkley, John W., 81
Winternheimer, Clarence, 101, 155 (photo)
Winternheimer, P. Louis, 103, 150, 151 (photo)

Winternheimer, Wilma, 160
Wise, Dale, 128, 129
Wolf, April, 290
Wolf, Jeffery, 236, 237
Wolfe, Ben, 93
Women's studies, 276
Wood, George W., 18
Wooding, Charles, 181
Woody, Allen, 304
Worthington, Betty and Wayne, 145, 226
Worthington, John, 295
Worthington, Steve, 295
Wrench, David, 257
Wrestling, 221
Wright, David, 165, 265
Wright, George P., 68 (photo)
Wright, Jane Elizabeth, 42
Wright, Rachel, 290
Wright, Wayne, 199
WUEV-FM, 315-316, 281
   see also: Radio
Wulf, Linda, 157
Wyatt, Ima S., 61 (photo)
Wylie, Mary Ellen, 264

Yearbook
   see: Melange and LinC
Youngblood, Linda, 130

Zausch, Jo Willa, 170
Zeta, Elinore, 149, 182
Zifer, Timothy, 268
Ziliak, Jake, 290
Zimmer, Michael, 156, 293
Zimmer, Molly, 156
Zion, Marjorie, 181
Zminkowski, Thomas, 139
Zoph, Oscar P.N., 51, 73
Zuehsow, Dalen, 246 (photo)